MODERN RELIGIOUS MOVEMENTS IN INDIA

MODERN RELIGIOUS MOVEMENTS IN INDIA

BY

J. N. FARQUHAR, M. A.

GYAN

Published by

Gyan Publishing House
5, Ansari Road
Daryaganj, New Delhi-110002
Phone: 011-47034999, 9811692060
E-mail: books@gyanbooks.com

Distribution Network
gyanbooks.com
India, USA, Canada, UK, Australia, France

ISBN : 978-81-212-9960-2 (PB)
First Published, 1915

2nd Impression 2021

Printed at: Gyan Press, Delhi.

Modern
Religious Movements in India
Author: J. N. Farquhar

MODERN RELIGIOUS MOVEMENTS IN INDIA

BY

J. N. FARQUHAR, M.A.

LITERARY SECRETARY, NATIONAL COUNCIL OF YOUNG MEN'S CHRISTIAN ASSOCIATIONS, INDIA AND CEYLON

AUTHOR OF
"A PRIMER OF HINDUISM," "THE CROWN OF HINDUISM"

New York
THE MACMILLAN COMPANY
1915

From life-size portrait by Biggs in Bristol Museum.

By permission of the Committee of the Museum and Art Gallery.

RAJA RAM MOHAN RAY

Founder of the Brāhma Samāj.

THE HARTFORD-LAMSON LECTURES ON "THE RELIGIONS OF THE WORLD" ARE DELIVERED AT HARTFORD THEOLOGICAL SEMINARY IN CONNECTION WITH THE LAMSON FUND, WHICH WAS ESTABLISHED BY A GROUP OF FRIENDS IN HONOUR OF THE LATE CHARLES M. LAMSON, D.D., SOMETIME PRESIDENT OF THE AMERICAN BOARD OF COMMISSIONERS FOR FOREIGN MISSIONS, TO ASSIST IN PREPARING STUDENTS FOR THE FOREIGN MISSIONARY FIELD. THE LECTURES ARE DESIGNED PRIMARILY TO GIVE SUCH STUDENTS A GOOD KNOWLEDGE OF THE RELIGIOUS HISTORY, BELIEFS AND CUSTOMS OF THE PEOPLES AMONG WHOM THEY EXPECT TO LABOUR. AS THEY ARE DELIVERED BY SCHOLARS OF THE FIRST RANK, WHO ARE AUTHORITIES IN THEIR RESPECTIVE FIELDS, IT IS EXPECTED THAT IN PUBLISHED FORM THEY WILL PROVE TO BE OF VALUE TO STUDENTS GENERALLY.

PREFACE

TOWARDS the close of 1912 Dr. W. Douglas Mackenzie, President of Hartford Theological Seminary, Hartford, Conn., invited me to deliver, as Lamson Lecturer for 1913, a course of eight lectures on Modern Religious Movements in India. The subject was extremely attractive. It was clear that to bring these many movements together, arrange them in related groups, and set them forth as varying expressions of a great religious upheaval would be a far more illuminating piece of work than the description of them as units ever could be. But the difficulties involved in the proposed investigation were so great that it was only after much inward questioning as to whether I ought to dare the task that I decided to attempt it.

The first difficulty of the subject lies in the fact that the majority of these numerous and very varied movements, scattered over every part of India, have never been described before. In the case of a few of the more noteworthy, excellent monographs do exist. The following books and pamphlets proved of signal service in my investigation:

Śāstrī, *History of the Brāhma Samāj* (including the Prārthanā Samāj); Griswold, art. *Ārya Samāj* in *ERE.;* Griswold, *The Chet Rami Sect;* Griswold, *Mirza Ghulām Aḥmad, the Mehdī Messiah of Qadian;* Griswold, *The Rādhā Swāmī Sect;* Griswold, *Paṇdit Agnihotṛi and the Deva Samāj;* Chirol, *Indian Unrest.* There are also several valuable biographical works — notably, Max Müller's *Rāmakṛishṇa*, Prof. M. N. Gupta's *Gospel of Śrī-Rāmakṛishṇa*, Dayānanda's *Autobiography*, and Solovyoff's *Modern Priestess of Isis*, — which enable the student to see, in a measure, the genesis of the movements to which they are related. But, apart from these two groups of good authorities, it was necessary to conduct the investigation almost entirely by personal visits and interviews, or, less satisfactorily, by correspondence. By these means nearly all the fresh matter in the following chapters was gathered. A small amount of the new material comes from another source, *viz.*, the apologetic and propagandist literature of the various movements; but, with the exception of certain systematic statements of creed (e.g. *Rādhā Soāmi Mat Prakāsh*, *A Dialogue about the Deva Samāj*, and Leadbeater's *Textbook of Theosophy*), these innumerable booklets, pamphlets and tracts in many tongues have provided only a scanty gleaning of significant facts.

But the subject carries within it a still more intimate difficulty. Even if abundance of information were forthcoming about any one of these most noteworthy uprisings of the Indian spirit, there would still remain the difficulty of *understanding* it, the possibility of totally misconceiving the forces that have created it, of fastening one's eyes on externals and failing to feel the beatings of the heart.

Others must decide whether I did right in attempting the task, and how far I have succeeded in it. What weighed with me was the fact that my past experience had given me a partial preparation for the work, and that my present circumstances afford me unusual facilities for getting the necessary information.

I spent in Calcutta eleven years as a Professor in a Missionary College and five as an Association Secretary among educated non-Christians. During those sixteen years I was constantly in touch with Chaitanyas, Brāhmas,

Āryas, Theosophists, followers of Rāmakṛishṇa and young men interested in other North India movements. Two pieces of work arose from this contact: *Gītā and Gospel* (1903), a booklet dealing with the Neo-Kṛishṇa Movement in Bengal, and art. *Brāhma Samāj* in *ERE.* (1909).

During the next five years my duties required me to travel all over India with little intermission and to deliver religious addresses in all the important towns. I was thus brought into personal contact with men of almost every type of religious belief; while my one study was Hinduism.

A recent modification of my work has given me special opportunities for interviewing individuals and learning facts with a view to these lectures. Fresh arrangements, made by Dr. J. R. Mott and the Committee in New York, have enabled me since the spring of 1912 to spend the summers in England in literary work and the winters in India lecturing and teaching. The invitation to give the Lamson Lectures reached me late in 1912. That winter I visited Bombay, Jubbulpore, Allahabad, Benares, Lahore, Calcutta, Puri, Madras, Conjeeveram, Bangalore, Mysore City, Palamcottah, Madura, Trichy, Tanjore, Kumbakonam, Pudukottai; and almost everywhere I was able to have long conversations with intelligent men about the sect or movement they were interested in, to visit buildings, and to pick up literature and photographs. The summer of 1913 was spent in Oxford, preparing the lectures. This enabled me to use the Bodleian Library and the British Museum and to consult many men in and about London who have special knowledge of certain of the movements dealt with. After delivering the lectures in Hartford, Conn., in October, 1913, I returned to India, and visited Poona, Hyderabad (Deccan), Bangalore, Madras, Trichy, Madura, Palamcottah, Nagarcoil, Trevandrum, Quilon, Calicut, Tellicherry, Calcutta, Jamalpore, Jubbulpore,

Allahabad, Cawnpore, Lucknow, Agra, Lahore, Rājkot (Kathiawar), Bombay. I thereby gained much fresh information, and was able to settle scores of questions which had arisen in my mind in the course of writing the lectures.

Thus, one way or another, I have had personal intercourse with adherents of all the movements described in this book, with the exception of a few of the smallest and most obscure.

I have felt cramped for want of space. To deal with the whole subject adequately would have required two volumes instead of one. I have thus been compelled to compress the matter very seriously everywhere. I trust this has not resulted in making my sentences and paragraphs unintelligible. It certainly has reduced the last chapter to rather an arid catalogue of facts. Necessarily, the eight lectures delivered in Hartford contained far less material than the book does.

Though I have done my utmost to secure accuracy and to avoid misrepresentation, the movements are so varied and so intricate that there must be many omissions and mistakes. Criticism will therefore be very warmly welcomed. Letters calling attention to errors and omissions, or suggesting fresh points of view, may be sent either to 86 College Street, Calcutta, or to Oxford.

So many friends in every part of India, and also in England and America, have helped me in conversation and by correspondence that it would be impossible to make a complete list of them. I wish here, however, to express my heartfelt gratitude to every one who has given me personal assistance, whether much or little; for, without them, the book could never have been written. I mention in the footnotes the names of those who have helped me at the most critical points, because in these cases it is necessary to give the source of my information. But my gratitude is quite as great to those whose names are not mentioned.

The portraits scattered through the text may help readers to seize in a more vivid way the character and temperament of the men and women who created these religious movements. A few of them are new, but all the others have been published before. Of these, some are quite well known; but the rest, having appeared only in obscure Indian books and periodicals, must be quite new to the general reader. In any case it seems worth while bringing them together as a series of religious leaders.

I wish here to express my most grateful thanks to those whose kindness has made possible the publication of these portraits; first to the following for gifts of photographs and leave to publish them:

Donors	*Portraits*
The Committee of the Museum and Art Gallery, Bristol	Raja Ram Mohan Ray
Mr. N. C. Sen, Private Secretary to the Maharani of Cooch Behar . . .	Keshab Chandra Sen (father of the donor)
Sir R. G. Bhandarkar	His own
Sir N. G. Chandavarkar	His own
Mr. M. N. Katrak, Bombay . . .	Mr. K. R. Cama
Dr. H. D. Griswold, Lahore . . .	Mirza Ghulam Aḥmad
Mr. Sasipada Banerjea, Calcutta . .	The symbolic picture, Plate X.
Mr. Mansukhlal Ravjibhai Mehta, Bombay	Mr. Rajchandra Ravjibhai (brother of the donor)
Mr. G. K. Devadhar, Bombay . . .	The Hon'ble Mr. G. K. Gokhale, C. I. E.

I owe very special thanks to Mr. Satyendra Nath Tagore, I. C. S., Retired, who gave me permission to take a photographer into the Tagore Residence, Calcutta, and photograph the beautiful portraits of his grandfather and father (Plates I and II).

Grateful thanks are also due to the following for permission given to publish photographs:

	Portraits
Mrs. Ramabai Ranade, Poona .	The late Mr. Justice Ranade
The Ārya Samāj, Lahore . .	Svāmī Dayānanda Sarasvatī
The Rādhā Soāmi Satsaṅg .	The gurus
The Deva Samāj . . .	The guru
The Rāmakṛishṇa Mission .	Rāmakṛishṇa Paramahaṁsa and Svāmī Vivekānanda
The Theosophical Society . .	Madame Blavatsky and Mrs. Besant
Mr. Rabindra Nath Tagore .	His own

My debt to my friend Dr. H. D. Griswold of Lahore is very great; for considerable sections of my third chapter are built upon his scholarly monographs mentioned above; and he revised the whole work for me in manuscript. To him and to another friend, the Rev. John McKenzie of Bombay, who kindly did for me the troublesome work of revising the proofs, I offer my unfeigned gratitude and thanks.

11 Frenchay Road, Oxford,
October 30, 1914.

CONTENTS

LIST OF PORTRAITS

ABBREVIATIONS USED IN THE NOTES

A Historical Retrospect.	*A Historical Retrospect of the Theosophical Society*, by H. S. Olcott.
Chhajju Singh.	*The Life and Teachings of Swami Dayanand Saraswati*, by Bawa Chhajju Singh.
Collapse.	*The Collapse of Koot Hoomi*, a reprint of articles from the Madras Christian College Magazine.
Dubois.	*Hindu Manners, Customs and Ceremonies*, by J. A. Dubois.
ERE.	*Encyclopædia of Religion and Ethics.*
Gospel of R.	*Gospel of Śrī Rāmakṛishṇa*, by M.
HBS.	*History of the Brahmo Samaj*, by Siva Nath Sastri.
IRM.	*The International Review of Missions.*
ISR.	*The Indian Social Reformer.*
Karaka.	*History of the Parsees*, by Dosabhai Framji Karaka.
Miss Collet.	*Life and Letters of Raja Rammohun Roy*, by Sophia Dobson Collet.
MPI.	*A Modern Priestess of Isis*, by V. S. Solovyoff.
ODL.	*Old Diary Leaves*, by H. S. Olcott.
Proceedings.	*Proceedings of the Society for Psychical Research.*
Ranade, *Essays.*	*Religious and Social Reform, A Collection of Essays and Speeches*, by M. G. Ranade.
Richter.	*A History of Missions in India*, by Julius Richter.
Sinnett, *Incidents.*	*Incidents in the Life of Madame Blavatsky*, by A. P. Sinnett.
Social Reform in Bengal.	*Social Reform in Bengal*, by Paṇḍit Sītānātha Tattvabhushaṇa.

MODERN RELIGIOUS MOVEMENTS IN INDIA

CHAPTER I

HISTORICAL OUTLINE OF THE PERIOD

1. Our subject is *Modern Religious Movements in India*, that is, the fresh religious movements which have appeared in India since the effective introduction of Western influence. There are two great groups of religious facts the presence of which we must recognize continuously but which are excluded from our survey by the limitations of our subject. These are, first, the old religions of India, Hinduism, Buddhism, Jainism, Zoroastrianism and Muḥammadanism, so far as they retain the form and character they had before the coming of Western influence; and, secondly, Christian Missions, which are rather a continuation of Church History than a modern movement. The old religions are the soil from which the modern movements spring; while it will be found that the seed has, in the main, been sown by Missions. Thus, though these great systems are not included in our subject, we must, throughout our investigation, keep their constant activity and influence in mind.

It seems clear that the effective interpenetration of India by the West began about 1800. The first fresh religious movement appeared in 1828; the intellectual awakening of India began to manifest itself distinctly about the same time; and the antecedents of both go back to somewhere about the beginning of the century. The period we have to deal with thus extends from 1800 to 1913.

In 1800 India was in a pitiable plight. Early Hindu governments seldom succeeded in securing settled peace even in the great central region of the country for any extended period of time; but matters became much worse when the flood of Muhammadan invasion came at the end of the twelfth century. When the nineteenth century dawned, India had scarcely known peace for six hundred years. Even under the best of the Mughals there was frequent fighting, and a good deal of injustice; under all other Muslim rulers there was practically constant war and frequent outbreaks of barbarity; while the eighteenth century piled misery on misery. It is heartbreaking to read descriptions of India at that time.

We can now see that British supremacy began to assert itself with the battle of Plassey in 1757; yet the rulers had scarcely a definite policy until the opening of the new century; and, even then, Britain had not by any means awaked to the greatness and the splendour of the task set before her in India. We must never forget that the East India Company went to India exclusively for commerce, and that the British Empire sprang altogether from the necessity, which was only very gradually realized, of providing a settled and just government in order to make commerce possible.

2. In 1800 Hinduism, which was the religion of at least three-fourths of the population of the peninsula, consisted, in the main, of two great groups of sects and a mass of wandering celibate ascetics, who were held to be outside society. The two great groups of sects are the Vishṇuite and the Śivaite. The Vishṇuite sects were very numerous, both in the North and in the South, and they were perhaps, on the whole, more homogeneous than the worshippers of Śiva. The

leading Vishṇuite sects declare Vishṇu to be the one God, and yet they recognize the existence of all the other divinities of the Hindu pantheon. They also hold that Vishṇu has been incarnate among men a great many times, the latest and chief incarnations being Rāma and Kṛishṇa. Worshippers of Śiva declare that Śiva is the one God, but recognize also all the other gods. A special group of Śivaite sects has to be noticed, namely, those who pay honour to the wife of Śiva as Kālī or Durgā. Both Vishṇuites and Śivaites worship idols, but among Śivaites the phallic symbol is more usual than images of the god. Both sects worship their gurus, that is, their teachers, as gods. Both are fully orthodox in the sense that they retain and enforce with great strictness the ancient Hindu rules of conduct which are summed up under the word *dharma*. Both sects claim to be Vedāntists, but each has its own interpretation of the philosophy. Around the Hindu community in every part of the country there lived multitudes of degraded Outcastes, held down in the dirt by Hindu law. They number about fifty millions to-day.

When the century dawned, Hindus were in a pitifully backward condition. Their subjugation by the Muḥammadans about 1200 A.D. had been a very serious trampling under foot; and, while the reasonable rule of the Mughals had given them a breathing-space, the terrific convulsions of the eighteenth century had more than undone all that had been recovered. Learning had almost ceased; ordinary education scarcely existed; spiritual religion was to be met only in the quietest places; and a coarse idolatry with cruel and immoral rites held all the great centres of population. The condition of South Indian Hinduism at the end of the eighteenth century is very vividly reflected in l'Abbé Dubois' famous work, and the Hinduism of the North at the beginning of the nineteenth in the writings of Ram Mohan Ray. The reader may make a rough guess at the state of the Hindu community from the long list of reforms, social and religious, which the early missionaries felt driven to demand [1] and which all the finer spirits within Hinduism have since then recognized as altogether necessary.

Buddhism, which came to the birth about 525 B.C., attained extraordinary greatness before the Christian era, and during the next six centuries not only spread over the whole of Eastern and Southern Asia, but struggled with Hinduism for the primacy in India. Thereafter it steadily declined in the land of its origin; the Muḥammadan conquest all but destroyed it; and Hinduism gradually absorbed what remained. Thus there were practically no Buddhists in India proper at the opening of the nineteenth century; but on the Himalayas, in Burma and in Ceylon the faith was still supreme.

Jainism was originally an agnostic philosophy which arose a little earlier than Buddhism, and, like Buddhism, became transformed at an early date into a religion and a rival of Hinduism. By the beginning of our period the ancient Jain community had shrunk to small proportions. They were scattered over a large part of the country, and were wealthy and prosperous; but there was no vigour in Jainism; and there was a slow, continuous drift towards Hinduism; so that the community was steadily dwindling in numbers.

The Parsees are a small community of Zoroastrian Persians who fled from Persia to India in the eighth century A.D., and have since then remained a prosperous business community, very exclusive socially and very faithful to their ancient religion. They originally settled in Gujarāt; but, since early last century, Bombay has been their chief centre.

In 1800 Muḥammadanism in India was very orthodox and very ignorant, and was steadily deteriorating. The collapse of the Muḥammadan governments and the steady fall of Muslim character had worked sad havoc in the religion itself.

[1] See p. 15.

Muḥammadans formed perhaps one-sixth of the population. They were necessarily discontented and crushed, having been conquered both by the Marāṭha Hindus and by the British. Yet they were not so cowed nor so weak as the Hindus. The British had entered into the heritage of their administration; multitudes of Muslims were still government officials; and Urdu, the hybrid tongue which had grown up as a medium of communication in the Muḥammadan camp, was still the official language in the law-courts and elsewhere. The bulk of public education was thus still Muḥammadan in character; and what men studied most was the Persian and Urdu languages. Yet the Muslim community was steadily declining. There was no living movement of thought and no spiritual leader among them.

3. Can we see what was the cause of the great Awakening which began about 1800 and since then has dominated the life and history of India? How was the Muslim period so barren as compared with the nineteenth century? How is it that European influence produced practically no results between 1500 and 1800? Why did the Awakening begin at that particular point?

The answer is that the Awakening is the result of the co-operation of two forces, both of which began their characteristic activity about the same time, and that it was quickened by a third which began to affect the Indian mind a little later. The two forces are the British Government in India as it learned its task during the years at the close of the eighteenth and the beginning of the nineteenth centuries, and Protestant Missions[1] as they were shaped by the Serampore men and Duff; and the third force is the work of the great Orientalists. The material elements of Western civilization have had their influence, but, apart from the creative forces,

[1] Catholic Missions have been continuously of service, especially in education, but they have had no perceptible share in creating the Awakening.

they would have led to no awakening. The proof of all this will gradually unfold itself in our chapters.

It was necessity that drove the East India Company to assume governmental duties. They had no desire to rule India, far less to reform the intellectual, social and religious life of the people. They were driven to undertake first one and then another administrative duty, because otherwise they could not obtain that settled government and those regular financial arrangements without which profitable commerce is impossible. But every step they took led to another; and gradually the conscience of Britain awoke and began to demand that India should be governed for the good of the people. It was during the last decades of the eighteenth century that the old trading company was gradually hammered into something like a government. The men who did the work were Clive, Hastings and Cornwallis. A succession of changes transformed its civil-servant traders, whose incomes depended on their business ability, into administrators living on a salary and strictly forbidden to make money by trading; while the Government itself steadily assumed new functions, and grew in knowledge of the people.

Protestant missionary history in India opens with the Danish Mission, which did very remarkable work in the Tamil country throughout the eighteenth century; but it was the toil of Carey and his colleagues that roused first Britain and then America and the Continent to a sense of their duty to the non-Christian peoples of the world. William Carey, an English Baptist, arrived in Calcutta on the 11th November, 1793, and, after many wanderings, settled as an indigo-planter near Malda in North Bengal. Here he studied Bengali and Sanskrit, began the work of translating the Bible into Bengali, gained his experience and developed his methods. In 1800 he settled in Serampore under the Danish flag; and in the same year he began to teach Sanskrit and Bengali in

Lord Wellesley's College in Calcutta. Then it was not long before the wiser men both in Missions and in the Government began to see that, for the immeasurable task to be accomplished, it was most necessary that Missions should take advantage of the advancing policy of the Government and that Government should use Missions as a civilizing ally. For the sake of the progress of India coöperation was indispensable.

The rise of Orientalism is contemporaneous with the beginnings of good government in North India and with the development of the new Mission propaganda, but it did not touch the Indian mind until later.[1] It was Warren Hastings who took the steps which led to Europeans becoming acquainted with Sanskrit and Hinduism. By his orders a simple code of Hindu law was put together and translated into English in 1776. In 1785 Charles Wilkins, who had been roused to the study of Sanskrit by Hastings, published a translation of the *Bhagavadgītā;* and Sir William Jones, the

[1] At first sight it seems very extraordinary that our real knowledge of India should have begun so late. Europe has known of India superficially from time immemorial; and from a very early date Indians have had scraps of information about the West. Long centuries before the Christian era, it seems certain that Solomon sent his navy from the Gulf of Akabah to Western India; and Indian merchants sailed to the Persian Gulf and brought home Babylonian goods and ideas. The conquest of the Panjab by Darius the Persian brought a small amount of knowledge to Greece; and Alexander's matchless raid led to the establishment of direct communication between India and the Greek kingdoms. Roman traders carried on large commerce with the mouths of the Indus, and also with Southern India, in the first and second centuries A.D. Occasionally travellers from the West penetrated to India during the Middle Ages; and a great trade both by caravan and by sea went on uninterruptedly. Modern intercourse begins with Vasco da Gama, the famous Portuguese explorer, who sailed round the Cape of Good Hope and reached the coast of India at Calicut in Malabar in 1498. From that date onward, Portuguese, Dutch, French and English went to India by sea, and a large trade was carried on; yet until the end of the eighteenth century no serious attempt was made to understand India and its civilization.

first great Sanskritist, published in 1789 a translation of *Śakuntalā*, the finest of all Indian dramas. Another Englishman, named Hamilton, happened to be passing through France on his way home, in 1802, and was arrested. During his long involuntary stay in Paris he taught Sanskrit to several French scholars and also to the German poet, Friedrich Schlegel. Thus was the torch handed on to Europe. The discovery of Sanskrit led to a revolution in the science of language. About the same time English scholars began the study of the flora and fauna of India, and also of her people.[1]

4. But, though history has shown decisively that it was the British Government and Protestant Missions working together that produced the Awakening of India, we must note carefully that, at the outset, the Government vehemently opposed Missions. In order to understand their attitude, we must realize that their only object was trade, and that it was purely for the safeguarding of their trade that they had interfered with the politics of the land. In consequence, they regarded themselves as in every sense the successors of the old rulers and heirs to their policy and method, except in so far as it was necessary to alter things for the sake of trade. There was another point. They had won their territory by means of an Indian army composed mainly of high-caste Hindus, who were exceedingly strict in keeping all the rules of caste and of

[1] We ought also to mention the wonderful work done by two Frenchmen. Anquetil du Perron went to India and ultimately prevailed upon the Parsee priests to teach him the language of the *Avesta*. He brought his Mss. and his knowledge to Europe in 1771, and thus became the pioneer of Zoroastrian research in the West. Four years later he translated into Latin a Persian version of a number of the Upanishads, produced under the orders of a Mughal Prince in the seventeenth century. It was through his almost incomprehensible Latin that Schopenhauer received his knowledge of the Vedānta philosophy. L'Abbé Dubois, a Catholic missionary who lived and wandered in the Tamil country from 1792 to 1823 wrote *Hindu Manners, Customs and Ceremonies*, one of the most vivid and reliable descriptions of a people that has ever been penned.

religious practice. Further, every competent observer was deeply impressed with the extraordinary hold Hinduism had upon the people. Every element of life was controlled by it.[1] In consequence, the Government believed it to be necessary, for the stability of their position, not merely to recognize the religions of the people of India, but to support and patronize them as fully as the native rulers had done, and to protect their soldiers from any attempt to make them Christians. Accordingly, they adopted three lines of policy from which, for a long time, they stubbornly refused to move:[2]

a. They took under their management and patronage a large number of Hindu temples. They advanced money for rebuilding important shrines and for repairing others, and paid the salaries of the temple officials, even down to the courtesans, which were a normal feature of the great temples of the South.[3] They granted large sums of money for sacrifices and festivals and for the feeding of Brāhmans. Salvoes of cannon were fired on the occasion of the greater festivals; and government officials were ordered to be present and to show their interest in the celebrations. Even cruel and immoral rites, such as hook-swinging, practised in the worship of the gods, and the burning of widows, were carried out under British supervision. In order to pay for all these things, a pilgrim-tax was imposed, which not only recouped the Government for their outlay, but brought them a handsome income as well. Reformers in England and India found it a long and toilsome business to get this patronage of idolatry by a Christian Government put down. The last temple was handed over as late as 1862.

[1] During the many years that I studied Hindu customs I cannot say that I ever observed a single one, however unimportant and simple, and, I may add, however filthy and disgusting, which did not rest on some religious principle or other. Dubois, p. 31.

[2] Richter, 185–192.

[3] See below, pp. 408–9.

b. They absolutely refused to allow any missionary to settle in their territory. Carey got a footing in Bengal by becoming an indigo-planter; and he was not able to devote his whole time and energy to Christian work, until he settled at Serampore, twelve miles north of Calcutta, under the Danish flag. Many missionaries, both British and American, landed in India, only to be deported by the authorities. This policy was reversed by Act of Parliament in 1813.

c. They refused to employ native Christians in any capacity, and they enforced all the rigours of Hindu law against them. In the Bengal army, if any native soldier wished to become a Christian, he was forcibly prevented by the authorities; or, if by any chance he became baptized, he was expelled from the service. This fierce prejudice was so strong even at the time of the Mutiny that the services of thousands of Indian Christians were refused by the Government.

Yet from quite an early date there was a certain amount of collaboration between the Government and Missions. When Lord Wellesley founded, in 1800, the College of Fort William in Calcutta, to give his young Indian Civilians a training in Indian languages and literature, Carey was the only man who could be found to teach Sanskrit and Bengali. He was accordingly appointed Professor; and for many years, though his chief work was in Serampore, he spent one-half of each week in Calcutta, lecturing to Indian Civilians in the morning, and preaching to the poor in the evening. Government also took advantage of the Mission Printing Press at Serampore, where, for the first time in history, Indian languages were printed in their own script; and they departed in one instance from their strict rule of deporting every missionary landing in India, because the new man was a skilled type-founder, and was about to cut, for the mission, Chinese type which the Government would be glad to use. At a later date the great problem of education drew the Government and Missions together.

The present wise policy of absolute religious neutrality was not reached until 1857, when, in the throes of the Mutiny, the East India Company came to an end, and the home Government became directly responsible for India. Since that moment, though many individual government officers, both civil and military, have misinterpreted British neutrality to mean what it certainly meant under the Company, namely, favour to the old religions and opposition to Christian work, yet the attitude of Government as such has been right. Every Christian to-day ought to rejoice that the policy of strict neutrality was adopted when India came under the Crown. Some people wished the Government to take a definite stand in favour of Christianity and to use its money and influence for the bringing of India into the Church; but it is as clear as noonday that that could have brought only disaster to the cause of Christ. No government can ever do the work of the Church; the government official as such cannot be an Apostle.

5. This discussion will enable us to sympathize with a number of ideas which have been influential in certain sections of Anglo-Indian society for a hundred and fifty years, and are still held by some. We can see how it is that men in business and in government have come to believe that we had better not touch the religion and civilization of India, that it is impossible to alter them, or to produce any lasting influence on Indian thought, and that every attempt to introduce change is bad for the people, on the one hand, and a grave danger to British trade and government, on the other.

It is well to notice that from time to time men of scholarship and character have held to the old policy and ideas in these matters. Horace Hayman Wilson, the famous Sanskrit scholar, was opposed to Bentinck's abolition of *satī*,[1] and seriously believed that it would cause the Government grave

[1] Below, p. 17.

difficulty.[1] As a matter of fact, Bentinck's judgment was justified. No difficulty of any kind arose. Many noteworthy persons, and masses of business men throughout the nineteenth century have been opposed to educating the Indian. Lord Ellenborough, when Governor-General,

> regarded the political ruin of the English power as the inevitable consequence of the education of the Hindus.[2]

Many a business man in Calcutta echoes this belief to-day, but no serious statesman holds such an opinion. Here is how the attitude of the people of Calcutta to missions was described in 1812:

> All were convinced that rebellion, civil war, and universal unrest would certainly accompany every attempt to promote missionary enterprise, and, above all, that the conversion of a high-caste native soldier would inevitably mean the disbanding of the army and the overthrow of British rule in India.[3]

Gradually the policy of Government was brought into consonance with the political and religious convictions of the people of Britain; yet, in circles little touched by Christian enthusiasm and democratic feeling, the old ideas still persist, and find frequent expression in conversation and public addresses, in articles and books.

Probably no thinking man to-day believes that Western influence is producing no serious effect on the Indian mind; yet we must not forget that one of the greatest publicists who ever lived and wrote in India, Meredith Townsend, held, throughout a long life, that all the efforts of Britain to modify Indian thought and behaviour were absolutely hopeless. Here are two brief quotations from his volume of Essays, *Asia and Europe*:

[1] Compare also Ram Mohan Ray's attitude. See below, p. 33 n.
[2] Richter, 183. [3] *Ib.*, 131.

All the papers are directed to one end, a description of those inherent differences between Europe and Asia which forbid one continent permanently to conquer the other. . . . It is rather a saddening reflection that the thoughts of so many years are all summed up by a great poet in four lines:

"The East bowed low before the blast,
In patient deep disdain;
She let the legions thunder past,
Then plunged in thought again."[1]

As yet there is no sign that the British are accomplishing more than the Romans accomplished in Britain, that they will spread any permanently successful ideas, or that they will found anything whatever. It is still true that if they departed or were driven out they would leave behind them, as the Romans did in Britain, splendid roads, many useless buildings, an increased weakness in the subject people, and a memory which in a century of new events would be extinct.[2]

Dubois held similar opinions:

I venture to predict that it (*i.e.* the British Government) will attempt in vain to effect any very considerable changes in the social condition of the people of India, whose character, principles, customs and ineradicable conservatism will always present insurmountable obstacles.[3]

It is necessary, for the understanding of the history of the nineteenth century, to realize how influential these ideas were for many years, though they begin to seem rather old-world and bloodless in the light of the Awakening, and especially of the religious upheaval we have to deal with.

LITERATURE.—*The Rise and Expansion of the British Dominion in India*, by Sir Alfred Lyall, London, Murray, 1894. *Hindu Manners, Customs and Ceremonies*, by J. A. Dubois, Oxford, Clarendon Press. *A History of Missions in India*, by Julius Richter, London, Oliphant. *Asia and Europe*, by Meredith Townsend.

We shall divide the period of one hundred and thirteen years with which we deal into four sections.

[1] P. xxi. [2] P. 27. [3] P. xxiii.

FIRST SECTION: 1800–1828

1. In this year 1800, from which we date the effective interpenetration of India by the West, a large part of the country was already under British rule, and Lord Wellesley was busy bringing the independent native princes within the scope of the empire by means of peaceful treaties. His policy proved very successful, and extended the empire far and wide. In the wars which arose his brother, later known as the Duke of Wellington, played a great part. His policy may be said to have completed itself in 1849, when the last remaining portion of India proper was added to the empire.

2. We have already seen that Carey, his apprenticeship over, had settled under the Danish flag at Serampore in 1800 and had at once become a Government professor in Calcutta. He gave a great deal of time to the translation of the Bible into the vernaculars of India and even into the languages of countries outside India; but it was chiefly by the winning of actual converts from Hinduism, by his schools, newspapers and literature, that he was able to bring Christian thought effectively to bear on the Indian spirit. But it would have been impossible for him to make his work varied and effective had it not been for his two great colleagues, Marshman and Ward. Carey had been a cobbler, Marshman a Ragged-School teacher and Ward a printer. They were all largely self-taught. They differed greatly from each other, but differed in such a way as to supplement one another. Their methods of work were partly those which had been developed by Danish missionaries in South India in the eighteenth century, partly new. The basis of all their work was preaching and translation of the Bible. To this they added the publication of literature of many types, and very effective journalism. They had a printing press, and in it Indian type was first founded and used. They laid great stress on education, and opened numerous

schools around them for both boys and girls. They opened boarding-schools and orphanages. They even attempted medical work, and did not neglect the lepers. They were most eager to send out native missionaries to preach throughout the country, and with that in view built a great college at Serampore, and received from the King of Denmark authority to confer degrees. Their study of Hinduism and the Hindu community convinced them that, for the health of the people, many social and religious reforms were necessary, for example, the total abolition of caste, the prohibition of widow-burning, of child-marriage, of polygamy and of infanticide, the granting to widows of the right to remarry, the prohibition of human sacrifice, of the torturing of animals in sacrifice, of human torture in worship, and of the gross obscenity practised in the streets. They took great care that caste should be utterly excluded from the Church of Christ.

In 1813, when it was necessary to renew the Charter of the East India Company, Parliament insisted, in spite of the opposition of the Directors of the Company, on inserting a clause in the Charter, giving missionaries full freedom to settle and work in India. There can be no question that this was largely a result of the wonderful work done at Serampore. Soon afterwards there was a great influx of missionaries into the country.

During these years a number of individual Europeans did what they could to start Western education in the great cities of India apart from missionary associations. David Hare, a Scotch watchmaker, was the pioneer of English studies among boys in Calcutta; and a Civil Servant, Mr. Drinkwater Bethune, succeeded in starting a school for Hindu girls in the same city. The Hon'ble Mr. Mountstuart Elphinstone led both the Hindu and the Parsee community in Bombay to modern education. His name is perpetuated in the Government College of that city.

3. Three men stand out as pioneer Orientalists during these years, the great Colebrooke, to whom almost every aspect of Sanskrit and Hindu study runs back, H. H. Wilson, who published a number of very useful works, and Tod, a military officer, who studied the poetry, traditions and customs of the Rajputs so thoroughly that his *Rājasthān* is to this day the greatest and most beautiful work upon that people and their country.

4. But for our subject the most interesting name is that of Ram Mohan Ray, the founder of the Brāhma Samāj. We shall deal with his work in our next chapter. Here we note simply that the years from 1800 to 1828 were the years that formed him, and that while he was influenced by Hinduism, Islam and Buddhism, the forces which proved creative in him were unquestionably Christianity and the influence of the West in general. During these years he published almost all his books and conducted a vigorous agitation in Calcutta against widow-burning, which proved of great practical value.

No fresh religious movement worthy of notice appeared during these years.

LITERATURE. — Lyall, as above. Marshman's *History of India. Wellesley* and *Hastings* in Rulers of India Series, Oxford University Press. *Life of William Carey*, by George Smith, in Everyman's Library. *Carey, Marshman and Ward*, by George Smith. For the rise of Orientalism see Macdonell's *Sanskrit Literature*, chap. I.

SECOND SECTION: 1828–1870

1. The British Empire in India continued to expand during these years until it covered the whole of India. The last portion to be added, namely the Panjab, was annexed in 1849, at the conclusion of the second Sikh war.

The Mutiny of 1857–1858 extends across the middle of our period like a dark bar, but we need not, in this brief historical outline, attempt to deal with it. It was essentially a reaction, a natural and almost inevitable result of the rapid conquest of the country and of the numerous reforms imposed on a most conservative people. So far from checking the process of the building up of the empire, the Mutiny, in the long run, produced most beneficial results; for the Crown became directly responsible for India; and both policy and method were clarified and simplified, to the immeasurable benefit of India.

Apart from the completion of the empire, the whole activity of the Government throughout this section might be described as one long programme of reform; and this aspect of its work is of more importance for our subject than the extension of the frontiers and the wars that shook down the old rulers. We take the beginning of the Governor-Generalship of Lord William Bentinck as the date of the opening of this section of our period, because he initiated the policy of reform, and began to apply in serious earnest the conviction, which had taken hold of the best minds at home, that Britain must govern India for the good of India. The reforms which he introduced may be best understood if we take them in three groups.

The first group consists of a list of cruel practices which had long been customary in India, and were closely connected with the religious life of the people. The principle on which the government decided to interfere with these religious customs is this, that to interfere with religion as such is beyond the province of rulers, but to prohibit customs which are grossly immoral and revolting to humanity is a most serious duty, even though these customs, through superstition and long tradition, have come to be regarded as most sacred. The chief of these customs prohibited were *satī*, the burning of a widow along with her husband's body, *thagī*,[1] the strangling and robbery of travellers, female infanticide and human sacrifice.

[1] See below, p. 425 n.

The second group of reforms comes under the head of the recognition of human equality. It was decided that no native of India should suffer in any way because of his religious opinions, but that all should be absolutely equal before the law. The same idea found practical expression in the largely extended employment of Indians in Government service; but the reason the Directors had for asking Lord William to initiate the reform was the necessity of economy.

The third set of reforms gathers round the English language. For years there had been a serious controversy among government officials as to whether Government should support Oriental or Western education. The great success of Duff's work in Calcutta, which we shall notice below, and the powerful advocacy of Macaulay, who was Legal Member of Council under Lord Bentinck, enabled the Governor-General to decide in favour of modern education. The English language became the official tongue of the empire, and the vehicle of instruction in all higher education. No more momentous decision was ever taken at the Indian Council Board. The working out of a new policy in education was necessarily left to Lord Bentinck's successors. Government schools and colleges grew and multiplied; medical education was introduced; vernacular education was not neglected; and, in the midst of the throes of the Mutiny, the new system was crowned by the establishment of universities at Calcutta, Bombay and Madras.

The results produced by English education in India are revolutionary in the highest degree. The following pages will give much evidence of the extraordinary changes in progress; but, so far as one can see, we have not nearly reached the end of the evolution; and no man can foretell what the ultimate result will be.

Other reforms of considerable magnitude followed. In 1843 an act was passed to render slavery in India illegal;

and, in consequence, during the following years vast numbers of people who had been born and brought up in slavery gradually acquired liberty. Lord Dalhousie (1848–1856) introduced many reforms into the administration. His acts led to great improvements in the life and prosperity of the people throughout the vast empire. Amongst these was a law prohibiting certain gross obscenities which hitherto had been common in the streets of Indian cities. A clause had to be inserted excluding the temples, images and cars of Hindu gods from the operation of the law.

But the most far-reaching and precious reform of this section of history was the assumption of the government of India by the Crown. Every part of the service was quickened, purified and invigorated under the new system.

2. In Missions these decades are marked chiefly by great activity in education, especially in English education, and by a brilliant development of missionary method in many directions. The number of missionaries engaged in the Empire increased very greatly during those years; and the area covered by missions expanded with the Empire.

In 1830 a young Scotch missionary named Alexander Duff arrived in Calcutta. He decided to open a school for the teaching of English, believing that nothing would do so much for the opening of the Hindu mind as intercourse with the spirit of the West through the medium of the English language. Ram Mohan Ray obtained rooms for him in which to start his school and brought him some of his earliest pupils. His work rested on two convictions. The first of these was this, that the highest form of education is Christian education, namely, a thoroughly sound intellectual and scientific training, built on the moral and religious principles of Christ. To him the teaching of the Bible was the most essential element in the education he gave. Apart from that, mere intellectual drill might do more harm than good. His second conviction was that a modern education could be given to the Indian only through the medium of English, because their own vernaculars did not contain the books necessary for a modern education. His work opened a new missionary era in India. His school became extraordinarily popular; all the most promising young men of the city flocked to him; and the results of his teaching were very remarkable. Western thought caused a great ferment in their minds, breaking down the old ideas with great rapidity; and the daily Scripture lesson filled them with Christian thought. Soon a stream of fine young fellows began to pass out of Hinduism into the Christian Church, and Duff's work and Christianity became the most absorbing topic of conversation throughout the Hindu community. Dr. John Wilson started similar work in Bombay and John Anderson in Madras. These were followed by other missionaries in other centres.

During these decades the Christian education of girls was pushed rapidly forward, and its methods well worked out. It was the desire to spread girls' schools far and wide that led to the rapid increase of women missionaries and finally to a great influx of unmarried lady missionaries. Further contact with the people showed the piteous needs of the women of the upper classes shut up in zenānas; and consequently from about 1854 there was developed a new method of missionary service, the visitation of zenānas by women missionaries and their assistants. It was during this section of our period also that medical missions took shape. During all the previous years a little medical help had been given at various points; but now the Christian conscience of Europe and America was stirred to bring medical help to the millions of the common people of India, for whom no skilled assistance in the time of trouble and death was available. Gradually the idea took shape, and produced the Medical Mission, *i.e.* a Christian medical man, sent out to heal and to preach, well equipped with knowledge, with medicine and with surgical implements, and backed also with a dispensary, hospital and assistants. Here again the sufferings of the women of India led to something new. Men could not enter the zenānas, and yet in them much of the tragedy of Hindu pain and death took place. Such was the origin of the woman medical missionary, one of the most precious forms of help ever sent to India. Orphanages, widows' homes and famine relief were all used to some extent during these years, but their full development comes later.

3. The years 1828–1870 saw the flowering of Oriental scholarship. Hodgson discovered the literature of Northern Buddhism during his residence in Nepal from 1833–1844. Roth published his epoch-making treatise on *The Literature and the History of the Veda* in 1846, and, in collaboration with Böhtlingk, began the issue of the great Petersburg Lexicon in 1852. Max Müller's Text of the *Ṛigveda* was issued between 1849 and 1875. Meantime Prinsep and Cunningham laid the foundations of our knowledge of Indian art, epigraphy and archæology. Even at this date the work of Oriental scholars did not influence the Indian mind seriously.

4. The new educational policy of the Government created during these years the modern educated class of India. These are men who think and speak in English habitually, who are proud of their citizenship in the British Empire, who are devoted to English literature, and whose intellectual life has been almost entirely formed by the thought of the West. Large numbers of them enter government service, while the rest practise law, medicine or teaching, or take to journalism or business. We must also note that the powerful excitement which has sufficed to create the religious movements we have to deal with is almost entirely confined to those who have had an English education.

It was in Bengal and Bombay that the results of the new

policy became first conspicuous. The Bengalis in the East and the Parsees and Marāṭhas in the West took very eagerly to English education. Madras followed, and took quite as much advantage of the new situation. The Muḥammadans on the whole held back, but one prominent man, Sir Syed Aḥmad Khan, was far-sighted enough to see the folly of this attitude and did all he could to bring his people into line.

5. We have already noticed Ram Mohan Ray's activity as a writer and social reformer. His greatest achievement coincides with the opening year of this section of our period. In 1828 he founded the Brāhma Samāj, a theistic society, opposed to polytheism, mythology and idolatry, the first and most influential of all the religious movements we have to deal with. But, eighteen months after it was founded, he sailed for England and never returned. The new society would have died, had it not been for the financial support of one of his friends, Prince Dwarka Nath Tagore. In 1842 Debendra Nath Tagore, the youthful son of Rama Mohan Ray's friend, entered the Samāj, and soon became recognized as its leader. A new period of growth and fruitful labour followed. For nearly twenty years longer the Brāhma Samāj continued to be the most prominent indigenous religious movement. Just after the Mutiny a young Bengali, named Keshab Chandra Sen, became a member, and soon displayed remarkable powers. He led the little community into social reform, philanthropy and also, in some degree, into discipleship to Christ.

From the Brāhma Samāj there sprang in 1867 a kindred organization in Bombay, known as the Prārthanā Samāj. Its most prominent leaders belong to a later day. The Parsees of Bombay were busy at the same time with educational and social reform, but no organization sprang up among them.

We ought also to notice that in 1856, largely as a result of the agitation of a Calcutta Brāhman, Paṇḍit Īśvara Chandra

Vidyāsāgara, the Government passed a law legalizing the remarriage of Hindu widows.

Sir Syed Aḥmad Khan, whose influence on the Muḥammadan community we have already noted, was an eager social and religious reformer, but his most notable achievement was the foundation of the Muḥammadan College at Aligarh, which has done a great deal to rouse the Muḥammadans of North India to accept modern thought and to take their rightful place in government and education in these modern days.

LITERATURE. — Lyall, as above. *India under Victoria*, by L. J. Trotter, London, Allen, 1886, 2 vols. *Bentinck, Dalhousie* and *Canning* in Rulers of India Series. Trevelyan's *Life of Macaulay*. *The Administration of the East India Company*, by J. W. Kaye, London, Bentley, 1853 (describes the great reforms). *The Suppression of Human Sacrifice, Suttee and Female Infanticide*, Madras, C. L. S. I., 1898, two and a half annas (abridged from Kaye). Richter's *History of Missions in India;* and George Smith's Lives of Duff and Wilson.

THIRD SECTION: 1870–1895

1. Continuous progress in the adaptation of British administration to the needs of India may be said to sum up the policy and the work of the government during those thirty years. A few points ought to be definitely mentioned. Perhaps the greatest social advance made by Government has been the elaboration of the Famine Code, whereby provision is made from year to year for the possible arrival of serious famine. Elaborate instructions, the reasoned outcome of very wide and very varied experience, are also laid down for the guidance of officers who have to deal with famine conditions. A Local Self-government Bill was passed by Lord Ripon's Government with the definite purpose of educating the people in self-government. Good has certainly resulted

from it but not quite so much as was looked for. The only other act which we need notice is the Age of Consent Act, passed in 1891, which prohibits a husband from living with his wife before she reaches the age of twelve.

2. From the very birth of missionary work in India there had been devoted men who had given their lives to toil amongst the Outcastes, but for a long time comparatively little fruit appeared. From 1876 to 1879 the South of India suffered from an appalling famine. Everywhere missionaries threw themselves into the work of saving life and alleviating distress; and this piece of disinterested service brought its reward. From 1880 onwards great masses of the Outcastes of South India passed into the Church of Christ. The movement has since spread to the North. It has proved the most signal of all the object-lessons given to India by Christians.

Women's work for women, and medical work, both of which took shape, as we have seen, before 1870, have become greatly expanded and still further improved in method since then. These years have also seen the organization of systematic Christian work for lepers. Numerous hospitals have been built for them; and in many places badly managed shelters have been brought under Christian care, and are now doing wonderful work. A large proportion of the lepers cared for by Christians become Christians.

The rapid spread of English education has produced a very large student class, studying in three different types of institutions, government, missionary and native schools and colleges. The attention of Christians has been drawn to the moral and religious needs of this interesting group of young men in a number of ways, and also to the still larger group who are beyond the student stage. Methods of work have been steadily improved in Christian institutions. Hostels for non-Christians have been built in considerable numbers, and, under devoted Christian management, have produced such excellent results that there is a loud cry for the extension of the hostel system throughout the country. The student's magazine, whether connected with a single college or meant for the students of a province, is also a creation of these years. The Young Men's Christian Association, which had been working among Europeans for several decades, began to reach out to Indians, both Christian and non-Christian, in the year 1889, and has proved singularly popular and efficient. The young Indian Christian likes the Association because of its democratic government and the variety of its activities. To the young Hindu the Association has proved a very great boon in many a town. It is to him at once a happy social club and a centre of religious instruction. Its organization and methods have been copied by every religious group throughout India.

3. If Oriental study flowered before 1870, we may say that its fruit was plucked during the next thirty years. Great masses of the knowledge acquired by the leading scholars in previous decades were made available for the ordinary man during these years. We need only refer to these magnificent series of volumes, *The Sacred Books of the East*, Trübner's *Oriental Series*, *The Harvard Oriental Series* and M. N. Dutt's long list of translations. Several of the books published during these years have climbed to fame, notably Edwin Arnold's *Light of Asia* and *The Song Celestial*. Childers, a young civil servant in Ceylon, published in 1875 a Dictionary of Pali, and thus laid the basis of the scientific study of the literature of early Buddhism. Since 1870 Oriental study has reacted very powerfully on the Indian mind in various ways. Indian scholars, trained in European methods, have done brilliant service both in the editing of texts and in translation.

4. The reason why we date this section of our period from 1870 is that from about that date a great change manifests itself in the spirit of the educated classes of India. Hitherto

they have been docile pupils: now they begin to show the vigour and independence of youth. There is a wonderful outburst of freshness, energy and initiative. Many forms of new effort and organization appear. The most pronounced line of thought is a growing desire to defend Hinduism, and an increasing confidence in its defensibility. The movement is now shared by Muslims, Buddhists, Jains and Parsees, but it appeared first among Hindus. Rather later, new political aspirations began to be expressed; the Indian National Congress came into being; and the native press climbed to great influence. About the same time the Social Reform Movement was organized. The first college organized by Hindus was opened in Calcutta in 1879.

5. Religiously, the new feeling created what was practically a Counter-Reformation. A large number of religious movements sprang into being, all of them quite as distinctly opposed to the Brāhma Samāj and the Prārthanā Samāj as to Christianity. We divide these movements into two groups, those which insist on a good deal of reform, and those which lay all their emphasis on defence of the old faiths.

Of the group which seeks reform the most noteworthy movements have their home in the Panjab. There is first the Ārya Samāj, the founder of which was an ascetic named Dayānanda Sarasvatī. A Muḥammadan, named Mirza Ghulam Aḥmad, resident in a village in the Panjab, founded a body which holds much the same place in Indian Muḥammadanism that the Ārya Samāj does in Hinduism. He proclaimed himself the Muslim Maḥdi, the Christian Messiah and a Hindu incarnation. There is, lastly, the Deva Samāj, an atheistic body with its centre in Lahore, the leader of which receives divine honours.

The other group contains a large number of movements, of which we shall mention only a few at this point. The first is the teaching of an interesting ascetic who lived and taught in a temple a few miles north of Calcutta. He is known as Rāmakṛishṇa Paramahaṁsa. Svāmī Vivekānanda, who represented Hinduism at the Parliament of Religions in Chicago, was a pupil of his. The next movement is Theosophy, which was founded by a Russian lady, named Madame Blavatsky, in New York in 1875. The headquarters were moved to India in 1879, and have remained there since. Madame Blavatsky declared that the system was taught her by certain beings of superhuman knowledge and power who, she said, resided in Tibet. It is rather remarkable that another Russian, a man named Notovitch, created, in similar fashion, a myth about Jesus in connection with Tibet [1]; and an American has started in Chicago an eclectic form of Zoroastrianism which he declares he was taught by the Dalai Lama himself.[2]

All the leading Hindu sects, both Vishṇuite and Śivaite, have formed defence associations; and Jains, Buddhists, Parsees and Muḥammadans have followed their example. We need not deal with these in detail here.

These two groups of movements, taken together, form a very striking revival of the ancient religions, parallel to the revival which the faiths of the Roman Empire experienced in the early centuries of the Christian era.

LITERATURE. — Trotter's *India under Victoria*. R. C. Dutt's *Victorian Age in India*. The Lives of Ripon, Dufferin and Lansdowne. Richter's *History of Missions in India*. Phillip's *Outcastes' Hope*, London, Y. P. M. M., 1912. *India, Fifty Years of Progress and Reform*, by R. P. Karkaria, Oxford Press, 1896.

FOURTH SECTION: 1895–1913

This brief space of eighteen years is but a fragment of a period; but it has proved so different in character from the foregoing time that it would be misleading not to set it by it-

[1] P. 140, below. [2] P. 346, below.

self. What gives it its peculiar colour is the new national spirit, which will be discussed in our fifth chapter.

For our purposes the most significant events of the decade, 1895–1905, are the serious preparations for revolutionary action which were made during these years, especially in the Marāṭha country, but also to some extent in the Panjab and Bengal. Meantime, the national movement was steadily gaining in strength, and men were becoming furiously urgent to reap results. The educated Indian was becoming a full-grown man. Towards the close of the decade there came the Russo-Japanese war, the result of which was to enhance the self-respect and the sense of independence and strength of every thinking Asiatic. It happened, then, that, while these three series of events were moving to their climax, we had in India as the representative of Britain Lord Curzon, a man of high aims, of will and knowledge, of industry and eloquence, but also a man whose temperament and action were as a mustard-blister to educated India.

Those who had been preparing for ten years got their opportunity in the Partition of Bengal in October, 1905; and thus the whole length of Lord Minto's viceroyalty (1905–1910) was filled with the horror of anarchism. But he also has the honour of having proposed the new Councils, which have served to give Indians a new place in the Government of India. The King's visit in 1911–1912, and the restoration of the unity of central-Bengal greatly helped the healing process.

Since the time when the majority of the educated class came to recognize that anarchism was the worst enemy the people of India have, the new national feeling, touched as it is with religious feeling, has led men into new forms of activity and service, which promise to bear rich fruit.

LITERATURE.—*Lord Curzon and After*, by Lovat Fraser, London, Heinemann, 16s. *Indian Unrest*, by Sir Valentine Chirol, London, Macmillan, 1910, 5s. net. *Indian Nationalism*, by Edwin Bevan.

CHAPTER II

MOVEMENTS FAVOURING VIGOROUS REFORM

1828–1913

We have already seen that the earliest religious movements of our period were very radical in character, seeking both religious and social reform with great earnestness, and that organizations which sprang from them at a later date were usually filled with the same spirit. All these movements oppose both idolatry and caste; and none of the leaders have been ascetics.

1. The Brāhma Samāj

1. Of all the religious movements of the nineteenth century the Brāhma Samāj has, without doubt, proved the most influential. *Brāhma* is an adjective formed from Brahman, the God of the Upanishads and the Vedānta philosophy, and *samāja* is a noun meaning society. Throughout its history it has been sternly theistic and opposed to idolatry, and has always had a policy of reform. Looked at from one side, it is one of a long series of attempts to found a spiritual religion on a genuine Hindu foundation, which have marked the religion of India from a very early date; while, from the other side, it is a new creation, finding the sources of its vitality in Christian faith and practice.

Ram Mohan Ray (Rāmamohana Rai) (1772–1833), the founder of the Samāj, is the pioneer of all living advance, religious, social and educational, in the Hindu community during the nineteenth century. He was born in a Kulīn

Brāhman family, which had long been connected with the Muḥammadan government of Bengal. The family were followers of Chaitanya,[1] the Bengali Vishṇuite leader, but his mother came of a Śākta[2] family. Both his parents were deeply religious. He was married when quite a boy; but his girl-wife soon died, and his father married him to two other little girls; so that until 1824[3] he was a polygamist.

When he was about twelve years old, he was sent to study at Patna, at that time a famous seat of Muḥammadan learning, which was then the passport into Government service. The effect of the education he received there is thus described by the historian of the Brāhma Samāj:

> He is said to have been specially enchanted with the writings of the *Sufi* school of Mahomedan philosophers, whose views tallied to a large extent with those of the Vedantic school of the Hindus and who accordingly were regarded as little better than heretics by the narrow and orthodox school of Mahomedans. Throughout his subsequent life, Ram Mohun Roy never entirely shook off these early Mahomedan influences. In private life, through a long course of years, his habits and tastes were those of a Mahomedan, and in private conversation he always delighted to quote freely from his favourite *Sufi* authors.[4]

It is probable that he also made the acquaintance of the rationalistic school of Muslim thought, the Mu'tazilites,[5] as B. C. Pal suggests.

On his return, about the age of fifteen, he discovered that the differences between himself and his father on the subject of idolatry were very serious, and he decided to leave home. For some years he lived a wandering life. There is a story that he visited Tibet to study Buddhism and held discussions with the Lamas, but the truth of it is uncertain. But finally his father recalled him. He then settled in Benares, and

[1] P. 293, below.
[2] P. 303, below.
[3] Miss Collet, 115.
[4] *HBS.*, I, 16–17.
[5] P. 96, below.

studied Sanskrit and certain of the Hindu books. In 1796 he began the study of English.

In 1803 his father died, and Ram Mohan removed to Murshidabad, where he published, in 1804, a pamphlet in Persian, *Tuḥfatul Muwaḥḥiddin*, A Gift to Deists. Here the rationalistic and somewhat hard character of the deistic thought which he had imbibed from his study of the Muḥammadan doctors makes itself manifest.

Shortly after, he entered the service of the East India Company under Mr. John Digby. This gentleman, noting Ram Mohan's studious disposition, became his friend, and helped him to acquire a better knowledge of English and English literature. He still continued his religious inquiries and his discussions with those round about him. He served the Government as a revenue officer for nine or ten years, and amassed a fortune. During his stay at his last station, Rungpur, he spent a good deal of time in religious discussion with the Hindus and Jains of the town.

From this time onward his mother opposed and persecuted him, and for some considerable time his wives refused to live with him on account of his heterodoxy.[1]

Originally, Ram Mohan had only hatred for the English; but his practical experience of the Government, his intercourse with Digby and further study of English literature led to a change of feeling and conviction.[2]

On retiring from the service in 1814, he settled in Calcutta, with the definite purpose of devoting his whole time and strength to the propagation of his religious convictions. He established in 1815 a society called the *Ātmīya Sabhā* or Friendly Association. Meetings were held weekly, at which texts from the Hindu scriptures were recited and hymns were sung: but the society ceased to meet in 1819. He studied very seriously, giving his chief attention to the Upanishads

[1] Miss Collet, 33–4, 115. [2] Müller, *Biographical Essays*, 17n., 47.

and the *Vedānta-sūtras* of Bādarāyaṇa. Between 1816 and 1819 he published, in both Bengali and English, an abstract of the *Vedānta-sūtras*, translations of four of the verse Upanishads, and two pamphlets in defence of Hindu theism. His position was that the Upanishads taught pure theism, uncontaminated by idolatry; and he summoned his fellow-countrymen to return to the pure religion of their forefathers. His vigorous action brought him not only controversy but serious persecution. The publication of these works created extraordinary excitement in Bengal and even beyond.

Shortly after settling in Calcutta, he made the acquaintance of the Serampore Missionaries. He also set himself to study Christianity seriously, learning both Hebrew and Greek in order to get at the sources. The result of his reading was thus expressed by himself:

> The consequence of my long and uninterrupted researches into religious truth has been that I have found the doctrines of Christ more conducive to moral principles, and better adapted for the use of rational beings, than any other which have come to my knowledge.

In order to give practical effect to this conviction he published, in 1820, a very remarkable volume, *The Principles of Jesus, the Guide to Peace and Happiness*, being a series of extracts from the Gospels, covering the bulk of Christ's teaching given by Matthew and Luke, with a few pages from Mark and still fewer from John. In the preface to this volume he says:

> This simple code of religion and morality is so admirably calculated to elevate men's ideas to high and liberal notions of one God, . . . and is also so well fitted to regulate the conduct of the human race in the discharge of their various duties to God, to themselves and to society, that I cannot but hope the best effects from its promulgation in the present form.

His position is that Christ was a theist like himself, that His disciples misunderstood Him, and that the whole edifice of

Christology is a huge mistake. Despite this attitude, we can now see what a striking and prophetic advance in the growth of the Hindu spirit the book indicates, and can rejoice that Ram Mohan was able to come so far; but, necessarily, his friends at Serampore felt that the Gospels were mangled and used in an utterly unfair and unhistorical way, in order to bar the progress of Christianity in India. Hence Ram Mohan was now involved in serious controversy on the Christian side.

But he was almost as keenly interested in education and in the reform of the Hindu family as in the establishment of his religious views. In the matter of English education his help proved of great value. He was one of those who formed the scheme of the Hindu College, which was opened in Calcutta in 1819; and, when Duff arrived in the city in 1830, Ram Mohan not only secured a suitable house for his English school, but also brought him a number of pupils. He realized that caste was indefensible and required to be opposed; but, for various reasons, he carefully guarded his own caste, retained his sacred thread, and wrote in defence of the observance of caste; so that he did no service to the crusade.

With regard to the family he felt strongly. The influence of the Serampore men moved him decisively here. It was chiefly the wrongs of women that stirred him. He denounced widow-burning and polygamy, and pleaded for a return to earlier practice in the matter of the rights of women according to the Hindu law of inheritance.

His efforts proved fruitful in several directions. The agitation against the burning of widows, in which he had taken a great part,[1] found its conclusion in Lord Bentinck's famous order of the 4th of December, 1829, forbidding the cruel practice.

[1] Strangely enough, Ram Mohan, though eager to see the practice cease, was opposed to Lord Bentinck's proposal, and endeavoured to persuade him not to carry it out. See Miss Collet, 146.

But it was in religion that his work was most effective. Through his friendship with the Serampore Missionaries he was led to help them in their great task of translating the New Testament into Bengali. In the course of the work serious discussions arose, and collaboration ceased; but one of the Missionaries, the Rev. W. Adam, sided with Ram Mohan, and became a Unitarian in May, 1821. This led to the formation in September, 1821, of a Unitarian Mission in Calcutta under a Committee of Europeans and Indians. A house was rented, and Unitarian services were conducted in English. A printing-press and education were also used as auxiliaries; and a Vedant College, meant to turn out *Hindu* Unitarians, was opened. But Ram Mohan and Adam did not pull well together, and little success was attained. The mission was given up.

2. *First Period of the Samāj, 1828–1842: Deistic Theology and Christian Ethics.* Since the weekly service in English had failed, some friends suggested a more distinctly Indian service in the vernacular. Feringhi Kamal Bose's house in Upper Chitpore Road was rented, and the first meeting was held on the 20th of August, 1828. The name chosen at first was *Brahma Sabhā*, Brahman Association, but it was soon altered to *Brāhma Samāj*. His chief supporters were three wealthy men, of whom the most notable was Prince Dwarka Nath Tagore (*Dvārikānātha Ṭhakkura*), and a group of learned Brāhmans. The society met every Saturday evening from seven to nine. The service was in four parts, the chanting of selections from the Upanishads in Sanskrit (this was done in a small room curtained off by itself into which only Brāhmans were admitted), the translation of these passages into Bengali, a sermon in Bengali, and the singing of theistic hymns in Sanskrit and Bengali composed by Ram Mohan and his friends. There was no organization, no membership, no creed. It was merely a weekly meeting open to any who cared

to attend. Ram Mohan believed he was restoring Hindu worship to its pristine purity.

Soon afterwards a building was erected in Chitpore Road for the Samāj; and it was opened on the 23rd of January, 1830. The Trust Deed is rather a remarkable document. The following are a few sentences from it:

> To be used . . . as a place of public meeting of all sorts and descriptions of people without distinction as shall behave and conduct themselves in an orderly sober religious and devout manner for the worship and adoration of the Eternal Unsearchable and Immutable Being who is the Author and Preserver of the Universe but not under or by any other name designation or title peculiarly used for and applied to any particular Being or Beings by any man or set of men whatsoever and that no graven image statue or sculpture carving painting picture portrait or the likeness of anything shall be admitted within the said building . . . and that no sacrifice . . . shall ever be permitted therein and that no animal or living creature shall within or on the said premises be deprived of life . . . and that in conducting the said worship and adoration no object animate or inanimate that has been or is . . . recognized as an object of worship by any man or set of men shall be reviled or slightingly or contemptuously spoken of . . . and that no sermon preaching discourse prayer or hymn be delivered made or used in such worship but such as have a tendency to the promotion of the contemplation of the Author and Preserver of the Universe to the promotion of charity morality piety benevolence virtue and the strengthening the bonds of union between men of all religious persuasions and creeds.

3. In November, 1830, Ram Mohan sailed for England. He had long wished to take the journey. He was fully conscious of the momentous changes destined to arise in India from the introduction of British government, Western civilization and Christianity; and naturally wished to study life and religion in England. He also hoped to be of some service to his coun-

try politically, since the Charter of the East India Company fell to be renewed in 1833. The representative of the Mughal dynasty, now a pensioner of the Company, entrusted him with a personal petition, and conferred on him the title of Rāja. He took two servants with him, in order that he might keep caste on the sea and in England.

He was received with the utmost cordiality and respect in England, and exercised a greater influence than he can have ever hoped to do, but he died in Bristol in 1833. In Bristol Museum there hangs a portrait by Biggs, which is reproduced as the frontispiece to this volume.

4. He was a man of large intellect, of wide sympathies and of both courage and force. He was the first Indian who realized the great good which the country would reap from its connection with Britain and from the leaven of Christianity. But [1] he realized to the full that no real blessing could come to India by the mere adoption of Western things unchanged. India, he said, would inevitably remain Indian. No gift from the outside could be of any real value except in so far as it was naturalized. His long bold struggle, on the one hand, for religious and social purity, for educational progress and journalistic freedom, and his brilliant literary work and unchanging fidelity to Indian ideals, on the other, had made him not only the most prominent of all Indians, but the one man able to stand between Indians and Englishmen as interpreter and friend.

But he was neither a philosopher nor a theologian. He thought out no system. Faced with the superstitions and the immoralities of popular Hinduism, on the one hand, and seeing distinctly, on the other, the truth contained in Islam and Christianity as well as in his own Hindu Upanishads, he found a plain man's solution of the complicated problem. He

[1] The following sentences to the end of the paragraph are from the author's article on the Brāhma Samāj in *ERE*.

seized on the theistic elements common to the three faiths, and declared them to be at once the original truths of Hinduism (corrupted by the populace in the course of the centuries) and the universal religion on which all men could unite. We must not be astonished at the crudeness of his work. The Vedas from which alone a true knowledge of the rise of Hinduism can be obtained were inaccessible to him, only the Upanishads being available; and the science of religion had not yet gathered its stores of comparative knowledge to illuminate the whole problem of the religions and their relation to each other.

He believed he was restoring the Hindu faith to its original purity, while, as a matter of fact, what he offered was a deistic theology and worship. Deism was very popular among European rationalists in the eighteenth century, and it harmonized well both with what he found in the Upanishads and with what he had learned from Muḥammadan rationalists. The Upanishads teach that Brahman is actionless; that he has no purpose or aim which could lead him to action; that all his activity is sport; that he is beyond the range of thought and speech; and therefore cannot be reached by man's meditations and prayers. That Ram Mohan's conception of God was seriously deistic we may realize clearly from the lack of prayer in the worship of the Samāj in his day, and also from the definitions of worship given in his writings. Here is a passage from his *Religious Instructions founded on Sacred Authorities:*

Question — What is meant by worship?
Answer — Worship implies the act of one with a view to please another; but when applied to the Supreme Being, it signifies a contemplation of his attributes.
Question — In what manner is this worship to be performed?
Answer — By bearing in mind that the Author and Governor of this visible universe is the Supreme Being, and comparing

> this idea with the sacred writings and with reason. In this worship it is indispensably necessary to use exertions to subdue the senses, and to read such passages as direct attention to the Supreme Spirit. . . . The benefits which we continually receive from fire, from air, and from the sun, likewise from the various productions of the earth, such as the different kinds of grain, drugs, fruit and vegetables, all are dependent on him: and by considering and reasoning on the terms expressive of such ideas, the meaning itself is firmly fixed in the mind.[1]

Contrast with these statements the following lines from a little manual used at present by the Sādhāran Brāhma Samāj:

> Worship is the communion of the soul with God; on the part of man, it is the opening of his soul, the outpouring of his aspirations, the acknowledgement of his failures and transgressions and the consecration of his life and work to God as his Lord, Refuge and Guide; and on the part of God, the communication of His light, strength, inspiration and blessing unto the longing soul.[2]

This is a living theism: the above is a dry deism.

But there is another element in Ram Mohan's teaching which, in the subsequent history, has proved of infinite importance, namely this, *that he did not believe in transmigration.* Here he broke absolutely with Hinduism. Transmigration and karma are the very essence of the religion. The one aim of the philosophy of the Upanishads is the attainment of *release from transmigration.* It is thus only the simple truth to say that Ram Mohan was no longer a Hindu, that the orthodox were quite right in their suspicions, although they failed to lay stress on the crucial point. That this is a just judgment is made plain by the fact that the historical evolution of his principles has ended in separating the Brāhmas from Hindu society. The Brāhma to-day is as distinctly outside Hinduism as the Christian is.

[1] *English Works*, 135, 137. [2] *The religion of the Brahmo Samaj*, 40.

PLATE I

From life-size portrait by Baron de Schweter.

PRINCE DWARKA NATH TAGORE

We must also note that the form of the service arranged by Ram Mohan is Christian. Congregational worship is unknown in the ancient Hinduism which he believed he was restoring. Further, the ethics which Ram Mohan recommended were drawn from the teaching of Christ.

The death of the Founder was almost fatal to the infant society; but the munificence of his friend Prince Dwarka Nath Tagore enabled it to exist until a better day dawned.

5. *Second Period, 1842–1865: Debendra Nath Tagore: Theism and Religious Reform.* In 1838 Debendra Nath Tagore, the youthful son of the prince who had been Ram Mohan's great friend, passed through a very decided spiritual change, which made him a consecrated man for the rest of his life. The following year he formed, along with a few friends, the *Tattvabodhinī Sabhā*, or Truth-teaching Association, which met weekly for religious discussion, and once a month for worship.

Then in 1842, nine years after Ram Mohan's death, he and his young friends joined the Brāhma Samāj; and, for some years, the two societies worked side by side for common objects. Debendra was soon recognized as leader, and, being a Brāhman, became the *Āchārya* or minister of the Samāj. A monthly, called the *Tattvabodhinī Patrikā*, or Truth-teaching Journal, began to appear; and a Vedic school, the *Tattvabodhinī Pāṭhśāla*, was established, partly to train Brāhma missionaries, partly with a view to check Christianity, now making considerable progress in Calcutta under Duff's[1] leadership. Debendra followed Ram Mohan in his belief that original Hinduism was a pure spiritual theism, and in his enthusiasm for the Upanishads, but did not share his deep reverence for Christ. He believed India had no need of Christianity; and he was never known to quote the Bible.

6. He saw that the Samāj needed organization. Hitherto

[1] P. 19, above.

it had been merely a weekly meeting. It had exercised little influence on the private life of those who attended; and they were bound by no lasting tie to the Society. He therefore drew up, in 1843, what is known as the Brāhma Covenant, a list of solemn vows to be taken by every one on becoming a member of the Society. The chief promises made are to abstain from idolatry, and to worship God by loving Him and by doing such deeds as He loves. The members of the *Tattvabodhinī Sabhā* were the first to take the vows. This fresh organization greatly strengthened the Samāj.

At the same time a brief form of prayer and adoration, drawn up by Debendra and called *Brahmopāsanā*,[1] worship of Brahman, was introduced. This addition of prayer and devotional exercises to the service of the Samāj was a notable enrichment. It was a living fruit of Debendra's own religious experience. He was as far as possible from being a deist. He lived a life of constant prayer and worship of God; and the direct communion of the human soul with the supreme Spirit was the most salient point in his teaching.

These changes and the vigorous preaching of Debendra and several young missionaries in Calcutta and many places round led to considerable growth. The Samāj began once more to take a prominent place in the life of Bengal.

But there were difficulties. The Vedas were recognized as the sole standard of the faith of the Samāj; and most of the members believed them to be verbally inspired. Duff was therefore justified in criticizing the Samāj for holding the plenary inspiration of such documents. A few of the more advanced members saw that it was no longer possible to hold the belief. In order that the matter might be settled on a sure basis, four students were sent to Benares, that each might study and copy one of the four Vedas, and bring back the fruits of his labour. They reached Calcutta in 1850; and the final

[1] Published in *Brāhma Dharma*.

result was that the inerrancy of the Vedas was altogether given up. Thus the rationalism implicit in Ram Mohan's teaching from the beginning became fully explicit; and the Samāj, left without any authoritative standard of doctrine, was thrown back on nature and intuition. Yet the Upanishads did not cease to be the chief scripture of the society; for, just at this crisis, Debendra compiled a series of extracts from Hindu literature, the bulk of them being from the Upanishads, for use in public worship and private devotion. This volume is called *Brāhma Dharma*, i.e. Brāhma Religion.

7. In 1857 a young man joined the Samāj who was destined to prove its third leader. This was Keshab Chandra Sen (*Keśavachandra Sena*), a Calcutta student, who came of a well-known Vishṇuite family of Vaidya caste, and had had a good modern education. For two years he did nothing, but in 1859 he became an active and successful worker. Debendra formed a great liking for his gifted young friend, while Keshab looked up to him with reverence and tenderness as to a father.

In 1860 Keshab founded the Saṅgat Sabhā,[1] or Believers' Association, which met regularly for devotional purposes and for the discussion of religious and social questions. In this weekly meeting the problem of the sacraments, *saṁskāras*, celebrated in Hindu homes on the occasion of births, marriages and other family events, was discussed; and their idolatrous character stood out so clearly that the members came to the conclusion that Brāhmas could not conscientiously take part in them. In consequence, Debendra decided that no idolatrous sacrament should ever be celebrated in his own home, and prepared, for the use of the Samāj, a set of modified ceremonies from which everything heathen and idolatrous had been eliminated. These are known as Brāhma rites; the manual is called the *Anushṭhāna Paddhati;* and Brāhmas who use them are known as Anushṭhānic Brāhmas. The worship

[1] The word *Saṅgat* is used by the Sikhs for a company of pious people.

of Durgā, which until now had been held every year in the Tagore residence, was given up, and the chamber in which the idol stood was converted into a chapel for family worship. The Sabhā also discussed caste, with the result that the members gave it up once and for all, and Debendra discarded his own sacred thread. At Keshab's suggestion, the Samāj began to follow the example of Christian philanthropy, and gathered money and food for the famine-stricken. He was daily coming more and more under the influence of Christ, and felt in the depths of his spirit that social service and social reform were the bounden duty of every serious theist.

Keshab had had a good English education and had obtained a post in the Bank of Bengal. In 1861 he and several of his young friends gave up their positions, in order to become missionaries of the Samāj. Shortly afterwards, Keshab, though he was not a Brāhman, was formally made a minister of the Samāj with the title of Āchārya.[1] At this time also it was arranged that no minister of the Samāj, whether Brāhman or non-Brāhman, should wear the sacred thread.

Amongst the new activities of the movement were the Brāhma Vidyālaya, a sort of informal theological school, and a fortnightly English journal, *The Indian Mirror*, which soon became influential.

In 1864 Keshab made a long tour extending as far as Madras and Bombay, and preached with great power and success wherever he went. As a result of his labours, a new society called the Veda Samāj was founded in Madras that same year. From this society the present Brāhma Samāj of Madras has grown. During this tour the welcome which he received far and near, and the many openings which he saw, suggested to him the possibility of a Brāhma Samāj for the whole of India.

[1] This led to the secession of a number of the older members of the Samāj, including Īśvara Chandra Vidyāsāgara. They formed a new society, the Upāsanā Samāj, which did not last long.

Three years later the men whom he had influenced in Bombay formed themselves into the Prārthanā Samāj.[1]

8. But all the changes and reforms which had come through Keshab's activity proved too much for the older members of the society; and Debendra himself, though he felt like a father towards his gifted young helper, was very much afraid that spiritual religion would be sacrificed to the new passion for social reform. To him the latter was of very little consequence as compared with the former. He was still very much of a Hindu in feeling; he believed that, however evil caste might be, members of the Samāj ought not to be compelled, in the circumstances of those days, to give it up. He was opposed to marriages between people of different castes; and he could not endure the thought of widow-remarriage. Keshab's Christian studies, on the other hand, had led him and his associates to see that the overthrow of caste and the complete reform of the Hindu family were altogether necessary for the moral and religious health of India. There were religious differences between them also. Debendra was a deeply devotional spirit, but the fact of sin and the need of repentance had made very little impression upon him; while, through the teaching of Christ, Keshab and his party had become fully alive to the supreme importance of the ethical side of religion, both for the individual and the country.

The consequence was the formation of two parties within the Samāj, each eager to be friendly with the other, and yet each unable to yield to the other; and suspicion grew apace. On the 5th of October, 1864, a very violent cyclone visited Calcutta and Bengal, and so damaged the Brāhma building that it became necessary to hold the services in Debendra's house. He seized this opportunity to allow ministers wearing the sacred thread to officiate. Keshab and his party protested

[1] P. 74, below.

against this breach of the rules, while Debendra would not budge. Negotiations were carried on for some time, but without result. Consequently, early in 1865, Keshab and his party withdrew, leaving Debendra and his followers with all the property of the Samāj. Keshab was only twenty-four years of age. There were already fifty Samājes in Bengal, three in North India and one in Madras.

9. Since the secession, the old Samāj has become more Hindu than before. Its ambiguous theological position is reflected in its undecided attitude to caste. On this latter point one of its leaders wrote:

> In conformity with such views, the Ādi Samāj has adopted a Hindu form to propagate Theism among Hindus. It has therefore retained many innocent Hindu usages and customs. . . . It leaves matters of social reformation to the judgments and tastes of its individual members. . . . If it be asked why should such social distinctions as caste be observed at all, the reply is that the world is not yet prepared for the practical adoption of the doctrines of levellers and socialists.[1]

10. We may here sum up what we have to say about Debendra Nath Tagore; for, though he preached from time to time, and now and then published something, during the forty years that intervened between the secession and his death in 1905, yet he no longer occupied his old prominent position. He spent most of his time in retirement and devotional exercises, either on the Himalayas or in his own home in Calcutta. His great and noble character and his lofty spiritual nature so impressed his fellow-citizens that he was universally known as the *Maharshi*, the great Ṛishi or Seer; and he was looked up to by all sections of the Samāj as the saintly patriarch of the movement. I had the pleasure of seeing and talking with him a few months before his death.

[1] *HBS.*, I, 189.

PLATE II

From portrait by W. Archer, R.A.

MAHARSHI DEBENDRA NATH TAGORE

The bleached complexion and massive architecture of his face revealed even then, at the age of eighty-seven, the lofty spiritual nature and the sensitive heart which had done so much in the far-away years.

He regarded himself as a true Hindu, standing in the long noble succession of the thinkers and rapt devotees of the Vedānta; and it is indeed true that a large measure of their reverence and inspiration had descended to him. But he failed to realize that the rejection of the authority of the Vedas, and above all of the doctrine of transmigration and karma, had set him outside the nexus of the peculiar beliefs and aspirations of Hinduism. Since he was unwilling to learn from Christ, and since he stood apart from the chief source of Hindu religious passion — the desire for release from rebirth, — his Samāj has barely succeeded in keeping afloat amid the fierce currents of modern thought and practical life.

11. *Third Period, 1865–1878: Two Samājes: Theism and Social Reform.* At this time Keshab read a great deal of Christian literature and came more and more under Christian influence. Dean Stanley's *Works*, Robertson's *Sermons*, Liddon's *Divinity of our Lord*, the *Theologica Germanica* and Seeley's *Ecce Homo* were among the volumes which touched him most deeply. The influence of Seeley can be very distinctly felt in the lecture delivered in 1866 on *Jesus Christ: Europe and Asia.* He called attention to the fact that Jesus was an Asiatic, and spoke very freely of Christ's greatness and his supernatural moral heroism. The chief point of the lecture, however, is a straightforward, manly appeal, addressed to Europeans as well as his fellow-countrymen, to follow the moral precepts of Jesus. His enthusiasm for Christ led many to believe that he was about to become a Christian.

Many of his followers turned enthusiastically to the study of the Bible at this time; and the touch of Christ produced a new seriousness among them, which showed itself in an eager desire to lead a pure and holy life, and a passion for saving souls. It was this that formed the temper of the missionary body. These men, seven or eight in number, all of them attached by the closest personal ties to Keshab, were the strength of the new movement. They were great in enthusiasm and self-sacrifice. They lived lives of simplicity and hard work, and suffered both privation and persecution. They went about preaching, and many individuals were won to the cause. Yet the seeds of future difficulty were already visible. There was no organization; and so, although each missionary was bound to Keshab by strong religious ties, lack of definite arrangement and rule led to frequent quarrels amongst them, which Keshab found it hard to compose.

12. At the end of 1866 he formed a new society, called the Brāhma Samāj of India, and invited all Brāhmas throughout the country to join it. Henceforward the original Samāj was called the Ādi Brāhma Samāj, or original society. A number of the steady old members held by Debendra, but nearly the whole of the younger and more enthusiastic men followed Keshab; and many noteworthy Brāhmas in other parts of India also adhered to him. Unfortunately there was no constitution, no governing body, no rules. Everything was left in Keshab's hands. Very soon afterwards a selection of theistic texts from the Hindu, Buddhist, Jewish, Christian, Muḥammadan and Chinese Scriptures was published, under the title *Ślokasaṅgraha*, or Collection of Texts, for use in the services of the Samāj. The wider, freer outlook of the new body thus received very vivid expression. The society held its weekly service in Keshab's own house on Sundays, while the leaders still attended the regular service of the Ādi Samāj, which was held on Wednesday.

13. The separation from Debendra depressed Keshab, and threw him back on God. Hence, he and his fellow-mission-

aries spent long days of fervent prayer and adoration in his house, seeking strength and courage from God. Ever since his conversion he had been a man of prayer, but he now entered into a deeper experience of its joy and power than ever before.

Set free from old restraints, and having round him a large body of enthusiasts who were ready for progress, he adopted a number of new practices which were meant to deepen and strengthen the religious life of the Samāj. The sources of his new methods were the Vishṇuism of Chaitanya,[1] which was traditional in his own family, and Christianity, which was now influencing him so deeply. He began to use the old Vishṇuite word *bhakti*, which covers both love for God and faith in Him, and to stir the members of the Samāj to live by it. One of his missionaries, Bijay Kṛishṇa Gosvāmī, was a lineal descendant of one of the companions of Chaitanya. Keshab commissioned him to introduce the instruments used in the old sect, and begin *saṅkīrtana*,[1] the enthusiastic singing in chorus, with musical accompaniments, of hymns of praise and devotion. Chaitanya had also taught his followers to move in procession through the streets of a town, dancing and singing praise to God, with flags flying and drums beating. This *nagarkīrtana*,[1] town-praise, was adopted and used in Calcutta with much success. He also drew up a new liturgy for use in the services, which is still widely used. From this time too the Brāhmas have held several annual festivals, each lasting two or more days. The whole time is spent in prayer, worship and the hearing of religious addresses. Keshab thus did all in his power to start the new society in a living experience of God and His service.

14. In August, 1869, a building in Machua Bazaar Street was opened for the use of the new Samāj with great rejoicings. Then, just as Ram Mohan did, after the opening of the original

[1] P. 293, below.

building, Keshab suddenly announced, to the amazement of his friends, his intention of going to England. The Samāj was altogether without organization, and all its activities depended entirely on Keshab himself; so that it seemed rather unwise for him to go away. But some sort of arrangement was made, and Keshab took the journey. He was received in England with the utmost cordiality, delivered addresses in all parts of the country, met many noteworthy people, and made many new friends. The visit was also a great experience for Keshab: he returned to India with a new sense of the priceless value of the Christian home, and with his head filled with fresh schemes for social reform.

15. The younger members of the new Samāj had been very busy socially from the very outset. They were, above all, enthusiastic advocates of the education of girls and of the emancipation of women. Some of them began to take their wives with them to call on Christians and to social gatherings. They invented a new and becoming dress, more suited for outdoor wear and social intercourse than the rather scanty clothing of the stay-at-home Bengali wife. A new form of marriage-ritual was created, more truly expressive of progressive Brāhma feeling than the form in use in the old Samāj, and in it were included marriage-vows to be taken by the bride and bridegroom, in imitation of Christian marriage. They struggled to put down child-marriage. Several widows were remarried and more than one marriage between persons of different castes was solemnized. Philanthropy was not neglected. In time of famine or epidemic they were ready to help.

Later, it became clear that there was no law in existence under which Brāhma marriages could come. Hence Keshab appealed to the Government, and, after much discussion and difficulty, an Act was passed in 1872 which legalized them. Paṇḍit S. N. Śāstrī remarks:

The passing of this Act may be justly regarded as the crowning success of the prolonged efforts of the reformers for the amelioration of their social life. It abolished early marriage, made polygamy penal, sanctioned widow marriages and inter-caste marriages. As such it was hailed with a shout of joy by the progressives; but ever since it has been one of the principal causes that have alienated the Brahmos from the sympathies of their orthodox countrymen.[1]

The new social activities which Keshab inaugurated on his return from England included a Normal School for girls, an Industrial School for boys, the Victoria Institution for women, and the *Bhārat Āśram*, a home in which a number of families were gathered together for the cultivation of a better home-life, and for the education of women and children. Journalism was also eagerly pursued. *The Indian Mirror* became a daily paper, and the *Sulabh Samāchār*, the Cheap News, a Bengali weekly published at a farthing, began to appear.

The movement was very successful. The tours of the missionaries in country towns, Keshab's tours to distant cities, and his great lectures in English drew great numbers of men to theism and rapidly built up the membership of the Samāj. Several of the other missionaries, notably Pratap Chandra Mozoomdar, were growing in strength and spiritual power.

16. Yet Keshab began to be conscious that all was not well in the Samāj. An opposition party was being formed. There were several reasons for their dissatisfaction. While Keshab was in most things very progressive, he was opposed to giving women much freedom, and was very much afraid of the effects which a university education would produce on them. He had already done much to release them from the restraints of Hinduism, and he was in favour of giving girls a simple education; but a large and growing party were coming more

[1] *HBS.*, I, 251.

and more under the spell of Western ideals, and they were determined that their daughters should receive a good modern education. The second point of difference sprang from the supremacy of Keshab in the Samāj. He was so much bigger than any other Brāhma, and his addresses showed so much inspiration, and influenced men so deeply, that he began to believe himself different from other men, dowered with a constant inspiration from heaven; and some of his youthful followers began to fall at his feet and to address him as Hindus have been accustomed to address their gurus for many centuries. The party of progress and freedom were very sensible of the extreme dangers of guruism in a modern body like the Samāj, and they protested seriously against it. Two of the missionaries actually left Keshab. It seems clear that he rebuked his young disciples when their enthusiasm carried them to extremes; yet in his lectures he used expressions which might well lead people to treat him as different from other men; and Mozoomdar tells us frankly that he always favoured those who regarded him as the divinely commissioned leader of the movement, and severely criticized the opposite party. The worst point of all was his doctrine of *adesh* (*ādeśa*). He declared that from time to time a direct command from God was laid upon him by special revelation. The want of organization in the Samāj made matters still worse. It is probably true that he had no desire to be an autocrat; yet, since there was no constitution, and since he objected to every form of popular government proposed by the other party, everything depended upon him, and he occupied, as a matter of fact, the position of master of the Samāj, whether he deserved to be charged with autocracy or not.

17. In a temple a few miles to the north of Calcutta there lived an ascetic known as Rāmakṛishṇa Paramahaṁsa, of whom we shall hear later.[1] Keshab made his acquaintance,

[1] P. 188, below.

went frequently to see him, and now and then took a large company of his followers with him. There can be no doubt that Keshab's appreciation of the man and his frequent praise of his devotion and his stimulating conversation did much to bring Rāmakṛishṇa into public notice, and to draw to him the crowds of disciples who listened to his words. We do not know when Keshab made his acquaintance, but Rāmakṛishṇa's latest biographer states that it was about the year 1875; and that seems, on the whole, the most likely date.[1] Rāmakṛishṇa was a man of deeply religious nature. He was a true Hindu, little touched by Western influences, holding the Vedānta philosophy, ready to worship any Hindu idol, and prepared to defend any Hindu belief or practice against all comers, yet also convinced that all religions are true and that no man should leave the faith into which he has been born.

Feeling very distinctly the growing opposition in the air around him, Keshab sought once more by prayer, consecration and new forms of renunciation to unite and strengthen the missionary body, and to fill the whole Samāj with such enthusiastic devotion as to preclude the possibility of disunion. The practices which he adopted himself and which he induced his missionaries to adopt at this time are so very different in spirit from the methods of devotion that he employed earlier, and are so distinctly Hindu, that one is tempted to see in them evidence of the influence of Rāmakṛishṇa. Here is the account given by Śāstrī:

> It was not entirely the asceticism of the spirit that he inculcated at this time; for he countenanced, both by precept and example, some of the external forms of it. For instance, he himself gave up the use of metallic drinking cups, substituting earthen ones for them, his example being followed by many of the missionaries; he took to cooking his own food and constructed a little thatched kitchen on the terrace of the third

[1] P. 194, below.

story of his Kalutolah house for that purpose; and introduced the *ektara*, a rude kind of musical instrument and the mendicant's drinking bowl, well-known to a sect of Vaishnavas. . . . One thing, however, was remarkable. Along with the development of these tendencies there was visible a decline of the old philanthropic activities of the Samaj. The educational and other institutions started under the *Indian Reform Association*, for instance, began to decline from this time. Very great stress was laid on meditation and retirement from the world. With a view to giving practical effect to these ideas, Mr. Sen purchased a garden in the village of Morepukur, within a few miles of Calcutta, in 1876, and duly consecrated it to that purpose on the 20th of May that year, under the name of *Sadhan Kanan*, or "Forest Abode for Religious Culture." Here many of the missionaries of the Samaj spent with him most of the days of the week in meditation and prayer, in cooking their own food, in drawing water, in cutting bamboos, in making and paving roads, in constructing their cabins, in planting and watering trees, and in cleansing their bedrooms. As marks of their asceticism they began to sit below trees on carpets made of hides of tigers and of other animals, in imitation of Hindu mendicants and spend long hours in meditation. . . . It was towards the end of this year that Mr. Sen introduced a fourfold classification of devotees. He chose from amongst his missionaries four different sets of men to represent four types of religious life. The *Yogi*, or the adept in rapt communion, the *Bhakta*, or the adept in rapturous love of God, the *Jnani*, or the earnest seeker of true knowledge and the *Shebak*, or the active servant of humanity. These four orders were constituted and four different kinds of lessons were given to the disciples of the respective classes.[1]

He succeeded by these means in binding the missionaries to himself, but he failed with a large section of his followers.

18. Yet things might have continued as they were for some time, but for a chance occurrence, which led to a serious practical application of the doctrine of *adesh*[2] by Keshab, and which

[1] *HBS.*, I, 269–71. [2] P. 50, above.

convinced the opposing party that they were absolutely right in their estimate of him. The Government of Bengal had had the young heir to the native state of Kuch Bihar (in North Bengal) carefully educated under English officials, so that he might become a capable modern ruler, and they had arranged that he should proceed on a visit to England. But his mother demanded that he should be married before leaving India; and the Government officials who were responsible for his training were most anxious that he should be married to a cultured girl who would be a help and not a hindrance to him. Consequently, the proposal was made that he should marry Keshab's daughter. Now, the Brāhma leader had been fighting idolatry and child-marriage for many years; and, through his influence, a special Marriage Act had been passed for Brāhmas.[1] The young prince and Keshab's daughter were both under age from the point of view of the Brāhma Marriage Law. Further, the Kuch Bihar family were Hindus; and, consequently, the prince could not be married as a Brāhma. His marriage would necessarily be a Hindu marriage; and there could be no guarantee that he would not marry other wives. It was thus perfectly clear that Keshab could not consistently agree to the marriage. But several things conspired to make it difficult to refuse. The Government were most eager to see it carried out. Already tentative proposals had been made with regard to the daughter of another Brāhma, with whom the alliance would be made, if Keshab declined it. The young man himself declared that he was a theist, and that he would not marry more than one wife; yet, as he was not a member of the Samāj, that could not alter the character of the marriage. Indeed, since Kuch Bihar is a native state, the Brāhma Marriage Act was altogether inapplicable. Government, however, extracted promises from the Kuch Bihar family, that everything idolatrous

[1] P. 48, above.

would be excluded from the ceremony, and that the marriage would be in fact a betrothal, as the parties would not live together until the young man returned from England, when both would be of age. But what decided Keshab was the doctrine of *adesh*. He believed that he had received from God a command to go on with the wedding; and therefore, in spite of all the facts already mentioned, and in spite of the vehement protests of a large party in the Samāj, he gave his consent.

As was to be expected, the Kuch Bihar family did not carry out their promises. The wedding as celebrated was a Hindu marriage; idolatrous implements and symbols were in the pavilion; and, though Keshab and his daughter both withdrew before any idolatrous ceremonies took place, the ritual was completed by the Hindu priests in the presence of the bridegroom in the usual way.

19. A tremendous storm followed in Calcutta. The opposing party did their best to depose Keshab, and to seize the building, but failed in both attempts. Finally, they left the Samāj, a great body of intelligent and influential men. For many years a fierce controversy raged round the details of the wedding; but the facts are now quite clear. A little pamphlet, called *A Brief Reminiscence of Keshub Chunder Sen*,[1] written by Miss Pigot, the pioneer Zenāna Missionary of the Church of Scotland, who was most intimate with Keshab and his family, and accompanied the little bride to the wedding, gives a clear and intelligible account of all that happened.

20. *Fourth Period, 1878–1884: Three Samājes: Keshab's New Dispensation.* Most of the missionaries, a number of outstanding men and a section of the rank and file held by Keshab, but the major portion of the membership went out. All the provincial Samājes were consulted, and the majority fell in with the new movement. The name chosen was the

[1] Published in Calcutta in 1910.

PLATE III

KESHAB CHANDRA SEN

Sādhāran Brāhma Samāj; and great care was taken to organize the society in a representative way, so as to avoid the single-man government and the consequent changes of teaching which had caused so much trouble in the old body. The word *sādhāran* means "general," and is clearly meant to suggest that the society is catholic and democratic. With regard to doctrine and practice, they were anxious to continue the old theistic teaching and the social service and philanthropy which had characterized Keshab's Samāj to begin with. They were especially eager to go forward with female education. It was the easier to organize a representative government and to secure continuity of teaching, because, while there were many able men among them, there was no outstanding leader. Of the four missionaries appointed the most prominent was Paṇḍit Śiva Nāth Śāstrī. On the 22nd of January, 1881, their new building in Cornwallis Street was opened.

Yet, despite the great schism, Keshab retained the primacy in Brāhmaism by sheer genius and force of character until his death in 1884. His achievements during the last six years of his life are very remarkable, the extraordinary freshness of his thinking and writing, and the many new elements he introduced into his work. Yet, though very brilliant, these innovations have not proved nearly so fruitful and lasting as his early contributions to the cause. They will be more intelligible grouped under three heads, than set out in chronological order.

21. The first group comes under the head of his own phrase, the *New Dispensation*. For some years it had been clear that he thought of himself as having a special divine commission. That idea now becomes explicit. There have been a number of divine dispensations in the past: he is now the divinely appointed leader of the New Dispensation, in which all religions are harmonized, and which all men are summoned to enter as their spiritual home. He and his missionaries are

the apostles of this new and universal church. But this claim, which, if logically carried out, would have set him, as the centre of the final religion of all time, far above Christ, Buddha, Muḥammad and every other leader, is crossed and hindered by two other thoughts, each of which influenced him powerfully during the last section of his life; first, the idea that all religions are true, which he took over from Rāmakṛishṇa Paramahaṁsa, and, secondly, a belief in the supremacy of Christ as the God-man. Consequently, all his teaching about the New Dispensation lacks consistency and grip.

On the anniversary day in January in 1881 he appeared on the platform, with twelve of his missionaries around him, under a new red banner, on which were inscribed the words Naba Bidhan (*Nava Vidhāna*), that is, New Dispensation, and also an extraordinary symbol made up of the Hindu trident, the Christian cross and the crescent of Islam. On the table lay the Scriptures of the four greatest religions of the world, Hinduism, Buddhism, Christianity and Muḥammadanism. Four of the apostles were specially appointed that each might study the Scriptures of one of these religions. Henceforward, the phrase Brāhma Samāj falls into the background, and Keshab's body is known as *The Church of the New Dispensation.*

Feeling now more confident of his own inspiration, he frequently issued proclamations in the name of God, calling upon all men to accept the New Dispensation, and pronouncing those who had left him infidels, apostates and disobedient men. In keeping with the universality ascribed to the New Dispensation, the faithful were exhorted to turn their thoughts to the great men of all nations. One of the methods employed was to go on pilgrimage in imagination to see one of the great ones, and to spend some time in meditation on his teaching, achievements and virtues. Men and women were formed into orders of various kinds, and solemn vows were laid upon them.

22. The second group of innovations comes from Hinduism.

How far Keshab had moved from his early theism may be seen from the following facts. In his early days he was a stern theist, and vehemently denounced polytheism and idolatry of every type. He was seriously opposed to all coquetting with other systems, believing that it was dangerous. When Mr. Sasipada Banerjea founded at Baranagar, near Calcutta, in 1873, the *Sādhārana Dharma Sabhā*, i.e. the General Religious Association, the platform of which was open to Hindus, Buddhists, Muslims and Christians as well as to Brāhmas, Keshab roundly condemned it, as the following sentences from his own paper show:

> We cannot but regard this new Society as a solemn sham before God and man. The members seem to have no fixed religion in them, and, in endeavouring to commend every creed, they only betray their anxiety to mock and insult everything sacred. Such dishonest latitudinarianism ought to be put down.[1]

But somewhere about 1875 Keshab made the acquaintance of Rāmakṛishṇa, and thereafter saw him frequently and listened with great pleasure and interest to his teaching. Now one of the most outstanding ideas of that gifted man was this, that all religions are true.[2] In January, 1881, the New Dispensation was formally announced, as described above; and in the *Sunday Mirror* of October 23rd the following sentences appeared:

> Our position is not that truths are to be found in all religions; but that all the established religions of the world are true. There is a great deal of difference between the two assertions.
>
> The glorious mission of the New Dispensation is to harmonise religions and revelations, to establish the truth of every particular dispensation, and upon the basis of these particulars

[1] This quotation occurs in an article in the *Indian Mirror* of Oct. 15th, 1896, called *Prof. Max Müller on the Paramhansa.*

[2] P. 197, below.

to establish the largest and broadest induction of a general and glorious proposition.[1]

One of Rāmakṛishṇa's friends had a picture painted symbolizing the dependence of Keshab on Rāmakṛishṇa in this matter. It is dealt with below.[2]

It was doubtless this idea, that all religions are true, and that their harmony can be demonstrated, which prompted Keshab to adopt a number of ceremonies from both Hinduism and Christianity and to seek so to interpret a great deal of Hindu doctrine and practice as to make it appear consistent with theism. He called God Mother. He adopted the *homa* sacrifice and the *ārati* ceremony (the waving of lights) into Brāhma ritual. He expounded polytheism and idolatry as if they were variant forms of theism. He found spiritual nourishment in the Durgā Pūjā, *i.e.* the annual festival held in October in Bengal in honour of the demon-slaying Durgā, the blood-thirsty wife of Śiva. In imitation of the 108 names of Vishṇu, a Sanskrit hymn of praise, recounting 108 names of God, was composed, and became an integral part of the liturgy of his Church.[3] Chaitanya's religious dance was introduced to express religious joy.[4] Prayers were addressed to the Ganges, to the moon and to fire, as creatures of God and expressions of His power and His will.

23. The third group of innovations come from Christianity. Baptism and the Lord's Supper were both introduced into New Dispensation ritual. But of far more importance than these ceremonies were the new pieces of Christian doctrine adopted, above all, certain new convictions about the person of Christ.

Ram Mohan Ray recognized clearly that Christ had a great contribution to make to Indian religion. He believed that

[1] I owe these quotations to *HBS.*, II, 96.
[2] P. 198.
[3] *HBS.*, II, 66.
[4] P. 293, below.

the ancient Vedānta was all that India needed in the way of theology; but in the matter of ethics he saw the supremacy of Jesus; and in *The Precepts of Jesus*[1] he laid the ethical teaching of Christ before his fellow-countrymen, and told them plainly that they required to study it and live by it. To him these precepts were the path to peace and happiness.

Keshab from the very beginning realized the truth which Ram Mohan had expressed; but, even in his early lectures, he went far beyond Ram Mohan's standpoint, and that in three directions.

a. The first of these is the recognition of the glory of *the character of Christ,* and its value as an example to man. We quote from Keshab's lecture, *Jesus Christ: Europe and Asia:*

What moral serenity and sweetness pervade his life! What extraordinary tenderness and humility — what lamb-like meekness and simplicity! His heart was full of mercy and forgiving kindness: friends and foes shared his charity and love. And yet, on the other hand, how resolute, firm, and unyielding in his adherence to truth! He feared no mortal man, and braved even death itself for the sake of truth and God. Verily, when we read his life, his meekness, like the soft moon, ravishes the heart and bathes it in a flood of serene light; but when we come to the grand consummation of his career, his death on the cross, behold he shines as the powerful sun in its meridian splendour!

Christ tells us to forgive our enemies, yea, to bless them that curse us, and pray for them that despitefully use us; he tells us, when one smites the right cheek, to turn the left towards him. Who can adequately conceive this transcendent charity? The most impressive form in which it practically manifests itself is in that sweet and tender prayer which the crucified Jesus uttered in the midst of deep agony — "Father, forgive them, for they know not what they do."[2]

[1] P. 32, above.

[2] *Lectures in India*, 25–6.

b. The second is *the sense of sin* and all it leads to. We quote from the historian of the Brāhma Samāj. He remarks:

> Keshub Chunder opened his heart to the Christian spirit, and it begat a sense of sin and the spirit of earnest prayer.[1]

> The infusion of the Christian spirit brought into the field another characteristic Christian sentiment, namely, an enthusiasm for saving fellow-sinners by carrying to them the new gospel. . . . The spirit of utter self-surrender in which the new missionaries took up their work after the schism was a wonder to all. . . . Amongst the new principles imbibed from the study of the life of Christ was one, "Take no thought for the morrow," which they wanted to carry literally into practice. . . . Their young wives, most of them below twenty, touched by the new enthusiasm, shared in all their privations with a cheerful alacrity. The memory of these days will ever remain in our minds as a truly apostolic period of Brahmo history, when there was a spirit of real asceticism without that talk of it, in which the Church abounded in subsequent times.[2]

c. The third is *the Christian attitude to social life*. We again quote from the history:

> Mr. Sen tried to view social questions from the standpoint of pure and spiritual faith, making the improvement of their social life an accessory to men's progress in spiritual life. Social reform naturally came as a part of that fundamental conception. Under the influence of their leader the progressive party tried to abjure those social abuses that tended to degrade society or encourage vice or injustice. The conviction became strong in them that it was only by raising and ennobling man's social life that a pure and spiritual religion like theism could establish itself as a social and domestic faith of man and convert human society into a household of God. This conviction took firm possession of Mr. Sen's mind and he unfurled the banner of social reform by systematic efforts for the abolition of caste

[1] *HBS.*, I, 133.

[2] *Ib.*, I, 209–11.

and also by trying to communicate new light and new life to our womanhood.

We may justly ascribe this passion for social reform to the influence of Mr. Sen's Christian studies. The reason for my ascribing it to Christian influence is that it is so unlike the Hindu teaching on the subject, with which we are familiar.[1]

These three aspects of Christ scarcely appear in Ram Mohan's teaching, but they were the very pith and marrow of Keshab's doctrine. Indeed, as the last extracts shew, they were the source of all the life and vigour which Keshab succeeded in pouring into his missionaries and followers during the first twenty years of his public life. This fact was very vividly present to Keshab's mind. Here are his own words:

Christ has been my study for a quarter of a century. That God-Man — they say half God and half man — walks daily all over this vast peninsula, from the Himalayas to Cape Comorin, enlightening and sanctifying its teeming millions. He is a mighty reality in Indian history. He is to us a living and moving spirit. We see him and commune with him. He permeates society as a vital force, and imbues our daily life, and is mixed with our thoughts, speculations and pursuits.[2]

24. But from 1879 onward there is a further advance. Thus far Christ had been to Keshab only a religious leader, distinctly the greatest of all the prophets, but in no sense divine. From now the problem of the person of Christ occupies a large place in his mind. He began the discussion of the question in his lecture, *India asks: Who is Christ?* delivered in 1879. He starts from the words, "I and My Father are one," and explains them as follows:

Christ really believed that he and his Father were one, or he would not have said so. He spoke the truth, unmixed and pure truth, when he announced this fact. "I can of mine

[1] *HBS.*, I, 296–7.

[2] *Lectures in India*, 330.

own self do nothing," "I am in my Father, and my Father in me."

I am, therefore, bound to admit that Christ really believed that he and his Father were one. When I come to analyse this doctrine, I find in it nothing but the philosophical principle underlying the popular doctrine of self-abnegation, — self-abnegation in a very lofty spiritual sense.[1]

Therefore, I say this wonderful man had no thought whatever of self, and lived in God. This unique character of complete self-surrender is the most striking miracle in the world's history which I have seen, and which it is possible for the mind to conceive.[2]

He declares that God sent Christ to be the perfect example of sonship to men:

An example of true sonship was needed. . . . Perfect holiness dwelt in the Father, the eternal fountain-head of all that is true, and good and beautiful. It comprehended all manner of holiness. It had in it the germs of all forms of virtue and righteousness. Purity of life dwelt in Him in its fulness and integrity. Out of this substance the Lord took out only one form of purity, that which applies to the son in his relations to the Father and his brethren, and comprises the whole round of human duties and virtues, and having given it a human shape, said, — Go and dwell thou in the world and show forth unto nations divine sonship.[3]

He also declares that Christ fulfils Hinduism:

He comes to fulfil and perfect that religion of communion for which India has been panting, as the hart panteth after the waterbrooks. Yes, after long centuries shall this communion be perfected through Christ.[4]

Then in his lecture on the Trinity, in 1882, Christ is definitely called the Logos, the Son of God, the second person of the Trinity:

[1] *Lectures in India*, 245–6.
[2] *Ib.*, 249.
[3] *Ib.*, 251–2.
[4] *Ib.*, 258.

> You see how the Lord asserted His power and established His dominion in the material and the animal kingdom, and then in the lower world of humanity. When that was done the volume of the Old Testament was closed. The New Testament commenced with the birth of the Son of God. . . . Having exhibited itself in endless varieties of progressive existence, the primary creative Force at last took the form of the Son in Christ Jesus.[1]
>
> Gentlemen, look at this clear triangular figure with the eye of faith, and study its deep mathematics. The apex is the very God Jehovah, the Supreme Brahma of the Vedas. Alone, in His own eternal glory, He dwells. From Him comes down the Son in a direct line, an emanation from Divinity. Thus God descends and touches one end of the base of humanity, then running all along the base permeates the world, and then by the power of the Holy Ghost drags up regenerated humanity to Himself. Divinity coming down to humanity is the Son; Divinity carrying up humanity to heaven is the Holy Ghost.[2]

Through Israel came the First Dispensation; in Christ we have the Dispensation of the Son; while Keshab's own movement is the Dispensation of the Holy Spirit:

> The Old Testament was the First Dispensation; the New Testament the Second; unto us in these days has been vouchsafed the Third Dispensation.[3]

25. But all this inevitably raises the question, How could Keshab teach in this strain and yet declare all religions true, and introduce Hindu ceremonies into the ritual of his services? — There is only one way of accounting for it: we must recognize that Keshab was not a consistent thinker, far less a systematic theologian. Illustrations of inconsistency are sown thick in his lectures. Thus in 1876, six years before the lecture on the Trinity, while he was still pledged to the doctrine that Christ is a mere man, the very first sentence of one of his lectures runs:

[1] *Ib.*, 336. [2] *Ib.*, 338. [3] *Ib.*, 356.

> I verily believe that, when Jesus Christ was about to leave this world, he made over the sacred portfolio of the ministry of his Church to the Holy Spirit.[1]

What manner of man is this who stands in official relations with the Spirit of the Universe? — The truth is that he was dazzled with the glitter of Rāmakṛishṇa's idea of the harmony of all religions; and, having once accepted the thought, he proceeded, in confidence in it, to attempt to hold in his own mind, at the same moment, the essential principles of Hinduism, the Christian doctrine of the Trinity, and his own old theism. Perhaps the most amazing example of inconsistency occurs within the limits of a single paragraph in his lecture *We Apostles of the New Dispensation*, delivered in January, 1881, when the New Dispensation was announced. He first sets his own Dispensation on a level with Christ's:

> Is this new gospel a Dispensation, or is it simply a new system of religion, which human understanding has evolved? I say it stands upon the same level with the Jewish dispensation, the Christian dispensation, and the Vaishnava dispensation through Chaitanya. It is a divine Dispensation, fully entitled to a place among the various dispensations and revelations of the world. But is it equally divine, equally authoritative? Christ's Dispensation is said to be divine. I say that this Dispensation is equally divine.[2]

He then sets himself on a level with Christ:

> If Christ was the centre of his Dispensation, am I not the centre of this?[3]

And immediately thereafter there follows this most touching piece of self-humiliation:

> Shall a sinner vie with Christ for honours? God forbid. Jesus was a born saint, and I am a great sinner. Blessed Jesus! I am thine. I give myself, body and soul, to thee. If

[1] *Lectures in India*, 161. [2] *Ib.*, 298. [3] *Ib.*, 299.

India will revile and persecute me, and take my life-blood out of me, drop by drop, still, Jesus, thou shalt continue to have my homage. I have taken the vow of loyalty before thee, and I will not swerve from it, — God help me! These lips are thine for praise, and these hands are thine in service. Son of God, I love thee truly. And, though scorned and hated for thy sake, I will love thee always, and remain an humble servant at thy blessed feet. Yet, I must tell you, gentlemen, that I am connected with Jesus' Gospel, and occupy a prominent place in it. I am the prodigal son of whom Christ spoke, and I am trying to return to my Father in a penitent spirit. Nay, I will say more for the satisfaction and edification of my opponents. I am not Jesus, but I am Judas, that vile man who betrayed Jesus into the hands of his infuriated persecutors. That man's spirit is in me. The veritable Judas, who sinned against truth and Jesus, lodges in my heart. If I honour Jesus, and claim a place among his disciples, is there not another side of my life which is carnal and worldly and sinful? I am Judas-like so far as I love sin. Then tell me not I am trying to exalt myself. No. A prophet's crown sits not on my head. My place is at Jesus' feet.[1]

No further proof is wanted of the unsystematic character of Keshab's thinking. Clearly, he had not worked the contents of his mind into any kind of consistent unity.

26. But another problem remains, his relation to Christ. His habitual want of consistency explains how he could hold self-contradictory ideas, but the extraordinary place which Christ holds in his teaching needs explanation. The needs of the time, and the wonderful way in which the teaching of Christ meets them, account for the hold which Christ's ethical and social teaching have taken of the Brāhma Samāj as a whole; but they do not account for the tenderness and passion which mark Keshab's every reference to Jesus nor for his interest in the problem of Christology. The simple fact is that Keshab's religious experience was from beginning to

[1] *Ib.*, 299.

end rooted in Christ; and he was thereby driven steadily forward, steadily nearer an adequate account of Christ's person and His relation to God. His lectures show quite clearly that his religious experience depended largely on Christ:

My Christ, my sweet Christ, the brightest jewel of my heart, the necklace of my soul — for twenty years have I cherished him in this my miserable heart. Though often defiled and persecuted by the world, I have found sweetness and joy unutterable in my master Jesus. . . . The mighty artillery of his love he levelled against me, and I was vanquished, and I fell at his feet.[1]

The Father cannot be an example of sonship. Only the Son can show what the son ought to be. In vain do I go to the Vedas or to Judaism to learn sonship. That I learn at the feet of my sweet Christ, my Father's beloved Son.[2]

All over my body, all through my inner being I see Christ. He is no longer to me a doctrine or a dogma, but with Paul I cry, For me to live is Christ. . . . Christ is my food and drink, and Christ is the water that cleanses me.[3]

There can be no doubt as to the meaning of these words. Further, the solution of the problem of the three amazing passages quoted on page 64 lies here, that in his theory of the New Dispensation we have his loose but brilliant thinking, while in the touching sentences where he contrasts himself with Christ we have a living transcript from his religious experience. Practically every difficulty which Keshab's life presents to the student (and they are not few) becomes comprehensible when we realize to the full these two facts: he was not a systematic thinker, and his religious experience sprang from Christ.

But we may go one step farther still. Keshab's richest religious experience came from Christ, and, in consequence, in the latter part of his life, his deepest theological beliefs

[1] *Lectures in India*, 260. [2] *Ib.*, 344. [3] *Ib.*, 393.

were fully Christian, but he never surrendered himself to Christ as Lord. He retained the government of his life in his own hands. I also believe that this is the only way in which we can explain the spiritual experience of his friend and biographer, Pratap Chandra Mozoomdar, and of two or three others of the missionaries.

The theological position of these men stands out quite clear from a number of facts.

The late Registrar of Calcutta University, Mr. K. C. Banurji, a Bengali Christian universally loved and respected, was very intimate with Keshab; and he maintained, with great consistency and earnestness, that Keshab died a Christian. Had Mr. Banurji been an ordinary man, it might have been said that he had been misled by some chance expression, such as one meets in Keshab's published writings, and the inconsistency of which the leader was so often guilty would have been sufficient explanation. But Mr. Banurji was no ordinary man; and he had no hazy, indistinct conception of Christian faith. He had followed Keshab's history closely for many years, and was most intimate with him. It is thus certain that, in conversation with Mr. Banurji, Keshab gave expression to a full, clear, distinct faith in Jesus Christ.

Mr. P. C. Mozoomdar, one day, had a long unhurried conversation with a friend of the writer, a missionary in the North. In the course of the talk my friend gave expression to the deepest convictions of his Christian life. Mr. Mozoomdar assured him that his own faith, and Keshab's also, was precisely the same, and said that the reason why he and Keshab did not give public expression to these beliefs was that they held they would be more likely to bring their fellow-countrymen to full faith in Christ by a gradual process than by a sudden declaration of all they believed.[1]

[1] He must have spoken in the same way in South India. *Madras Decennial Miss. Conf. Report*, 310.

Some eleven or twelve years ago, in a brief article, I had ignorantly spoken of all Brāhmas as Unitarians. In a courteous note, the only letter I ever received from Mr. Mozoomdar, he protested against the statement so far as the Church of the New Dispensation was concerned, declaring himself and his fellow-believers to be Trinitarians. During the last twenty years articles have frequently appeared in the pages of *Unity and the Minister* (a weekly published under the New Dispensation), which, if taken seriously from the standpoint of theology, undoubtedly imply the full Christian faith. My own personal intercourse with several of the leaders would also tend to prove that they had learned from Keshab to regard Christ as the Son of God and the Saviour.

Yet, so far as my experience and reading reach, there is no evidence that these men ever allowed their faith to rule their life. There was never the full surrender of the soul to the Saviour. There was something that restrained. They regarded Jesus as the eternal Son, but they lived the life of theists, following now one master, now another. An incident in Keshab's life fits in well with this judgment. One of the missionaries of the New Dispensation, who was very intimate with him, and who believed that he was a servant of Christ and would remain such to the end, went to see the great leader as he lay dying in his home, Lily Cottage, Calcutta. He found him rolling on his bed in great pain, crying aloud in prayer to God in Bengali. Great was his friend's astonishment to catch the following words repeated over and over again:

Buddher Mā, Śākyer Mā, nirbāṇ dao,

i.e. "Mother of Buddha, Mother of the Sākyan, grant me Nirvāṇa." What an extraordinary mixture of ideas this sentence bears witness to! Thus Keshab's deepest convictions were Christian beliefs, yet he was not a Christian.

He passed away on the 8th of January, 1884, leaving his Samāj shepherdless.

27. *Fifth Period, 1884–1913: the Sādhāran Brāhma Samāj.* It has been already stated that, from the beginning, there were disputes, and even quarrels, among the missionaries, which Keshab found it difficult to control. One day, in Lily Cottage, when some little difference of this kind was being talked about, Keshab pointed to a velvet pincushion, and said, "You are like the pins, united in the pincushion. When I am taken away, there will be nothing to hold you together." The words were prophetic. Ever since the leader's death, his whole following has been reduced to the utmost weakness by the quarrels of the missionaries. There are three sub-divisions, each of which holds a separate service on Sunday, and there are individuals who will unite with none. But it is not personal differences only that have led to this state of affairs; the irreconcilable elements in the leader's teaching, now held by different minds, render real union impossible. It was largely because P. C. Mozoomdar was so much of a Christian that his brethren refused to make him their leader. The tendency to make Keshab an inspired guru, which led to the Kuch-Bihar marriage and the great secession, operated most disastrously. After his death one party declared that he was still their leader, and that no one could ever take his place in the Samāj building, while the others opposed vehemently. Some still keep up this foolish idea. They call the anniversary of his death the day of "the Master's Ascension";[1] and the room in which he died, kept precisely as it was then, is entered reverently, as if it were a shrine. For nine and twenty years the Samāj has been dismembered and rendered impotent by divisions and brawls; and there is no sign of betterment.

28. The Ādi Brāhma Samāj still holds steadily on, but there

[1] A recent book calls him "God-man Keshub" and "Lord and Master."

are few members apart from the family of Debendra Nath Tagore. The saintly old leader lived to the age of eighty-seven, passing away in 1905. After his death a fragment of an *Autobiography* in Bengali was published, and later still was translated into English by one of his sons. It is a very modest document but contains a remarkable spiritual record. It is one of the most valuable pieces of literature the Ādi Samāj has produced. Debendra's fourth son, Mr. Rabindra Nath Tagore, now so famous as a poet,[1] frequently preaches in the building.

29. The Sādhāran Brāhma Samāj, on the other hand, has made steady, solid progress since its formation in 1878. It has now a large body of members and adherents in Calcutta, and its services are well attended. Most of the provincial Samājes are connected with it. It is the only section of the Brāhma Samāj whose missionaries are able from time to time to go on preaching tours. It is a living, effective body, though not large. Its history need not detain us. A brief sketch of its organization and its teaching must suffice.

The Samāj is under the control of a General Committee of a hundred members elected both from Calcutta and the provinces. The President, the Secretary with three Assistant Secretaries, and the Treasurer, together with thirteen others chosen by the General Committee from among its members, form the Executive. This form of organization has succeeded in making the government of the Samāj representative and democratic. This body governs the Sādhāran Brāhma Samāj of Calcutta and its missionaries, and also bears relations to the majority of the provincial Samājes. Forty-one of the provincial Samājes are called "Associated Samājes": they pay a certain annual subscription to the central body, and are entitled to receive help from the missionaries. The majority of the other Samājes are in fellowship with the Sād-

[1] P. 383, below.

hāran Samāj of Calcutta, although some have closer relations with the Ādi Samāj or the New Dispensation or the Prārthanā Samāj in Bombay.

The bulk of the work of the Samāj is carried on by the nine missionaries; but a good deal is also done by the *Sevak Mandali* or Circle of Laymen. The heaviest work undertaken is the tours made in the provinces by the missionaries, to strengthen existing work and win new adherents. Apart from these, the chief forms of effort are the Sunday Services in the building, the Students' Weekly Service, the Saṅgat Sabhā (a sort of Methodist Class Meeting), the Working Men's Mission at Baranagar, near Calcutta, the Brahmo Young Men's Union, and the Samāj newspapers, the *Indian Messenger* and the *Tattva Kaumudī*. The Calcutta congregation has more than 800 members and a very large number of adherents. The mission on the Khasi Hills in Assam is perhaps the most notable piece of work being done outside Calcutta. The Khasis are a very simple race, who had no education or literature until the Welsh Calvinistic Mission waked them to an altogether new life. The Brāhmas have won some fifty families.

In 1911 there were 183 Brāhma Samājes in India; and 5504 persons were entered as Brāhmas in the Census.

30. The following is a brief summary of the beliefs of the Ādi Samāj[1]:

(1) God is a personal being with sublime moral attributes.

(2) God has never become incarnate.

(3) God hears and answers prayer.

(4) God is to be worshipped only in spiritual ways. Hindu asceticism, temples, and fixed forms of worship are unnecessary. Men of all castes and races may worship God acceptably.

(5) Repentance and cessation from sin is the only way to forgiveness and salvation.

(6) Nature and Intuition are the sources of knowledge of God. No book is authoritative.

[1] *ERE.*, II, 816.

The following is the official statement of the principles of the Sādhāran Samāj[1]:

(1) There is only one God, who is the Creator, Preserver and Saviour of this world. He is spirit; He is infinite in power, wisdom, love, justice and holiness; He is omnipresent, eternal and blissful.

(2) The human soul is immortal, and capable of infinite progress, and is responsible to God for its doings.

(3) God is to be worshipped in spirit and in truth. Divine worship is necessary for attaining true felicity and salvation.

(4) To love God and to carry out His will in all the concerns of life constitute true worship.

(5) Prayer and dependence on God and a constant realisation of His presence are the means of attaining spiritual growth.

(6) No created object is to be worshipped as God, nor is any person or book to be considered as infallible and as the sole means of salvation; but truth is to be reverently accepted from all scriptures and from the teaching of all persons without distinction of creed or country.

(7) The Fatherhood of God and the Brotherhood of man and kindness to all living beings are the essence of true religion.

(8) God rewards virtue, and punishes sin. His punishments are remedial and not eternal.

(9) Cessation from sin accompanied by sincere repentance is the only atonement for it; and union with God in wisdom, goodness and holiness is true salvation.

The following statement of the faith and principles of the New Dispensation is from Keshab's *Laws of Life:*[2]

(1) God. I believe that God is one, that He is infinite and perfect, almighty, all-wise, all-merciful, all-holy, all-blissful, eternal and omnipresent, our Creator, Father, Mother, Friend, Guide, Judge and Saviour.

(2) Soul. I believe that the soul is immortal and eternally progressive.

[1] From the Report for 1910.

[2] Published in the *World and New Dispensation*, of July 27, 1910.

(3) Spiritual Law. I believe in natural inspiration, general and special. I believe in providence, general and special.

(4) Moral Law. I believe in God's moral law as revealed through the commandments of conscience, enjoining perfect righteousness in all things. I believe that I am accountable to God for the faithful discharge of my manifold duties and that I shall be judged and rewarded and punished for my virtues and vices here and hereafter.

(5) Scriptures. I accept and revere the scriptures so far as they are records of the wisdom and devotion and piety of inspired geniuses and of the dealings of God's special providence in the salvation of nations, of which records only the Spirit is God's, but the letter man's.

(6) Prophets. I accept and revere the world's prophets and saints so far as they embody and reflect the different elements of divine character, and set forth the higher ideals of life for the instruction and sanctification of the world. I ought to revere and love and follow all that is divine in them, and try to assimilate it to my soul, making what is theirs and God's mine.

(7) Church. I believe in the Church Universal which is the deposit of all ancient wisdom and the receptacle of all modern science, which recognises in all prophets and saints a harmony, in all scriptures a unity and through all dispensations a continuity, which abjures all that separates and divides and always magnifies unity and peace, which harmonises reason and faith, *yoga* and *bhakti*, asceticism and social duty in their highest forms, and which shall make of all nations and sects one kingdom and one family in the fulness of time.

(8) Synopsis. My creed is the science of God which enlighteneth all. My gospel is the love of God which saveth all. My heaven is life in God which is accessible to all. My church is that invisible kingdom of God in which is all truth, all love, all holiness.

LITERATURE. — HISTORY: *History of the Brahmo Samaj*, Sivanath Sastri, Calcutta, Chatterji, 1911–1912, two vols. Rs. 6. *The Theistic Directory*, by V. R. Shinde, Bombay, Prārthanā Samāj, 1912. THE ĀDI SAMĀJ: *Life and Letters of Raja Rammohun Roy*, by Sophia Dobson Collet, Edited by Hem Chandra Sarkar, Calcutta, 1914, Rs. 2, as. 8. *The English Works of Raja Ram Mohan Ray*, Allahabad, Panini Office, 1906, Rs. 2, as. 8. *The Complete Works of Raja Ram Mohan Ray, Sansk it and Bengali*, Calcutta, 1880. *The Autobiography of Maharshi Devendranath Tagore*, Translated by Satyendranath Tagore, Calcutta, Lahiri, 1909, Rs. 2 as. 8. *Brāhma Dharma*, by Devendranath Tagore, Calcutta, K. K. Chakravarti, 1850. KESHAB AND THE NEW DISPENSATION: *The Life and Teachings of Keshab Chundra Sen*, by Pratāp Chandra Mozoomdar, Calcutta, Baptist Mission Press, 1887, out of print. *Keshub Chunder Sen's Lectures in India*, Calcutta, the Brahmo Traet Society, 1899. (Most of Keshab's writings, whether Bengali or English, can be got through the Brahmo Tract Society, Lily Cottage, Upper Circular Road, Calcutta.) *Keshab Chandra Sen in England*, Calcutta, 1881. *The Oriental Christ*, by P. C. Mozoomdar, Calcutta, Brahmo Tract Society, Rs. 3. *Ślokasaṅgraha*, A Compilation of Theistic Texts, Calcutta, K. P. Nath, 1904, Rs. 1. THE SĀDHĀRAN SAMĀJ: *The Religion of the Brahmo Samaj*, by Hem Chandra Sarkar, Calcutta, Kuntaline Press, 1911, as. 6. *The Philosophy of Brahmaism*, by Paṇḍit S. N. Tattvabhūshaṇa, Madras, Higginbotham, 1909, Rs. 2–8.

2. THE PRĀRTHANĀ SAMĀJ

1. We now turn our attention to Western India, the modern history of which begins in 1818 when, at the close of the last Marāṭha war, British authority became supreme in the great territory now known as the Bombay Presidency. The Hon. Mr. Mountstuart Elphinstone, who became Governor of Bombay in 1819, founded the very next year the Bombay Native Education Society, which did much to plant Western education in the city. When he retired in 1827, the leaders of the city, both Hindu and Parsee, in order to commemorate his work, raised a great fund which was used to found professorships, and became the nucleus of the Elphinstone College, the Government College in Bombay.

John Wilson of the Church of Scotland founded in 1835 the college which bears his name to-day. Wilson's work was on the same lines as Duff's; and under his teaching a number of young men, both Hindu and Parsee, passed into the Christian Church. The whole of Western India was moved by the baptism of three Parsees in 1839,[1] and again by the baptism of a Brāhman, Nārāyaṇa Śeshādri in 1843. Wilson's vital influence may also be traced in many men who remained in Hinduism and Zoroastrianism. In 1842 the London Society for the Promotion of Female Education sent out a lady missionary to work among the Parsee women in Bombay.[2]

2. Progressive movements among both Hindus and Parsees sprang from these educational and religious efforts. The earliest organization was a secret society called the *Gupta Sabhā*. The members were Hindus [3] and they met for worship and religious discussion, but nothing further is known of its work. It was succeeded in 1849 by the *Paramahaṁsa Sabhā*.[4] It too was a secret society, but social reform held a rather more prominent place in its discussions than religious questions. After their discussion was over the members sang hymns from the *Ratnamālā* and joined in a common meal, the food for which had been prepared by a low-caste cook. No one could become a member, unless he were willing to eat bread made by a Christian, and drink water brought by a Muḥammadan. The influence of the society was necessarily rather limited, as everything was kept secret. Yet there were branches in Poona, Ahmadnagar and elsewhere. But in 1860 some one stole the books, and the whole thing was made public. There was great indignation against the members; and the society broke up.

[1] P. 84, below.

[2] Richter, 338 n.

[3] Amongst them were Moroba Vinoba and Baba Padmanji, who became a Christian at a later date.

[4] Amongst its members were N. M. Paramanand and B. Mangesh Wagle. It is interesting to note that a secret society was formed in Calcutta by Hindus "for instructing their young daughters and other female relatives." Richter, 337.

The more earnest men, however, held by their convictions and watched with great interest the Brāhma movement in Bengal. In 1864 Keshab paid his first visit to Bombay, and many were delighted with both the man and his message. But his visit came at an unfortunate moment; Bombay was in a fever of excitement over share speculation; and no result followed.

3. Three years later, however, in 1867, a theistic society was actually formed and called the *Prārthanā Samāj*, Prayer Society, the leader being Dr. Atmaram Pandurang (1823–1898), who was a personal friend of Dr. Wilson and had been deeply influenced by him. Other members were Dadoba Pandurang, Bhaskara Pandurang (brothers of the leader), Ram Bal Krishna, N. M. Paramanand, Bhare Mahajan, W. B. Naorangi, V. A. Modak and B. M. Wagle. A weekly prayer-meeting was started, rules for the society were drawn up, and a managing committee appointed. The aims were theistic worship and social reform. Next year Keshab visited Bombay for a second time, and considerably strengthened the organization. In 1870 the first marriage celebrated according to theistic rites took place; and about the same time R. G. Bhandarkar (now Sir R. G. Bhandarkar) and M. G. Ranade (later Mr. Justice Ranade) joined the young Samāj. In 1872 P. C. Mozoomdar came from Calcutta, and spent six months in Bombay, building up the congregation, and starting night-schools for working people and the journal of the Samāj, the *Subodh Patrikā.* In 1874 the Samāj erected its own building in Girgaum, Bombay. Paṇḍit Dayānanda Sarasvatī came to Bombay the same year,[1] and his lectures roused much interest, but his ideas about the Vedas prevented the Prārthanā Samāj from following him. The following year he founded the Ārya Samāj in Bombay. A little later there was a proposal to change the name of the society

[1] P. 109, below.

PLATE IV

Mr. Justice Ranade

Sir N. G. Chandavarkar

Sir R. G. Bhandarkar

Kharshedji Rustamji Cama

to the Bombay Brāhma Samāj, but on account of the dissensions in the Brāhma Samāj in Calcutta the Bombay leaders were unwilling to identify themselves with it. In 1882 S. P. Kelkar became a missionary of the Samāj; and in the same year N. G. Chandavarkar, now Sir Narayan Ganesh Chandavarkar, began to take an active part in the work. Paṇḍitā Ramabai, who had not as yet become a Christian, did valuable work among the women of the Samāj in 1882–1883, and founded the Ārya Mahila Samāj, or Ladies' Society. During recent years a number of younger men, the chief of whom are K. Natarajan, S. N. Gokhale, V. R. Shinde, V. A. Sukhtankar, and N. G. Velinkar, have joined, and have done valuable work in various ways.

The Prārthanā Samāj has never had such groups of missionaries as have toiled for the Brāhma Samāj. They have usually had only one or two. For this reason the movement has not spread widely; yet there are associated Samājes at Poona, Kirkee, Kolhapur and Satara. Several societies, originally connected with the Prārthanā Samāj, now call themselves Brāhma Samājes. On the other hand, the milder policy of the Prārthanā Samāj has commended itself to many in the Telugu country and further south. Out of the twenty-nine Samājes in the Madras Presidency eighteen bear the name Prārthanā Samāj.

Nor has the Prārthanā Samāj produced much literature. This failure is, doubtless, largely due to the impression so common among its members that definite beliefs and theological thought are scarcely necessary for a free theistic body. Of this serious weakness Ranade wrote [1]:

Many enthusiastic leaders of the Brāhma Samāj movement have been heard deliberately to declare that the only cardinal points of Theism necessary to constitute it a religion of mankind, the only articles of its confession of faith, are the Father-

[1] *Essays*, 251–3.

hood of God, and the Brotherhood of man. These are the only points which it is absolutely necessary to hold fast to for purposes of regeneration and salvation. And with fifty years of working history, our leaders seem content to lisp this same story of early childhood. There is no attempt at grasping in all earnestness the great religious difficulties which have puzzled people's faith during all time, and driven them to seek rest in revelation. . . . To come nearer home, our friends of the Prarthana Samaj seem to be perfectly satisfied with a creed which consists of only one positive belief in the unity of God, accompanied with a special protest against the existing corruption of Hindu religion, viz., the article which denounces the prevalent idolatry to be a sin, and an abomination; and it is ardently hoped that a new Church can be built in course of time on such a narrow foundation of belief. . . . It is time, we think, to venture on an earnest attempt to remove this reproach.

His own *Theist's Confession of Faith*[1] is a brave attempt to give the thought of the Samāj something more of a theology. In February, 1913, Mr. N. G. Velinkar, one of the most capable thinkers in the Samāj, gave expression in conversation with the writer to his regret that there is so little definite teaching in the Samāj. A vigorous effort is being made at present by Mr. Velinkar and a few other leaders to produce theological and devotional books to enrich the life of the society.

4. Speaking practically, the beliefs of the Samāj are the same as those held by the Sādhāran Brāhma Samāj. They are theists, and opposed to idolatry. Their theism rests largely on ancient Hindu thought; yet, practically, they have given up the inspiration of the Vedas and the doctrine of transmigration. The latter is left an open question, but few hold by it. The Samāj draws its nourishment very largely from the Hindu scriptures, and uses the hymns of the old Marāṭha poet-saints in its services.

If theistic worship is the first interest of the Samāj, social

[1] *Essays*, p. 250.

reform has always held the next place. Four reforms are sought, the abandonment of caste, the introduction of widow-remarriage, the encouragement of female education, and the abolition of child-marriage. Yet some of the diffidence of the Paramahaṁsa Society still clings to the members. There has never been amongst them the rigid exclusion of idolatry, which has marked the Brāhma Samāj since Debendra Nath Tagore became leader, nor is the breaking of caste made a condition of membership, as in the two younger Samājes of Calcutta. Even though a man be a full member of the Samāj, caste may be observed and idolatry may be practised in his house. Miss S. D. Collet wrote in her Brāhma Year Book in 1880:

> The Theistic Church in Western India occupies a position of its own. Although in thoroughly fraternal relations with the Eastern Samajes, it is of indigenous growth and of independent standing. It has never detached itself so far from the Hindu element of Brahmaism as many of the Bengali Samajes, and both in religious observances and social customs, it clings far more closely to the old models. It is more learned and less emotional in its tone, and far more cautious and less radical in its policy than the chief Samajes of Bengal. But it is doing good work in its own way and it has enlarged its operations considerably within the last few years.[1]

A writer in the *Indian Social Reformer*[2] says:

> The *Prarthana Samaj* may be said to be composed of men paying allegiance to Hinduism and to Hindu society with a protest. The members observe the ceremonies of Hinduism, but only as mere ceremonies of routine, destitute of all religious significance. This much sacrifice they make to existing prejudices. Their principle, however, is not to deceive anyone as to their religious opinions, even should an honest expression of views entail unpopularity.

[1] I owe this quotation to Shinde, *Theistic Directory*, 33.

[2] Vol. XX, 317.

The following is the official statement of the faith of the Samāj:

Cardinal Principles of Faith

(1) God is the creator of this universe. He is the only true God; there is no other God beside him. He is eternal, spiritual, infinite, the store of all good, all joy, without parts, without form, one without a second, the ruler of all, all-pervading, omniscient, almighty, merciful, all-holy and the saviour of sinners.

(2) His worship alone leads to happiness in this world and the next.

(3) Love and reverence for him, an exclusive faith in him, praying and singing to him spiritually with these feelings and doing the things pleasing to him constitute His true worship.

(4) To worship and pray to images and other created objects is not a true mode of divine adoration.

(5) God does not incarnate himself and there is no one book which has been directly revealed by God or is wholly infallible.

(6) All men are His children; therefore they should behave towards each other as brethren without distinction. This is pleasing to God and constitutes man's duty.[1]

5. The religious activities of the Samāj are the Sunday services, the Sunday School, the Young Theists' Union (a sort of Endeavour Society), the Anniversaries, the work of the missionaries, the Postal Mission, which sends religious literature by post, and the *Subodh Patrikā*.

There are eight night-schools for working-people financed and conducted by the Samāj; there is a Free Reading Room and Library in the Samāj building; and there is a Ladies' Association for spreading instruction and culture among women and girls. The Students' Brotherhood, a theistic replica of a Young Men's Christian Association, is loosely

[1] *Prārthanā Samāj Report*, 1911–1912.

associated with the Samāj. In Pandharpur an Orphanage and Foundling Asylum supported by the Samāj has done good work for many years.

But the greatest service which the Samāj has done to India has been the organization of the Social Reform Movement. Though not officially connected with the Samāj, nearly every vigorous effort made in favour of social reform during the last thirty years has been started, and largely carried on, by its members. The same is true of the Depressed Classes' Mission. We deal with these great movements below.[1]

An All-India Theistic Conference is held annually which brings the Brāhma and Prārthanā Samājes together.

LITERATURE. — HISTORY: Vol. II, pp. 411–456 of *History of the Brahmo Samaj*, by Sivanath Sastri, Calcutta, Chatterji, 1911–1912, two vols. Rs. 6; and pp. 33–42 of *The Theistic Directory*, by V. R. Shinde, Bombay, Prarthana Samaj, 1912. TEACHING: *Religious and Social Reform*, by M. G. Ranade, Bombay, Claridge, 1902. *The Speeches and Writings of Sir N. G. Chandavarkar*, Bombay, Manoranjak Grantha Prasarak Mandali, 1911, Rs. 2 as. 8.

3. PARSEE REFORM

1. One great branch of the Indo-European race lived long before the Christian era somewhere in Central Asia to the south of the Oxus River. This group finally broke in two, the eastern wing passing into India, and creating its civilization, the western colonizing Iran, and producing the Zoroastrian religion and the Persian Empire. On the rise of Islam, Arab armies marched both east and west, conquering every power that came in their way. The overthrow of Persia was complete. In their new zeal for their religion, the Muslim warriors offered the Persians the choice of Islam or the sword. Only a remnant of the people were able by escaping to the wilds of the North to retain both life

[1] P. 372 and Chapter VI.

and religion. Even there, they were so much harassed that a great company of them left Persia altogether, and found their way into the province of Gujarāt in Western India. There the Hindus allowed them to settle under very definite conditions. The exiles took root, and prospered. Bombay is now their greatest centre, but they are still found in Gujarāt, and small groups reside in each of the great commercial centres of the country. They call themselves Parsees, *i.e.* Persians; and they number about one hundred thousand.

They brought with them certain copies of their sacred books, but the disasters of their country had played terrible havoc with its sacred literature. The people ascribe their most serious losses to Alexander the Great; but it is not known how far the destruction of the *Avesta* is due to him, or to later conquerors. In any case there has been most pitiable loss. Professor Moulton says:

> The faithful remnant who in the next century (*i.e.* after the Moslem conquest) took refuge on the hospitable shores of India, to find there a liberty of conscience which Mohammedan Persia denied them, brought with them only fragments of the literature that Sassanian piety had so laboriously gathered. Altogether, Prof. William Jackson calculates, about two-thirds of the Avesta have disappeared since the last Zoroastrian monarch sat on the Persian throne.[1]

As the Hindus and the Parsees are sister-peoples, so the Zoroastrian religion and the Hindu faith have a good deal in common. The religious reform introduced by Zoroaster did for the Persians a larger and more fruitful service than that done for the Hindus by the Vedānta philosophy. But, though the monotheism and the ethics of Zoroaster had worked a greater revolution than the Vedānta produced, yet the religions still shewed their ancient kinship. Consequently,

[1] *Early Religious Poetry of Persia*, 14.

when a small band of hunted fugitives, carrying with them the precious fragments of their national literature, settled in a Hindu environment, they found themselves in somewhat congenial company; and, despite their exclusiveness, their life and conceptions necessarily felt the influence of the powerful community in the midst of which they were settled. Child-marriage and the Zenāna became universal among them. Polygamy was not uncommon. The men ate separately from the women. Many were ready to recognize Hindu festivals and worship. The Parsee priesthood became a hereditary caste. Religious, social and legal questions were settled, according to Hindu custom, by a small body called the Panchāyat.

2. If we consult Parsee writers as to the state of the Parsees at the beginning of the nineteenth century, we shall be told that the community was living in great ignorance, that the ordinary Parsee received little education and did not understand a word of his prayers or of the liturgy of Parsee worship, and that very few of the priests were scholarly. They knew the ritual and the liturgy, and were able to spell their way through certain books of the *Avesta;* but there seems to have been no thought-movement among them, and no vivid realization of the importance of the spiritual elements of their religion as compared with the ritual. The whole people tended to stand aloof from the other communities of India, making pride in their religion and race the reason for their exclusiveness.

In material things the Parsees were very prosperous. They held a great place in Indian commerce, and many families had risen to opulence. They were highly respected alike by Hindus and Muḥammadans.

3. We have seen above[1] that Western education was introduced into the Bombay Presidency in 1820, and that in 1827 money was raised which finally created the Elphinstone Col-

[1] P. 74, above.

lege. In 1835 John Wilson began Christian College education in Bombay; in 1839 three Parsees were baptized; and in 1843 Wilson's work on the Parsee religion appeared. In a letter to me Mr. R. P. Karkaria writes:

> This work, which mercilessly exposed the weak points of the popular system believed in by the laity and the clergy in their ignorance, was really epoch-making, not only for its scholarship — it was the first European book based on a first-hand knowledge of Parsi sacred language and books — but for the effect it has had on our religion itself, which it helped materially to purify. It put Parsis on their mettle. Numerous were the criticisms and replies, mostly ignorant and some downright stupid. In a few years sensible Parsis set to work to put their house in order, so to say.

In 1849 they started schools for the boys and girls of the community, so that no child should have to go without education. As the Panchāyat had lost all power over the community, and reform was seriously needed, a group of influential and wealthy Parsees and a number of young men fresh from Elphinstone College formed, in 1851, the *Rahnumai Mazdayasnan Sabhā*, or Religious Reform Association, which had for its object "the regeneration of the social condition of the Parsees and the restoration of the Zoroastrian religion to its pristine purity." The more notable men in this group were Dadabhai Naoroji, J. B. Wacha, S. S. Bangali and Naoroji Furdonji. They established at the same time the *Rast Goftar*, or Truth-teller, a weekly journal, which proved a powerful instrument in their hands. By lectures, meetings and literature they stirred the community to its depths with their proposals of reform. At first they encountered a great deal of opposition from the orthodox.[1] But they persevered, and at last achieved considerable success:

> These early reformers were very cautious, discreet, sagacious and tactful in their movement. They rallied round them

[1] See below, p. 343.

as many Parsi leading priests of the day as they could and submitted to them in a well-formulated form specific questions under specific heads, asking their opinion if such and such practice, dogma, creed, ceremony, etc., were in strict conformity with the teachings of the religion of Zoroaster, or contravened those teachings. Fortified by these opinions, the reformers carried on their propaganda in the way of lectures, public meetings, pamphlets and articles in the *Rast Goftar*. One cannot rise from the perusal of these articles without being thoroughly impressed with a sense of candour, thorough independence and an unmixed desire to extricate their co-religionists from the thraldom of all those practices, rituals and creed for which there was no warrant within the four corners of the authentic Zoroastrian scriptures.[1]

In 1858 a group of educated Parsees started a movement for helping their brethren, the remnant of the old Zoroastrians of Persia, now known as the Gabars,[2] who were very seriously oppressed by the Shah's government. After twenty-four years of agitation, they were released, in 1882, from the poll-tax, *jīzya*, which weighed heavily upon them. The Parsees have also assisted them financially.

A little later a new element was introduced. A young man belonging to one of the great commercial families, Kharshedji Rustamji Cama,[3] went to Europe on business; and, before he returned to Bombay in 1859, proceeded to the Continent, where he studied the *Avesta* in the original under the greatest Avestan scholars of Europe.[4] What he did in Bombay from 1861 onwards had better be told in the words of one of my correspondents:[5]

On his return he began teaching to a few disciples the *Avesta*, the Parsi scriptures, by the Western methods — comparative

[1] *ISR.*, XXII, 113.

[2] See art. *Gabars* in *ERE*.

[3] See his portrait, Plate IV, facing page 76.

[4] For the rise of Avestan scholarship, see p. 8 n. above.

[5] Professor P. A. Wadia.

study of the Iranian languages and grammar. The most famous of his disciples were Sheriarji Bharucha, who is still alive, Temurasp Anklesaria, a most distinguished scholar of Pahlavi, who died about ten years ago, and Kavasji Kanga. He also helped largely in the foundation of two Madressas, or institutions devoted to the study of the Iranian languages and scriptures.

His main purpose was to create a new type of Parsee priests who, by their education and character, might be able to lead the community, and also by study to realize what the real teaching of Zoroaster was, and so be able to show authority for casting off the many superstitious accretions which the religion had gathered in the course of the centuries.

Meantime, through the encouragement of the reformers, English education had laid hold of the Parsee community. They built schools for themselves. The education of girls made great progress. A certain amount of religious instruction was given in the schools. The age of marriage was gradually raised; and, within a comparatively short space of time, Parsee women achieved their emancipation. They began to move about freely in the open air, both on foot and in carriages, while in former years, if they went out at all, the blinds of the carriage were always closely drawn. English dress came more and more into use; the European mode of dining at table was accepted; and men and women began to eat together:

> The Parsi mode of life may be described to be an eclectic *ensemble*, half-European and half-Hindu. As they advance every year in civilization and enlightenment, they copy more closely English manners and modes of living.[1]

Many hold that Western influence has gone too far. Thus, Mr. R. P. Karkaria, writing of Government education, says:

[1] Karaka I, 123.

> It helped the reformers, but went much farther than they intended, and has bred up a generation which is too reformed, a generation which is not quite strictly Parsee or Christian or anything in religion.

This has helped the conservative movement dealt with below.[1]

4. Mr. B. M. Malabari, a Parsee government servant, who later became a journalist, exercised a very wide and powerful influence in the cause of women and children in India. His pamphlet on *Infant Marriage and Enforced Widowhood*,[2] published in 1887, stirred public opinion to the depths. In his journal, *The Indian Spectator*, he continued the struggle for more humane treatment for the women and children of India. When in England in 1890, he published, in pamphlet form, an *Appeal on behalf of the daughters of India*, which powerfully moved English feeling. Finally, in 1908, in conjunction with his biographer, Mr. Dayaram Gidumal, he founded the Seva Sadan.[3]

5. The culture and wide business relations of the Parsees have brought them into very close relations with Europeans, and there have been several intermarriages. One wealthy Parsee married a French lady. She declared herself a Zoroastrian by faith; and, wishing to be a true wife in all things to her husband, sought admission to the Parsee community, that she might share his religious life with him to the full. The advanced party wished to agree to the proposal; but necessarily opposition arose; for the Parsees have not admitted (except stealthily) any foreigner to their ranks for centuries; and the priests refused her admission.[4] For, though reform has done much for the Parsee community in general, the priests have lagged pitiably behind. Very few of them are men of education; and, even if they know their own Scriptures, they have no knowledge of the West, and are therefore quite unfit to lead the community to-day. In consequence,

[1] P. 343. [2] Below, pp. 389 and 396. [3] P. 380, below.

[4] A great lawsuit followed, but it did not result in a clear decision.

a new demand has arisen for educated priests. Parsees contrast their priests with the missionaries they see around them. A valued correspondent writes:

> There is an increasing demand for educated priests, capable of satisfying the spiritual needs of an educated community, which is no longer content with accepting everything on authority. Amongst us hitherto the priests have been illiterate, ignorant, and therefore unfit for the new demands created by the times. They have to depend not upon fixed salaries or endowments but upon fees and payments received for reciting prayers and performing ceremonies. There is an increasing demand for priests who by preaching and example can set up an ideal for the faithful to follow. Hitherto we have had little of preaching or sermonizing, or even of philosophical exposition of tenets.[1]

The most advanced party are also convinced that there is still much required in the way of religious and social reform.

But a number of the leading men of the community have come to believe that the Parsees are losing their primacy in India, that they no longer control commerce to the extent they used to do, and that physical degeneration has set in amongst them. Strangely enough, one of the boldest and most cultured of modern Parsees, the Hon. Justice Sir Dinshaw Davar, puts down this supposed degeneracy to modern education. Others have, however, no difficulty in answering him. It is clear that it is city life, sedentary occupations and the want of regular exercise which is producing the phenomena referred to.

6. A Parsee priest named Dhala went to America and studied in the University of Columbia under Professor Jackson, the famous Zoroastrian scholar. He returned to India in 1909, and, in order to focus the reform movement, proposed a Zoroastrian Conference. The following quotation gives the main facts:

[1] Professor Wadia.

A couple of years ago, Dr. Dhala, a young energetic Parsi divine, fresh from his long and arduous studies of the Parsi Religion at the University of Columbia, as elucidated by scholars and savants of English, European and American reputation, whose labours and researches in the field of Avesta literature have thrown a flood of light on the philosophical teachings and speculations of our revered prophet, conceived the idea of having a Conference on some such lines as the Indian Social Conference held every year by our sister community, the Hindus. The *raison d'être* of the Conference was to inaugurate a liberal movement for the purpose of restoring Zoroastrian religion to its pristine sublimity and simplicity, in other words, to weed out all practices, beliefs, creeds, rituals, ceremonies and dogmas that have clustered round the true original religion, and to instruct and guide the community accordingly.[1]

The Conference was held in April, 1910, and a variety of questions, religious, social and educational were discussed. The need of an educated priesthood, and the need of serious moral and religious education in schools, were strongly emphasized. But the conservatives[2] opposed, and violent scenes interrupted the proceedings, the result being that the gathering which had been created by the reformers for the sake of securing a great advance became rather a rallying centre for the conservative party. The Second Conference, held in 1911, also suffered seriously from the same causes.

The third and fourth Conferences, held in 1912 and 1913, were largely attended and very successful, and were not marred by violent opposition. The membership has grown to 500. The Conference is pressing forward the following schemes for the betterment of the community:

1. Lectures. Dr. Dhala and Mr. D. H. Madan, advocate of the Bombay High Court, and several others, have delivered lectures on Zoroastrianism in the vernacular to very large audiences in Bombay and throughout Gujarat.

[1] *ISR.*, XXII, 113. [2] P. 345, below.

2. Revision of the Calendar.

3. Education of Parsee priests. Money is available for this project, but the scheme is not yet ripe.

4. Industrial and Technical Education. A sub-committee has been appointed for this purpose.

5. Medical Inspection of School Children. The special Committee on this subject has 35 doctors to carry out the work.

6. Charity Organization. A scheme was proposed by Professor Henderson of Chicago but it is still in embryo.

7. Dairy Scheme. A limited liability company is being organized to supply sterilized milk, first to Parsee children, then to others.

8. Agricultural Scheme. A proposal has been made to purchase land for a new organization to conduct farming.

The leaders of the progressive party are Dr. Dhala, Sir P. M. Mehta, Sir Dinshaw Petit, the three Tatas, Mr. H. A. Wadia and Dr. Katrak. The paper that represents their position is *The Parsee.*

The rise and growing influence of the propaganda of the Theosophic party[1] led in 1911 to the organization within the reforming party of a society to resist and expose it. It is called The Iranian Association. The following are the objects the members have in view:

1. To maintain the purity of the Zoroastrian religion and remove the excrescences that have gathered around it.

2. To expose and counteract the effects of such teachings of Theosophists and others as tend:

(*a*) to corrupt the religion of Zarathushtra by adding elements foreign to it, and

(*b*) to bring about the degeneration of a progressive and virile community like the Parsis, and make them a body of superstitious and unpractical visionaries.

3. To promote measures for the welfare and advancement of the community.

[1] P. 344, below.

Since March, 1912, the Association has published the *Journal of the Iranian Association*, a small monthly, partly in English, partly in Gujarātī.

LITERATURE.—*History of the Parsis*, by Dosabhai Framji Karaka, London, Macmillan, 1884, 2 vols., 36*s*. *The Pārsī Religion*, by John Wilson, D.D., Bombay, American Mission Press, 1843, out of print. *The K. R. Cama Memorial Volume*, by Jivanji Jamshedji Modi, Bombay, Fort Printing Press, 1900. *Dadabhai Naoroji, A Sketch of his Life and Life Work*, Madras, Natesan, as. 4. *B. M. Malabari, a Biographical Sketch*, by Dayaram Gidumal, with Introduction by Florence Nightingale, London, Fisher Unwin, 1892. *Infant Marriage and Enforced Widowhood in India*, by B. M. Malabari, Bombay, Voice of India Press, 1887.

4. Muḥammadan Reform

1. By the opening of the nineteenth century the collapse of the Muḥammadan empire in India was complete, although the name and the shadow continued to exist in Delhi for half a century longer. Necessarily, the fall of this mighty empire, which had wielded so much power and controlled so much wealth, produced the direst effects upon the Muḥammadans of North India. True, the Empire collapsed through inner decay, so that serious evils were there before the fall; yet the actual transference of the power and the prestige produced widespread degradation. The whole community sank with the empire. Necessarily, there was very bitter feeling against the European who had so unceremoniously helped himself to the empire of their fathers. The old education and culture rapidly declined; and for many decades Muḥammadans failed to take advantage of the new education planted by the conqueror. The consequence was that, throughout North India, the relative positions of the Hindu and Muḥammadan communities steadily changed, the former rising in knowledge, wealth and position, the latter declining.

2. Syed Aḥmad Khan came of an ancient noble family which had long been connected with Government. After receiving a Muḥammadan education, he had found a position under the British administration. In these and other particulars of his life and experience he was very like Ram Mohan Ray, only he came about forty years later, and was connected not with Calcutta but Delhi. While he was still young, he began to see how matters stood. During the Mutiny his loyalty never wavered, and he was instrumental in saving many Europeans. As soon as peace returned, he wrote a pamphlet, called *The Causes of the Indian Mutiny*, but, unfortunately, it was not published until five years later. That piece of work showed most clearly what a shrewd, capable man the writer was, and how invaluable he might be as an intermediary between the Government and the Muḥammadan community.

But the Mutiny opened Syed Aḥmad's eyes also. It showed him, as by a flash of lightning, the frightful danger in which his community stood. He had early grasped the real value of British rule in India, and had thereby been led to believe that it would prove stable in spite of any such storm as the Mutiny. He now saw clearly that the Muḥammadans of India must absorb the science and the education of the West, and must also introduce large social reform amongst themselves, or else fall into complete helplessness and ruin. He therefore at once set about making plans for persuading his brethren of the truth of his ideas. He talked incessantly to his personal friends, published pamphlets and books, and formed an association for the study of Western science. He frankly said, "All the religious learning in Muḥammadan libraries is of no avail." He established English schools, and struggled in every possible way to convince his community of the wisdom of learning English and absorbing the culture of the West. But he saw as clearly that Englishmen also required to learn. It was most necessary that they should know Indian opinion and sympathize with Indian aspirations. Hence in 1866 the British-Indian Association was founded, in order to focus Indian opinion on political questions, yet in utmost loyalty to the British Government, and to represent Indian ideas in Parliament. Then, in order to further his plans, both educational and political, he visited England with his son in 1869, and spent seventeen months there, studying English life and politics but giving the major part of his time and attention to education.

When he returned to India, he began the publication of a monthly periodical in Urdu, the *Tahzību'l Akhlāq* or Reform of Morals. It dealt with religious, social and educational subjects in a courageous spirit. He combated prejudice against Western science, advocated greater social freedom, and sought to rouse the Muḥammadan community to self-confidence and vigorous effort. He urged that there was no religious reason why Muslims should not dine with Europeans, provided there was no forbidden food on the table, and boldly put his teaching into practice, living in European style, receiving Englishmen as his guests and accepting their hospitality in return. In consequence, he was excommunicated, slandered and persecuted. He was called atheist, renegade, antichrist. Men threatened to kill him. But he held bravely on.

3. The climax of his educational efforts was the creation of the Anglo-Muḥammadan College at Aligarh. He conceived the institution, roused public opinion in its favour and gathered the funds for its buildings and its endowment. His idea was to create an institution which should do for young Muslims what Oxford and Cambridge were doing for Englishmen. He believed that a good education on Western lines, supported by wise religious teaching from the Koran, would produce young Muḥammadans of capacity and character. Aligarh is thus the first college founded by an Indian that follows the

missionary idea, that education must rest on religion. The founder did his best to reproduce in India what he had seen in Oxford and Cambridge. The students reside in the College; there are resident tutors who are expected to develop character as well as intellect; athletics are prominent; and religion is an integral part of the work of the College. The Principal and several members of the staff are always Europeans. The prospectus states that the College was founded with the following objects:

1. To establish a College in which Musalmans may acquire an English education without prejudice to their religion.

2. To organize a Boarding-House to which a parent may send his son in the confidence that the boy's conduct will be carefully supervised, and in which he will be kept free from the temptations which beset a youth in big towns.

3. To give as complete an education as possible, which, while developing intellect, will provide physical training, foster good manners, and improve the moral character.

The following sentences from the Prospectus show how religious instruction is given:

A Maulvi of well-known learning and piety has been specially appointed to supervise the religious life of the students and conduct the prayers in the College Mosque.

Religious instruction is given to Musalman students, to Sunnis by a Sunni, and to Shias by a Shia; the books of Theology taught are prescribed by committees of orthodox Sunnis and Shias, respectively.

The first period of each day's work is devoted to the lectures on Theology, and attendance at these lectures is enforced by regulations as stringent as those regulating the ordinary class work of the College.

Attendance at prayers in the College Mosque is also compulsory, and students who are irregular are severely punished. Students are expected to fast during the month of Ramzan.

On Friday, the College is closed at eleven so as to allow the students to attend at Juma prayers, after which a sermon is delivered by the Resident Maulvi.

All Islamic festivals are observed as holidays in the College.

The College has proved truly successful. It has given the Muḥammadan community new courage and confidence. A striking succession of English University men have occupied the position of Principal, and have succeeded in producing something of the spirit and tone of English public school and University life among the students. A steady stream of young men of education and character passes from the College into the service of Government and the professions. It has convinced thoughtful Muḥammadans of the wisdom of accepting Western education. It has proved a source of enlightenment and progressive thought. But, it must be confessed, the religious influence of the College does not seem to be at all prominent or pervasive.

In 1886 interest in modern education had made so much progress that Syed Aḥmad Khan was able to start the Muḥammadan Educational Conference, which meets annually, now in one centre and now in another. It has done a great deal to rouse Muḥammadans to their own backwardness and pitiable need. In recent years a Conference of Muslim ladies has met alongside the main Conference to deal with female education.[1]

4. With the Syed also began the permeation of the Muḥammadan community in India with modern ideas in religion.

After the death of Muḥammad, Muslim teachers gathered all the traditions about him, and sought to form a systematic body of doctrine and of law for believers. Orthodoxy gradually took shape. The doctrine of the divine will and the divine decrees was stated in such a form as to make human freedom almost an impossibility. The Koran was declared to be the eternal and uncreated Word of God. Crude concep-

[1] *ISR.*, XXII, 247.

tions of God and His attributes became crystallized in Muslim doctrine. Rules for family and social life were fixed in rigid form.

But as conquest brought vast territories of both the East and the West under Islamic rule, the conquerors came into close touch with Greek and Christian civilization. At Bagdad, especially, the science and philosophy of Greece were carefully cultivated. Christian monks taught and translated. From this living intercourse there arose, in the eighth century A.D., a great movement of Muḥammadan thought. Learned teachers began to defend the freedom of the will, to speculate on the nature of the Godhead, and to discuss the Koran. A new school, the Mu'tazilites, arose, characterized by freedom of thought, great confidence in reason, and a keen sense of the importance of the moral issues of life. They held the freedom of the human will, pronounced against the doctrine of the resurrection of the body, and declared that the Koran was created in time, and that there was a human element in it alongside the divine. They were opposed to polygamy. But this enlightened school was soon pronounced heretical, and passed out of existence.

It is most interesting to note that Western thought produced almost identical results in India in the nineteenth century. Early in life Syed Aḥmad Khan openly abandoned the charge, which is so often made by orthodox Muḥammadans, that Christians have seriously corrupted the text of the Old and New Testaments. He urged his fellow-believers that they should not consider Christians as Kafirs and enemies, and declared that the Bible and the Koran, when rightly understood, did not contradict one another. Readers will note how closely his position approximates to the teaching of Ram Mohan Ray. The resemblance in many respects is very striking: the Hindu leader published *The Precepts of Jesus:* the Muḥammadan reformer published a fragment of a

Commentary on *Genesis*, which has been of real service in opening Muḥammadan minds. He held that in the Koran, as in the Bible, we must acknowledge the presence of a human element as well as a divine. The rest of his religious conceptions have been outlined by a trustworthy scholar as follows:

> But his thought (system we cannot call it) is more influenced by the conceptions of *conscience* and *nature*. Conscience, he says, is the condition of man's character which results from training and reflection. It may rightly be called his true guide and his real prophet. Still, it is liable to mutability, and needs to be corrected from time to time by historic prophets. To test a prophet we must compare the principles of his teaching with the laws of nature. If it agrees with these we are to accept it, and he quotes with approval the remark of a French writer, that Islam, which lays no claim to miraculous powers on the part of the founder, is *the* truly rationalistic religion. Muhammad, he claims, set forth the Divine unity with the greatest possible clearness and simplicity: first, Unity of Essence, which he promulgated afresh; second, Unity of Attributes, which the Christians had wrongly hypostatized in their doctrine of the Trinity; third, Unity of Worship in the universal and uniform rendering of that devotion which is due to God alone, thus securing the doctrine of the Unity against all practical encroachments through corrupt observances.[1]

He made much of reason. One of his phrases was, 'Reason alone is a sufficient guide.' He spoke and wrote in favour of Natural Religion. Hence his followers are called *Naturis*. The word has been corrupted into *Necharis*, and occurs in this form in Census Reports and elsewhere. The Syed won the confidence of Government, became a member of the Viceroy's Legislative Council, and was knighted.

His principles have been accepted and carried farther by several writers, notably Moulvie Chiragh Ali and The Right

[1] Weitbrecht, *Indian Islam and Modern Thought*, 5 (Church Congress, 1905).

Hon. Syed Amir Ali. Their work is almost entirely apologetic. They have a double aim in view, first, to defend Islam from Christian criticism and the corroding influences of Western thought in general, and, secondly, to prove that the religious, social, moral and political reforms, which, through Christian teaching, modern thought and the pressure of the times, are being inevitably forced on Muḥammadan society, are in full consonance with Islam. As the practice of Muḥammad himself, Muḥammadan Law and orthodox teaching are all unquestionably opposed to these things, the line of argument taken is that the spirit [1] of Islam is all in their favour, and that everything else is to be regarded as of the nature of concessions to human frailty. This theory is elaborately worked out in Syed Amir Ali's *Spirit of Islam.* There we are told that the Koran in reality discourages slavery, religious war, polygamy and the seclusion of women. Of this writer a competent scholar [2] says:

> The Syed is at the stage of explaining things away, and it is fair to say that he does it at the expense of much hardly ingenuous ingenuity and a good deal of *suppressio veri.*

But the very hopelessness of these positions from the critical point of view may be to us the measure of the forces that are driving the writers to plead for the reforms and to find justification for them. Syed Amir Ali definitely identifies himself with the Mu'tazilite school, both in their theology and their social ideas, and believes that large numbers of Indian Muḥammadans are with him in his opinions.

As to the results of the movement the following statement may suffice:

> The energies of the reform movement at present find their vent in the promotion of education and of social reforms.

[1] Cf. p. 334, below. [2] D. B. Macdonald in *IRM.*, April 1913, p. 377.

The Aligarh College, under a series of capable English principals and professors, is training up a new generation of Muḥammadan gentlemen in an atmosphere of manly culture and good breeding, with high ethical ideals. The yearly meeting of the Educational Conference both works practically for the advancement of enlightenment among Indian Muḥammadans and also affords an opportunity for exchange of thought and propagation of reforming ideas. Thus some years ago a leading Muḥammadan gentleman known as the Agha Khan, when presiding over the Conference at Madras, trenchantly impressed upon his hearers that the progress of the community was chiefly hindered by three evils: by the seclusion and non-education of women, by theoretical and practical fatalism, and by religious formalism; an enlightened self-criticism which commands sympathy and admiration. The questions of polygamy and female seclusion are being actively debated in the press and otherwise, and some leading Muḥammadan gentry have broken the ordinance of the veil and appear in public with their wives and daughters in European dress.

As far as regards theological thought, competent Indian observers are of opinion that the rationalism of Sir Syed Ahmad is not at present being developed; but that there is rather a relapse towards a passive acceptance of Muslim orthodoxy.[1] Still, there is no doubt that the movement has tended to increase openness and fairness of mind among the educated classes.[2]

A few educated Indian Muḥammadans during recent years have reached a more advanced position. Mr. S. Khuda Bukhsh, M.A., one of the Professors of the Presidency College, Calcutta, has published a volume entitled, *Essays, Indian and Islamic*, which the present writer has not seen, but which is characterized as follows by one of our best scholars:

He has read his Goldziher and accepts his positions. He knows what a monogamous marriage means and confesses frankly the gulf between it and marriage in Islam; and he does not try to prove that Islam does not sanction polygamy.

[1] P. 347, below. [2] Weitbrecht, p. 7.

With similar candour he views the other broad differences of East and West. How, then, is he a Moslem? He would go back to the Koran and Mohammed and would sweep away all the labours of the schoolman by which these have been overlaid. Above all he is fascinated by the music and magic of the Koran. That book and a broad feeling of loyalty to the traditions of his ancestors are evidently the forces which hold him.[1]

It is probably true, as the Right Hon. Syed Amir Ali said to me, that there are very few indeed who are ready to follow Mr. Bukhsh. For the modern conservative movement among Muslims see p. 347.

LITERATURE.—*Sir Syed Ahmad Khan*, by General Graham, London, Hodder, 1909. *Sir Syed Ahmed Khan*, Madras, Natesan, as. 4. *The Spirit of Islam*, by Syed Amir Ali, Calcutta, Lahiri and Co., 1890. *Essays, Indian and Islamic*, by Khuda Bukhsh, London, Probsthain, 1912, 7*s*. 6*d*. net.

[1] D. B. Macdonald, *IRM*., April, 1913, p. 378.

CHAPTER III

REFORM CHECKED BY DEFENCE OF THE OLD FAITHS

1870–1913

We have seen in the historical outline that about 1870 a great change began to make itself manifest in the Hindu spirit. The educated Indian suddenly grew up, and shewed that he had a mind of his own. Religiously, the change manifested itself in a disposition to proclaim Hinduism one of the greatest religions. The same temper appeared among Buddhists, Jains, Muslims and Parsees; but the movement shewed itself, first of all, among Hindus. It also took many forms. We propose to divide the many movements and organizations incarnating this spirit into two groups, according as they defend only a part or the whole of the ancient faith. This chapter will deal with those that defend only a part. Every movement in this group opposes Hindu idolatry; but several of them worship their gurus, a practice which leads to idolatry. The attitude to caste in all cases is very ambiguous.

1. The Ārya Samāj

1. This powerful body, which during the last twenty years has expanded rapidly in the Panjab and the United Provinces, is so completely the creation of its founder that a brief sketch of his life is the indispensable introduction to a study of the movement.

For the first thirty-three years of his life we have a very clear and informing witness, a fragment of an autobiography, dictated by him, and published in the *Theosophist*, in October and December, 1879, and November, 1880.[1] This sketch seems to be on the whole trustworthy. It certainly enables us to trace in some degree the growth of his mind during the period which it covers.

In the small town of Taṅkārā,[2] belonging to the native state of Morvi, Kathiawar, Western India, there lived early last century a wealthy Brāhman, named Ambā Śaṅkara. He held the position of Jamadar of the town, which his fathers had held before him, and was a banker besides. He was a devout Hindu, an ardent and faithful worshipper of Śiva. To this man was born, in 1824, a son, whom he named Mūla Śaṅkara. The father was above all things anxious that the boy should prove a religious man and should accept his father's religion. Accordingly he was careful to give him a Hindu education. By the time he was fourteen the boy had learnt by heart large pieces of the Vedas and had made some progress in Sanskrit grammar.

At this time the first crisis in his life occurred. As the incident is one of the most vivid episodes in the *Autobiography*,[3] we give it in his own words:

When the great day of gloom and fasting — called Śivarātrī — had arrived, this day falling on the 13th of Vadya of Magh, my father, regardless of the protest that my strength might fail, commanded me to fast, adding that I had to be initiated on that night into the sacred legend, and participate in that night's long vigil in the temple of Śiva. Accordingly, I followed him along with other young men, who accompanied their parents. This vigil is divided into four parts, called *praharas*, consisting of three hours each. Having completed my task, namely, having sat up for the first two *praharas* till the hour of mid-

[1] Republished as an introduction to the English translation of the *Satyarth Prakash*, by Durga Prasad.

[2] For the name of the town I am indebted to Mrs. Sinclair Stevenson of Rajkot, and also for the names of the father and the son.

[3] Pp. 2–3.

night, I remarked that the *Pujaris*, or temple servants, and some of the lay devotees, after having left the inner temple, had fallen asleep outside. Having been taught for years that by sleeping on that particular night, the worshipper lost all the good effect of his devotion, I tried to refrain from drowsiness by bathing my eyes now and then with cold water. But my father was less fortunate. Unable to resist fatigue, he was the first to fall asleep, leaving me to watch alone.

Thoughts upon thoughts crowded upon me, and one question arose after the other in my disturbed mind. Is it possible, — I asked myself, — that this semblance of man, the idol of a *personal* God that I see bestriding his bull before me, and who, according to all religious accounts, walks about, eats, sleeps and drinks; who can hold a trident in his hand, beat upon his *damaru* drum, and pronounce curses upon men, — is it possible that he can be the Mahādeva, the Great Deity, the same that is invoked as the Lord of Kailash, the Supreme Being and the Divine hero of all the stories we read of him in his Puranas? Unable to resist such thoughts any longer, I awoke my father, abruptly asking him to enlighten me, to tell me whether this hideous emblem of Śiva in the temple was identical with the Mahādeva, of the scriptures, or something else. "Why do you ask it?" said my father. "Because," I answered, "I feel it impossible to reconcile the idea of an omnipotent, living God, with this idol, which allows the mice to run upon its body, and thus suffers its image to be polluted without the slightest protest." Then my father tried to explain to me that this stone representation of the Mahādeva of Kailash, having been consecrated with the Veda mantras (verses) in the most solemn way by the holy Brāhmins, became, in consequence, *the* God himself, and is worshipped as such, adding that, as Śiva cannot be perceived personally in this Kali-Yuga — the age of mental darkness, — we hence have the idol in which the Mahādeva of Kailash is worshipped by his votaries; this kind of worship is pleasing to the great Deity as much as if, instead of the emblem, he were there himself. But the explanation fell short of satisfying me. I could not, young as I was, help suspecting misinterpretation and sophistry in all this. Feeling faint with hunger and fatigue, I begged to be allowed to go home.

My father consented to it, and sent me away with a Sepoy, only reiterating once more his command that I should not eat. But when, once home, I had told my mother of my hunger, she fed me with sweetmeats, and I fell into a profound sleep.

Every one will feel the beat of conviction in this fine passage; and the results of it are visible in the crusade of the Ārya Samāj against idolatry to this day. But every one who knows India will also agree that what happened is scarcely comprehensible in a Hindu boy of fourteen years of age, unless he had already heard idolatry condemned. Brooding over the problem, I wrote to my friend, Mrs. Sinclair Stevenson of Rajkot, Kathiawar, and asked whether Sthānakavāsī influence could be traced in or about the boy's birth-place at that time. The Sthānakavāsīs are a group of Jains who gave up idolatry and broke away from the main Śvetāmbara sect in the fifteenth century.[1] Mrs. Stevenson writes:

Taṅkārā is fourteen miles south of Morvi, and about twenty-three miles north of Rajkot. In the thirties, the father of the present Thakur Saheb of Morvi was ruling. He was very devoted to a certain Sthānakavāsī monk, and the Prime Minister also was a Sthānakavāsī; so that the sect was then very powerful and influential in the Morvi state. All monks and nuns, travelling from the town of Morvi to Rajkot (another Sthānakavāsī stronghold), passed through Taṅkārā, where Ambā Śaṅkara and his son lived.

This clearly gives the environment which prepared the boy for his experience in the temple.

Four years later the sudden death of a sister convulsed him with grief, and made him realize to the full the horror of death. He thereupon resolved that he would allow nothing to restrain him from winning *moksha*, that is, emancipation from transmigration, the Hindu idea of salvation. Consequently, he returned to his studies with redoubled energy, and made up his

[1] P. 326, below.

mind to allow no such entanglement as marriage to impede him in his quest. In 1846, when he was twenty-one or twenty-two, his parents determined to get him married; but he fled from home. Thus ends the first section of his life.

2. In his wanderings he met a number of ascetics, who received him into their order. His father came out to seek for him and caught him, but he escaped once more. He then met with a sannyāsī named Brahmānand, and by him was convinced of the truth of the Vedānta doctrine of the identity of his own soul and God. This he gave up at a later date. For two years he wandered about, seeking good teachers.

In 1848 he proceeded to Chānoda Kanyāli on the banks of the river Nerbudda, and met several groups of scholarly ascetics, some of them followers of the Yoga system, others of the Vedānta. He was most anxious to become an initiated *sannyāsī*, that is, a Hindu monk who has renounced the world completely. He gives up caste, home, marriage, property, the use of money and of fire, and is expected to live a wandering life. If he were once received into one of the recognized orders of sannyāsīs, his parents could no longer bring pressure upon him to marry. At length he begged an ascetic known as Paramānanda, belonging to the Sarasvatī order of Śaṅkara's Daṇḍīs, to receive him. At first he refused, but, after much persuasion, he initiated him, giving him the name Dayānanda. Since he had thereby become a member of the Sarasvatī order, he was henceforward known as Dayānanda Sarasvatī. Until the day of his death he would tell no one his real name.

From this time onwards for eight years he wandered about from place to place, trying to find trustworthy teachers of Yoga. His *Autobiography* does not tell us why he was so eager to learn Yoga methods; but he probably regarded them as the proper means for reaching the emancipation which he was so desirous to reach.

Either at the time of his initiation as a sannyāsī, or at some point during these years, he lost faith in the teaching of Śaṅkara, and came to believe that God is personal, that the human soul is distinct from God, and that the world is real. He does not tell us who the teachers were who led him to these opinions. They are probably the outcome of the modern influences he came under, and of his original belief in Śiva. In any case he continued to worship Śiva, and believed in the personality of God.

His books on Yoga contained anatomical accounts of the human body. Reading in these volumes long and intricate descriptions of nerve-circles and nerve-centres which he could not understand, he was suddenly filled with suspicion. As it happened, a dead body was floating down the river on the banks of which he was walking. He drew the corpse to the shore, cut it open, satisfied himself that the books were false, and in consequence consigned them to the river along with the corpse. From this time his faith in many works on Yoga gradually dwindled.

The *Autobiography* stops short at the beginning of 1857, and we are without information of his activities until 1860. Thus there is no echo of the Indian Mutiny whatsoever in his life.

He had been greatly disappointed in his search for competent teachers.[1] In 1860, however, he came across a blind Brāhman in the city of Mathurā (Muttra), and became his disciple for two and a half years. His master, whose name was Virajānanda, was a great authority on Pāṇini's Grammar. He believed implicitly in the authority of the ancient books, but condemned all modern Sanskrit religious works as worthless lies. He would not accept Dayānanda as a disciple until the latter had sunk all his modern books in the river Jumna. Blind and learned though he was, he was a very irritable man,

[1] For the remainder of Dayānanda's life see his *Life* by Bawa Chhajju Singh.

and would now and then give his disciple corporal chastisement. One day he struck him on the hand with a stick with such violence that he carried the mark of it all his life. This man influenced Dayānanda more than any other. He read with him Pāṇini's Grammar and Patañjali's Commentary on it. We are also told that he studied the *Vedānta-sūtras* and many other books, but what these other books were, we do not know. Whether it was from Virajānanda that he learned the extraordinary method of expounding the Vedas which he used in writing his Commentaries in later years, we do not know. But his teacher certainly sketched his mission for him. When he was leaving, Virajānanda said to him:

> The Vedas have long ceased to be taught in Bhāratvarsha, go and teach them; teach the true Shastras, and dispel, by their light, the darkness which the false creeds have given birth to. Remember that, while works by common men are utterly misleading as to the nature and attributes of the one true God, and slander the great Rishis and Munis, those by the ancient teachers are free from such a blemish. This is the test which will enable you to differentiate the true, ancient teaching from the writings of ordinary men.[1]

It was in May, 1863, that he took leave of his master and began his wanderings once more. He now regarded himself as a learned man, and usually conversed in Sanskrit rather than in the vernacular Hindī. Although he had many a conversation and discussion during those years, he still thought of himself as a religious student and not as a teacher. When he started out, he was still a devotee of Śiva, wearing the necklace of *rudrāksha* berries, and the three lines of white ash on the forehead, which distinguish the pious Śaiva. But in the course of his wanderings his mind altered, and he laid these things aside once for all. Henceforward he worshipped God, and recognized Śiva as only one of the many names of the

[1] Chhajju Singh, 77.

Supreme. This change seems to have come in the year 1866, which was clearly a time of crisis for him. During that year he came in contact with various missionaries, and had long conversations with them. The same year finds him not only preaching against idolatry at Hardwar, but telling the pilgrims there that sacred spots and ceremonial bathing are of no religious value whatsoever, and denouncing the great Vaishṇava book, the *Bhāgavata Purāṇa*, as immoral.

3. A further change came in the year 1868. Virajānanda and he seem both to have felt that it was now his duty to begin the public exposition of his ideas. From this time, then, Dayānanda's public life may be said to have begun. His biographer speaks of him as trying several methods of work, and finding them each more or less a failure.

His first plan was to talk to the paṇḍits in Sanskrit, in the hope that, if he convinced them of the truth of his ideas, they would spread the light all over the land. But these old-fashioned conservatives, no matter how often convicted of error, were of the same opinion still. So he gave the course up in despair.

He next decided to adopt one of the methods which he had seen in use in Christian missions, namely education. He found some well-to-do men to finance several schools for him. The curriculum was to be confined to early Sanskrit literature. He hoped that pupils trained in this way would become missionaries of his ideas. The schools were opened, and continued for some time; but, though the paṇḍits were quite willing to receive his pay and become schoolmasters, they did not teach the new ideas; and the work came to nothing.

Consequently, he determined to appeal to the people themselves, both by lectures and by books. He published a number of books, and went from town to town, delivering lectures, in Sanskrit, on the right interpretation of the Vedas and the teaching which he believed they gave. This method was

PLATE V

Dayānanda Sarasvatī
As a sannyāsī

Dayānanda Sarasvatī
After his visit to Calcutta

more successful. He found it quite possible to draw huge audiences wherever he went, and to get the ear, not only of ordinary men, but of the wealthy. He had many conversations with individuals, but consistently refused to speak to women. Wherever it was possible, he met the paṇḍits in discussion. He was specially anxious to prove in every place, in public discussion with the most learned men, that idolatry has not the sanction of the Vedas. His followers declare he was always victorious in these discussions. All those who met him in discussion declared him to be violent, loud-tongued and overbearing. He still lived like a sannyāsī, wearing only a minimum of clothing. He was a large, powerful man with striking features, and rather a remarkable voice.

In the end of 1872 he went down to Calcutta, and spent four months there, lecturing, speaking and discussing. He had been above all things anxious to meet Keshab Chandra Sen; and it is clear that Keshab and the Samāj exercised a very wonderful influence over him. Two changes in his method date from this time. He began to wear regular clothes; and a picture which still survives shows that he must have copied the Brāhma leaders, whose dress was a modification of missionary costume. Secondly, he realized, from the great influence exercised by Keshab and the other Brāhma leaders through their addresses in Bengali, that he ought to give up using Sanskrit in his public lectures and speak in Hindī instead.

4. His fame and influence continued to spread and become deeper, as he taught far and wide throughout North India. At Allahabad in 1874 he completed his *Satyārth Prakāsh*, with which we shall have to deal later. In the end of 1874 we find him in Bombay, in close touch both with the Hindu community and the young Prārthanā Samāj.[1] He seems to have had more than usual success in the city; for he returned early in 1875, and there launched his great scheme, the foun-

[1] P. 76, above.

dation of the Ārya Samāj. The members of the Prārthanā Samāj had hoped to be able to unite with him, but the differences were too deep. It is clear, however, that the main features of his society were borrowed directly from the Brāhma and Prārthanā Samājes, as he saw them working in Calcutta, Bombay and elsewhere. The common name covers common features. This may be taken as the end of the third, and the beginning of the last, stage of his life.

On the first of January, 1877, Queen Victoria was proclaimed Empress of India in a magnificent Durbar held by the Viceroy, Lord Lytton, at Delhi. Dayānanda was present as the guest of one of the native princes, and met some Hindus from Lahore, who gave him a pressing invitation to visit the Panjab. Shortly after he visited Ludhiana and Lahore. So great was his success in this latter city, that the Ārya Samāj founded there very speedily eclipsed the society founded in Bombay; and Lahore became the headquarters of the movement.

For six years longer Dayānanda lived and worked, touring throughout North India, and steadily extending the Samāj. There are just two matters to be noted during these years. The first is his connection with the Theosophical Society which had been founded in New York in 1875. In 1878 the founders, Col. Olcott and Madame Blavatsky, wrote to Dayānanda and suggested a union of the two movements, on the ground that their aim was the same; and Dayānanda accepted the proposal. The Theosophist leaders came to India in January, 1879; and the strange union continued until 1881, when it was broken off, both parties feeling bitter and aggrieved.[1]

The other matter is a living part of his general policy. He consistently sought to recall the Hindus to what he conceived to be the ancient faith, and as consistently stirred them up to vehement opposition to Christianity and Muḥammadan-

[1] Chhajju Singh, 476–532; *ODL.*, I, 135; 396 ff. Below, pp. 218, 226.

ism. In the first edition of the *Satyārth Prakāsh*,[1] published in 1874, he approved of beef-eating under certain conditions, but in the second edition it is condemned. In 1882 he formed the *Gaurakshinī Sabhā*,[2] or Cow-protecting Association, and about the same time published his book, *Gokaruṇanidhi*,[3] on the same subject. The purpose was to rouse Hindu feeling against Christians and Muḥammadans on account of the killing of cows and oxen, and to present a monster petition to Government,[4] begging that the practice might be prohibited. Dayānanda died before the movement had spread very far; but later it attained great proportions, as we shall see.[5] In this connection Sir Valentine Chirol has suggested [6] that Dayānanda was a political schemer. This we believe to be a complete mistake, although, as we shall show, his unhealthy teaching has produced very unhealthy political fruit.[7]

He passed away on the 30th of October, 1883, at the age of fifty-nine.

5. The following sketch of his position and aims by Dr. Griswold of Lahore is so vivid and convincing that we cannot do better than transcribe it:

> Paṇḍit Dayānand Sarasvatī became finally emancipated from the authority of Brahmanism in some such way as Luther became emancipated from the authority of the Church of Rome. Luther appealed from the Roman Church and the authority of tradition to the Scriptures of the Old and New Testament. Paṇḍit Dayānand Sarasvatī appealed from the Brahmanical Church and the authority of *Smṛiti* to the earliest and most Sacred of Indian Scriptures. The watchword of Luther was 'Back to the Bible': the watchword of Paṇḍit Dayānand was '*Back to the Vedas.*' With this religious watchword another watchword was implicitly, if not explicitly, combined, namely

[1] P. 302. Also *Saṅskār Vidhi*, 11; 42.

[2] Chhajju Singh, 726–30.

[3] *Ib.*, 721.

[4] *Ib.*, 730.

[5] P. 358, below.

[6] *Indian Unrest*, 109 ff.

[7] P. 358, below.

'*India for the Indians.*' Combining these two, we have the principle, both religious and political, that *the religion of India as well as the Sovereignty of India ought to belong to the Indian people;* in other words, Indian *religion* for the Indians, and Indian *Sovereignty* for the Indians. In order to accomplish the first end, Indian religion was to be reformed and purified by a return to the Vedas, and foreign religions as Islam and Christianity were to be extirpated. Thus the program included *reform* for indigenous religion and *extirpation* for foreign religion. With regard to the second end, the founder of the Arya Samaj seems to have taught that a return to the pure teachings of the Vedas would gradually fit the people of India for self-rule and that independence would ultimately come to them. I am not charging Paṇḍit Dayānand Sarasvatī with disloyalty. Every sincere well-wisher of India hopes that the time will come when the Indian people through the spread of education and the removal of bad social customs and above all through the prevalence of true religion will be *fitted* for Self-government. It is evident from all this that Paṇḍit Dayānand Sarasvatī was a man of large views. He was a dreamer of splendid dreams. He had a vision of India purged of her superstitions, filled with the fruits of Science, worshipping one God, fitted for self-rule, having a place in the sisterhood of nations, and restored to her ancient glory. All this was to be accomplished by throwing overboard the accumulated superstitions of the centuries and returning to the pure and inspired teachings of the Vedas. Thus the founder of the Ārya Samāj was a kind of Indian Elijah or John the Baptist, who felt himself called to turn the hearts of the degenerate children of modern India to their fathers of the glorious Vedic age, to reconcile the present with the past. The character of his mission helps to account for the violence of his methods of controversy. Elijah was not specially gentle in his dealings with the prophets of Baal; nor was Luther very tender toward the Roman Church. In like manner Paṇḍit Dayānand Sarasvatī stood with his back to the wall, facing on the one hand the attacks of the Brahmanical hierarchy and on the other the assaults of the foreign religions, Islam and Christianity. Under these circumstances we can hardly wonder that he struck back as hard as he could. Luther dealt heavy blows at the Roman Church as Paṇḍit Dayānand did at the Brahmanical Church. Suppose now that while Luther was fighting with Rome, an extensive and powerful Mohammedan propaganda, which threatened to devour all the fruits of the Reformation, was found all over Europe. What would Luther have done under these circumstances, but smite the apostate Roman Church at home and the Mohammedan propaganda from abroad with impartial zeal and violence and with no great effort to be fair and appreciative. This illustrates exactly Paṇḍit Dayānand's attitude toward the degenerate Brahmanical Church, on the one hand, and the foreign faiths Christianity and Islam on the other. In his opinion, the one needed to be purged and pruned; the others, to be extirpated. The sections in the *Satyārth Prakāsh* which deal with the criticism of Islam and Christianity are evidently intended to be the literature of such extirpation, *i.e.*, to be the means of rooting out all such foreign superstitions from the hearts of the sons of India. For extreme unfairness, for inability to state the position of opponents without caricature, and for general crudeness, these sections can hardly be matched in the whole literature of religious controversy.[1]

6. Dayānanda's chief convictions may be summed up as follows:

a. There is one God only. He alone is to be worshipped; and he must be worshipped spiritually, not by images.

b. The four Vedas are God's knowledge. They contain all religious truth, and also all science, at least in germ. They are the eternal utterance of God. There is nothing temporary or local in them. Everything which seems a reference to particular times and places only seems such through misconception. There is no polytheism in the Vedas. The many divine names which occur in them are all epithets of the one true God. These statements apply only to the collections of hymns. The Brāhmaṇas have less authority. Many other Hindu books are of value, because they were written by

[1] *Indian Evangelical Review*, January, 1892.

ṛishis and other inspired men, but they are not authoritative in the same sense as the Vedas; and they are not to be followed where they contradict the Vedas.

c. The Vedas teach transmigration and karma.

d. Forgiveness is for ever impossible.

e. Salvation is emancipation from transmigration.

The following are Dayānanda's chief works:

(1) *Satyārth Prakāsh*, a Hindī work, setting forth his teaching on marriage, the bearing of children, education, the ascetic orders, government, God, the Vedas, the world, man, salvation and food, and a long and interesting description of the various creeds of India with Dayānanda's criticism of them.

(2) *Veda Bhāshya*, a Vedic Commentary in Sanskrit. It is incomplete, yet covers the whole of the *Yajurveda* and the major part of the *Ṛigveda*.

(3) *Ṛigvedādi Bhāshya Bhūmikā*, an Introduction to his Vedic Commentary, partly in Sanskrit, partly in Hindī, a controversial work in which he condemns all existing commentaries as false, and expounds his own principles.

7. The most amazing of Dayānanda's ideas is his conception of the Vedas. In order to understand how he came to hold it, we must recognize what the traditional Hindu doctrine about them is. Since the Veda is the eternal utterance of God, there can be no temporal references in it. As Max Müller says:

> If any historical or geographical names occur in the Vedas, they are all explained away, because, if taken in their natural sense, they would impart to the Vedas an historical or temporal taint.[1]

This violent method of exegesis, whereby hundreds of allusions to places and events in these most human documents are distorted and misexplained, already finds clear expression

[1] *Biographical Essays*, 170.

as the only right principle of Vedic interpretation in the earliest treatises on the subject that have come down to us, some of which come from dates five or six centuries before Christ.

Dayānanda held fast by the old dogma, that the Vedas are God's eternal utterance. Several other Hindu ideas, notably the doctrines of transmigration and karma and of the sanctity of the cow, remained firmly seated in his mind.

But in his long, stormy career of wandering and disputing with all sorts and conditions of men, the facts of life, as they stared him in the face in North India under the British Government, had driven certain very modern and un-Hindu ideas into his mind with great force. The most important of these was the group of related convictions, that there is but one God, that all the gods (*devas*) of the Hindu pantheon have no existence, that idolatry is irrational and degrading, and that the sacrifice of animals and the offering of food as practised in Hindu temples are silly superstitions. Next in importance was his perception of the practical value of Western science and invention as made plain in the railway, the telegraph and modern weapons of war. Amongst his other fresh convictions may be mentioned the folly and danger of caste as practised in modern times, and of child-marriage.

Now these two groups of ideas, Hindu and modern, seem to have been both firmly implanted in his mind. He had had no modern education. He did not know sufficient English to read English books; so that he had no grasp of modern methods of thought and criticism. Nor had he had a thorough Hindu training. He had read with his blind teacher the best that Hindu literature contained on grammar and philosophy, but he had had no complete Vedic education. The time he spent with Virajānand was insufficient for the purpose. Hence, believing the Veda to be God's knowledge, he necessarily concluded that it corresponded with his own convictions as to truth, *i.e.* that it taught monotheism, transmigration and modern science, and that it did not recognize the gods of Hinduism nor sacrifice; and, being a Hindu born and bred, and filled with Hindu methods of thought, he proceeded, like the earliest Hindu scholars, by violent methods of interpretation to expel from the Vedas what he held to be false and to import into them what he held to be true. Max Müller writes:

> To him not only was everything contained in the Vedas perfect truth, but he went a step further, and by the most incredible interpretations succeeded in persuading himself and others that everything worth knowing, even the most recent inventions of modern science, were alluded to in the Vedas. Steam-engines, railways, and steam-boats, all were shown to have been known, at least in their germs, to the poets of the Vedas.[1]

Naturally he took full advantage of the principle stated by the ancient scholars, which we have just referred to, as justification of his methods.

Yet, though he claims to have restored the ancient interpretation, in reality he departs from it in two large and most important matters. The ancient scholars recognize the gods in the Vedas and all the details of their worship, while he removes all the gods, and leaves only the One. To the ancient teachers the Brāhmaṇas with their appendices, the Āraṇyakas and the Upanishads, are as truly the eternal word of God as the Hymns are; but Dayānanda makes the claim only for the *Saṁhitās*, *i.e.* the collections of Hymns, and recognizes the presence of a human element in the Brāhmaṇas. He thus stands absolutely alone as an interpreter of the Veda. No Hindu, ancient or modern, ever taught what he teaches; and we need scarcely say that every Western scholar repudiates both his methods and his results.

It is thus quite possible to follow the process of thought

[1] *Biographical Essays*, 170.

by which the Svāmī reached his doctrines. Yet, when one turns to the hymns themselves and to his interpretation of them, it becomes exceedingly difficult to believe in his straightforwardness and sincerity. One can hardly imagine any mind believing what he says. In order to give the ordinary reader some indication of his methods, we here transcribe the first five stanzas of the first hymn of the *Ṛigveda*, as translated by Hopkins.[1] It is a hymn of praise to the god *Agni*, *i.e.* Fire, regarded as the great priest, because sacrifices were wafted to the gods on the flames and smoke of the altar-fire.

To Agni

I worship Agni; house-priest, he,
And priest *divine* of sacrifice,
Th' oblation priest, who giveth wealth.

Agni, by seers of old adored,
To be adored by those to-day —
May he the *gods* bring here to us.

Through Agni can one wealth acquire,
Prosperity from day to day,
And fame of heroes excellent.

O, Agni! whatsoe'er the rite
That thou surround'st on every side,
That sacrifice attains the *gods*.

May Agni, who oblation gives —
The wisest, true, most famous priest —
This *god* with (all) the *gods* approach!

The meaning expressed in the above translation is precisely what is given by all Hindu scholars, ancient and modern;

[1] *Religions of India*, 108. For the materials used in this discussion I am indebted to Dr. Griswold's pamphlet, *The Dayānandī Interpretation of the word Deva.*

and all Western scholars agree. There are five words in the translation printed in italics. In the original the word in each case is *deva*, god, either in the singular or the plural. In the first stanza it is translated as an adjective, elsewhere as a substantive.

Dayānanda, like certain early Christian exegetes, is an advocate of the method of dual interpretation. Agni is not a god, but is at once a name of the one God, and the name of the material element, fire. Taken as a name of God, it means "giver and illuminator of all things." Taken as the material element, it means "fire which gives victory in battle by means of skilfully contrived weapons." This last is an allusion to modern firearms. In the first stanza he takes the word *deva* as an epithet of the one God and as meaning "Giver." In the second he translates it "excellent sense-organs" or "excellent qualities of knowledge," or "excellent seasons," or "excellent pleasures." Of the fourth and fifth stanzas he gives two translations, the one taking Agni as "God," the other taking it as "fire." In the fourth stanza, if God is addressed, *devāh* means "learned men"; if fire is addressed, *devāh* means "excellent things." In the fifth stanza, if we take Agni to mean God, the last line runs, "May this self-luminous One approach with learned men"; if we take Agni to mean fire, the meaning is, "May this illuminator approach with excellent qualities." This needs no comment. As translated by Hindu and by Western scholars, the poem is a polytheistic hymn, but clear, comprehensible, human. Dayānanda's translation reduces the lines to nonsense.

It ought to be stated here that Paṇḍit S. N. Agnihotṛi,[1] the founder of the Deva Samāj, published in 1891 a pamphlet called *Paṇḍit Dayānand Unveiled*, in which he avers that a number of men, some belonging to Gujarāt, others to Bengal, others to the Panjab, declared to him, either in conversation

[1] P. 173, below.

or by letter, that Dayānanda, in personal conversation with them, had acknowledged that his statements about the Veda were not matters of conviction but of diplomacy, that a religion must have some superstition as its basis, and that he had chosen the infallibility of the Vedas, because nothing else would be accepted by Hindus. Dayānanda had been dead eight years when the pamphlet appeared; and one of his followers attempted to demolish the writer by means of another pamphlet.[1] As the evidence was not carefully sifted by an impartial scholar at the time, it is not possible to say precisely how much weight ought to be attached to it; yet two or three of Agnihotṛi's witnesses were religious men of known probity; so that it would be hard to set their testimony aside. I have also received myself, from an altogether different source, another piece of evidence which strikingly corroborates their statements. The Rev. P. M. Zenker of the Church Missionary Society, Muttra, writes of an incident which occurred when he was in Brindaban preaching at a spring festival. He cannot vouch for the year, but it was 1884, 1885 or 1886. One of the leaders of the local Ārya Samāj had a long and serious conversation with him in the afternoon. Mr. Zenker returned his call the same evening; when they had another long talk. I quote Mr. Zenker's report of the conversation, so far as it refers to the Ārya Samāj:

> My informant stated that Dayānand's real object was to obtain for India all the advantages which Western civilization has conferred on the nations of Europe and America. But, being fully acquainted with the character of his Hindu fellow-countrymen, he knew they would hardly accept as a guide one who presented *this* as the sole aim and object of all the laborious training they would have to undergo. He therefore cast about for an expedient to gild the pill; and he thought he had found it in the cry, "Let us return to the pure teaching of the Veda."

[1] *Agnihotṛi Demolished*, by Rambhaj Datta.

This conversation, which occurred only some two or three years after Dayānanda's death in 1883, corroborates the statements of Agnihotṛi's witnesses, who had had personal intercourse with the leader himself. The evidence is not absolutely conclusive; but, taken along with the amazing character of Dayānanda's commentaries on the Vedas, it will have considerable weight with the open-minded student.[1]

8. The following is the official creed of the Samāj:

i. God is the primary cause of all true knowledge, and of everything known by its name.

ii. God is All-Truth, All-Knowledge, All-Beatitude, Incorporeal, Almighty, Just, Merciful, Unbegotten, Infinite, Unchangeable, without a beginning, Incomparable, the Support and the Lord of All, All-pervading, Omniscient, Imperishable, Immortal, Exempt from fear, Eternal, Holy, and the Cause of the Universe. *To Him alone worship is due.*

iii. The Vedas are the books of true knowledge, and it is the paramount duty of every Ārya to read or hear them read, to teach and preach them to others.

iv. One should always be ready to accept truth and renounce untruth.

v. All actions ought to be done conformably to virtue, *i.e.* after a thorough consideration of right or wrong.

vi. The primary object of the Samāj is to do good to the world by improving the physical, spiritual, and social condition of mankind.

vii. All ought to be treated with love, justice, and due regard to their merits.

viii. Ignorance ought to be dispelled and knowledge diffused.

ix. No one ought to be contented with his own good alone, but every one ought to regard his prosperity as included in that of others.

x. In matters which affect the general social well-being of the whole society, one ought to discard all differences and not allow one's individuality to interfere, but in strictly personal matters every one may act with freedom.

[1] Cf. the Tiyas, below, p. 313.

But these sentences omit many of the points which it is most important to know.

9. The following are the leading theological ideas of the Samāj. Orthodox Hindus allow only men of the three highest castes to study the Vedas: Āryas invite all, both men and women, to study them. On the other hand, they condemn modern Hindu literature. They teach that there are three eternal existences, God, the soul and elemental matter. The soul undergoes transmigration according to the law of karma. Forgiveness is altogether impossible. Salvation comes only by continued well-doing; and the soul, even when released from transmigration, is not absorbed in God. The doctrine of *avatāras*, or divine incarnations, is denied. Idolatry is vehemently condemned, and also the practice of killing animals in sacrifice or of offering food on the altar to God. The fire-sacrifice of the Vedas is retained, but is explained as a means of purifying the air. The Hindu form of ancestor-worship, known as the *śrāddha*, is condemned as useless; and pilgrimage is given up as superstitious.

10. A careful reading of the *Satyārth Prakāsh* shews that the ethical system of the Samāj is crude in the extreme. Many of the laws of Manu in all their barbarity are laid down for use in modern life. For example, the individual is encouraged to kill those whom he regards as monstrously evil men;[1] and the king is advised to have the adulterer burned alive on a red-hot iron bedstead, and the adulteress devoured alive by dogs, in the presence of many men and women.[2] But it is in its marriage laws that the book goes farthest astray. Child-marriage is prohibited,[3] and virgin widows and widowers are allowed to remarry,[4] excellent regulations, as all will agree. But widows and widowers who have lived with their spouses are told not to remarry.[5] Yet, for their relief, and for the

[1] Durga Prasad's translation, 203.
[2] *Ib.*, 204, 207. [3] *Ib.*, 132. [4] *Ib.*, 156. [5] *Ib.*, 156.

relief also of husbands and wives in certain circumstances, the law of *niyoga* is laid down.[1] *Niyoga* is simply sexual relationships without marriage. The details are too horrible to transcribe. They may be seen in the book. In 1892 some Āryas brought a law-suit against a Hindu who wrote against *niyoga*, calling it adultery, but the case was dismissed.[2] One is glad to hear that many members of the Samāj would now like to repudiate this most immoral legislation, which is equally repulsive to the Hindu and the Christian.

There is another feature of the *Satyārth Prakāsh* which has attracted wide attention. All the outstanding Hindu sects, and Jainism, Sikhism, Islam, and Christianity as well, are mercilessly criticized in it, and here and there with a good deal of malice and injustice. This section of the book has encouraged Āryas and provided them with very useful ammunition for their controversies, but it has also created vehement hatred against the Samāj in many quarters. Dayānanda's stinging taunts have been effective in rousing a number of the sects to retaliation and defensive organization. This is noticeably true of the Sikhs,[3] the Jains,[4] the Aḥmadīyas,[5] the Muḥammadans,[6] and also of Paṇḍit Dīn Dayāl,[7] the founder of the Bhārata Dharma Mahāmaṇḍala.

Dayānanda's own methods of controversy, shewn in his public addresses and debates and also in his writings, have naturally been adopted by his followers. Wherever they go, one hears of slander, passion, and unfair methods; and disturbances in the streets and squares have been pitiably common.

11. I had the privilege of being present, in company with Dr. Griswold, at an Ārya Samāj Sunday morning service in

[1] Durga Prasad's translation, 156–161.

[2] Ruchi Ram Sahni, *The Niyoga Doctrine of the Ārya Samāj*, 35–6.

[3] P. 340, below. [4] P. 329, below. P. 137, below.

[6] P. 351, below. [7] P. 316, below.

Lahore in December, 1912. The place of meeting is a large oblong hall without seats, with a platform at one end and a high narrow gallery at the other. In the floor, in front of the platform, there is a square pit, measuring perhaps two feet each way. This is the altar. On one side of the hall a small platform for singers and a harmonium had been placed. When we entered, there was only one man in the hall, and he was laying some pieces of wood in order at the bottom of the square pit. When that was done, he set up a stick of incense on end on the floor at each corner of the pit. Some packets of aromatic herbs and several sacrificial vessels lay on the floor. Men came dropping in, and squatted in front and on the two sides of the altar. When there were perhaps twenty present, those next the altar began to intone some Sanskrit verses, amongst which we could distinguish some of the verses of *Ṛigveda*, X, 129. This continued about twenty minutes. By that time there were about thirty present. The fire and the incense sticks were then lighted; the aromatic leaves were shed on the fire; and *ghī* (melted butter) was rubbed on the outer edges of the altar. Other verses were now chanted, while the flames rose nearly two feet above the level of the floor. This is the *havana*, which Āryas are recommended to perform every morning, at the time of their devotions, for the purification of the air. This continued for about fifteen minutes. All then rose to their feet and sat down in various places in the hall. A young man mounted the platform to lead the service, one sat down at the harmonium and a few others gathered round him to sing. There were forty-eight present.

The second part of the service then began. It consisted of the singing of hymns, the repetition of texts (one of them the *Gāyatrī*), prayer and a sermon, all in Hindī except a few texts which were in Sanskrit. It was just like a Protestant service, and totally unlike any Vedic observance. During this part of the service many boys came in. Before the sermon began there were perhaps two hundred present. Later the number rose to two hundred and fifty. There was no woman or girl present. I am told they are not excluded, but a special service, conducted by a lady, is held at another time and place, which they attend in fair numbers.

12. The death of Dayānanda was a great blow to the members of the Samāj; yet the work was carried on with enthusiasm; and the movement has continued to grow at a rapid pace since then. Large sums of money were collected to perpetuate the memory of the founder, and in 1887, the Dayānanda Anglo-Vedic College was opened in Lahore. This great foundation, in which the flower of the youth of the Ārya Samāj receive a modern English education, and also instruction in the religion of the Samāj, forms a very worthy memorial to Dayānanda's devotion and energy.

In 1892 the Ārya community fell in two. This division is parallel to the first split in the Brāhma camp. As Keshab led out the progressives, and left Debendra and the conservatives behind; so the Ārya Samāj broke up into the College or "Cultured" party and the Vegetarian or "Mahātma" party. The former are progressive, stand for modern education and for freedom in diet, and declare that the Ārya Samāj is the one true universal religion, which must be taught to all the world; while their opponents favour the ancient Hindu education, stand by vegetarianism and declare that the teaching of the Samāj is pure Hinduism, but not the universal religion.

13. I have failed to obtain printed reports of the work of the Samāj, so that it is rather hard to estimate what they are doing. Their methods, however, are well known. Those members of a local Samāj who pay 1% of their income to the funds elect the managing Committee of the Samāj. Then the Samājes in each Province elect representatives who form the *Pratinidhi Sabhā*, or Representative Assembly, of the Prov-

ince. Since the split in 1892 there have been duplicate organizations. There are missionaries and preachers of the Samāj, some paid, others honorary. Most of the paid men were originally Hindu paṇḍits; most of the honorary workers are men who have had an English education. The Samāj also copies other forms of Christian effort. They have their Tract Society, their Strī Samāj or Women's Ārya Samāj, their *Ārya Kumār Sabhā*, or Young Men's Ārya Association (a copy of the Y. M. C. A.), their Orphanages, and their work among the Depressed, which will be noticed elsewhere.[1]

The Samāj is doing a good deal of education. Lala Lajpat Rai writes with regard to the schools and colleges of the progressive party:

> At Lahore it has founded and maintains a first-class College, preparing scholars up to the highest standard and for the highest University examinations. This was created in 1886 in sacred memory of its founder, and is called "The Dayanand Anglo-Vedic College." Its objects are to encourage and enforce the study of (*a*) Hindi literature; (*b*) classical Sanskrit and the Vedas; and (*c*) English literature and sciences, both theoretical and applied; and, furthermore, "to provide means for giving technical education." It owns considerable property, and has endowments yielding an annual income (including tuition and admission fees, etc.) of over Rs. 60,000 (£4000). The Principal is honorary, and has held the post with remarkable success since the foundation. On the staff are several of its own alumni, working in a missionary spirit on mere subsistence allowances. Directly or indirectly connected with the College are a number of secondary and primary schools maintained by the Samaj throughout the province, some of which receive the usual grants from the Educational Department. In the United Provinces, also, the Samaj maintains several schools on the same lines as the Anglo-Vedic or Anglo-Sanskrit Schools of the Punjab, their principal Anglo-Vedic school being at Dehra Dun.[2]

[1] P. 371, below.

[2] *Contemporary Review*, May, 1910.

The centre and crown of the educational efforts of the Mahātma party is the *Gurukula Mahāvidyālaya* at Hardwar, a great institution, founded in 1902, in which an attempt is being made to give a true Hindu education and to save students from the contaminations both of Hindu home and city life and of Western civilization. It is a most interesting and promising experiment. The situation is all that could be desired; good food is provided, and the physique of the students receives a good deal of attention. Here is what a Christian writes of the conditions of life and study:[1]

> The students are admitted at the age of eight years, and the parents are under written pledge not to remove their sons from the school till the expiry of the 17 years' course, *i.e.* till they have reached the age of 25. During the whole of these 17 years they may never once go home or leave the school. Indeed, they are only allowed to have a quarter of an hour's interview once a year with their parents, and that in presence of their teachers. . . . During the whole of their long course they are watched day and night by their teachers and house-fathers. Without these they may not go out even for a walk. No woman may approach the Gurukula. They live a simple, hardy life, on strictly vegetarian diet. . . . They wear the saffron dress of the religious orders.

There are many points to admire in the life and the methods of study. Almost all the work is done in the vernacular, not in English. Great care is taken to train the character as well as the mind, and the foundation of a true love of India is laid from day to day. One wonders, however, whether the exclusion of home influence is wise, and whether anything like a sound literary education can be given, while Dayānanda's interpretation of the Veda is retained. There are other Gurukulas at Gujranwala, Farukhabad and elsewhere.

The Samāj does also a good deal for the education of girls. They have a very successful boarding school at Jullundur.

[1] Rev. W. E. S. Holland in *East and West*, June, 1907.

Lala Lajpat Rai, struck with the work of the Salvation Army, started recently in Lahore the Vedic Salvation Army.

In the Panjab and the United Provinces the Samāj has done valuable work by its testimony to monotheism, its opposition to idolatry and to other superstitions and by its educational work. Its polemic against caste, child-marriage, priestcraft, pilgrimage, and self-torture in the name of religion, is all to the good, although members of the Samāj are still bound by caste,[1] and many have not given up child-marriage. In these matters there is far more talk than action. The great expansion of the Samāj in recent years[2] gives promise of still farther growth, and the zeal of the members is proved by the very generous way in which they subscribe to the funds. Dayānanda's praise of all things Indian, and his defence of the Vedas and of transmigration have proved very popular.

Yet there is no risk involved in prophesying that the Samāj will not have a great history. In the very sources of its present strength there is that which will inevitably lead to its ruin. The false interpretation of the Vedas, on which the whole structure rests, will inevitably crumble as enlightenment proceeds. The attempt to retain much that is old and outworn, instead of transcending it, is another source of weakness. The retention of the doctrine of transmigration and karma is in itself most dangerous. So long as that remains, a healthy monotheism is impossible,[3] and caste cannot be rooted out.[4]

On the 30th of November, 1907, at the Samāj Anniversary in Lahore, Prof. Lala Sain Das, M.A., gave an address in which he asked the assembly to realize how little work they were doing in comparison with Christian Missions, how weak they

[1] A low-caste man wanted to send his son to the D. A. V. College, Lahore, but there was so much opposition that the authorities kept him out.

[2] The last census shows that they now number 243,000.

[3] See the author's *Crown of Hinduism*, 392–407.

[4] *Ib.*, 179–181; 191.

were spiritually and how impotent socially through the caste system. He added:

> Two new forces are now at work in India (1) English education, and (2) Christian evangelisation. The first, formerly a source of weakness to the Hindu society, has now proved a source of strength to the Ārya Samāj. Superstition at once gave way before the scientific education. In order, therefore, to fully avail ourselves of the former and to nullify the effect of the latter, we should open as many schools as possible where all the latest discoveries in science should be taught and education on national and modern lines should be imparted free to as large a number as our funds permit, and, secondly to carry the torch of Vedic light to the remotest corners of India at least where the Ārya Samāj is still unrepresented. But then there comes in the question of funds. Our rich men are not going to part with their money, because they have to minister to their own wants, to those of their sons and daughters and relations. Then there is a question of time. Now those who can spare time, won't do it, because they have to attend to this business and to that business.[1]

An article appeared in Lahore in December, 1912, by Dr. Gokal Chand, Barrister, Lahore, in which he declares that the Samāj is gradually losing its intensity, and tries to discover the causes of this weakening. He puts it down, first, to the want of a Scripture, a book of spiritual instruction which the ordinary man can take up and find help in: "the members of the Ārya Samāj do not read the Vedas." Secondly, he notes they have no religious ministers doing pastoral work among the people. Thirdly, they want missionaries settled each in his district with an organization and assistants, just like Christian missionaries. Fourthly, they want men who have renounced the world and will live only for the Samāj.

LITERATURE. — GENERAL: Dr. H. D. Griswold, art. *Ārya Samāj* in *ERE*. *Hand-Book of the Ārya Samāj*, by Pandit Vishun

[1] Reported in the *Bombay Guardian*, Dec. 14, 1907.

Lal Sharma, Allahabad, the Indian Press, 1912, 6 as. (The best official account of the rise of the sect, its opinions and work.) BIOGRAPHY: The Autobiography is published in Durga Prasad's translation of the *Satyarth Prakash* (see below). *Maharshi Swāmī Dayānand Sarasvatī Jī Mahārāj Kā Jīvan Charitra*, by Pandit Lekh Ram and Lala Atma Ram, Lahore, 1897 (the standard biography; in Hindī). *The Life and Teachings of Swami Dayanand Saraswati*, by Bawa Chhajju Singh, Lahore, Addison Press, 1903, two vols., Rs. 2. DAYĀNANDA'S WORKS: *Ṛigvedabhāshya* (a Hindī commentary on the *Ṛigveda*). *Ṛigvedādibhāshya Bhūmikā* (Hindī introduction to the commentary on the *Ṛik*). *An English Translation of the Satyarth Prakash* by Durga Prasad, Lahore, Virjanand Press, 1908, Rs. 2. *The Ocean of Mercy* (an English translation of Dayānanda's tract on Cow-killing), by Durga Prasad, Lahore, Virjanand Press, 1889. CRITICISM: Chirol's *Indian Unrest*, chap. VIII. *The Niyoga Doctrine of the Ārya Samāj*, by Ruchi Ram Sahni, Lahore, 1896, one half-anna. *Pandit Dayānand Unveiled*, by S. N. Agnihotri, Lahore, The Tribune Press, 1891, out of print. *The Dayānandī Interpretation of the Word "Deva" in the Ṛig Veda*, by H. D. Griswold, Ludhiana, 1897. DEFENCE: *The Ārya Samāj, Its Aims and Teachings*, by Lala Lajpat Rai, *Contemporary Review*, May, 1910. *The Ārya Samāj and its Detractors*, by Munshi Ram and Ram Deva, Hardwar, Satya Dharm Pracharak Press, 1911, Rs. 3. *Agnihotri Demolished* by Rambhaj Datta, Lahore, 1891, out of print.

2. ŚIVANĀRĀYAṆA PARAMAHAṀSA[1]

1. We take next another wandering ascetic whose teaching bears quite a close resemblance to Dayānanda's.

Śivanārāyaṇa was the son of a Benares Brāhman, born perhaps about 1840. At home he seems to have received no education, and he remained practically illiterate to the end. While still a child, he was agitated with religious questions which his father could not help him with. He left home, according to his own account, when he was twelve years of age, and spent the rest of his life wandering all over India, at first only asking questions, afterwards teaching every one who

[1] For the word Paramahaṁsa see below, page 191.

would listen to him. He dressed in the simplest way, and lived practically like a sannyāsī, yet he never called himself such, and he does not seem to have been initiated into any order. We have no means of learning how he came to form the opinions he held. Mr. Mohini Mohan Chatterji of Calcutta, to whom I owe all the information I have about him, and who was one of his best friends, writes:

> So far as his thoughts were not the results of his musings and meditations, they were due to his contact with all sorts and conditions of men he came across in his wanderings all over India.

He spent most of his time during the last years of his life in Bengal. In 1884 or 1885 he went to the temple of Kālī at Dakshineśvara near Calcutta and met Rāmakṛishṇa, but the two men were not drawn to each other. In July, 1888, Mr. Chatterji, who had already published his well-known translation of the *Bhagavadgītā*, met Śivanārāyaṇa; and to this circumstance we owe the preservation of the latter's teaching. Mr. Chatterji listened to him eagerly, and took notes of what he said. A few tracts in Bengali, in Hindī and English were first published. Then in 1902 Mr. Chatterji edited the *Amṛita Sāgara*, a volume in Bengali, containing the main elements of his teaching arranged in systematic form. The volume was published in Hindī also. Mr. Chatterji then took down from his lips an account of his wanderings and of the conversations he had with the people he met. This appeared in 1907 in English, a volume of 146 pages, published by Luzac, and called *Indian Spirituality; or the Travels and Teachings of Śivanārāyaṇa*. Quite apart from the religious teaching, the book makes very pleasant reading, for it contains many interesting particulars about Hindu temples and the life of ascetics. He died at Kālīghāt, Calcutta, in 1909.

Mr. Chatterji writes,

> Those who came under his influence were common people in the main;

and again,

> He expressly prohibited the formation of a sect. But there is a large number of men and women in Calcutta and other places, specially among the Mech tribe of Assam, who look upon him as a source of spiritual inspiration.

He taught as seriously as Dayānanda did that there is but one God; but he attempted to conceive Him as having two aspects, the one unknowable, inactive, and tending to be impersonal, the other distinctly personal and active. He lays more stress on the will of God than any other Hindu thinker of the nineteenth century. There is one rather curious survival in his thought, viz., that God is specially manifested in light. Perhaps in connection with this same thought, he affirms that it is God's will that all men should make to Him offerings in fire of things fragrant and sweet. Like Dayānanda, he holds that this form of sacrifice purifies the air.

He condemns idolatry with quite as much vehemence as Dayānanda; but he goes further, and, like a prophet of the Old Testament, proclaims that the worship of idols degrades man and works ruin to the nation as a whole. His teaching on this point is most penetrating. He also condemned man-worship. Consequently, though he visited all the great shrines of India, he would not bow down to idols, nor would he prostrate himself before religious authorities, as Hindus are wont to do. He held most sincerely that the weakness of modern India was the result of idolatry and superstition. As he wandered through the country, he saw how gross the ordinary worship of the temples was, and how frequently fraud was employed to increase the popularity of a particular god or shrine. All this he condemned very frankly.[1] His

[1] See *Indian Spirituality*.

attitude to social questions was also practically the same as Dayānanda's. He opposed caste, condemned child-marriage, advocated female education, and declared woman to be equal with man. He says:

> Similar reasons will show you the injustice of the treatment to which your women are subjected. Man and woman are equally related to the all-comprehending supreme Being, manifested as light. It is pleasant in His sight that each should be free to realise the perfection possible to the human individual.[1]

His teaching is distinctly better than Dayānanda's in two particulars. First, he did not press the doctrine of transmigration and karma. Clearly he had not realized what an incubus it had been on the theology of Hinduism and on the life of the common people; so that he occupied rather an ambiguous position towards it. Mr. Chatterji writes:

> Transmigration did not receive much attention from Śivanārāyaṇa. He thought it had no bearing upon a man's spiritual life or his *mukti* or salvation. He neither asserted nor denied its reality. He left the question open and practically ignored it.

The other point on which he advanced beyond Dayānanda was this: he did not hold the infallibility of the Veda, but recognized the value of many sacred books.

He believed that, if men would only recognize the true import of the two aspects of God, peace would come amongst all religions, and good will would be established in place of evil. At one time he urged the advisability of holding a great religious Conference with the object of bringing all men to one opinion with regard to God. The following is another of his proposals, which, if not very practical, gives us a peep into his mind:

[1] *A Word in Season*, 14.

Let all mankind have a common speech. Compile from all the scriptures of the world, in that common human tongue, a scripture, containing all that is useful for man to know concerning his spiritual and temporal welfare. Preserve that one and burn all the rest, burying their ashes out of sight.[1]

He insists on the duty of training the body to be the obedient servant of the spirit, and he makes practical service of our neighbours an essential part of spiritual religion. The following summary is given at the end of one of his latest tracts:

1. Keep this world pure, so that no uncleanness may attach, within or outside, to the physical body, the senses, mind, food, raiment, dwellings, roads, bathing-places and so forth. Prevent the adulteration of food in every form.

2. Be "equal-sighted" to sons and daughters, and educate them equally; secure equal rights to man and woman. Looking on all individuals as God and your own soul, cherish them, so that want and suffering may come to none.

3. Let each, to the extent of his power, lovingly, in God's name, make offerings in the fire of things fragrant and sweet, such as clarified butter, sugar, etc., and help and encourage others to do so. This purifies the air, secures timely rain and abundant crops. Such is God's law.

4. His name is the mantra, Om Sat guru. Let every man and woman call upon Him by inwardly repeating this name. By His favour all will attain the fourfold objects of desire, — religious merit or ethical perfection, possessions on earth, enjoyment and salvation.

5. Light or the sun and moon is His expression. Let all men at the rising and the setting of light with love and reverence bow down with folded hands and adore Him who is light, craving forgiveness of sins.

When you perceive the true nature of light, you will understand all phenomena of life and movement, such as birth and death, eclipses and the waxing and the waning of the moon.

6. Knowing Him to be all-comprehending and complete, keep your hearts well established on Him.[2]

[1] *Take-Heed unto Yourselves*, 5.

[2] *A Word in Season*, 22–23.

Christian influence is very distinctly visible in his teaching at several points, notably in his attitude to idolatry, his freedom from the grip of transmigration, and his conception of the equality of man and woman.

2. A number of intelligent people in Calcutta still confess his influence; the Īsāmoshipanthīs are the outcome of the teaching of one of his disciples;[1] and a new sect has sprung from his teaching in Assam.[2] The Kacheris are a Burma-Tibetan race scattered throughout Upper Assam. One branch of the Kacheris are known as the Mech tribe. The word Mech is simply a corruption of the Sanskrit word *Mleccha*, which means "barbarian," "unclean," "foreign." There is a good deal of unrest up and down the country; and the Mech tribe, having grown in knowledge and intelligence during recent years, very naturally dislike their tribal name.

Shortly after Śivanārāyaṇa's death, a member of this tribe, Kali Charan by name, went to Calcutta and met some of his followers. He picked up the teacher's main ideas, and carried away one of his Bengali books with him, *Sār Nityakriyā, i.e.* "Essential Daily Duties." When he reached Assam, he taught the new doctrines as a means of changing the status of the tribe. He received a ready response, and the movement grew apace. He teaches the people that by accepting the new teaching they become *Brahmas*, or, as they pronounce it, *Bormhos*. He means they will become Brahman, God. Those who follow him call themselves Bormhos instead of using the old name Mech. They do their best to follow the teaching of *Sār Nityakriyā*, but they do not understand it well. They are setting themselves up as a caste, at least thus far that they will not eat with others. They have neither temples

[1] P. 156, below.

[2] All my information about this Assamese movement I owe to the Rev. A. C. Bowers of Goalpara, Assam. There is a brief mention in *Census of India*, 1911, vol. 1, 125.

nor idols, but worship fire, earth, air, water and sun in a spot prepared for the occasion. These are supposed to be God. They offer fruits and vegetables, and sacrifice certain sweet-smelling substances in fire.

Kali Charan is their leader. He has some half a dozen *chelas*, disciples, who assist him. They use the Bengali literature published by Śivanārāyaṇa's disciples in Calcutta. They are aiming at the economic development of the tribe, and therefore are collecting money for the erection of a technical school, shops and such like. They say that there are about two thousand families in the movement, but that is probably an overestimate. In any case it is now losing ground.

LITERATURE. —*Indian Spirituality or the Travels and Teachings of Śivanārāyaṇa*, by M. M. Chatterji. London, Luzac, 1907. *Amṛita Sāgara* (the teaching of Śivanārāyaṇa in Bengali), edited by M. M. Chatterji, Calcutta, Sanyal & Co., 1911, Rs. 2.

3. The Vedic Mission

In 1886 a movement called Sādhārana Dharma arose in Madras, and has continued active until to-day. The adherents of Sādhārana Dharma declare their belief in Paramātman, or the Supreme Self, his government of the world and of individuals, and the possibility of realizing him by the development of one's moral or physical powers and the use of them for the good of humanity; and they promise to work for their own progress and the advancement of humanity. The following sentences come from the prospectus of the organization:

> The Common Path (Sadharana Dharma) is open to people of any creed. Those who profess other faiths need not disclaim them when they adopt Sadharana Dharma. Sadharana Dharma aims not to establish uniformity but unity in variety throughout the different cults and sects of India, and by and by of the whole world.

In 1909 this organization was included in a wider body called the Vedic Mission. This new organization has two divisions, Vedic Dharma and Sādhārana Dharma, the former purely Hindu, the later for everybody and anybody. For a time they were affiliated with the Bhārata Dharma Mahāmaṇḍal,[1] but its orthodoxy was too stiff for the Vedic Mission. The following sentences allude to that fact:

> We take this opportunity of informing the public that our Mission has nothing to do with so called Hindu orthodoxy and priesthood. Nothing short of thorough religious reform based on "Vedic monotheism" will satisfy us.
>
> We do not want to please those orthodox people that may be indifferent or opposed to the spread of Sanskrit and Religious Education as well as the right kind of spiritual knowledge among the non-Brahmin castes and the depressed Classes.

The work is as follows:

> The Mission has three branches of work, viz., (i) Educational — for spreading secular and useful religious knowledge among the masses, (ii) Medical — pertaining to the Ministry of Healing (the sick in body and mind), and (iii) Literary — including the study of comparative Mythology, Theology and Philosophy. The Mission advocates the cause of Vedic Religion and philosophy.

They have what they call a Vedic Mission College for training preachers and teachers, and they publish a good deal of literature.

The leaders are Paṇḍit G. Kṛishṇa Śāstrī and an Australian. There is a branch in Delhi, under Svāmī Śivagaṇāchārya. Work is also being done in Australia. I find it impossible to make out how much is being done.

The movement seems to stand nearer the Ārya Samāj and Śivanārāyaṇa's teaching than anything else.

[1] P. 316, below.

4. A Castle in the Air

A Muḥammadan, who shall be nameless, has written a little book which it is perhaps kindest to regard as the product of a diseased mind. It is worthy of mention merely as another indication of the present state of affairs in India. Its folly may also serve to relieve my sober narrative. It is an attempt to fuse Islam, Christianity and Hinduism. A pantheistic theology and transmigration are mingled with Muḥammadan ideas and diluted Christian ethics. The writer calls himself the Holy Ghost, the very God and such like. Like Śivanārāyaṇa, he proposes one language and one Scripture for all men, and also a universal religious conference. From that there might emerge a universal religious empire. Constantinople would be the centre of this empire; the English would be its guardians; and the Promoter himself would be the spiritual teacher and head of the whole!

We now turn to a group of movements which have one striking feature in common, namely, their use of the person of Christ. They are a peculiarly interesting and instructive group; for two of them are Muḥammadan in origin, and two are Hindu.

5. The Aḥmadīyas of Qadian

1. The first is a very successful and combative sect which arose in the Panjab in the eighties, largely as a reaction from the striking success of a Christian mission in the Central Panjab and from the fierce onslaught of Dayānanda and his Samāj.

In the village of Qadian[1] in the Gurdaspur district of the Panjab, there was born, about 1838, in an ancient Muḥamma-

[1] I am indebted for most of my information about this sect to Dr. Griswold of Lahore. See his pamphlet, *Mirza Ghulam Ahmad*, and his article in *The Moslem World* for October, 1912.

dan family which had long been known for its attachment to the mysticism of Islam, viz., Sufiism, a boy called Mirza Ghulam Aḥmad. Very little is known about his youth or education; so that it is not possible to trace the growth of his mind, as may be done in the case of Dayānanda. He began to teach about 1879, and died in 1908.

2. The whole movement rests on his personal claims. He declared himself to be the Christian Messiah, the Muḥammadan Mahdi, and the final *avatāra* or "Incarnation" of the Hindus. In one of his latest utterances he said,

> My advent in this age is not meant for the reformation of the Mohammedans only, but Almighty God has willed to bring about through me a regeneration of three great nations, viz., Hindus, Mohammedans and Christians. As for the last two I am the promised Messiah, so for the first I have been sent as an Avatar.[1]

The last claim, to be Hindu *avatāra*, was made for the first time towards the end of his life, and has had no results. He spent his life in trying to prove himself the Mahdi of Islam as well as the Christian Messiah, in seeking to shew that in him Christianity and Islam unite and culminate.

The conception is rather an unusual one for a Muslim; for, according to ordinary Muḥammadan belief, the Messiah and the Mahdi are distinct persons;[2] and the common expectation is that the Mahdi will be a man of blood, a character which it would be impossible to combine with Christ. The Mirza gets over this last difficulty by declaring that the traditions which speak of the Mahdi as a man of blood are all forgeries, that the Guided One (*i.e.* the Mahdi) is to be a man of peace. Thus, the controlling idea of his conception of himself as a prophet is the character and work of Christ. It

[1] *Review of Religions*, November, 1904, p. 410.

[2] Yet some groups assert that Jesus is the only Mahdi that will ever come.

PLATE VI

MIRZA GHULAM AHMAD

seems almost as if he had first come to believe himself to be the Messiah, and had then added the idea that he was the Maḥdi as a sort of inference from his position in Islam. In any case, nearly the whole of his apologetic is built up with the object of proving himself the Messiah. With that, then, we begin.

He does not profess to be Jesus Christ returned *in propria persona*. He claims to be the fufilment of the prophecy of the Second Coming, on the ground that he has come in the spirit and power of Jesus. In order to make this claim seem reasonable, he uses two series of arguments.

A. He first sets about proving that Christ did not die on the Cross, rise from the dead, and ascend to Heaven.[1] He acknowledges that, if Jesus really died, rose, and went to heaven, then Christianity must be true, and he himself must be an impostor:

> If Christ was in reality exalted in bodily form alive to heaven, then there is no need of further controversy, and my claim to be the promised Messiah is in vain. The reason is that my claim is based upon the natural death (wafat) of the Son of Mary.[2]

He avers that, while Jesus was truly crucified, He was taken down from the cross seemingly dead, but really in a swoon, recovered from His wounds, came to India, lived for many years and finally died in Cashmere like any ordinary mortal. The materials he uses to establish these propositions are as follows:

a. He revives the old swoon theory of the death of Jesus, citing as confirmation the facts, that He was on the cross for only a few hours and that His legs were not broken. He also uses the phrase, "Why seek ye the living amongst the dead?"

[1] He asserts that the Gospels were deliberately corrupted by Christians.

[2] Griswold, *Mirza Ghulam Ahmad*, 5.

and urges that the appearances of Jesus to His disciples after the crucifixion are those of a living man and not of a disembodied spirit. Christ's own use of the experience of Jonah as a parallel to Himself is pressed into service. As Jonah was alive in the whale's belly, so Jesus must have meant that He Himself would be alive in the tomb.

b. He cites the so-called *Gospel of Barnabas*, a mediæval Muḥammadan forgery, as a witness that Jesus did not die on the cross.

c. He asserts that over a thousand medical books, Jewish, Christian, Parsee and Muḥammadan, describe the *Marham-i-Īsā*, or Ointment of Jesus, and extol its powers. He asserts that after three days Jesus recovered from the swoon, and that the disciples applied this wonderful ointment to His wounds with such success that, within the space of forty days, He was entirely healed and ready for foreign travel.

d. In 1887 a Russian, named Nicolas Notovitch, travelled through Cashmere to Leh in Ladak and spent some time in friendly intercourse with the Buddhist Lamas of the monastery of Himis. Seven years later, he published a book in which he declared that the Abbot of the monastery had brought out and read to him an ancient manuscript, according to which Jesus, in the interval between His visit to the Temple of Jerusalem at the age of twelve and his baptism by John, travelled from Palestine to India, and studied under the Jains, Buddhists and Hindus of those days. The book appeared in French and in English and made a considerable stir both in Europe and India for some time. In an article in *The Nineteenth Century* for October, 1894, Max Müller, who saw clearly that the tale was false, suggested that M. Notovitch had been so persistent in trying to get information that the Lamas, having nothing better to give him, had invented the story to satisfy him. But Prof. J. Archibald Douglas of the Government College, Agra, was inclined to think that

Max Müller was too rash in concluding that the whole story was false, and therefore used his hot-weather holiday in 1895 to take a journey to Ladak in the hope of finding the Ms. But when he reached the monastery and told his tale, the indignation of the Abbot knew no bounds. No such Ms. is in the library, nor indeed in Tibet anywhere. The whole story was an impudent lie. Professor Douglas described his journey in *The Nineteenth Century* for April, 1896; and M. Nicolas Notovitch was recognized to be an unscrupulous adventurer. Yet many Hindus and Muḥammadans still make use of his lies.

The prophet of Qadian sets forth this *false* story of a journey to India undertaken by Jesus *before* He began His ministry as proof that He travelled to India *after* His crucifixion. Could futility proceed to greater extremes?

e. The meaning of the Ascension, he argues, is that Jesus was separated from his disciples in order to preach in Afghanistan and Cashmere, the inhabitants of which countries, he avers, are the ten lost tribes.

f. In Khan Yar Street, Srinagar, Cashmere, there stands a tomb, perhaps a couple of centuries old, known to the people of the vicinity as the tomb of *Yus Asaf.* Clearly it is the tomb of some obscure Muslim saint. There is no tradition attached to the building.

The prophet maintains, however, without adducing the slightest evidence, that it is the tomb of Jesus, that *Yus* is a corruption of *Yasu*, which he equates with Jesus, and that *Asaf*, coming from the Hebrew *asā̆f*, to gather, designates Him as the "Gatherer" of the ten lost tribes of Israel.

g. Lastly, he asserts that Christianity is spiritually dead, and argues that, if Jesus had really risen from the grave, and ascended to heaven, to reign there in spiritual power, His Church would exhibit His energy and life. Hence we can infer that He did not rise.

It ought to be noticed that, in denying the Ascension of

Christ, the Mirza is a heterodox Muslim; for the Muḥammadan belief is that God took Him to heaven, that He is now there, and that He will return at the end of the world to slay the Antichrist.

B. Having thus in his own way set Christ aside, he proceeds to give positive arguments in support of his assertion that he is the Messiah himself.

a. As the Old Testament prophecy of the second coming of Elijah was fulfilled in John the Baptist, who was not Elijah, so the New Testament prophecy of the second coming of Christ will be fulfilled, not by a personal return of Jesus, but by the appearance of one coming in the spirit and power of Jesus.

b. In the Koran Christ's prophecy of the coming of the Comforter is referred to. The Greek word in John 16, 7 is *paracletos*, advocate, defender, comforter. Muḥammad seems to have got this word mixed up with the similar Greek word *periclytos*, which means famous, and took it as a prophecy of his own name, which, whether in the form Muḥammad or or Aḥmad, means praised, glorified. Hence the words of the Koran,[1]

> And remember when Jesus the son of Mary said, "O children of Israel! of a truth I am God's apostle to you to confirm the law which was given before me, and to announce an apostle that shall come after me whose name shall be Ahmad!"

Our prophet could not fail to seize upon this text, despite the fact that his own name is not Aḥmad but Ghulam Aḥmad, *i.e.* the servant of Aḥmad (Muḥammad). He uses it, as several other self-styled prophets of the name of Aḥmad have done, as a definite prophecy of himself.

c. He bases another argument on the doctrine of the millennium taught in the Apocalypse. Counting by lunar years, he divides the time since the appearance of Jesus into two

[1] *Sura*, LXI.

millenniums, and makes his own appearance the beginning of the third. The first is the millennium of the devil's imprisonment, during which time Muḥammad appeared. The second is the millennium of the devil's freedom, marked by the declension of Islam and a frightful growth of evil. The third, which the new Messiah introduces, is the millennium of the Kingdom of God.

d. He draws out a great many parallels between Jesus and himself. There is first the political parallel: the Indians under British rule are in very much the same condition as the Jews were under the Romans. Next comes the moral and religious parallel: the corruptions of India to-day are in many respects like the corruptions of Palestine in the time of Christ. Thirdly, he describes himself as a divinely appointed mediator between God and man, a true intercessor for man, and a perfect image of God. On the ground of these parallels he claims that his mission is altogether like the mission of Christ.

e. He also claims that he is able to prove the truth of his Messiahship by miracle. The only facts seriously put forward as miracles are certain prophecies which he made.

It is said that he predicted the death of no less than one hundred and twenty-one persons. Of these we need refer only to two. He predicted the death of Paṇḍit Lekh Ram, his chief antagonist in the Ārya Samāj. The man was murdered soon afterwards, under circumstances which gave rise to the strong suspicion that it was the deed of a Muḥammadan who had managed to become intimate with the paṇḍit on the pretence of being an enquirer. Again, he predicted that his Christian antagonist, Deputy Abdullah Atham, would die within the space of fifteen months. Precautions were taken by Mr. Atham's friends to protect him from possible assassination, and he outlived the time assigned to him. These prophecies went on for some time; but they proved so mischievous and dangerous that, on the 24th of February, 1899, the Government of the Panjab issued an order, ordering him to cease making such prophecies. The prophet, under grave pressure from the Government, solemnly promised:

(1) To refrain from publishing any prediction involving the disgrace of any person, or in which anyone should be represented as an object of God's displeasure.

(2) To refrain from publishing any challenge to appeal to God to indicate by the signs of His displeasure, such as disgrace, etc., the party in a religious controversy which is in the wrong.

(3) To refrain from publishing any writing purporting to be an *inspiration*, the object of which can be reasonably taken to be the disgrace of any person, or the representing of him as an object of the Divine wrath.[1]

He also predicted the birth of sons to certain friends, but, unfortunately, fulfilment did not always follow. Sometimes there was no birth at all, sometimes the sons turned out to be daughters, to the disgust of the parties and the discomfiture of the prophet.

In 1898 he published a pamphlet called, *A Revealed Cure for the Bubonic Plague*, in which he declared the *Marham-i-Īsā*, or Ointment of Jesus, mentioned above, to be a perfect remedy for bubonic plague, on the ground that it had been "prepared solely under the influence of divine inspiration." Hakīm Muḥammad Husain of Lahore was the manufacturer of the ointment. Unfortunately, the Government again interfered with the action of his "divine inspiration," and prohibited the exploitation of the specific.

He also prophesied that his people would be immune from pestilence without plague inoculation.

His own death from cholera in 1908 formed a fitting climax to this series of fraudulent impostures.

f. His claim to be the Second Adam is another of his arguments for his Messiahship. Dr. Griswold writes:[2]

[1] *Akhbar i Amm* of Lahore, March 17th, 1899. [2] Pp. 6–7.

At the close of the sixth day, God created the first Adam. But one day is with the Lord as a thousand years. Therefore at the close of the sixth millenium or the beginning of the seventh, the second Adam is to appear. We are now at the beginning of the seventh millenium, if we reckon according to the lunar year, which is the inspired mode of reckoning; and so the time is fulfilled for the second Adam to be manifested. Where is the Second Adam to appear? "In the East and not in the West," says the Mirza Sahib; "for from Gen. ii. 8 we learn that God had put the first Adam in a garden *eastward*. It is therefore necessary that the second Adam should appear in the East, in order to have a resemblance with the first in respect of his locality."

g. Towards the end of his life he began to claim that he was greater than Christ:

> I swear by the Lord . . . that the words expressing my dignity revealed from God . . . are far more weighty and glorious than the words of the Gospels relating to Jesus. . . . My superiority lies in being the Messiah of Muhammad, as Jesus was the Messiah of Moses.[1]

He also began to carp at the character of Christ, accusing Him of drunkenness, lack of philanthropy and several other such things.

He has not so much to say in proof that he is the Maḥdi, yet a couple of arguments may be noted.

i. There is a saying traditionally ascribed to Muḥammad which runs:

> What will be your condition when the Son of Mary shall descend among you, and your Imān from you?

Clearly the Messiah and the Maḥdi are here regarded as distinct personalities, the Messiah coming from heaven, the Maḥdi arising among Muslims. Hence the Mirza translates the passage:

[1] P. 15.

> What will be your condition when the Son of Mary shall descend among you? Who is he? He will be your Imān, who will be born from among you.

This opens the way for his own claims.

ii. He cites the passage from the Koran quoted above[1] as a proof that he is the Maḥdi, declaring himself the *Burūz* or spiritual reappearance of Muḥammad.

3. Apart from these personal claims, his teaching is an attempt to find, amidst the irresistible inrush of Western education and Christian thought, a middle path between impossible orthodoxy and the extreme rationalism of Sir Syed Aḥmad Khan.[2] He is opposed to *jihad*, i.e. Muslim religious warfare, and the spirit of the *ghāzī*, or religious fanatic, as well as to a bloody Maḥdi; and he condemns tomb-worship. He says the Koran teaches that slavery ought to be gradually abolished. He says polygamy, the veiling of women and divorce were permitted by Muḥammad to prevent worse evils.

His sect, which, in organization, is like a Samāj, has its headquarters in Qadian, and is called the *Sadr Anjuman-i-Aḥmadīya*, or Chief Society of Aḥmad.

His success shews that he was in some respects an able man, but one can scarcely say more than that. The reasoning which we have given above as advanced in support of his claims is a fair sample of his teaching and of his thought. One might illustrate his scholarship by the puerilities he advanced to shew that Arabic is the mother of all languages. He was probably self-deceived in the matter of his Messiahship rather than a conscious impostor, but one can scarcely believe him to have been honest in all his pretensions and assertions.

He was as eager for disputation as Dayānanda himself, and as violent and unscrupulous in controversy. He was a most

[1] P. 142. [2] P. 92, above.

vehement opponent of Christianity. He did not shew the genius for practical organization that his great rival did, but he founded a high school and a few other institutions. He edited two papers, one in the vernacular, the *Al-Hakam*, and one in English, the *Review of Religions*, and published large quantities of tracts, open letters, challenges, memorials to Government and such like. The sect has its own regular weekly services and its conferences, like the Samājes.

The likeness of the movement to Persian Babism is very striking, and well worth study.

The whole movement is outside orthodox Islam. Dr. Griswold writes: [1]

> In the numerous *fatwas*, which Muhammadan Associations all over India have issued against the Mirza Sahib, the strongest words of denunciation are used. Thus he is called *Kafir* 'unbeliever,' *Dajjal* 'Anti-Christ,' *mulhid* 'heretic,' *murtadd* 'apostate,' *kazzab* 'liar,' *be-iman* 'faithless,' *dag habaz* 'deceitful,' etc., etc. With such epithets as these is the 'certificate' filled, with which Muhammadan orthodoxy has dismissed the Mirza Sahib from its fellowship and service.

His successor, Hakim Nur-ud-Din, was not a man of the same strength and capacity as the founder, yet the sect went forward steadily. Nur-ud-Din died recently, and the community has fallen into two very hostile parties.

The sect has also a branch in Shorapur in the Deccan. A man named Abdulla has been the leader there for many years, but he now declares that he himself is the prophet; so that his followers have fallen into two companies, one loyal to the original founder, and one loyal to Abdulla. Feeling runs very high; orthodox Muslims oppose both parties; and three lawsuits are pending against Abdulla.

4. A member of the sect, Mr. Khwaja Kamal-ud-Din, a

[1] Pp. 26–7.

Pleader of the Chief Court, Lahore, began a Muslim Mission in England some two years ago. He settled first at Richmond, but has recently gone to Woking, where he has his office close by the Muḥammadan Mosque erected by the late Dr. Leitner, formerly Principal of the Oriental College, Lahore. The chief means whereby Mr. Kamal-ud-Din carries on his propaganda is a monthly magazine called *Muslim India and Islamic Review*. Lectures are also delivered from time to time in different places. A new English translation of the *Koran* is being prepared for use in England. Recently, Lord Headley, who for years has proclaimed himself to be more in sympathy with Islam than with Christianity, formally accepted Muḥammadanism in connection with the mission. This accession has caused great rejoicing in the Panjab. Two Moulvies have been sent to England from Delhi to strengthen Mr.Kamal-ud-Din's hands.

Naturally orthodox Muslims do not quite like to have Islam represented in England by such a heterodox group as the Aḥmadīyas. A pamphlet has recently been written by the Secretary of the Anjuman-i-Himayet-i-Islam [1] in Lahore, which violently denounces the mission.

LITERATURE. — *Mirza Ghulam Ahmad*, by Dr. H. D. Griswold, Ludhiana, The American Tract Society, 1902, one anna. *The Ahmadīya Movement*, by Dr. H. D. Griswold in *The Moslem World* for October, 1912. Also *The Review of Religions*, an English monthly published in Qadian, and many little pamphlets. *The Unknown Life of Christ*, by N. Notovitch, London, Hutchinson & Co., 1895.

6. THE NAZARENE NEW CHURCH

This short-lived organization sprang from the Aḥmadīya movement, but was so different in its teaching that it must be kept distinct.

[1] See below, p. 347.

In 1890 Mr. E. J. S. White, a Government servant, then stationed at Kurnool in South India, who was keenly interested in Muḥammadanism, paid a visit to Qadian and was greatly influenced by the prophet. But he could not follow him completely; for as he said in a letter to a friend of the writer recently:

> My view of Islam has always been that it is the mere perverted continuation of the Nazarene or Ebionite sect, the immediate community of disciples of our Lord, which contained the descendants of the Lord's brethren and His own disciples, and maintained the pure doctrine derived from Him, having nothing to do with the Gentile churches founded by Paul, in the midst of which it became a heresy and was crushed out of existence.

So he started the Nazarene New Church, seeking to mingle what he considered to be the purer elements of both Islam and Christianity in a Unitarian doctrine. He published a book of prayers in Urdu, so that Muḥammadans might be able to understand their prayers, which is scarcely possible while they use the Arabic. He also maintained the freedom of women and the duty of allowing them to join, under restrictions, in the worship of the mosque. A Eurasian named Snow became a Muḥammadan in Hyderabad, Deccan, in 1892 and became one of White's helpers. In 1893 a number of pamphlets were issued. In these we find it stated that members of the Nazarene New Church should adhere strictly to the Law of Moses "as perfected by our Master Jesus." They are to accept the Gospel of Matthew and some other parts of the New Testament, but not the writings of John or Paul. They are recommended to read the Koran as a perfect exposition of the Unitarian doctrine. Pilgrimage to Nazareth is enjoined as one of the principal duties. The following sentence occurs in one of these pamphlets:

The Church in India is directed by an apostle who, until the Spirit shall send one more worthy, is John White in the Blood of the Lamb.

Snow was guilty of a good deal of abusive language with reference to Christianity. The founder, who is still alive and resides at Cocanada in South India, writes:

> The late Daud Khan Bahadur, head of the Kurnool family, and a few other Muḥammadans were very sympathetic supporters of the movement. After I left Kurnool I endeavoured to form a Nazariah or Qadiani Jamaat at Ellore, at Secunderabad and in Madras, but nothing came of it.

So the movement soon ended.

The two Hindu movements which use the person of Christ are small groups, almost altogether confined to the common people.

7. The Chet Rāmīs [1]

In a village in the Lahore district of the Panjab, Chet Rām was born about 1835. The family were Vishṇuites by sect, and belonged to a class of shop-keepers and money-lenders. Chet Rām was uneducated, and almost illiterate. He could keep his shop accounts but that was all. He spent some two years in China, from about 1858 to 1860, as a camp-follower in the second Chinese war. When he returned, he settled down in his father-in-law's village Buchhoke, and kept a shop and sold opium and liquor.

To this shop there came from time to time a Muḥammadan ascetic of the Chisti order, named Syed Mahbub Shah. He was given to drink, and was often seen in the village in a dull intoxicated condition. Clearly, the man's teaching was

[1] All my information about this sect is derived from Dr. Griswold's pamphlet, *The Chet Rami Sect*, Cawnpore, Christ Church Mission Press, 1904. The references are to its pages.

eclectic; for he gathered Hindu as well as Muḥammadan disciples, and he was accustomed to speak about Christ. Up to this time Chet Rām was an idolater. Then, probably when he was about twenty-seven years of age, he became fascinated by Mahbub. He became his disciple, and henceforward followed him everywhere, and served him with the utmost faithfulness. We have no record of what Mahbub taught him; but it seems clear that he led him to reverence Christ and the Bible.

Mahbub died when Chet Rām had been his disciple for some three or four years, probably about 1865 or 1867. He was buried at Buchhoke; and, for three years, Chet Rām haunted the tomb, sleeping on it every night, or actually inside it, as tradition now goes. Then one night he had a vision of Jesus Christ, and received a command from Him to build a church on that very spot and to place a Bible therein. A simple Panjabi poem, ascribed to Chet Rām, describes the vision. We quote a few of the stanzas of a translation made by the Rev. G. L. Thakur Dass of Lahore:

1. Upon the grave of Master Mahbúb Shàh
Slept Sàín Chet Rām.

2. O dear (*reader*) it was midnight,
Full moon, stars were as hanging lamps;

3. Unique was that night, surpassing the *shab qadr;*
Rays were falling from the full moon.

4. There appeared a man
Whose description is without bounds;

5. A man came in a glorious form
Showing the face of mercy;

6. His countenance beautiful as the full moon,
No man could look at that beauty;

7. Glorious form, tall in stature and erect,
Appeared as if a clear mystery of the Deity.

8. Sweet was his speech, and simple his face,
Appearing entirely as the image of God.

9. Such a glory was never seen before,
The coming of the Lord Himself was recognized in it.

. . . .

25. Afterwards I began to think,
What was all this which Omnipotence did?

26. Then my soul realized
That Jesus came to give salvation.[1]

The date of the vision must have been somewhere between 1868 and 1870. From that time Chet Rām became, in his own way, a follower of Christ. He built a small church and placed a Bible in it, and began to gather disciples "in the name of Christ." He succeeded in inducing a number of men and women, both Hindu and Muḥammadan, to attach themselves to him. He lived a wandering life, moving about the country with a number of his followers, everywhere proclaiming Jesus as Lord, and suffering much persecution from both Hindus and Muḥammadans. He sought the friendship of Christians and missionaries in a general way, but did not join the Christian church. One Sunday in 1897, Chet Rām and his followers came to the American Mission Compound in Lahore; and both the Rev. C. W. Forman and the Rev. C. B. Newton give accounts of the appearance and the behaviour of the leader and his disciples. Mr. Newton went with them to Buchhoke, and saw the church. We have also a report from a missionary in Ludhiana of the year 1888.

Chet Rām died at Buchhoke in 1894 and was cremated; and his bones were buried beside his master's.

[1] Pp. 4–6.

Of Chet Rām's character Mr. Newton gives us a very pleasing picture, though it is clear that he had but little knowledge of Christ:[1]

> During my stay, I had an opportunity of observing Chet Rām's conduct and character; and certainly the case is a remarkable one, though the good in him is so obscured by superstition and ignorance, that one can scarcely call his case a very hopeful one. He manifests on all occasions a strong feeling of love and reverence for Christ, and undergoes persecution and contumely for His name. His treatment of others is marked by a spirit of rare kindness and generosity. One day a *faqir*, a total stranger, from some distant place, came to the *takyà*, and told a story of his sufferings, having been robbed of some article of clothing. Chet Rām at once pulled off his own principal garment, and gave it to him. He never refuses appeals of this kind.

He was no real student of the Bible. He was ignorant and had no desire to read. Sometimes his talk was quite incoherent.

Chet Rām's daughter was appointed his successor and the head of his sect, while the leader was alive. She is an unmarried woman, and is pledged to lifelong celibacy. She lives at the headquarters of the sect, which are now in Lahore.

> Just outside the Taxali Gate, Lahore, and at a distance of only two or three hundred feet from the Royal Mosque is a small garden thickly planted with trees and flowers and trailing vines and containing a tiny square building and several faqirs' huts. The square building has one room, perhaps fourteen feet by ten, and contains certain relics of Chet Rām such as his bed and his Bible. In front of the building is a pole surmounted by a cross. Such are the monastic headquarters of the Chet Rami Sect in Lahore.[2]

The only other leader whose name is known is one Munshi Nathu, who has been called the theologian of the sect. He has interpolated large pieces into Chet Rām's poem.

[1] P. 9.   [2] P. 1.

The creed of the sect is quite short. It is engraved on a tablet over the door of Chet Rām's cell at headquarters. The translation is as follows:

> Help, O Jesus, Son of Mary, Holy Spirit, Lord God Shepherd. Read the Bible and the Gospels for salvation. Signed by Chet Rām and the followers.[1]

In this we note the recognition of the Trinity, the duty of reading the Bible and the belief that salvation is made known in the Gospels.

The sect teaches another doctrine of the Trinity besides that contained in the above creed. They believe in the existence of Allah the Creator, Parameśvara the Preserver, and Khudā the Destroyer; and they use this trinity to set forth the supremacy of Jesus. Allah represents Muḥammadanism, Parameśvara Hinduism, and Khudā, who is the greatest of the three, is Jesus. Jesus is the true God. He is the giver of all gifts. All the Muḥammadan prophets and saints and the Hindu gods and incarnations were sent by Jesus. He is the supreme ruler over all. He is the Son of God. The Father and the Son are of one nature.

Now that Chet Rām is dead, his followers give him a very exalted place. They say he is not dead, but is present now and works in the hearts of his followers. As Hindus recognize their guru to be God, they consider Chet Rām to be Christ Himself. They praise Chet Rām as much as they praise Christ. They are accustomed to say:

> There is a God, if Chet Rām says so;
> There is no God, if Chet Rām says no.

After his cremation, his ashes were mixed with water and eagerly swallowed by his disciples. It is their veneration for their Teacher which keeps them from joining the Christian Church.

[1] P. 13.

The followers of Chet Rām are either householders or monks. When a man joins the community, there is a ceremony of baptism. When a birth takes place, the creed is recited in the ears of the child, and also the names of the twelve Apostles. When a member wants to become a Chet Rāmī monk, he tears off his clothes, casts dust upon his head and thus becomes a monk. This is known as Earth-baptism. The monks get their living by begging; and they are the only clergy of the sect. It is their business to preach the Gospel of Chet Rām. Like most modern Indian ascetics, they are addicted to the use of intoxicating drugs, such as bhang, charas, opium.

As to the Chet Rāmī worship Dr. Griswold writes:[1]

> There does not seem to be any fixed form of worship among the Chet Rāmīs. One old *faqir* declared that for the enlightened there is no need of religious worship. 'We have received,' said he; 'worship is for those who have not received.' I invited Munshi Nathu to attend our Church services in Lahore. He proceeded to tell me that all such worship is man-made worship. I have spent many hours at the Chet Rami *Khanqah* in Lahore, conversing with Munshi Nathu. He said to me on one occasion, 'This conversation of ours is worship: no other worship is needed.' All Chet Rāmīs are supposed to own a Bible, and the few who can read doubtless read it. Ghulam Muhammad one day said to me: 'I read the Bible every day and especially on the Sabbath. I was just reading the first chapter of John's Gospel, when you arrived.' The Chet Rāmī creed is repeated as an act of worship, and the Hymn of Chet Rām is chanted. There are some forms of worship which show decidedly the influence of Hinduism and Mohammedanism. At the *Khanqah* in Lahore are preserved with great care certain relics of Chet Rām. At evening lighted lamps are placed before the Cross and the Bible. On one occasion I noticed the evening worship of two Chet Rāmī women. They came and bowed themselves to the ground first before the cross and then before the Bible, and so went their way. A

[1] Pp. 21–2.

considerable use is made of amulets. Charms are made and inscribed with the Chet Rāmī Creed and with the names of the Twelve Apostles, and hung about the neck.

Most of the members of the sect are poor, illiterate people. They are a small body, probably less than a thousand in number. There is a good deal of brotherly feeling amongst them. Yet caste remains among them, and Hindu converts do not mix with Muḥammadan converts. The duty of philanthropy, and of the endurance of persecution, has been carefully taught them, but, apart from that, there does not seem to be much emphasis on morality. They frequently carry a long rod surmounted by a cross. On the horizontal bar of the cross there is usually inscribed the creed of the sect.

8. The Īsamoshipanthīs

A group of Hindus in South Behar, mostly cobblers and masons, have formed a new sect and call themselves *Īsāmoshipanthīs*, i.e., the Jesus-Messiah-followers.[1] Besides these simple people, there are a few educated ascetics who are identified with the sect. They study the Bible, and lay a good deal of stress on the teaching of Jesus. They do not class Christ with the incarnations of Vishṇu; yet they have mixed up His life with the story of Kṛishṇa. Christ's death is of more importance to them than His resurrection. They meet for worship on Fridays. It is said that the sect is the result of the teaching of one of the disciples of Śivanārāyaṇa Paramahaṁsa.[2] I am told they number two to three thousand.

The four movements which close this chapter are grouped together, because, though they have all accepted a good deal that is new, the system in each case is very distinctly

[1] My informant is Mr. B. C. Sircar, M. A., one of the National Secretaries of the Y. M. C. A. in India.

[2] Above, p. 129.

Hindu, and the worship of the teacher as God is prominent in all. The first pair are closely related in the elements they borrow from the West and in the claim that their teaching is scientifically trustworthy and verifiable.

9. The Rādhā Soāmi Satsaṅg

1. The word *satsaṅg* seems to come from the Sikhs, among whom it means "a company of pious people." The phrase Rādhā Soāmi cannot be explained apart from the history of the sect. It is dealt with below.[1]

In order to secure a reliable account of this society and its teaching, a few paragraphs are here transcribed from a manual of doctrine published by the second guru.[2]

1. The Rādhā Soāmi faith derives its name from its original Founder, the Supreme Being, Rādhā Soāmi, who appeared in this world in human form and designated Himself Sant Satguru or perfect Saint or true Guide and Preceptor, and preached holy doctrines to sincere enquirers of Truth for the deliverance of their spirit from the bondage of body and its surroundings, as well as from the pains and pleasures of this world, and for the ultimate admission of their spirit into the Holy Presence of the Supreme Being after traversing and breaking through the trammels and impediments in the material spheres.

2. The Holy name Rādhā Soāmi has been given out by the Supreme Being Himself. It resounds in splendid refulgence in the higher spheres, and can be heard within themselves by those who perform devotion by practising Surat Śabd Yoga according to the instructions given by the Supreme Being Himself.

4. This Holy name Rādhā Soāmi signifies both the Supreme Being and the original Spirit or Sound current (or Word) which

[1] See p. 167.

[2] *Rādhā Soāmi Mat Prakāsh.* The numbers of the sections are retained.

emanated from His Holy Feet, and which is the prime factor and principal agent in the whole creation.

6. The three degrees or grand divisions, comprised in the entire creation, according to Rādhā Soāmi faith are:

1. SPIRITUAL
2. SPIRITUAL-MATERIAL
3. MATERIAL-SPIRITUAL

Pure spirit, uncontaminated with matter, exists in the first grand division. Here the Supreme Being reigns over absolutely spiritual life. This, the purest possible form of life, has no desire but to love and serve the Supreme Being. The joys — the very existence — of this pure spirit-life are derived from the Supreme Being who is the Ocean of spirit, love and joy. Nothing concerning this degree is known or has been known to the founder of any religious creed. It comprises six sub-divisions and is called the Dayāl Desh or the Regions of Mercy.

7. The second or Spiritual-Material degree or grand division is entirely free from all worldly passions and desires of the lower order. Likening the Supreme Being to an Ocean, the president of the second degree is a tide from that Ocean. He is a kind of Viceroy who rules over all life existing in the space comprised in the second and third grand divisions committed to his care. As its name indicates, the spiritual-material degree contains both spirit and matter. But matter is, comparatively speaking, pure and is subject to, and controlled by spirit. Life here is very pure, and, though clothed in pure material forms, spirit predominates. This degree also comprises six subdivisions and is called the Brahmāṇḍa or the regions of Universal Mind and pure matter.

8. In the third or Material-Spiritual degree matter predominates over spirit. Life is composed of spirits wholly clothed in coarse matter. Having quite forgotten the higher abode from which they originally sprang, the spirits here have acquired carnal desires and passions. This also comprises six

sub-divisions and is called the Piṇḍa or the regions of Individual Mind and coarse matter.

9. This degree is dominated over by a wave emanating from the Supreme Being and flowing through the tide which has already been likened to a Viceroy. This wave or current may, for want of a better name, be called a Governor who presides over the Material Universe and controls matter.

12. The Supreme Being, as already said, is unknown. The Spirit or the Viceroy who presides over the second degree, is the Lord God of the Bible: he is the Sat or Sacchitãnand or Brahman of the Vedãnta, the Nirvãṇa of the Jains and the Buddhists and the Lãhut of the Mahomedan Saints. The Spirit or Governor who rules over the third degree is the Brahmã or Parmãtmã or God of most religions in the world.

13. The entire creation below the first degree is composed of two parts, namely, spirit which is all good and pure, and matter which is always more or less bad. Man is a drop from the Ocean, that is, the Supreme Being. This drop of pure good spirit is so mixed with matter that it becomes in bondage thereto, and unless aided by a Superior Spirit is always liable to yield to temptation and deteriorate or sink down in matter.

16. There are two streams in our solar system; the one ever improving, the other always deteriorating. The spirits of the first of these streams pass from plants through the lower creation till they reach man; they then become angels or heavenly spirits and ultimately merge into the Supreme Being or remain in His Presence. Maintenance of individuality in the changes later than man depends upon the practice of devotion according to Surat Śabd Yoga or the union of the Spirit with the Word — the Word being the emanation from the Supreme Being. If such devotion be not practised, the spirit loses its previous individuality and becomes merged into a lower stage fit for its reception. A devotee, when merged into the Supreme Being, can assume his individuality at pleasure. Such a being is called a perfect Sant, a Special and Beloved

Son of the Supreme Being. But the spirits who belong to the deteriorating stream are wholly under the influence of matter. At every change they get lower and lower until they reach the lowest form in the creation.

17. The Supreme Being has Special and Beloved Sons called Sants and Param Sants, who are full of mercy and love and who descend periodically upon the earth to deliver spirits from the bondage of matter and to carry them to the Presence of the Supreme Father.

18. Any one desirous of reaching the Supreme Being must search for a Sant Satguru (incarnation of the Supreme Being) or a Sadh Guru (one who has reached the top of the second grand division) and invoke His help, and receive instructions from one of these Superior Guides, as to the manner of his devotion and procedure.

21. The name of the Supreme Being is Rādhā Soāmi. He is impersonal, but personal in the second and third divisions and when He manifests Himself through humanity as Sant Satguru. His attributes are mostly met with in the Sant Satguru, who might be called an incarnation of Sat Purush Rādhā Soāmi, the true Supreme Being.

22. The deliverance of spirit from the bondage of body, senses and mind, and its gradual ascension and eventual entrance into the first or highest division by the practice of Surat Śabd Yoga is perfect salvation according to Rādhā Soāmi faith.

24. Rādhā Soāmi faith is not built on the basis of scriptures appertaining to Hindu or any other religion, but on the precepts or instructions of the Supreme Being Himself, Who appeared on this earth in human form and graciously performed the functions of a Sant Satguru for the benefit of degraded humanity.

25. The sound heard internally is a current which has originally emanated from the Supreme Being and is the means not

only of concentrating the will but also of raising the spirit to the source from which it emanated.

27. It must be clearly understood that by Śabd or Word or internal voice is meant the spirit or life current which enlivens every part of the body and is the main principle or essence which supports life in and gives activity to every being or body in the whole creation or Universe.

28. At present the spirit of man is residing in the third or material-spiritual region, and has, therefore, to do all the work here by means of the senses and the mind which are mediums between it and the material objects, and consequently, as a natural result, its power has become quite hampered. But as soon as it begins to ascend, the powers which are now lying dormant, become active and the spirit acquires ultra-material or higher powers.

29. The method for taking back the spirit to its Supreme source is first to concentrate at the focus of the eyes the spirit and mind which are diffused in our body and in a manner tied to external objects by desires and passions, and next to commence its journey homewards by attending to the internal sound, or in other words, by riding the life or sound current which has originally emanated from the Supreme source.

30. The current which has been instrumental in having brought it down here must naturally be the only true path for its return to the original source, and whoever finds this current is on the path of emancipation. This current which is the spirit and life current, is called in the Rādhā Soāmi faith, Sound (*Śabd*) or Word or Holy Name.

34. To approach the Supreme Being, there is absolutely no other means except the practice of Surat Śabd Yoga under the guidance of a Sant Satguru or a Sadh Guru, or a sincere lover of the Supreme Being who has received instructions from, and is helped in his practice by one of those Superior and Holy Spirits.

35. Prayer is necessary to obtain blessing and mercy to help man's perfect salvation, but it must be offered from the inmost heart and not confined to mere utterance. It must be also backed up by works of faith and charity performed through love and affection for the Supreme Being.

37. In following this mode of devotion the following restrictions are made with regard to diet and mode of living. No intoxicating drink or drug and animal food is to be taken and immoderate indulgence in any desire is to be avoided. Animal food is forbidden on account of its producing a material tendency in human nature, and intoxicating drink is detrimental to a calm and natural state of the brain and the nervous system. Other public and private duties should be carried on as usual.

38. The moral code appertaining to Rādhā Soāmi faith is comprised in two sentences:

(1) All acts including spiritual practice which tend to free the spirit from matter and raise it towards its source are good works.

(2) All acts which tend to degrade the spirit by weighing it downwards deeper and deeper into matter are bad works. Again any action done with a view to help the needy from unselfish motives is good work; and the contrary, bad work in this world.

147. A member of Rādhā Soāmi faith is strictly forbidden to divulge the secrets or mention to any one (even to a fellow member without express permission) the glory and wonder of the higher creation he sees now and then within himself, or the happiness and extraordinary joy he experiences during his practice, or the special Mercy, Grace and Protection extended to him from time to time on important occasions by the Supreme Father and Sant Satguru.

2. One fact stands out clear from the above statement of doctrine that the guru occupies a place of supreme importance in the sect. He is the centre of the whole; for he is not only the source of revelation but the essential means of salva-

tion. Thus the sect ought to have an unbroken succession of gurus. There have been already three, and a fourth is now required. The following facts are taken from a book by the third guru.[1]

The first guru was an Agra banker of Kshatriya caste, born in 1818. His name seems to have been Tulsī Rām, but he is better known as Śiva Dayāl Saheb. He came of a pious Vishṇuite family, and had his guru, whose name was Tulsī Saheb; yet, according to the sect, he did not learn any of the deep things from his guru, but brought his divine knowledge with him from the other world. He is said to have had the power of sending people into *samādhi*,[2] that is, a sort of religious trance, and of enabling them to see visions. He publicly proclaimed his doctrine in 1861. He left two books, each named *Sār Bachan*, i.e. "Essential Utterance," one in poetry and one in prose. He died in 1878. His ashes lie in a sacred tomb in the Rādhā Soāmi Garden, Agra.[3] His titles are *Rādhā Soāmi Dayāl* and *Soāmijī Mahārāj*.

The second guru was born in Agra in 1828, in a family of Kāyastha caste. He was a government official, serving in the Post Office, and finally rose to be Postmaster-General of the United Provinces, and received from Government the title Rai Bahadur. He was thus known as Rai Saligram Saheb Bahadur. Of his early life and his relations with the first guru, whom he met in 1856, Max Müller[4] writes:

> It seems that the horrors of the mutiny in 1857 made a deep impression on his mind. He saw thousands of men, women, and children butchered before his eyes, the rich reduced to poverty, the poor raised to unexpected and undeserved wealth, so that the idea of the world's impermanent and transient nature took complete possession of him and estranged him from all that had formerly enlisted his interest and occupied his

[1] *Discourses on Rādhā Soāmi Faith.*

[2] See p. 189.

[3] See below, p. 166.

[4] *Rāmakṛishṇa*, 20–1.

energies. From his very youth, however, his mind had been filled with religious and philosophical questions, and he is said to have devoted much time from his youth onward through all the years of his official life to the study of the Sacred Scriptures. No wonder therefore that after witnessing the horrors of the mutiny and its suppression, he should have wished to flee from this den of misery and to get happiness unalloyed and permanent where alone it could be found. He went to consult several Sannyāsīs and Yogīs, but they could not help him. At last one of his colleagues at the Post Office recommended his elder brother as a spiritual guide who could be trusted. For two years he attended his lectures, compared his teaching with that of the Upanishads and other holy writings, and then became his devoted pupil or Chela. During his stay at Agra he allowed no one else to serve his master. He used to grind the flour for him, cook his meals, and feed him with his own hands. Every morning he could be seen carrying a pitcher of pure water on his head for the Guru to bathe in, which he fetched from a place two miles distant. His monthly salary also was handed over to the Saint, who used it for the support of his pupils, wife and children, and spent the rest in charity.

In 1878, on the death of the guru, he became head of the sect, and retained his position until his death in 1898. His *samādh*, sacred tomb, is at Pipalmandi, Agra. He left behind him several works in poetry called *Prema Bāṇī*, "Love Utterances," and *Prema Patra*, "Love Letters," and a little manual in English called *Rādhā Soāmi Mat Prakāsh*, "Exposition of Rādhā Soāmi Doctrine," from which our exposition of the teaching of the sect is taken. Ḥe also wrote several small treatises in Hindī and Urdū. It seems certain that the sect owes a great deal to this man's clear intellect and power of expression. The first guru may have been the source of the leading ideas and of the religious practice of the sect; but one can scarcely doubt that the order and precision which now mark its teaching were the fruit of Saligram's vigorous and orderly mind. His title is Huzoor Maharaj.

The third guru was a Brāhman of Bengali extraction, named Brahmā Śaṅkar Misra. He was born in Benares in 1861, quite near the place where Kabīr taught. He received an English education, and was a Master of Arts of Calcutta University. He held a position in the Accountant General's Office, Allahabad. He joined the Satsaṅg in 1885. In 1898 he became the head of the sect. In 1902 he came to the conclusion that it was necessary, for the health of the Satsaṅg, to give it a well-expressed constitution and a definite organization. He created a Central Administrative Council, and had a Constitution and By-laws drawn up. He left a few poems in Hindī and he wrote two brief expositions of the faith for the Census Officers of the Panjab and of the United Provinces. When he died, he left, in manuscript, a volume of three hundred pages, called *Discourses on Rādhāsoāmi Faith*, which contains much more sound than sense. He left also a few letters in English which have been published under the title *Solace to Satsaṅgīs*. He died in 1907. In Benares, where he died, they have purchased a famous house and garden. It used to be called Nandeshwar Kothi, and at the close of the eighteenth century it was used as the residence of the British judge and magistrate of Benares. Here in 1799 Mr. Davis, the judge, was attacked by a body of native troops, who had just killed the British Resident. He placed himself at the top of a narrow staircase leading to the roof, and succeeded in defending himself, his wife and two children with a spear, until he was rescued by a regiment of cavalry. The garden is now called the Rādhā Soāmi garden. A fine building has been erected in it, which is used for the worship of the sect. It is a large hall with a gallery and a raised platform. At the back of the platform there is the tomb of the third guru, and on it there hangs his photograph, so that the faithful may look upon his face and adore him. His title is Mahārāj Saheb.

Since his death the community has been unable to agree

as to who is to be the next guru. Until 1913 there were two prominent candidates, Mr. Sircar Kamta Prasād of Murai, near Ghazipur, and Mr. Mādhava Prasād Saheb, who is the Chief Superintendent in the Accountant-General's Office, Allahabad. The former died in the autumn of 1913; so that Mr. Mādhava Prasād Saheb has now a far better chance of being chosen; but there are groups who are unwilling to follow him, and at least two other candidates.

3. Thus far we have relied on the literature published by the sect, but there are many important facts which do not appear in the official books. For this further information I am indebted to members of the sect or to people who were members but are no longer so.

The first guru was a man who had had no Western education and did not know English. We may compare him with Rāmakṛishṇa.[1] His wife, whose real name I have not discovered, was a woman of great piety and goodness. They acted together as religious teachers, although the guru was probably the greater of the two. There was no organization, no sect, in those days. Disciples came to them and received instruction; and the photographs of both the man and his wife were given them to contemplate during their private meditations.

The guru belonged to a Vaishṇava family, as we have already seen. His connections were with the Kṛishṇaite gurus of Brindaban. From time to time he and his wife dressed up as Kṛishṇa and Rādhā to receive the worship of their disciples. The second guru also got himself up as Kṛishṇa from time to time. Thus the guru-worship of the sect was probably borrowed unchanged from the practices of the gurus at Brindaban. In February, 1914, I was able to visit the Rādhā Soāmi Bāgh (*i.e.* Garden), some four miles outside Agra, where the tomb, *samādh*, of the first guru is. I was shown over the prem-

[1] Below, p. 188.

PLATE VII

RĀDHĀ
Wife of the first guru

SOĀMI
The first guru

The second guru

The third guru

ises by Mr. Tota Ram, who was educated at Roorki and served Government as a civil engineer for years, but has now retired, and is both architect and builder of a fine new marble structure being erected over the samādh. I was greatly interested to find two photographs hanging on the front of the samādh, a woman and a man. I asked my guide who they represented. He answered that the woman was Rādhā and the man Soāmi, and then explained that they were the first guru and his wife. He also said that Rādhā was not the woman's real name.

So far as my information goes, it was the second guru, Rai Saligram Saheb Bahadur, guru of the sect from 1878–1898, who organized the Satsaṅg, systematized the teaching and gave it its modern character. I have also been told that the sect owes its name to him. It is most noteworthy that this extraordinary name, Rādhā Soāmi, bears four significations in the sect. It is the name of God Himself; it is the name which the first guru bears, as the perfect incarnation of God; it is the sound which the spiritual sound-current (*Śabda*) makes as it rings through all regions; and it is the name of the sect. It is necessary also to realize that the real meaning of Rādhā-svāmī is Kṛishṇa, as Lord of Rādhā (his cowherd mistress in the latest cycle of the myth); and that Soāmi is only a curious phonetic misspell for Svāmī. How comes it that this name stands for God in a sect which rejects the whole Hindu pantheon? We can only conjecture, until some scholar explores the Hindī writings of the first guru; but it almost seems as if, in the first instance, it had been applied to the first guru and his wife, as they shewed themselves to their disciples in person and in portrait, and as they still appear on the samādh, and also in our reproduction of their portraits,[1] and had then been applied to God, of whom the guru was held to be the full and perfect revelation. The third guru quotes a Hindī

[1] Plate VII, facing this page.

couplet, said to be by Kabīr, which is supposed, by transposition, to say that the name of God is Rādhāsvāmī;[1] but the couplet is clearly a forgery: it nowhere occurs among the writings of Kabīr, published or unpublished; the language is of a later date than Kabīr; and the forger was a bungler, for, when transposed according to rule, the name reads *Ārādhsvāmī*, and not Rādhāsvāmī.[2]

The cosmogony is curiously like the Buddhist scheme, which also has three planes or worlds, the Formless World, the World of Form, and the World of Desire, each sub-divided into sections. We may also compare the Theosophic scheme, which sets forth reality as existing in seven distinct planes.

Most of the conceptions of the sect are Hindu, and of these the majority are Vishṇuite. God, the World, and the Soul are recognized as realities; the soul is an *aṁśa*, or portion of God; the spirit-current (*Śabda*), which streams from the Supreme and is the source of all things, corresponds to the *śakti*, or energy of God, in the Vaishṇava and Śaiva systems. Transmigration is retained. The doctrine of immortality shews traces of the Vaishṇava conception, that the soul retains its personality for ever; but the incarnation doctrine differs very seriously from the Vaishṇava idea; for it is men who become incarnate and not God Himself.

4. The practice of the sect is summed up in the phrase *Surat Śabd Yoga*, that is, union (*yoga*) of the human soul (*surat*) with the spirit-current or word (*Śabda*). The methods employed are unknown; for they are imparted by the guru to the disciple under a vow of secrecy; but it is clear that they are occult practices of a hypnotic nature such as are used in Theosophy. There are hints in the literature that the initiate sees wonderful lights and extraordinary scenes, and wins

[1] *Discourses of Rādhāsoāmi Faith*, 162.

[2] I owe this criticism to my friend the Rev. Ahmad Shah of Hamirpur, U. P.

supernatural powers. Instructions about the practice are given partly in meetings of the sect, in which the guru delivers lectures, partly in private, when he receives his disciples individually or in small groups. The guru gives his photograph to each disciple, that he may have it before him during his religious practice. The prescribed exercises (*sādhanāni*) ought to be practised from two to three hours every day.

As to the powers of the Sant Satguru Dr. Griswold writes:

> The incarnate Sant Satguru, even while on earth, has his citizenship in the Rādhā Soāmi Dhām (realm). He is not controlled by the forces and currents which come from low levels of earthly lives; for, "as in the state of somnambulism, all the functions of the body and senses are performed from a plane higher than that which the soul occupies in the wakeful state, so all the actions of the incarnations of the True Creator are regulated by the currents coming direct from the Supreme Being himself." The Sant Satguru who has attained to the highest stage of being might leave the body at any time and return to his own proper sphere; but he stays on earth a certain time for the salvation of believers. This is of his grace.

We are told in the books that the sect recognizes no temples, shrines or sacred places, except those sanctified by the presence of the guru or his relics: that the practice of the sect can be carried on anywhere. This is quite true; for the initiate can sit down, with the photograph of his guru in front of him, and practise his meditations and his exercises wherever he pleases, so long as he does it in secret. But for their meetings the members of the sect prefer to have their own buildings and the presence of either the living guru or the relics of one who has passed away. There are three relic-shrines already in existence, each called *gurudwāra* (the guru's chamber), two in Agra and one in Benares. Each guru's photograph hangs on his tomb.

In the daily meetings of the sect portions of their own

sacred books or of the writings of Kabīr and other Hindu saints are read. There is a prayer, hymn-singing and an address by the guru, if he is present, by some other one, if he is not present. Besides these common practices, there is the adoration of the guru or of his portrait;[1] but of that I have received no detailed description. Several things are clear, however. We are told in the books that each member brings to the meeting with him a wreath of flowers, which he places round the neck of the guru. The wreath is afterwards returned to him, filled with the spiritual power of the guru. Everything that has touched him is charged with his sanctity and influence. All relics from his body, such as clothing, hair, nail-parings or water in which he has washed his feet, are sacred and precious. There are some very disgusting practices connected with this idea, certain products of his body being actually eaten or drunk by his followers. When he dies, his body is burnt; and his ashes, mixed with water, are swallowed by the faithful. The place where he resided is considered holy; and contemplation of his image is held to be contemplation of the Supreme Being.

Rādhā Soāmis are taught that there is no need for them to give up their life as householders and become monks.[2] Indeed, the lives of the three gurus themselves show what is the ideal. Yet, in spite of this, in the Constitution of the Satsaṅg drawn up in 1902, a set of rules is given for the enrolment and conduct of Rādhā Soāmi monks.[3]

There is one side of Rādhā Soāmi influence which is very curious, their want of touch with modern movements. The gurus discourage study. The members shew no national feeling whatsoever, nor any serious interest in the life of the country. If any member were to accept a public position of

[1] Cf. the Deva Samāj, p. 179 below, and Theosophy, p. 261, below.

[2] *Rādhā Soāmi Mat Prakāsh*, 51.

[3] *Discourses of Rādhāsoāmi Faith*, 329.

any prominence, he would be looked down upon. Economic, literary or educational progress is no part of the ideal of the sect. This neglect of public affairs is what takes the place of the old ascetic renunciation.

5. The points that attract new members seem to be, first of all, the secrecy of the religious practice of the sect, with the hope connected therewith of gaining supernatural wisdom, enlightenment and power. The living guru, believed to be an incarnation of God in the fullest possible sense, is a distinct attraction. Within the meetings of the sect there is a good deal of freedom. Men of all castes mix freely together, and even on occasion, dine together in secret; and there is no strict separation of men and women. There is thus a sort of free happy fellowship within each group of Satsaṅgīs, as they call themselves. Finally, membership in the sect does not involve any breach with one's own religion. The fact that a man is a member of the sect is often kept secret. As in Theosophy, you may be a Rādhā Soāmi and yet remain a Hindu, a Muḥammadan or a Christian. People are taught that all religions are true, and that the Rādhā Soāmi faith is an extra, fit to be the complement of any religion, and supreme over them all. Membership is thus made quite easy. Yet it is definitely stated that the religion is for all, and that outside the Satsaṅg there is no salvation.

There is no proselytism in the sect, except in so far as the individual member may express his high appreciation of the guru to his personal friends. One Satsaṅgī tried to make me realize how many miracles had accompanied the gurus throughout their lives. They teach only people who wish to be taught; and they would rather win a few intelligent men than crowds of common people.

6. The affinities of the theology of the sect stand out quite clear. Most of the teaching is purely Hindu; it stands nearer to Vaishṇavism than to any other part of Hinduism, and is

perhaps most closely allied to the teaching of Kabīr. This is reflected in the practice of the sect. While they profess to find all truth in the books of their own gurus, they do use the writings of certain Hindu and Muḥammadan saints, and amongst these they give Kabīr the highest place. But, though the system is in the main Hindu and old, there are modern elements. There is an attempt to place religious leaders in the various spheres of the universe, according to their merit; and there are a number of Christian elements in the teaching. The unknown Supreme is constantly called the Heavenly Father; His will is frequently emphasized; and Satsaṅgīs are taught to seek His approbation. The Sant Satguru, who alone can reveal Him, is called His beloved Son. God created man in His own image. Love is emphasized in the teaching of the sect in such a way as clearly to reveal its Christian origin; for it goes far beyond the old ideas connected with *bhakti*. Works of faith and charity, the spirit of service and prayer, are laid down as necessary duties. Finally, the forms of worship in the regular services, apart from the adoration of the guru, are Christian.

In this connection, however, nothing is more noteworthy than the many points in which Rādhā Soāmi and Theosophical doctrine and practice coincide. The most important items are: the unknowable Supreme, the spheres and their regents, the human revealers of religion, the emphasis on the Word, reincarnation, the use of methodical exercises (*sādhanāni*) of a hypnotic character for the development of the spiritual powers and of the photograph[1] of the guru in meditation, the worship of gurus, the supernatural powers of the gurus, the claim that the teaching of the sect is scientifically accurate and verifiable in every particular, esoteric teaching, secret practice, and all the talk about astral and higher planes, adepts and such like.

[1] See above, pp. 169, 170; below, p. 261.

LITERATURE. — *Rādhā Soāmi Mat Prakāsh*, by Rai Salig Ram Bahadur, Benares, 1896, for private circulation, 10 annas. (This is by far the best presentation of Rādhā Soāmi Doctrine in English.) *Discourses of Radhasoami Faith*, by Pandit Brahm Sankar Misra, Benares, The Satsang, 1909. This very verbose volume has a Prefatory Note which contains details about the three gurus. For the other works of the gurus, see above, pp. 114, 115, 116. *The Radha Swami Sect*, by the Rev. H. D. Griswold, Ph. D., Cawnpore Mission Press.

10. THE DEVA SAMĀJ

1. Śiva Nārāyaṇa Agnihotṛi was born in a Kanauji Brāhman family in 1850, in a small town in the Cawnpore district of the United Provinces. When he was sixteen, he entered the Government Engineering College at Rurki, and got the degree of Overseer after some years of study and service there. Before the close of his course, he came greatly under the religious influence of the Curator of the Instrument Depot of the College, and through him became convinced of the truth of the Vedānta philosophy as taught by Śaṅkarāchārya, namely, that God is impersonal, and that the human spirit is God. In 1871, while he was acting as a master in the College, both he and his wife underwent a ceremony of initiation and became disciples of the Curator-guru. He also began to see clearly the need of religious and social reform. Hence he banished idolatry from his household and set his wife free from the restrictions of the zenāna.

In 1873, now 23 years of age, he was appointed Drawing-master in the Government School, Lahore; and in that city he has lived ever since. Here he at once came under the influence of the Brāhma Samāj, with its doctrine that God is essentially personal. Both he and his capable wife became active Brāhma workers. In 1875 he was appointed honorary minister of the Lahore Samāj, and soon became well known in the city as a man of character and a good speaker. Wherever he went, large audiences gathered to hear him. The Ārya Samāj was planted in Lahore in 1877, as we have already seen, and very soon rose to great influence. The following year, Agnihotṛi began a long-continued crusade against its false pretences about the Veda. In January, 1880, he attended the anniversary meetings of the recently founded Sādhāran Brāhma Samāj in Calcutta;[1] and he and three others were ordained as the first missionaries of the movement.[2] For two years longer he gave all his leisure to work for the Lahore Samāj; but in 1882 he gave up the post of Drawing-master in the Government School, in order that his full time might be devoted to missionary labour. We are also informed in the recent literature of the Samāj that on his birthday, the 20th of December of the same year, he took his great vow, expressed in a Hindī couplet, the translation of which runs:

> The supreme object of my Life is to serve the world by establishing the kingdom of Truth and Goodness on this earth and by destroying what is opposed to them; may I spend my whole life for the fulfilment of this supreme object!

In any case his full powers now began to make themselves manifest. He proved effective as a writer as well as a speaker. Books, pamphlets and tracts poured from the press. For a little time a sort of simple copy of the Salvation Army, called the Brāhma Sena or Brāhma Army, was used as an auxiliary. He made his influence felt in every section of public life in Lahore. But it was not long before difficulties arose within the Samāj. His methods displeased the quieter members; and his forceful will and autocratic temper led to constant friction with the other leaders. He wanted to rule. He would often be heard to say, "I am born to command not to obey." Most of the members were apprehensive that he would soon set up as the authoritative guru of the Samāj. The way his followers now express this is: "His life-mission was unique

[1] P. 55, above. [2] *HBS.*, II, 144.

and quite different from the object of the Brāhmo Samāj." A split became inevitable.

2. Accordingly, he seceded from the Brāhma Samāj, taking with him a fair number of followers, and organized, on the Queen's Jubilee day,[1] February 16th, 1887, a new society to be known as the Deva Samāj. The name was clearly chosen in order to distinguish the new society from the old, and yet to indicate its close relationship to it. Brāhma is an adjective formed from the word Brahman, the name of the supreme God of the Upanishads. Deva is the ordinary Sanskrit word for one of the innumerable gods of the Hindu pantheon, but is probably used in the name of the society as an adjective. So that the whole name means the Divine Society. A creed was soon issued, which showed that the aims and beliefs of the new community were very similar to those of the Brāhma Samāj; yet there were significant differences. The Deva Dharma, the divine religion of the divine society, is a special divine dispensation,[2] and so is distinct from the Brāhma Dharma. The doctrines are Brāhma doctrines; yet the beginnings of a guru-doctrine are perceptible; and, within a few years, the leader could say of himself, "My mission is unique"; "I am free from sin"; [3] and "I am a ship of hope and a leaven for elevating nations." The work of the Samāj ran along the usual lines: only Agnihotṛi dabbled in spiritualism.

In 1893 he became involved in a libel case which, dragging on for five long years, greatly hindered the work of the Samāj. During this period Agnihotṛi's mind underwent a very serious change; and at its close a new period opens.

3. From 1898 down to the present day the Deva Samāj has been an atheistic society, working for educational and moral ends. Yet the members attribute to the guru such a supreme place in human evolution and give him such a position in their

[1] As celebrated in India. [2] Cf. Keshab's idea, above, p. 55.

[3] *Dharma Jivan*, 4th October, 1892.

own minds and devotional practice that we are fully justified in saying that, practically, he is regarded and worshipped as a god. Indeed, they call him *sattya deva*, a real god.[1] The literature of the earlier period was at once withdrawn from circulation as far as possible; a new creed, quite different from the previous one was promulgated; and, for several years, there was no public preaching or disputation. The literature of the sect is now sold publicly and many of the meetings are public; but the devotional meetings and the worship of the guru are held in private. The chief book of the Samāj is called the *Deva Śāstra*, or Divine Scripture, and the teaching, *Deva Dharma*, or Divine Religion.

4. The teaching of the sect is that the universe consists of matter and force, which are uncreated and indestructible, and which manifest themselves in four forms, inorganic, vegetable, animal, human. Man's life or soul is the builder of his body, the most essential part of his existence. The soul develops if it possess the necessary capacity and unite with the right evolutionary environment; but if it lacks the capacity or fails to grasp the environment, it degenerates; and if degeneration is not checked, it will become extinct. A soul that rises to the Complete Higher Life is thereby raised above the danger of degeneration and extinction. The soul then survives in the form of a refined human body.

Good action leads to development, evil action to degeneration. When a man reaches a certain height of development, he is entirely beyond the danger of degeneration and dissolution. In order to reach this higher life, it is necessary to unite with one who has already risen to these heights. The guru of the Deva Samāj has risen to the highest possible heights, and thus is the true environment for souls eager for progress. He is an unprecedented manifestation of the powers of the highest life.

[1] He is so called in a letter sent me by the Secretary of the Samāj.

PLATE VIII

Mahamānanīya Pujanīya Śri Deva Guru Bhagavān
Paṇḍit S. N. Agnihotṛi

Since matter and force are the only reality that exists, there is no such thing as God or gods. Every conception of God that has been held among men is purely imaginative, and consequently harmful.

The teaching about the guru himself is the key to the whole life of the sect. He is the highest result of the evolution of the universe. He has evolved the highest powers that any being on this earth has ever had. Nay, he possesses in his soul all the powers of the Complete Higher Life and is its highest ideal. Hence many of the titles used of Hindu gods are conferred upon him. He is Mahāmānanīya Pūjanīya Śrī Deva Guru Bhagavān (the Most Reverend, Most Worshipful, Most Exalted, Divine Teacher and Blessed Lord). Since he became the god of the Samāj, he has tended to withdraw into seclusion. He no longer figures in the public life of Lahore. He seldom instructs any one except his own disciples, very seldom gives outsiders interviews, and delivers addresses only in meetings of the Samāj. Much is made of the vow he is said to have taken in 1882. Much is also made of his sacrifices.

The guru teaches and practises spiritualism. Being the summit of all evolution, he possesses powers whereby he is able to see into the other world, and to have personal dealings, through mediums, with souls there. He states that many of his own dead relatives have become convinced of the truth of his teaching, and have found salvation through him. He delivers addresses to spirits who assemble from time to time to hear him at the Samāj building.

Transmigration is denied. This is one of the elements of Brāhma teaching which have been carried over into the new period.

5. Those who wish to become members of the Samāj have to take the following ten vows.[1]

[1] *A Dialogue about the Deva Samāj*, 14–16.

1. I shall not commit the following four sins relating to my profession or calling: —

(*a*) I shall not take bribe.

(*b*) I shall not weigh or measure anything more or less, with a motive of cheating some one.

(*c*) I shall not substitute one thing for another with a view to cheating some one.

(*d*) When certain remuneration for a certain work or price of a thing has been agreed upon, I shall not dishonestly pay less or take more than is due according to the agreement.

2. I shall not commit theft.

3. I shall not withhold anything borrowed by or entrusted to me.

4. I shall not rob any person of his money, land or any other article by force or fraud.

5. I shall not gamble or do any act which involves loss or gain of money or property through betting.

6. I shall not lead a useless life when I am able to do some work.

7. I shall not commit adultery, polygamy, or any unnatural crime.

8. I shall not use, prepare, cultivate, buy or sell, or give to any person any intoxicant such as Wine, Opium, Bhang, Tobacco, Charas, Chandoo, Cocaine, etc., for the purpose of intoxication.

9. I shall not eat flesh or eggs myself, or give or direct others to eat flesh or eggs or anything made thereof.

10. I shall not kill any sentient being, barring certain right occasions.

When any one wants to become a member of the Samāj, he writes a letter to the guru, putting into it a catalogue of all his past sins, telling how he has been brought to a better mind by the guru, and promising to give them up. From time to time thereafter he writes in a similar strain. All these documents the guru preserves most carefully.[1]

6. The guru is seldom present at the regular devotional meetings of the Samāj, but his photograph hangs before the congregation. An image would be used; but hitherto the cost has stood in the way. When the people have assembled, all stand up, and the conductor offers a tray of flowers to the portrait,[2] or hangs a garland round it. All then bend low in adoration. The *stotra*, a Sanskrit hymn in praise of the guru, is then sung by all, and a Hindī translation is read by the conductor. All then prostrate themselves before the portrait. When all are seated, the conductor offers prayer to the guru. Then a hymn is sung. This is often followed by a sermon, or a meditation on the virtues of the guru, and another hymn; or a passage is read from the *Deva Śāstra*. The conductor or some other one then closes the meeting with another prayer. The burning of incense and the waving of lights (*ārati*) before the portrait were originally parts of the service, but they have been discontinued. When the guru himself is present, the service centres in him; and when members call on him, they prostrate themselves at his feet. His birthday is the anniversary of the Samāj.

7. The methods of the Samāj are practically all Christian. Many of them the guru brought with him from the Brāhma Samāj; the rest have been copied direct from Christian missions. The Samāj has missionaries, and also lay-workers, both men and women. They have two High Schools, a number of Primary Schools, a School for the Depressed Classes, and a Training College for mission workers, called the *Bikāshālai*, or House of Development. A good deal of attention is given to female education. They have a successful Board-

[1] Cf. p. 182, below.

[2] Cf. the Rādhā Soāmis, p. 169 f., above, and Theosophy, p. 261, below.

ing School for Girls at Firozepore, teaching up to the Matriculation Standard. They do a little medical work, have two Widows' Homes, and have held Industrial Exhibitions. They lay a good deal of stress on social reform, as we have already seen, and endeavour to do a little social service. They have a Temperance League and a Vegetarian League.[1]

Literature is much used in spreading the teaching of the Samāj. The guru's chief work is a Hindī book, the *Deva Śāstra*, i.e., the Divine Scripture, which, he believes, is destined to eclipse all the sacred books of the world. The portrait of the guru which forms the frontispiece of the *Deva Śāstra* is reproduced in the plate facing page 126. There are a few more books of some size in Hindī which expound the principles of their doctrine; and there are a great many pamphlets in Hindī, Urdū, Sindhī and English. A series of schoolbooks in Hindī has been published. Four journals are published: an English monthly, called the *Science-Grounded Religion*, an Anglo-Sindhī monthly, called the *Sindh-Upakārak*, an Urdū fortnightly, called *Jiwan Tattva*, and a Hindī monthly, called the *Sewak*, which is meant only for those belonging to the Samāj.

The Reports read at the Anniversary Meetings tell of steady expansion.[2] Lahore and Firozepore are the two chief centres of the work; but members from Sindh, Baluchistan, the N. W. Frontier Province and the United Provinces attend the annual meetings.

8. The sources and connections of the system stand out quite clear. The scientific elements are fairly prominent: the conceptions of life, seed, soil, growth, evolution, progress, degeneration, extinction, are scattered throughout the literature. Originally, the guru seems to have been considerably influenced by Drummond's *Natural Law in the Spiritual*

[1] All this may be found in the *Dialogue about the Deva Samāj.*

[2] *ISR.*, XX, 258; XXI, 207, 257; XXIII, 235.

World; but his later thought is drawn mainly from Spencer. Hinduism shews itself in the Samāj in the beliefs about the guru and in the worship, and lingers on in the practice of caste, though transmigration has been expelled, and in the stress laid on vegetarianism and on the preservation of animal life. The influence of Christianity is visible throughout, chiefly in the vigorous moral sense which characterizes the doctrine of salvation, and in the claim made in every report, that numerous individuals have been saved from various forms of vice by the teaching of the Samāj;[1] also in the rejection of transmigration, in the demand for social reform, and in the practical methods employed. The religious atheism of the Samāj reminds one of Comtism, but the position of the guru is distinctly Hindu. Curiously enough, his doctrine of conditional immortality is not unlike that preached by the Rev. Edward White in London, shortly before the rise of the Deva Samāj.

9. All went fairly well with the Samāj until 1913, when the guru took two measures which have raised a storm. He appointed his own second son, Devānand, who keeps an athletic store in Lahore, to succeed him. Naturally, Dev Ratan, who has been associated with him for twenty-four years, and for many years has been his right hand, did not think this quite the right appointment. In the second place he published a book, called *Bignan-Mulak Tattva Siksha*, in which he declared himself the perfect ideal, the perfect object of worship, the perfect giver of life, perfection and salvation for all mankind. No one has been equal to him in the past; no one will ever equal him in the future. The worship of all other beings, whether imaginary gods and goddesses or real men, should be abandoned as harmful.

The consequence is that Dev Ratan, the one considerable

[1] See, for example, the *Dialogue*, 19. Cf. Madame Blavatsky's boasts, below, p. 438.

man in the movement after the guru, has seceded from the Samāj; and one of the sons of the guru, his brother-in-law, his sister-in-law, two graduates and some others have come out with him. The bulk of the members have, however, remained. The seceders have formed *The Society for the Promotion of Higher Life*. Their position is the old teaching without the guru. Meantime the guru has published the letters of confession [1] written to him by Dev Ratan in former years, and seeks to show from them what a bad man he is; — a proceeding which suggests many thoughts. What the outcome of all this will be no one can tell.

LITERATURE. — OFFICIAL: *Devaśāstra*, by S. N. Agnihotṛi, Lahore, Jivan Press, Rs. 5. (The chief scripture of the Samāj; in Hindī.) *Dev Dharm*, Lahore, Deva Samaj Office, price 1½ as. (An account of the teaching of the sect, in English, in fifty pages.) *A Dialogue about the Dev Samaj*, Lahore, The Jivan Press, 1912, 1 an. (A brief account of the Samāj and its work.) CRITICAL: *Pandit Agnihotṛi and the Deva Samāj*, by Dr. H. D. Griswold, Lahore, 1906. (A clear account of the Samāj.) *A Lecture on Pandit S. N. Agnihotṛi and His Atheistic Propaganda*, by Kashi Ram, Lahore, N. W. Indian Press, 1908.

11. TWO MINOR GURUS

Two young Hindus, belonging to our own day, the one a Telugu, the other a Tamil, have each sketched a system and gathered a few disciples. Both have been deeply influenced by Christ; yet, the main teaching of each is Hindu; and they both wish to be worshipped as gurus. They are of no importance as leaders, but their teaching may be worth notice as further evidence of the character of Indian thought to-day.

1. The Telugu guru [2] is not quite ready yet to appear in public to expound his system. His thought, as it at present exists in his mind, seems to be fundamentally Hindu, but with

[1] P. 178, above.

[2] My informant is one of his disciples, whom I met in Madras.

a good deal of Christianity worked into it. He declares that his system is for all men, and that he selects what is good from all religions.

At present he seems to be a pantheist. The whole world is God, and we are part of God. God is not a Spirit. God is not *Sat, Chit, Ānanda*, except in so far as the universe deserves these titles. God is non-moral. He has no will. He does not act. He does not listen to prayer, and does not receive sacrifice. God does not answer prayer: prayer automatically answers itself.

He condemns idolatry entirely.

He finds all metaphysics in the *Ṛigveda*. He acknowledges that Hindu mythology is absurd, and explains Brahmā as *sthūla*, i.e., the material world, Vishṇu as *antaḥkaraṇa*, i.e. man's inner faculties, and Śiva as the first cause. He asserts that there is no mythology in the *Ṛigveda*. He is writing a Commentary on it. In his attitude to the *Ṛik* he stands very near Dayānanda.

He bids his followers concentrate the mind on certain words or phrases from the *Ṛigveda* (*e.g.* the Gayatrī, the most famous of Hindu prayers), because he holds they are instinct with meaning. They are to concentrate the mind on that, until only one thought remains. He believes in the power of Yoga methods, but says they are dangerous.

He calls Śaṅkara and Buddha great philosophers. He has not much respect for Muḥammad. He acknowledges that the *Gītā* is not an utterance of Kṛishṇa.

He says the world is eternal. He does not believe in the re-creation and destruction of the world. He believes in karma and transmigration; but he does not seek deliverance himself at all; nor does he admire men who seek deliverance. He desires rebirth, in order to work for the good of humanity. This is curiously like the attitude ascribed to the Bodhisattvas in Mahāyāna Buddhism.

Moral law is made by man. What is best for society is moral. In moral action he would advise us to copy Jesus. He holds that the life of Jesus was entirely given up to doing good; and he says that He died for men. He also declares that Jesus is now a living angel, who can answer the prayers of Christians.

He urges his followers above all things else to philanthropic action. He also urges them to prayer and moral action. He insists on moral asceticism.

He is a Brāhman; yet he eats with Christians in secret. He is in favour of mixed marriages, even between people of different races. He is anxious to make Brāhmans less conservative; but, as he has not yet appeared publicly as a teacher, he conceals his anti-caste tendencies. He is opposed to polygamy, but is not in favour of widow-remarriage, nor in favour of marrying girls after puberty. The age of the marriage of men ought to be raised. He is a married man with a family. He lays no stress on the monastic life, but makes working for humanity the prime thing.

Though he has not proclaimed himself a public teacher as yet, he has gathered a number of friends around him and formed a sort of society. Weekly or fortnightly a meeting is held. He presides; some one reads a paper in Sanskrit, and he comments on it.

The disciples consider him worthy of divine honour. Each bows down individually to him.

2. The young Tamil has been rash enough to publish a little book to explain his position. It is simply a rhetorical exercise, containing no systematic thinking. The elements contained in it are drawn mainly from the Śaiva Siddhānta and from Christianity, but Vaishṇavism is not quite neglected. The Christian elements are distinctly subordinate to the Hindu, and the need of the guru is one of the most prominent points. He describes, in a mystical way, his own meeting with his guru,

whom he calls the Anointed, and to whom he attributes his conversion. His language throughout is modelled on the Bible; but in every case Christian truth is volatilized, so as to become equivalent to Hindu doctrine. Baptism, the Holy Ghost, Regeneration, the Kingdom of God, Eternal Life, and other such phrases are scattered about his pages everywhere; and many texts are quoted from the Gospels; but all are emptied of their real meaning.

CHAPTER IV

FULL DEFENCE OF THE OLD RELIGIONS

1870–1913

At the beginning of our third chapter we noted the rise in India about 1870 of a new spirit, which generated many religious movements, roughly divisible into two series, one marked by defence of the old, tempered by reform, the other eager to defend the old in almost every particular. We deal with this latter series in this chapter.

1. Beginnings

The earliest stirrings of the new spirit appeared in and around Calcutta. In 1872 Raj Narayan Bose, one of the leaders of the Ādi Brāhma Samāj,[1] delivered a lecture on *The Superiority of Hinduism over all other Forms of Faith*,[2] which attracted a good deal of attention. The very next year, the idea of the equality of all religions, which has become so closely associated these last thirty years with the defence of Hinduism, found organized expression at Barahanagar, a few miles to the north of Calcutta. Mr. Sasipada Banurji, a Kulīn Brāhman, who had early turned to various forms of social service, and had become a member of the Brāhma Samāj in 1865, established a religious association, which he called the *Sādhāran Dharma Sabhā*, or General Religious Association, in which Hindus, Brāhmas, Christians, Buddhists

[1] P. 46, above.

[2] *HBS.*, I, 248.

and Muslims were allowed freely to express their own religious beliefs, so long as they condemned no one. The following is a description of its work:

> Its two main features were, first, a spiritual union, held every week, of the followers of various religions on the basis of commonly-accepted principles — a union in which prayers and other spiritual exercises took place and were joined in by all; and, secondly, a platform for the preaching of diverse opinions by their advocates, a platform where the most perfect freedom and toleration were allowed consistently with brotherly feeling and general co-operation; for no one was allowed to vilify or ridicule the beliefs and practices of another.[1]

The work has died out at Barahanagar. But, within recent years, Mr. Banurji has started it again in Calcutta. The institution is named the *Devālaya*, or "Divine House."[2] The building is his own, and stands in the compound of the Sādhāran Bārhma Samāj. He has made over this property to a group of trustees, so that it may be used for the purposes described by the donor. It is most curious to note how similar Sasipada's original idea is to those which, a few years later, were expressed by Rāmakṛishṇa, and later still, by Theosophists.

We may also note that in 1873, at the very time when he was starting his General Religious Association at Barahanagar, a group of Hindus formed in Calcutta the *Sanātana Dharma Rakshinī Sabhā*, or Association for the Defence of the Eternal Religion. They were anxious to found a Sanskrit School in the city to counteract modern tendencies. One of the reasons why Dayānanda Sarasvatī visited Calcutta was that he hoped to help this society.[3] A few years later the Hindus of the South began to move in the same direction, as we shall see.

[1] *The Devālaya*, by S. N. Tattvabhushan, 19.

[2] *Ib.*, 26.

[3] *Swami Dayanand Saraswati*, 28, Madras, Natesan. Cf. above, p.109.

2. Rāmakṛishṇa Paramahaṁsa

But the man who really made these ideas current coin in India was a Bengali ascetic, known as Rāmakṛishṇa Paramahaṁsa.

1. Gadādhar Chatterji[1] was born in the village of Kamarpukur in the Hoogly district of Bengal, on the 20th of February, 1834,[2] in a poor but orthodox Brāhman family. The accounts which are published of his life already tend to be mythical. Even the best biography that exists, which was written by one of his pupils, and published by Max Müller, decidedly tends here and there towards the marvellous; and a large volume, published by another of his disciples, and called the *Gospel of Śrī Rāmakṛishṇa*, imitates the Christian Gospels so carefully in many minor points that one wonders how far the assimilation has gone. Yet the main events of his life stand out quite clear, so that we can trace, in large measure, the growth of this gifted man's mind.

Even when quite a boy, he showed wonderful powers of memory and considerable interest in religious books and stories. He received no education. His father died when he was about seventeen; and he then went with his elder brother, Paṇḍit Ram Kumar, down to Calcutta, to try to make a living. For some time he was employed as *pūjārī*, or ministrant, in certain Hindu families in the northern part of the city, his duty being to see to the worship of the household idols. But a wealthy Bengali lady built rather a striking temple at Dakshineśvara, four miles north of Calcutta, on the bank of the Hugli River; and, when this temple was opened on the 31st of May, 1855, his elder brother was appointed chief priest. Soon after, Gadādhar was appointed one of the assistant priests.

[1] The details of his life are taken mainly from Max Müller's *Rāmakṛishṇa*. Where I differ from him, I give my authority.

[2] See the *Gospel of R.*, p. 1. Müller's date is clearly wrong.

The two brothers were now in comfortable circumstances; but almost at once religion began to assert itself in Gadādhar's life. The form which his religious passion took was a fervent worship of the image of Kālī in the temple. He thought of her as the mother of the universe, and as his own mother. The following quotation is from Max Müller's life:[1]

> He now began to look upon the image of the goddess Kālī as his mother and the mother of the universe. He believed it to be living and breathing and taking food out of his hand. After the regular forms of worship he would sit there for hours and hours, singing hymns and talking and praying to her as a child to his mother, till he lost all consciousness of the outward world.

In his religious ecstasy he would pass into that form of trance which is called in Hinduism *samādhi*. When this came on him, he became unconscious. He would sit in a fixed position for a short time, or it might be for hours, and would then slowly return to consciousness. When he was in this condition, the best doctors could find no trace of pulse or of heart-action.[2] It is also said that he already had the power of inducing *samādhi* in others. This trance is clearly a form of hypnotism.

His mother and brothers, thinking that marriage would make him more like ordinary people, took him home, and had him married. This was in 1859. He was then twenty-five years of age, while his little bride was only six. This Hindu marriage-ceremony is a full Hindu marriage, and completely binding: but the husband and wife do not live together until the little girl-wife is eleven or twelve years old.

Then he returned to the temple, leaving his little wife in her father's home. But, instead of getting rid of his religious ecstasy, he developed a new phase. He now had an overpowering desire to realize the existence and the presence of

[1] P. 36.

[2] *Rāmakṛishṇa*, 57.

his mother, the goddess. The following is from one of his disciples:

> "Oh Mother!" he would cry, "show me the truth! Art Thou there? Art Thou there? Dost Thou exist? Why then should I be left in ignorance? Why can I not realize? Words and philosophy are vain. Vain all this talk of things! Truth! It is truth alone I want to realize. Truth I would touch! Truth I seek to feel!"[1]

He believed that God can be seen. He felt that, until he had seen Kālī, he had not realized her, and that there was something wrong with his devotion. He would fall into *samādhi*, and remain unconscious for hours. His neglect of his duties as priest of the temple was so serious, that he had to be deprived of his position. He left the temple, and lived in a little wood near by. From now onwards for about twelve years he lived a life of prayer and supplication, of severe self-repression, and of unceasing effort to reach union with God:

> Looking back to these years of self-torture in his later days, he said, 'that a great religious tornado, as it were, raged within him during these years and made everything topsy-turvy.' He had no idea then that it lasted for so long a time. He never had a wink of sound sleep during these years, could not even doze, but his eyes would remain always open and fixed.[2]

The first person who understood him and helped him, was a Brāhman nun (*sannyāsinī*), who came and resided in the temple for some time. She was a woman of great beauty, and considerable learning. She knew and practised *yoga*, that is, various bodily postures, breathing exercises, and forms of intellectual drill, meant for the progressive restraint of both body and mind and the development of supernatural powers. The books she knew were the *Tantras*, old manuals written for the worship of Kālī, and the exposition of the theology con-

[1] *My Master*, 30. [2] *Rāmaskrishṇa*, 41.

nected with her name. She understood Gadādhar's religious condition, and her sympathy was of great service to him. She showed his friends old Vaishṇava books from which it appeared that the saints of Bengal of former days were afflicted just as he was. She taught him all she knew; and then, after a stay of some years, departed and was never seen again.

Gadādhar was still dissatisfied. He longed for higher knowledge; and, fortunately, there came to the temple a man named Ṭotā-puri who was able to help him. He was a tall, strong, muscular ascetic, who wore no clothing, and never slept under a roof, but kept up the use of the sacred fire. He was some sort of monk, *sannyāsī*, but he cannot have belonged to any of the great orders, else he would not have had a fire. The system of philosophy which he followed was the monistic Vedānta, as taught by Śaṅkarāchārya. The doctrines are that God is impersonal, that the human spirit is identical with God, and that the world is an illusion. This he expounded to Gadādhar; and the latter proved a quick pupil. He also taught him the highest stage of religious trance, *nirvikalpa samādhi*, in which not a trace of consciousness remains. But the master also learned much from the pupil; so that he stayed eleven months with him. He initiated Gadādhar as a monk, *sannyāsī*. As we have already seen, the *sannyāsī* gives up home, property, caste, ornaments, the work of the world, money and marriage. Gadādhar was able to take this vow, because he had forgotten that he was married. When a man becomes a sannyāsī, he takes a new name. From this time forward, then, he was known as Rāmakṛishṇa. At a later date his friends called him Paramahaṁsa, a title bestowed only on sannyāsīs of the most advanced knowledge and sanctity.

After the departure of Totā-puri, Rāmakṛishṇa desired to remain continuously in the exalted form of trance he had learnt; and we are told that, for six months, almost without a break, he lived in religious unconsciousness. His own account of these days is as follows:

> In those days I was quite unconscious of the outer world. My body would have died for want of nourishment, but for a *sādhu* (religious ascetic) who came at that time and stayed there for three days for my sake. He recognized my state of Samadhi, and took much interest to preserve this body, while I was unconscious of its very existence. He used to bring some food every day, and when all methods failed to restore sensation or consciousness to this body of mine, he would even strike me with a heavy club, so that the pain might bring me back to consciousness. Sometimes he succeeded in awakening a sort of partial consciousness in me, and he would immediately force down one or two mouthfuls of food before I was lost again in deep Samadhi. Some days when he could not produce any response, even after a severe beating, he was very sorrowful.[1]

The trance period passed away, ending in a serious illness, but Rāmakṛishṇa recovered.

He next sought to attain the Vaishṇava ideal of love for God. The method by which he tried to rouse the right feelings was to imagine he was some one of the great devotees of the old stories. For example, he imagined himself Rādhā, Kṛishṇa's cowherd mistress, wore woman's attire, spoke like a woman, and lived among the women of his own family, until he experienced something like her passionate love for Kṛishṇa. After some time he felt he had attained his ideal: he saw the beautiful form of Kṛishṇa in a trance, and was satisfied.

The twelve years of storm and stress had passed. He was at peace. It was the year 1871. His wife, who was now eighteen years of age, and had heard of his fame, came to see him. Rāmakṛishṇa explained that he could never be a husband to her. She replied that she was quite satisfied to live with him on his own terms, if he would only enlighten her

[1] *Rāmakṛishṇa*, 49.

mind, and enable her to see and serve God. So she took up her residence in the temple, and became one of his most devoted pupils. She survived him, and spoke in the warmest way of him afterwards. She revered him as a divine being.

The next impulse that came to him was to conquer his own feelings in matters of caste. Since he was a sannyāsī, he had no caste of his own left, according to the rules of his religion; yet the prejudices and instinctive feelings of his Brāhman birth remained; and he felt he must overcome his natural abhorrence of low-caste people. One of his disciples describes what he did:

> In order, then, that he might stand above none, our Brahmin sought to identify himself with the Chandāla, by doing his work. He is the street-cleaner, and the scavenger, touched by no one; and so, in the night, this man possessed himself of his brooms and utensils, and entering those hidden offices of the temple which it was the duty of pariahs to cleanse, he knelt down, and did the work of purification with his own hands, wiping the place with his hair! Nor was this the only abasement that he imposed upon himself. The temple gave food daily to many beggars, and amongst these were Mahommedans, outcasts, and people of no character. Waiting till all had finished eating, our Brahmin would collect the green leaves that had formed their plates, would gather together the broken fragments of food that they had left, would even eat from amongst their rejected morsels, and would finally cleanse the place where all sorts and conditions of men had had their meal.[1]

He was next seized by the desire to know and understand other religions. Here are two quotations which tell how he proceeded:

> He found a Mahommedan saint and went to live with him; he underwent the discipline prescribed by him, became a Mahommedan for the time being, lived like a Mahommedan, dressed like a Mahommedan, and did everything laid down in their codes.[2]

[1] *My Master*, 38–40. [2] *Ib.*, 41.

He had seen Jesus in a vision, and for three days he could think of nothing and speak of nothing but Jesus and His love.[1]

The result was that he came to the conclusion that all religions were true, that they were simply various paths leading to the same goal.

2. People now began to visit him. One of his chief friends was a paṇḍit, named Vaishṇava Charan, who often went to see him, and now and then brought him to Calcutta.[2] Dayānanda Sarasvatī met him during the time which he spent in Calcutta at the end of 1872 and the beginning of 1873.[3] About the year 1875, Keshab Chandra Sen made his acquaintance,[4] and became deeply interested in him. He talked about him to his friends, and also wrote about him. In consequence, educated men from Calcutta began to go to the temple to see Rāmakṛishṇa. From this time onward, he made the acquaintance of those young men who became his devoted disciples, and carried on his work after his death. Many famous Indians went to see him, and to listen to his brilliant conversation.[5] For seven years, from 1879 to his death in 1886, he talked almost incessantly. He wrote nothing, but his disciples took down his sayings in Bengali; and several collections of them have been published. The most convenient collection is that contained in Max Müller's *Rāmakṛishṇa*. *The Gospel of Śrī Rāmakṛishṇa*, written by Prof. M. N. Gupta, one of his disciples, consists of a brief introduction, containing the merest outline of his life, and a description of the temple precincts where he lived, and then 350 pages of conversations with friends and disciples. A good deal of the language is modelled on the language of the Gospels.

According to his most famous disciple, Narendra Nath Dutt,

[1] *Rāmakṛishṇa*, 51. [2] *Gospel of R.*, 6. [3] *Ib.*, 9, 182.
[4] *Ib.*, 7. Müller's date, p. 55, is manifestly wrong. P. 51, above.
[5] *Gospel of R.*, 8–10, 135, 182.

PLATE IX

Rāmakrishṇa Paramahaṁsa

Svāmī Vivekānanda

Madame Blavatsky

Mrs. Besant

usually called Svāmī Vivekānanda, he had two types of conversation, as may be seen from the following paragraph:[1]

> He was a wonderful mixture of God and man. In his ordinary state he would talk of himself as servant of all men and women. He looked upon them all as God. He himself would never be addressed as Guru, or teacher. Never would he claim for himself any high position. He would touch the ground reverently where his disciples had trodden. But every now and then strange fits of God-consciousness came upon him. He then spoke of himself as being able to do and know everything. He spoke as if he had the power of giving anything to anybody. He would speak of himself as the same soul that had been born before as Rama, as Krishna, as Jesus, or as Buddha, born again as Ramakrishna. He told Mathuranatha long before anybody knew him, that he had many disciples who would come to him shortly, and he knew all of them. He said that he was free from all eternity, and the practices and struggles after religion which he went through were only meant to show the people the way to salvation. He had done all for them alone. He would say he was a Nitya-mukta, or eternally free, and an incarnation of God Himself.

3. The character of Rāmakṛishṇa was singularly simple. He seemed to be capable of only a single motive, namely, a passion for God. That ruled and filled him. So completely did it dominate him that many regarded him as a useless, ineffective man, while others said he was mad. His idea of God seems crude and thin to a Christian; yet it had mastered him; and, when we follow that clue, every detail of his character and life falls into place. For this end he became a sannyāsī, renouncing caste, marriage, property, money. In order that his renunciation might be utterly real, he put himself through a tremendous discipline of repression, until his hatred of money had become so instinctive that his body would shrink back convulsively if he were touched with a coin, when asleep;[2]

[1] *Rāmakṛishna*, 58. [2] *My Master*, 61.

and he had so conquered the sex instinct that every woman was to him a mother. On this latter point P. C. Mozoomdar,[1] the Brāhma, says:

> For long years, therefore, he says, he made the utmost efforts to be delivered from the influence of women. His heart-rending supplications and prayers for such deliverance sometimes uttered aloud in his retreat on the river-side, brought crowds of people who bitterly cried when he cried, and could not help blessing him and wishing him success with their whole hearts.

This same passion for God, taken along with the Hindu idea of God, will explain also the more curious and eccentric points of his character. One of his own sayings is:

> A true devotee who has drunk deep of the Divine Love is like a veritable drunkard, and, as such, cannot always observe the rules of propriety.[2]

It is from this point of view that we can understand another of Mozoomdar's statements about him:

> His speech at times was abominably filthy.[3]

He believed God in His true essence to be impersonal, unknowable, beyond the reach of man. On the other hand, every human being, indeed everything that is, is a manifestation of God. Everything that happens is, in a sense, done by Him:

> God tells the thief to go and steal, and at the same time warns the householder against the thief.[4]

God is thus so truly all that is, that in Him moral distinctions become obliterated.[5] Here we get a glimpse of the radical distinction between Christianity and Hinduism. Another point in his conduct will enable us to understand still more clearly. Since every human being is a manifestation of God,

[1] *Paramahaṁsa Rāmakṛishṇa*, 13. [2] *Rāmakṛishṇa*, 121.
[3] *Ib.*, 62. [4] *Ib.*, 103. [5] *Gospel of R.*, 72.

if Rāmakṛishṇa happened to meet an unfortunate, he would bow down before her in adoration. Contrast with this the mind of Christ, who loved the unfortunate as a child of God, but could not be content, unless she came to repentance.

Like every ordinary Hindu, Rāmakṛishṇa regarded all deities as manifestations of the impersonal Supreme. He recognizes the goddess Kālī as one of the chief manifestations of God. She was to him the divine mother of the universe, and he worshipped her more than any other divinity. He worshipped her by means of idols; for he implicitly believed the Hindu doctrine, that the divinity fills every one of his own idols with his presence.[1] He also held the ordinary Hindu idea of the guru. Here is one of his sayings:

> The disciple should never criticise his own Guru. He must implicitly obey whatever his Guru says. Says a Bengali couplet:
>
> Though my Guru may visit tavern and still,
> My Guru is holy Rai Nityānanda still.[2]

He was thus a true Hindu, and was ready at any moment to defend the whole of Hinduism.

Thus far Rāmakṛishṇa was simply a very devoted Hindu. Had there been nothing more in him, he might have lived at any time during the last two thousand years. There have been multitudes of men like him in India. But the living forces which are making the new India pressed in upon him from every side. Though he had no English education, the new thought came to him by many channels. Christianity was demanding acceptance from Hindus, claiming to be the one religion for the whole world, urging its ethics on all men. Islam was also present, but far less active. What was his response to the situation? He declared that all religions were true, that in their inner essence they were identical, and that

[1] See above, p. 189, and *Gospel of R.*, 187. [2] *Rāmakṛishṇa*, 133.

each man should remain in the religion in which he had been born:

> A truly religious man should think that other religions also are paths leading to the truth.[1]
>
> Every man should follow his own religion. A Christian should follow Christianity, a Mohammedan should follow Mohammedanism, and so on. For the Hindus the ancient path, the path of the Aryan Rishis, is the best.[2]

4. One of Rāmakṛishṇa's disciples, a wealthy Calcutta man, named Surendranath Mitter, was keenly interested in the result produced on Keshab Chandra Sen by his master's teaching on this point,[3] and employed a painter to produce a symbolical picture, embodying the idea of the harmony of all religions and of the part played by Rāmakṛishṇa in introducing it to Keshab.[4] I have not been able to discover with certainty when the picture was painted, but it was already in existence on the 27th of October, 1882.[5] When it was shewn to Keshab, he exclaimed, "Blessed is the man who conceived the idea of this picture." At a later date the picture was reproduced and published as a supplement to *Unity and the Minister*, a weekly paper representing one of the sub-divisions into which the Church of the New Dispensation split up after the great leader's death. This picture is reproduced here. In the background are a Christian church, a Muḥammadan mosque, and a Hindu temple. In front of the church stand Keshab and Rāmakṛishṇa, Keshab carrying the symbol of the New Dispensation described above,[6] and Rāmakṛishṇa calling Keshab's attention to the group of figures arranged in front of the mosque and the temple. In the middle of this group Christ and Chaitanya, a Bengali religious leader of the sixteenth century,[7] are represented dancing together, while a

[1] *Rāmakṛishṇa*, 153. [2] *Ib.*, 177. [3] See above, pp. 57–8.
[4] *Janmabhumi*, Āsāṛha, 1317 Sal.
[5] *Gospel of R.*, 132, 164. [6] P. 56, above. [7] P. 293, below.

PLATE X

Rāmakṛishṇa teaching Keshab the Harmony of All Religions

Muslim, a Confucian, a Sikh, a Parsee, an Anglican clergyman and various Hindus stand round them, each carrying some symbol of his faith. It seems to me that nothing could be more fitting (for I am writing in Oxford and the subject is most apposite) than to dedicate this interesting piece of theological art to the versatile author of *Reunion All Round.*

5. It was his teaching on the religions that laid hold of his disciples. He impressed all who came in contact with him as a most sincere soul, a God-intoxicated man; but what distinguished his message from the teaching of others was his defence of everything Hindu and his theory that all religions are true. This gave his teaching a universalistic turn, and provided the ordinary Hindu with a defence which he could use to meet Christian criticism and the Brāhma Samāj.

His personal influence over all who came within his range was very remarkable. Mozoomdar says:

> My mind is still floating in the luminous atmosphere which that wonderful man diffuses around him whenever and wherever he goes. My mind is not yet disenchanted of the mysterious and indefinable pathos which he pours into it whenever he meets me.[1]

Over his personal disciples he exercised a still more wonderful power. Their love and reverence for him was boundless. They worshipped him. Vivekānanda once remarked to a well-known Calcutta citizen of high character, Dr. Sircar:

> We look upon the Master as a Person who is *like* God.[2]
> We offer to Him worship *bordering* on divine worship.[3]

Here we have ancient Hindu guru-worship checked in Vivekānanda's mind by the Christian teaching he had got in his college course. Apart from Christian influence, he would have said, "He is God, and we worship him as God."

[1] *Paramahaṁsa Rāmakṛishṇa*, 1. [2] *Gospel of R.*, 357. [3] *Ib.*, 360.

The picture given of him by his disciples is very pleasing and very vivid; yet there are not many personal traits to notice. Though he was a sannyāsī, he dressed like an ordinary Bengali, and lived like one.[1] Mozoomdar in describing him uses the words:

a child-like tenderness, a profound visible humbleness, an unspeakable sweetness of expression and a smile that I have seen on no other face that I can remember.[2]

He knew no Sanskrit and scarcely any English. His disciples would smile when he used the English words, "Thank you." Indeed he had no scholarly knowledge even of Bengali.[3] But his conversation was full of quaint, good sense, expressed in vivid homely phrases, and lighted up here and there with a broad kindly humour. He was fond of certain short alliterative phrases, which he had coined,[4] expressive of his main religious ideas, such as:

Nāham, nāham: Tuhu, tuhu.

that is, "Not I, not I, Thou, Thou." He was no formal teacher. Indeed he used to say, "I am nobody's teacher: I am everybody's disciple."[5] He was a conversationalist, pouring out his riches like Samuel Johnson.

6. After Rāmakṛishṇa's death,[6] his chief disciples decided that they must devote their lives to the spread of his teaching. So a group of them renounced the world and became sannyāsīs. Amongst these by far the most prominent has been Narenda Nath Datta, who took the name Vivekānanda, when he became a sannyāsī. Svāmī is a title of respect given to any sannyāsī. He was a Bengali, belonging to Calcutta, a Kāyastha by caste, born on the 9th of January, 1862.[7] He received

[1] *Gospel of R.*, 133. [2] *Paramahaṁsa Rāmakṛishṇa*, 3.
[3] *Rāmakṛishṇa*, 62; *Gospel of R.*, 194. [4] *Gospel of R.*, 196–7.
[5] *Ib.*, 337. [6] On the 15th March, 1886.
[7] See a brief biography published by Natesan, Madras.

a good English education, taking his degree from a Mission College in Calcutta, and distinguishing himself in philosophy. As a student, he came a good deal under the influence of the Brāhma Samāj. He had a fine voice, and wherever he went was in great request for the singing of Bengali hymns. After taking his degree, he began the study of law; but, early in 1882, an uncle took him to see Rāmakṛishṇa; and that moment became the turning-point in his life.

From the first Rāmakṛishṇa singled him out as one destined to do great things for God, and gave him a great deal of attention. On his master's death he became a sannyāsī, as we have said, and then spent some six years in retirement on the Himalayas, doubtless studying and thinking about many things. Among other places he is said to have visited Tibet, in order to study Buddhism. In 1892 he emerged from his retirement, and toured all down the western coast of India, going as far south as Trevandrum, whence he turned north again and went to Madras. Preparations were being made at that time for holding the Parliament of Religions in Chicago. Some friends in Madras proposed that Vivekānanda should be sent to the Parliament to represent Hinduism. Funds were collected, and he travelled to America by way of Japan.

The gathering was held in September, 1893; and Vivekānanda made a great impression, partly by his eloquence, partly by his striking figure and picturesque dress, but mainly by his new, unheard-of presentation of Hinduism. We shall deal with his thought later; so that we need not delay over it here. The following quotations from American papers show how far those who were most deeply influenced by the Svāmī went:

> He is an orator by divine right, and his strong, intelligent face in its picturesque setting of yellow and orange was hardly less interesting than those earnest words, and the rich, rhythmical utterance he gave them.[1]

[1] *The New York Critique.*

> Vivekananda is undoubtedly the greatest figure in the Parliament of Religions. After hearing him we feel how foolish it is to send missionaries to this learned nation.[1]

He stayed some time in America, lecturing and founding Vedānta societies in several places. Two American disciples joined him, Madame Louise, who became Svāmī Abhayānanda, and Mr. Sandsberg, who became Svāmī Kṛipānanda. From America he crossed to England, where he was joined by his most notable disciple, Miss Margaret Noble, who took the name Sister Niveditā (*i.e.* dedicated).

In January, 1897, the Svāmī arrived in Colombo with his small group of Western disciples, and from there made a triumphal progress all the way up through India. He was everywhere acclaimed by vast audiences of Hindus as the Saviour of the ancient faith; and it was generally believed that America and England were being rapidly converted to Hinduism. There was no limit to the thousands of disciples with which the Svāmī was credited.

He at once set about organizing regular work. Two monasteries were opened, one at Belur, near Calcutta, the other at Mayavati on the Himalayas, near Almora. These monasteries are meant to receive young men who have become sannyāsīs of the Rāmakṛishṇa Mission, as it is called, and to give them a training for their work. The monastery at Belur near Calcutta is the headquarters of all the work. The same year one of the most outstanding features of the Rāmakṛishṇa Mission, its philanthropic activity, was started. There was widespread famine in India then; and Vivekānanda was able to gather money, and to organize a number of enthusiastic followers at several centres for the relief of the famine-stricken.

But in 1898 Vivekānanda's health gave way, and he was

[1] *The New York Herald.*

advised to go to Britain and America for a change. He and Sister Niveditā sailed together. He spent but a short time in England, and went on to America. The climate of California helped his strength a good deal, and he soon began work again. It was at this time that the Vedānta Society was founded in San Francisco, and also the *Śānti Āśrama*, the Peace Retreat. He went to New York, and founded the Vedānta society there. It was then arranged that he should attend the Congress of Religions, which was to be held in Paris in 1900. After attending the Congress, he returned to India, but in very poor health.

Yet he could not be still; and, during the next two years, he organized a good deal of fresh work. A third monastery was founded, in Madras; and centres of philanthropic effort were formed in Madras, Benares and in the Murshidabad district of Bengal. He was deeply impressed with the need of work and self-sacrifice. He would not deliver lectures, but did all he could to set men to work.[1] He passed away rather unexpectedly on the 4th of July, 1902, at the early age of forty.

We may grasp his message most distinctly, if we take it in four parts.

A. All religions are true and good; and, therefore, every man ought to remain in his own religion.

B. God is impersonal, unknowable, non-moral. He is manifested in the whole world, in all men, in all gods and in all incarnations. The human soul is truly divine. All men are saints. It is a calumny and a sin to say that any human being can be guilty of sin. Idolatry is a very healthy and spiritual form of worship. Every particle of Hinduism is of value and must be retained. The reformers are mistaken. In trying to uproot the weeds, they are tearing up the precious wheat also:

[1] *ISR.*, XXI, 114.

The old ideas may be all superstition, but within these masses of superstition are nuggets of gold and truth. Have you discovered means by which to keep that gold alone, without any of the dross?[1]

C. Hindu civilization, since it springs from the oldest and noblest of religions, is good, beautiful and spiritual in every part. The foreigner fails altogether to understand it. All the criticism of European scholars is erroneous, and everything that missionaries say on the subject is wickedly slanderous. The Hindu nation is a spiritual nation. It has taught the world in the past, and will yet teach the whole world again.

D. European nations and Western civilization are gross, material, selfish and sensual; and therefore their influence is most seriously degrading to the Hindu. It is of the utmost importance that every Hindu should do all in his power to defend his religion and civilization, and save Hindu society from the poison of Western influence. Yet the Hindu requires to use Western methods and Western education. Nay, the Hindu must even give up his vegetarianism, and become a meat-eater, it may be a beef-eater, in order to become strong, and build up a powerful civilization once more on the soil of India.

Vivekānanda has no historical conscience whatsoever. He is ready to re-write the whole history of antiquity in a paragraph, to demonstrate in a sentence that China, in the East, and Greece and Rome, in the West, owed all their philosophical acumen and every spiritual thought they had to the teachers of ancient India. He learned the appeal to history from his Western education; but there is not the faintest reflection in his writings of the accuracy and careful research which are the very life-breath of modern scholarship.

He exercised a fine influence on young India in one direction. He summoned his fellow-countrymen to stand on their

[1] *My Master*, 13.

own feet, to trust themselves and to play the man; and his words were not without fruit.

It is striking to note the harvest that appeared in Vivekānanda from the seed sown by his master Rāmakṛishṇa. The latter dropped every moral restriction when thinking of God and his manifestations. Vivekānanda frankly drew the natural inference: "sin is impossible; there is no such thing as human responsibility; man can do no wrong." Rāmakṛishṇa's indiscriminate acceptance and uncritical defence of everything Hindu expanded in his disciple into unbounded laudation of everything Indian; and, while Vivekānanda himself bears witness that his master was genial and kindly, and condemned no one, the disciple, not unnaturally, was led by his unmixed praise of everything Hindu to the most violent and unjust condemnation of everything Western.

The final outcome of Vivekānanda's teaching will be discussed in another connection.[1]

7. Vivekānanda's English disciple, Sister Niveditā, settled in a small Hindu house in the northern part of Calcutta, and lived there a life of simple service for several years, visiting the Hindu homes around about her, conducting a school for girls in her own house, and leading young Hindus into practical service. She was a woman of deep romantic feeling and of considerable literary power. She readily picked up her master's method of glorifying Hinduism and Hindu life, and far exceeded him. Her chief work, *The Web of Indian Life*, shows, on the one hand, most remarkable sympathy with both the ideals and the actualities of Hindu life, and proves to every capable reader what a priceless help towards interpretation sympathy is, but, on the other hand, contains such exaggerated language in praise of Hindu customs and institutions, that many orthodox Hindus have protested against the book as altogether untrustworthy and as thoroughly unhealthy read-

[1] Below, pp. 357–8.

ing for young Hindus themselves. Yet Sister Niveditā had her reward. Though her book is unwise, she loved the Hindu people and served them; and they gave her their love. At her death, in October, 1911, there was an extraordinary outburst of feeling in the Hindu community of Bengal.

8. The work of the Rāmakṛishṇa Mission [1] has grown slowly since Vivekānanda's death. There have been no such results as one would have expected to spring from the unbounded enthusiasm with which the Svāmī was welcomed, when he returned from America. He summoned his countrymen to practical service, to self-sacrificing work for India. Had the myriads who acclaimed him really responded to his call, the work would soon have attained very great dimensions; but the truth is that ancient Hinduism does not teach the duty of service at all, and that all that the average educated Hindu wants is to get somebody to assure him that Hinduism is as good as Christianity, and that he does not need to become a Christian. Having heard this, amidst the flare of trumpets with which Vivekānanda returned from America, the average man gave a sigh of relief, and returned to his vegetating life as an ordinary Hindu. Vivekānanda's call to self-sacrificing service was just another of those troublesome appeals which they had heard over and over again from the missionaries and the Brāhma leaders; and they paid no more attention to it. Only a few responded; and these continue to carry on the work. There are now five monasteries, Belur, near Calcutta, Benares, Allahabad, Mayavati, on the Himalayas, and Bangalore. These institutions are meant for the residence and training of sannyāsīs. The whole mission is governed from the Belur monastery. At Benares, Hardwar, Allahabad and Brindaban, the four chief centres of Hindu pilgrimage, permanent charitable institutions, called *Sevāśrams*, Homes of Service, have grown up. Care for the poor

[1] It is described in the *Hindoo Patriot*, October 14, 1912.

and medical relief are their chief activities. Educational work is also attempted in a few places; and the mission is sensitive to need and ready to help, when distress arises through famine, plague or flood. There is a desire in the mission to build up a large educational activity, but this has not yet been found possible. Vivekānanda wished to combine Western and Hindu education.

The founder of the Ramakrishna Mission, Svāmī Vivekānanda, had his own ideal of national education. For, to him, as is evident from his Indian utterances, the national ideal was a thing already realized within. It is claimed by many, like the late Sister Nivedita, that he was the first representative of the synthetic culture which India must evolve, if she is to live.[1]

Vivekānanda's influence still lives in America. There are societies that teach Hinduism in various ways in New York, Boston, Washington, Pittsburg and San Francisco. His influence seems to be far stronger in San Francisco than anywhere else. There is a picturesque Hindu Temple there, in which classes are held and addresses given, and the literature of the mission sold. They have a little monthly magazine, called the *Voice of Freedom.* Two Svāmīs are in charge. There are three lectures every Sunday; and classes for the study of the *Gītā*, the Upanishads and Yoga are held on week days.

Vivekānanda started several magazines, which are still published in India. The *Brahmavādin*, which is published in Madras, and the *Prabuddha Bhārata*, which is published at Mayavati in the Himalayas, are both in English, and contain a good deal of useful matter on Hindu philosophy. A Bengali monthly, named *Udbodhan*, is published in Calcutta. Books written by Vivekānanda during his lifetime, and a few others, published by other members of the mission since then, are sold in the various centres.

[1] *The Hindoo Patriot*, October 14, 1912, p. 7.

LITERATURE. — LIFE: *Rāmakṛishṇa, His Life and Sayings*, by F. Max Müller, London, Longmans, 1910, 5*s*. (This book contains the best biography, and also a collection of his sayings.) *Gospel of Sri Ramakrishna*, according to M. (*i.e.* Prof. M. N. Gupta), Part I, Madras, Ramakrishna Mission, 1912, Rs. 2–8. (A picture of Rāmakṛishṇa's life with his disciples and his teaching: see above, p. 194.) *My Master* (a lecture), by Swami Vivekananda, Calcutta, Udbodhan Office, 1911, 8 as. VIVEKĀNANDA: *Swami Vivekananda, His Life and Teachings*, Madras, Natesan, 4 as. *Speeches and Writings of Swami Vivekananda*. Madras, Natesan, Rs. 2. NIVEDITĀ: *Sister Nivedita, A Sketch of her Life and Her Services to India*, Madras, Natesan, 4 as. *The Web of Indian Life*, by Sister Nivedita, London, Heinemann, 5*s*. An account of the Rāmakṛishṇa Mission appeared in the *Hindu Patriot* of October, 1912.

3. THEOSOPHY

Theosophy is a system of religion, science and practical life, first taught by Madame Blavatsky, and incorporated in a society founded by her and Colonel Olcott in New York in 1875, but carried much farther by Mrs. Besant and C. W. Leadbeater in recent years. It purports to be the final truth of the universe, taught in different lands and at different times by various founders of religion and teachers of philosophy, but revealed anew to Madame Blavatsky by certain Masters, or Mahātmas (*i.e.* Great Souls), said to live in Tibet and elsewhere. The system and the society are both of great interest because of the large literature which has sprung from the movement, and the very remarkable growth of the society in many parts of the world.

The attempt to write an unvarnished account of Theosophy is beset by a number of tantalizing difficulties. No trustworthy history of the movement, no reliable biography of the foundress, is in existence. Theosophic accounts both of Madame Blavatsky's life and of the history of the society are extremely unreliable.[1] Colonel Olcott and other leaders

[1] See Appendix, p. 447 ff.

of the movement themselves tell us with the utmost frankness that Madame Blavatsky was a liar, that she told lies at any time, both in fun and in earnest.[1] This habit of hers issued in two extraordinary myths, the story of the pretended Mahātmas in Tibet and their communications to her,[2] and the legend of her own virginity.[3] Since 1879 and 1885, respectively, these two myths have very seriously contaminated Theosophic literature. Every statement has to be checked by reference to other documents and authorities.

Fortunately, after her death, a number of letters, which she had written to two well-known Russian men of letters between 1874 and 1886, were published in Russia, and shortly afterwards were translated into English. These give us a great many peeps into her life. The first of these correspondents was M. A. N. Aksakoff, editor of the Leipzig *Psychische Studien*, who had long taken an interest in every kind of psychical question. Her letters to him run from the 28th of October, 1874, to the 6th of November, 1877, and there are a few from 1879 also. Her second Russian correspondent was M. V. S. Solovyoff, whose acquaintance she made in Paris in May, 1884. Her numerous letters to him all fall between that date and the spring of 1886. There is not the slightest question about the genuineness of these letters. They appeared originally in a series of articles, entitled *A Modern Priestess of Isis*, by M. Solovyoff in a Russian magazine. Madame Blavatsky's sister, Madame Jelihovsky, denied several of M. Solovyoff's own statements, but she did not challenge the authenticity of any of the documents which he had reproduced. The articles were published in book-form in Russia; and the book was then translated into English by Mr. Walter Leaf. Whoever wishes to understand Madame Blavatsky ought to read this brilliant and reliable work. We shall not use anything chal-

[1] *Hints on Esoteric Theosophy*, No. 1; *ODL.*, I, 264–5.

[2] P. 227, below.

[3] P. 260, below.

lenged by Madame Jelihovsky, and indeed shall rely almost entirely on the letters.

Similarly, for later periods, documentary evidence which enables the student to get somewhat nearer the facts, has become available in various ways. Thus, the full exposure of Judge would have been quite impossible, had it not been that one of the officials of the society, disgusted at the course of events, resigned, and then handed over copies of all the incriminating documents for publication;[1] and, in the Alcyone trials in Madras,[2] Mrs. Besant inadvertently handed over to the prosecution a bundle of letters written by Mr. Leadbeater, which threw much light on certain events.

It is very unfortunate that, at present, so far as I can make out, there is no scholar in England or America, outside the Theosophic circle itself, who has made any serious study of the literature and history of Theosophy. Hodgson, Coleman and Solovyoff are dead; and every scholar to whom I have spoken on the subject has said that the quality of Theosophic literature has altogether driven him away from the subject. This is greatly to be regretted.

I have had interviews with scores of people who are, or who were, Theosophists, and have learned much from them; but it is harder to get information of a helpful and reliable kind from Theosophists than from members of any other religious movement I have dealt with, except possibly the Rādhā Soāmis; and the pledge of secrecy exacted from those who join the Esoteric School makes it impossible to get light on Theosophic methods of occultism. I have learnt most of all from a few individuals who were once at the centre of things, but are now outside. Some have returned to Christianity, but most retain a larger or smaller amount of Theosophic belief.

I have been seriously hampered in writing my account

[1] See p. 270, below. [2] See pp. 276–7, below.

of Theosophy for want of space. An adequate outline of its history would fill the whole volume.

Madame Blavatsky

1. Helena Petrovna was born on the 12th of August, 1831, the daughter of Col. Peter Hahn, a member of a German family settled in Russia. She was connected with a number of the best Russian families. From her childhood she seems to have been a medium. Spiritualistic phenomena are said to have constantly attended her.[1] In 1848, when she was but seventeen, she married N. V. Blavatsky, a Russian official, a man a good deal older than herself,[2] but ran away from him three months after the marriage.

2. Of her life from 1848 to 1872 we have no connected and reliable account. It is clear that she travelled a great deal in many lands, but both dates and places are altogether doubtful. Two facts, however, are absolutely certain, both of great importance.

The first of these is that for many years she lived a very wild and evil life. Her relatives in Russia knew quite well the kind of life she led. M. Aksakoff wrote in the autumn of 1874, to Andrew Jackson Davis, an American journalist, interested in spiritualism:

J'ai entendu parler de Madame Blavatsky par un de ses parents, qui la dit un medium assez fort. Malheureusement ses communications ressentent de son moral qui n'a pas été des plus sévères.[3] (I have heard Madame Blavatsky spoken of by one of her relatives, who said she was rather a powerful medium. Unfortunately her communications bear marks of her morality, which has not been of the severest type.)

[1] Sinnett, *Incidents*, 33–37 (edition of 1913); Aksakoff in *MPI.*, 227.

[2] According to her story, he was nearer seventy than sixty in 1848 (Sinnett, *Incidents*, 39), but as he was still alive in 1892 (*MPI.*, 116), she must have greatly exaggerated his age.

[3] *MPI.*, 227.

Mr. Davis handed this letter to Madame Blavatsky herself to translate. Naturally the reference to her past caused her intense excitement; and she at once wrote a letter to M. Aksakoff from which we give a few sentences:

> Whoever it was told you about me, they told you the truth in essence, if not in detail. God only knows how I have suffered for my past. It is clearly my fate to gain no absolution upon earth. The past, like the brand of the curse of Cain, has pursued me all my life, and pursues me even here, in America, where I came to be far from it and from the people who knew me in my youth. . . . I hated hypocrisy in whatever form it shewed itself; ergo, I ran amuck against society and the established proprieties. Result: three lines in your letter, which have awakened all the past within me and torn open all the old wounds. . . .
>
> I have only one refuge left in the world, and that is the respect of the spiritualists of America, who despise nothing so much as 'free love.' [1]

Later she wrote again:

> I really cannot, just because the devil got me into trouble in my youth, go and rip up my stomach now like a Japanese suicide in order to please the mediums. My position is very cheerless; simply helpless. There is nothing left but to start for Australia and change my name for ever.[2]

In February, 1886, she sent a document, headed "My Confession," to M. Solovyoff, in which the following sentences occur:

> I have already written a letter to Sinnett *forbidding him* to publish my *mémoires* at his own discretion. I myself will publish them with all the truth. So there will be the *truth* about H. P. Blavatsky, in which psychology and *her own* and *others'* immorality and Rome and politics and all *her own* and *others'* filth once more will be set out to God's world. I shall conceal nothing. It will be a Saturnalia of the moral depravity

[1] *MPI.*, 228, 229, 230. Cf. also her later letters, 233, 268.
[2] *Ib.*, 268.

of mankind, this *confession* of mine, a worthy epilogue of my stormy life.[1]

Her sister, Madame Jelihovsky, also spoke and wrote to M. Solovyoff quite frankly on the subject.[2] Amongst her letters to Madame Coulomb [3] was one consisting of twelve closely written quarto pages, giving a detailed account of her life from 1851 to 1875. She spoke of it as a page which she wished to see "torn out of the book" of her life. For some considerable time she lived with a man named Metrovitch, and was known as Madame Metrovitch. There was also a boy whom she acknowledged as her son for several years; but in 1885, when she created the virginity myth, she told a new and wonderful tale about him.[4] There is thus the most irrefragable evidence that she lived a very immoral life for many years.

The other fact which stands out clear in these years is that in 1858 she returned to Russia for some time, and that spiritualistic phenomena followed wherever she went.[5]

3. From 1872 onward we can trace her life in outline without much difficulty. Some part of that year she spent in Cairo, endeavouring to make a livelihood by giving spiritualistic séances. There, she met an Englishwoman who later married a Frenchman, named M. Coulomb. This lady went to one of the séances, in the hope of hearing the voice of a dearly loved brother who had just died. The spirit-show was a complete failure, but the two women became friends. Madame Blavatsky was in great need of money, and the Englishwoman gave her a loan, which she was unable to repay during her stay in Egypt. In 1884, when the Coulomb letters made these facts public,[6] Madame Blavatsky denied them, but her

[1] *MPI.*, 181.
[2] *Ib.*, 193, 195, 202.
[3] See below, p. 239; also *Proceedings*, IX, 314–5.
[4] *MPI.*, 141.
[5] Sinnett, *Incidents*, chaps. III–VI.
[6] See below, p. 239.

own correspondence shews clearly that the séances were held and proved a failure.[1] A paragraph also appeared in *The Medium* for April 26, 1872, inviting mediums ready for engagements to apply to Madame Blawatsky (*sic*) in Cairo.

On the 7th of July, 1873, she arrived in New York, and settled down there. In her first letter to M. Aksakoff, written on the 28th of October, 1874, she said:

> I have been living in America for about a year and a half, and have no intention of leaving.[2]

She continued to reside in the States until the end of 1878, becoming a naturalized citizen in the interval. Clearly there was some reason for this decision to give up her wandering life and to settle down, not in Russia, but in an alien land. In her letters to M. Aksakoff she gives a clear intelligible reason for this policy. Her youth was now over; she was forty-two years of age. She wanted to escape from the results of her dissolute life; but that was impossible in Europe, above all in Russia, where her past was so well known.[3] So she decided to go to America "to be far from" the curse of her past life and "from the people who knew" her in her youth.[4]

No detailed account of how she spent her first fifteen months in America has been published. Events are clearly traceable only from October, 1874, onwards, when she began to correspond with M. Aksakoff. But her plan seems to have been to live by writing on spiritualism, which at that time was making a great noise in America. It is probable that it was this consideration which drew her to New York rather than to Melbourne, Calcutta, or some other city equally distant from the Russia which she longed for but

[1] *MPI.*, 131. [2] *Ib.*, 225. [3] *Ib.*, 228. [4] Above, p. 212.

dared not approach. At any rate, she made the acquaintance of several journalists and writers, one of whom was Andrew Jackson Davis, who has been already mentioned, and kept in close touch with spiritualism.

During the summer and autumn of 1874, a group of people interested in spiritualism had gathered round a family named Eddy, at Chittenden in the State of Vermont. Amongst those who were there to watch and to see what was to be seen was Henry Steel Olcott, who had served in the federal army during the Civil war and bore the title of Colonel, but who was now a journalist, and had been sent by the New York *Graphic* to report the happenings at Chittenden. Thither went Madame Blavatsky; and there, in October, she met Olcott.

On the 28th of the same month, at the advice of Davis, she wrote to M. Aksakoff, telling him of the great vogue of spiritualism in America, and asking whether she might not send him for publication from time to time Russian translations of articles on spiritist subjects appearing in American magazines. The proposal was accepted, and the correspondence continued for some years. In her first letter, the boom in spiritualism is represented as very great,[1] and the phenomena at Chittenden are described as most wonderful.[2]

The letter was scarcely despatched when Aksakoff's French letter to Davis about Madame Blavatsky's character already quoted,[3] arrived; and in her reply, an extract from which has been also quoted, she declares that she is a convinced spiritualist and has been such for more than ten years:

> I am a 'spiritist' and 'spiritualist' in the full significance of the two titles. . . . I have now been a spiritist for more than ten years, and now all my life is devoted to the doctrine.

[1] *MPI.*, 225. [2] *Ib.*, 226. [3] Above, p. 211.

I am struggling for it and trying to consecrate to it every moment of my life. Were I rich, I would spend all my money to the last farthing pour la propagande de cette divine vérité. But my means are very poor, and I am obliged to live by my work, by translating and writing in the papers.[1]

In later letters she wrote:

I was in deepest darkness, but I have seen the light, and to this light I have given myself up entirely. Spiritism is a great truth, and I will serve it to the grave. . . .

For spiritism I am ready to work night and day, so long as I have a morsel of bread, and that only because it is hard to work when one is hungry. . . .

I have already sacrificed myself for spiritualism, and in defence of my faith and the truth I am ready at any moment to lay my head on the block. . . .[2]

If you hear that the sinful Blavatsky has perished, not in the bloom of years and beauty, by some surprising death, and that she has dematerialised 'for ever,' then you will know that it is for spiritualism. In thee, Lord, do we put our trust, and we shall not be confounded for ever. . . .

I have quite ceased to get any letters from my aunts and sisters; they have evidently all forgotten me, and so much the better for them. I am no credit to them, to tell the truth. I shall now never go back again to Russia. My father is dead, nobody wants me, and I am altogether superfluous in the world. Here I am at least a human being; there, I am—Blavatsky. I know that everybody respects me here, and I am needed for spiritualism. Now the spirits are my brothers and sisters, my father and mother.[3]

From her letters it is plain that Olcott used every possible means to bring her into notoriety and popularity, raising her to the rank of Countess, mixing her up with "princes, boyards and imaginary governors-general,"[4] and making her out a second Livingstone in her travels in Africa and the

[1] *MPI.*, 228, 229. [2] *Ib.*, 236, 240–1. [3] *Ib.*, 242, 243. [4] *Ib.*, 244.

Soudan;[1] and she did him a like service. While the vogue of spiritualism lasted, things went well. Everything that they wrote was widely read, and they rose steadily in public estimation. There was a spirit who was peculiarly friendly with her. Here is what she says about him:

My John King alone is a sufficient recompense for all; he is a host in himself to me. And yet they call him the double of the medium, him and Crookes's Katie King. What sort of double can he be when the medium Williams is not here at all, but John King in his own person, with his own black beard and his white Chinese saucer-upside-down cap, going about here in America from one medium to another, and doing me the honour of visiting me incessantly, though he has not the least resemblance to me? No, John King is a personality, a definite, living, spiritual personality. Whether devil or good spirit, he is at all events a spirit, and not the medium's prototype.[2]

Olcott tells us that she had known John King since 1860, and had seen him and talked with him in different countries.[3]

But a peculiarly odious piece of fraudulent spiritism was exposed early in 1875, and public interest in the subject began to die down. The comrades tried various plans to keep their hold on the people, but it was useless. On May 24th, Madame Blavatsky writes:

Disaster has come upon us. Dr. Child has appeared in the character of the spiritist Antichrist, and, as the Judas of the seven councils, has destroyed spiritualism. Even the most advanced spiritualists begin to be afraid of public opinion, and their 'high respectability' induces many to continue to believe in spirits in secret only, and privately. . . .

I am ready to give my life for the spread of the sacred truth. Olcott is helping me as much as he can, both with his pen and with pecuniary sacrifices for the cause. He is as passionately

[1] *Ib.*, 245. [2] *Ib.*, 243. Cf. also 247; 253, 254.
[3] *People from the Other World*, 454.

devoted to spiritism as I am. But he is far from rich and has nothing to live on but his literary labours, and he has to keep a wife and a whole lot of children.

Olcott is sitting on heaps of his *People from the Other World*, like Marius on the ruins of Carthage, and thinking bitter things. Not a thousand copies of his book have been sold in five months.[1]

On the 18th of July she writes again:

Here, you see, is my trouble, to-morrow there will be nothing to eat. Something quite out of the way must be invented. It is doubtful if Olcott's 'Miracle Club' will help; I will fight to the last.[2]

Things were in a very bad way. Spiritualism was worked out, and the partners were threatened with want. Some new source of income had to be found. The Miracle Club was clearly meant to be something new and startling to catch public attention. But it did not succeed. Her letter of the 10th September is still very despondent.

4. Such were the circumstances in which the Theosophical Society was founded. Colonel Olcott gives us the dates and the steps in the following passage:

The formation of such a society was suggested by myself on the evening of September 7th, 1875, in the rooms of Madame Blavatsky, at 46 Irving Place, New York City, where a small gathering of her friends had assembled to listen to a discourse by a Mr. G. H. Felt on the lost canon of proportion of the Ancient Egyptians. My views as to the necessity of such a society were embodied in a short impromptu address and, receiving general assent, a motion was made by Mr. W. Q. Judge and adopted, *nem. con.*, that I be elected chairman of the meeting, and on my motion Mr. Judge was elected secretary. A committee to frame Bye-laws was chosen. A report of the proceedings including a digest of my little speech, was published in a local daily paper, copied into the *Spiritual Scientist*, of Boston, and thence transferred by Mrs. E. H. Britten into her large

[1] *MPI.*, 251, 250, 252. [2] *Ib.*, 253.

work, "Nineteenth Century Miracles" (p. 296), where the curious reader may find it in detail. No previous consultation had been held about the matter between Madame Blavatsky and myself or any body else; the suggestion was entirely unpremeditated and grew out of the discussion provoked by Mr. Felt's lecture. . . .

On the 17th November, the Society was launched as a perfected organization.[1]

Olcott became President, Judge Vice-president, and Madame Blavatsky Corresponding Secretary. To her friend in Russia Madame Blavatsky wrote on the 20th of September:

Olcott is now organising the Theosophical Society in New York. It will be composed of learned occultists and cabbalists, of philosophes Hermétiques of the nineteenth century, and of passionate antiquaries and Egyptologists generally. We want to make an experimental comparison between spiritualism and the magic of the ancients by following literally the instructions of the old Cabbalas, both Jewish and Egyptian. I have for many years been studying la philosophie Hermétique in theory and practice, and am every day coming to the conclusion that spiritualism in its physical manifestations is nothing but the Python of Paracelsus, *i.e.*, the intangible ether which Reichenbach calls Od. The Pythonesses of the ancients used to magnetise themselves — read Plutarch and his account of the oracular currents, read Cornelius Agrippa, Paracelsus, the Magia Adamica of Eugenius Philalethes, and others. You will always see better, and can communicate with the spirits by this means[1] — self-magnetisation.[2]

On December 6th she wrote:

It is the same spiritualism, but under another name. Now you will see if we shall not start the most learned investigations. Our vice-treasurer, Newton, is a millionare, and president of the New York spiritualists.[3]

[1] *A Historical Retrospect*, 2.
[2] *MPI.*, 256–7. [3] *Ib.*, 265.

These are most instructive paragraphs. It is, above all, to be noted that the purpose of the Theosophical Society is "to make an experimental comparison between spiritualism and the magic of the ancients." There is as yet no mention of Buddhism or Hinduism. There is no suggestion that the foundress receives her wisdom in ample measure, without trouble, through "Masters" from the ancient sources. She still struggles forward by experimental comparison; and her occult communications are not with living Masters in Tibet, but with the spirits of the dead. "Mahātma Morya" has not yet appeared above the horizon. "John King" is still "the Master of her dreams."[1]

The facts are simple and natural. Madame Blavatsky had been a medium from childhood, and had practised spiritualism since 1858, if not from an earlier date, though it does not appear that she ever worked as a hired medium. She started a spiritualist show in Cairo in 1872. She lived by spiritualist writing, and made the most serious protestations of belief in spiritualism from 1873 to September, 1875. The Miracle Club and the Theosophic Society were successive attempts to start something new and successful, when public interest in spiritualism declined. Theosophical doctrine at a later date became a blend of Buddhism, Hinduism and various forms of occultism; but, when first launched, it was merely an addition of the magic and mysticism of Egypt and of mediæval Judaism to spiritualism, with a view to stimulating the jaded appetite of the people of New York.

It is clear that she had been interested to some extent in all these mysterious things for years. She was a woman of most unusual temperament, possessing the powers of the medium, the clairvoyant, the clairaudient and probably also of the automatic writer. She had met "Eliphaz Lévy" in

[1] *MPI.*, 254. See below, p. 447.

Paris; and she had probably given some attention to juggling, devil-dancing and such like in Egypt and the East. The following sentences are probably quite reliable. We should not have had this curious passage in her letters at all, had it not been that her correspondent took in the American papers, and she felt she must apologize once more for Colonel Olcott's outrageous exaggerations:

> In a detailed account of the story of Katie King Olcott makes out of me something mysteriously terrible, and almost leads the public to suspect that I have either sold my soul to the devil or am the direct heiress of Count Germain and Cagliostro. Do not believe it; I have merely learnt in Egypt and Africa, in India and in the East generally, a great deal of what other people do not know. I have made friends with dervishes, and I do indeed belong to one mystic society, but it does not follow that I have become an Apollonius of Tyana in petticoats.[1]

She now began to study modern works on occultism seriously. About the same time she began to draw away from her old full belief in spiritualism and to hint that it was not spirits, but merely "shells" that caused the marvels. This theory comes from "Eliphaz Lévy." He taught that when a man dies, the spirit departs completely, leaving behind in this world only an empty "shell," which, however, has the power of producing phenomena.

Five months before the foundation of the Theosophical Society, on the third of April, 1875, Madame Blavatsky married in Philadelphia an Armenian, a Russian subject, named Michael Bettalay.[2] Yet N. B. Blavatsky was still

[1] *MPI.*, 246–7. The date is the 12th of April, 1875.

[2] The account of this marriage given by Olcott in *ODL.*, I, 54–57, having been written after the creation of the virginity myth (see below, p. 260), cannot be trusted. He is wrong even with the date. Solovyoff (*MPI.*, 165) tells how Madame once described the match to him. For the end of the marriage see below, p. 226.

alive; and there had been no divorce. It was a case of bigamy pure and simple. Doubtless she said she was a widow; for she practised that piece of deceit for many years. She put down her age in the marriage-register as thirty-six, while she was actually forty-three.[1]

The new society was scarcely started when serious trouble arose from her old spiritualist allies; for they felt that she was faithless to them. She had publicly declared that the spirits had brought her a medal and clasp from her father's grave, and Olcott had published in his *People from the Other World* a drawing of the medal and clasp. This enabled the medium Home to trace her antecedents and to obtain information about her private life. He had also got to the bottom of some of her fraudulent spiritualistic phenomena. He then attacked her publicly on both counts.[2]

The new society went fairly well for a time, and then interest steadily waned. Yet the comrades held on, never allowing the organization to fall to pieces.[3]

5. For two years Madame Blavatsky toiled at her new studies, and on the 2nd of October, 1877, her *Isis Unveiled* was published. It is a really noteworthy book, and that for two reasons. First, it was the earliest vigorous attempt made to defend the ancient religions against the harsh judgments still only too common at the time. Secondly, it took up a striking attitude to that great shady borderland which lies between jugglery and religion. Everything mysterious, weird, occult or magical, the unexplored powers of the human mind, and all suggestive, or symbolic words, acts or things, had an overpowering fascination for her. It

[1] I owe the facts in the text to Mr. W. Irving Lewis of the Young Men's Christian Association of Philadelphia, who did me the great kindness of searching the public records and copying out the details.

[2] *MPI.*, 267–8.

[3] *A Historical Retrospect*, 3.

is also clear that at a fairly early date she began to realize, in a more or less hazy way, certain facts which science has only recently perceived and acknowledged. The most important of these are (*a*) that spiritualism, clairvoyance, hypnotic trances, faith-healing and many of the phenomena of dreams and apparitions are, in essentials, identical with practices and occurrences which are vouched for in the literature of Classical and early Christian times, and with much which happens among modern savages; (*b*) that a considerable proportion of the marvels are genuine, whatever the ultimate explanation of their reality may be; and (*c*) that those who make such practices their profession sooner or later have recourse to fraud.[1] In the *Isis* these questions are not raised or treated in any scholarly fashion; and the evidence, good, bad and indifferent, is simply thrown down in indiscriminate heaps; so that the book as it stands is practically of no scientific value; yet the personal knowledge the authoress had of many of the practices dealt with, and her perception that there was something genuine in them, gave the book a certain value, and made it very attractive to many people.

One of the most notable characteristics of the book is its violent polemic against modern science and Christianity.

The authoress so wrote as to lead her readers to understand that she was a woman of vast learning, and that she had mastered all the great works on occultism in existence; while the truth is that all the learning it contains is borrowed, or rather stolen, from modern books; for in most cases there is no acknowledgment. Mr. Wm. Emmette Coleman of San Francisco spent three years in making an exhaustive analysis of the contents of Madame Blavatsky's writings. The following is his statement with regard to the *Isis:*[2]

[1] See art. *Clairvoyance* by Andrew Lang in *ERE.*

[2] *MPI.*, 354.

By careful analysis I found that in compiling *Isis* about 100 books were used. About 1,400 books are quoted from and referred to in this work; but, from the 100 books which its author possessed, she copied everything in *Isis* taken from and relating to the other 1,300. There are in *Isis* about 2,100 quotations from and references to books that were copied, at second-hand, from books other than the original, and of this number only about 140 are credited to the books from which Madame Blavatsky copied them at second-hand, The others are quoted in such a manner as to lead the reader to think that Madame Blavatsky had read and utilized the original works, and had quoted from them at first-hand, — the truth being that these originals had evidently never been read by Madame Blavatsky.

Col. Olcott stated in the *Theosophist*[1] that Madame Blavatsky's library contained about 100 books when she wrote the *Isis;* so that Mr. Coleman's critical judgment is confirmed. The following is a list of the books from which the largest numbers of quotations were taken:[2]

	PASSAGES
Dunlap's *Sod: the Son of the Man*	134
Ennemoser's *History of Magic*, English Trans.	107
Demonologia	85
Dunlap's *Spirit History of Man*	77
Salverte's *Philosophy of Magic*, English Trans.	68
Dunlap's *Sod: the Mysteries of Adoni*	65
Des Mousseaux's *Magie au Dix-neuvième Siècle*	63
Des Mousseaux's *Hauts Phênomènes de la Magie*	45
King's *Gnostics*, 1st edition	42
Supernatural religion	40
Mackenzie's *Masonic Cyclopaedia*	36
Zeller's *Plato and the Old Academy*	35

There are some students who, while recognizing frankly that the bulk of the *Isis* is built out of materials from modern works, are yet inclined to think that it may be true, as was stated by Madame Blavatsky and Col. Olcott,

[1] April, 1893, p. 387 f. [2] *MPI.*, 356.

that large sections of the book were written automatically. If this be true, then the explanation must be that her subconscious mind had retained all that she had read on these subjects, and gave out the materials when each fit of automatic writing came on.

The book contains innumerable errors, many of them of the most rudimentary type. The commonest Sanskrit words are misspelt; the Buddhist doctrine of transmigration is grossly misrepresented; and the *Bhagavadgītā* is confused with the *Bhāgavata Purāṇa*. The following sentences give a sample of the scholarship of the book:

> Apart from the now-discovered fact that the whole story of such a massacre of the Innocents is bodily taken from the Hindu *Bagavedgitta*, and Brahmanical traditions, the legend refers, moreover, allegorically to an historical fact. King Herod is the type of Kansa, the tyrant of Madura.[1]

Yet, to-day, we are asked to believe that all this is the wisdom of the Mahātmas. When Madame Blavatsky went to India, an elaborate myth was created, to the effect that for many years she had been receiving her wisdom from these Masters in Tibet. Thus all who accept this myth are compelled to explain the *Isis* as an early exposition of orthodox Theosophy. As a matter of fact, it represents the state of the writer's mind in 1877: it does not teach the doctrine of reincarnation;[2] it teaches that man is a being of a threefold nature, while the orthodox doctrine makes him sevenfold; there is no mention of the great doctrine of brotherhood; and a great deal of the furious attack on Christianity is contrary to the professed standards of to-day.

6. About the time when the *Isis* was published, Home's *Lights and Shadows of Spiritualism* also appeared, and its exposures of her frauds agitated her so much, and influenced public opinion so seriously, that she decided to leave Amer-

[1] II, 199.
[2] Olcott acknowledges this frankly, *ODL.*, I, 278.

ica for ever and go to India. Here is how she wrote in December, 1877, two months after the publication of the *Isis:*

> It is for this that I am going for ever to India, and for very shame and vexation I want to go where no one will know my name. Home's malignity has ruined me for ever in Europe.[1]

Home's evidence must have been irrefragable; for Olcott did not attempt to meet it, though asked to do so.[2]

In anticipation of their voyage to India, Olcott wrote to a Hindu friend, whom he had met some time before on a voyage across the Atlantic, and through him got into correspondence with Svāmī Dayānanda Sarasvatī, the founder of the Ārya Samāj. As a result of an interchange of letters, the two societies were connected the one with the other. This continued after the Theosophists reached India; but finally they separated in anger.[3]

On the 25th of May, 1878, Madame Blavatsky was divorced from her Armenian husband.[4] Olcott says that the husband obtained the divorce on the ground of desertion.[5]

7. In December, 1878, "the Theosophical Twins," as Madame Blavatsky had named herself and Olcott, sailed from New York. They arrived in Bombay in January; and that city, for almost three years, was the headquarters of the society. Madame Coulomb and her husband, who had meantime lost all their money, reached Bombay late in the spring of 1880, and were established at headquarters as friends and assistants of Madame Blavatsky.

The opinions and the teaching of the Twins now became much more distinctively Indian than they had been in America. They declared themselves Buddhists, and entered into close relations with Buddhism in Ceylon.

The Theosophic Myth also began to take definite shape.

[1] *MPI.*, 278. [2] *Ib.*, 278. [3] *ODL.*, I, 394–407. Above, p. 110.
[4] P. 221, above. [5] *ODL.*, I, 57. Cf. *MPI.*, 165.

They diligently taught the existence of the Great White Brotherhood and their Lodge in Tibet. The theory took shape gradually, and some of the more showy parts have been added only recently. The completed myth is as follows: A large number of men have reached the stage of Adepts in the Wisdom; and many have become members of the Hierarchy which governs this world.[1] These beings are far beyond death and transmigration; yet they live upon earth, mostly in Tibet; and a few of them are willing to take as apprentices those who have resolved to devote themselves to humanity. Since they take pupils, they are known as Masters. On account of their greatness they are called Mahātmas, great souls. Madame Blavatsky, we are told, was selected from the whole human race in our days to receive the ancient wisdom from these Masters. Her own particular master was Mahātma Morya; but Koot Hoomi and others were also ready to help. From them she received Theosophy: it was in no sense her own creation. As far back as 1851 she had met Mahātma Morya, "the Master of her dreams";[2] she had spent seven years in unremitting study in Tibet; and in the intervening years the wisdom had been poured into her mind in amplest measure.

Our narrative has provided sufficient disproof of the myth. As late as 1874 she was neither Buddhist nor Theosophist, but a Spiritualist, and was ready at any moment to lay her head on the block in defence of her faith.[3] Instead of learning from a living Master, she was the confidant of a disembodied spirit, John King.[4] Even when the Theosophical Society was founded, there was no mention of India but only of the Kabbala and the Hermetic system.[5]

[1] See below, pp. 279–80. [2] P. 447, below. [3] Pp. 215–6, above.
[4] P. 217, above. [5] P. 219, above.

The two travelled a great deal in various parts of India, and were usually received by the Hindu community with acclamation. The society steadily grew in numbers and popularity, largely as a result of the new theory of the Masters. For, wherever they went, miraculous events, which they called "phenomena," appeared; and Madame Blavatsky attributed all to her Masters, or to the occult knowledge she had derived from them. If some prominent European were inquiring about Theosophy, a letter from Koot Hoomi would be sure to fall on his head. Telegrams from the Masters would come tumbling through the air — "precipitated" in Theosophic phrase — but, strangely enough, bearing the stamp of the British Telegraph office. The Masters shewed themselves now and then in one of their bodies to selected people. Lost articles were found, and new things arrived in unheard-of ways. Half a cigarette, or a lock of Madame Blavatsky's hair, would be transported from one place to another by "occult" means. Probably a percentage of the phenomena were genuine, as we should expect in the case of a woman of Madame Blavatsky's powers; but no carefully sifted evidence has ever been given for any of them; while evidence exists which proves clearly that many of them were fraudulent; and, as to the Masters, nothing worth the name of evidence has ever been produced for their existence.[1]

8. One of the most famous occurrences took place at Simla. There was a dinner-party there one evening, in the house of Mr. A. O. Hume, a distinguished Indian Civilian, holding very high office under Government. After dinner it was proposed that Madame Blavatsky should give an example of her powers. After some talk she asked Mrs. Hume whether she had lost anything she would like very much to recover. In reply she described

[1] P. 447, below.

a brooch, which some little time before had passed out of the family. Madame Blavatsky indicated a spot in the garden where they might look for it. They looked, and the brooch was found.

Mr. and Mrs. Hume accepted the occurrence as a genuine occult phenomenon. It was described in glowing terms in the papers; and it has been continuously used by Theosophists ever since as evidence of the truth of their system. Yet the explanation is simple and undeniable. The truth came out in the following way:

The publication of the incident in the *Pioneer* gave rise to a good deal of discussion in the daily papers of the period. The *Englishman* pointed out a number of awkward lacunæ in the account given, and was especially anxious to know something of the "person" who had allowed the brooch "to pass out of their possession." It remarked —

"There is nothing to show to whom Mrs. Hume's friend, to whom she had given the brooch, parted with it. It might have been to some one who had communicated the fact and given the brooch to Madame. A very slight hint in the conversation might have turned Mrs. Hume's thoughts, almost unconsciously, towards her lost brooch," etc.

The *Bombay Gazette*, of October 13th, 1880, after noticing this article, went on —

"We can furnish the *Englishman* with a small item of intelligence. At the end of last and the commencement of this year, a young gentleman who had resided at Simla previously, and was, we believe, well known to the Hume family, sojourned for some months in Bombay, and was part of the time a guest of Madame Blavatsky at Girgaum. The latter lady's connection with this gentleman may or may not have had anything to do with the affair of the brooch, though to our mind it is as probable as that the presence of the brooch in the flower bed was due to 'occult' phenomena."

Three days later a correspondent of *The Times of India* wrote —

"It may interest some of your readers on the other side of

India to learn that some months ago an individual who had been immediately connected with some of the members of Mr. Hume's family at Simla arrived in Bombay. He was, I believe, hospitably received by Madame Blavatsky, if, indeed, he did not spend some weeks at her house in Girgaum, and when he left for England eventually, the arrangements for his passage were made through the agency of Colonel Olcott."

All this is very suggestive; but still more so is a pretty idyll narrated by the *Civil and Military Gazette* a month or two later:—

"Once upon a time a certain Daphnis had received as a gage d'amour from his Chloe, a brooch, an ancestral gem, formerly the property of Chloe's Mamma, which probably poor Chloe considered would in the course of happy time revert to her possession, when Daphnis and all that was his should be her own. But the course of true love never did run smooth, and the unhappy Daphnis, separated from Chloe, and driven by impecuniosity, deposited his pretty gift with an accommodating pawn-broker—for a consideration—meaning doubtless in future time to redeem the precious pledge. The trinket chanced, however, to attract the notice of a very famous spiritualist and medium, a lady who dealt in mysteries of psychic force and powers of disintegration and reintegration of matter. There is nothing to prevent a spiritualist, however magically endowed, from dealing also in mundane affairs after the usual humdrum and worldly fashion, and in this instance the famous lady chose to achieve the possession of the object of her fancy by the ordinary method of paying for it. Time rolled on, and it happened in the fulness thereof that the celebrated medium and Chloe's Mamma became acquainted, and under some circumstances, which attained perhaps an undeserved notoriety, the brooch became again the property of its original possessor.[1]"

Two further points came out after this account was printed. Mr. Hormusji Seervai, a Bombay jeweller, saw an account of the miracle in the papers, and realized from the description of the brooch that he had repaired it for Madame

[1] *Collapse*, 46–7.

Blavatsky.[1] Finally, the Rev. George Patterson, when on a visit to Bombay at the end of 1884, learned that Madame Blavatsky bought the pawn-ticket from the young man and redeemed the trinket.

There cannot be the slightest question as to the truth of the explanation; for not one of the facts has ever been so much as questioned. Mr. Hume himself publicly acknowledged that the famous phenomenon was a piece of well-planned fraud. Yet the Theosophical Society still uses this fraud, indefensible and undefended, as an example of occult agency.[2]

9. The Theosophic conception of the world, man and religion, which is nowhere given in the *Isis*, now gradually took shape. A brief analysis of the system is given below.[3] The main channel through which the fresh teaching found its way to Theosophists and the public was a series of long letters, which Madame Blavatsky averred were written and sent by the Master known as Koot Hoomi. Parts of these letters were published by Mr. Sinnett, an Englishman who was editor of the *Pioneer* and had become a Theosophist, in his books, *Esoteric Buddhism* and *The Occult World;* but much of the material was so poor that it had to be eliminated as rubbish.[4]

The Occult World was published in June, 1881. Mr. H. Kiddle of New York read the volume, and discovered in one of the letters a long passage copied almost verbatim from an address delivered by him at Lake Pleasant, August 15, 1880, and reported the same month in *The Banner of Light.* The date of the letter was two months later. When this was made public, a ridiculous reply, purporting to come

[1] Mr. Hodgson called and learned the facts from him personally. *Proceedings*, IX, 267.

[2] Sinnett's *Occult World*, pp. 66–79 (eighth edition, 1906).

[3] P. 278 ff.

[4] *Proceedings*, IX, 304.

from the Mahātma, was published, but no one was deceived. It was a case of deliberate plagiarism; and the final proof that it was so is found in the fact that in the more recent editions of *The Occult World* the passage is omitted.[1]

10. In December, 1882, the headquarters of the society were moved to Adyar, Madras. The Coulombs went along with the rest of the staff. M. Coulomb was Librarian, while his wife was Assistant Corresponding Secretary of the society. Besides that, Madame Coulomb acted as housekeeper, while her husband took charge of all repairs or additions to the buildings.

Madame Blavatsky occupied a large upper room in the main bungalow. See plan *B* on page 235. Early in 1883 a new room for occult purposes was built against the west wall of her room. There were two windows in the west wall. The south window, transformed into a door, became the ordinary entrance into the new room, which was called the Occult Room. The north window was removed, and a single layer of bricks filled up the aperture on the Occult Room side, leaving a recess about 15 in. deep on the other side, in Madame Blavatsky's bedroom. Part of the Occult Room was screened off by means of a curtain to form a small room for the Shrine. This was a wooden cupboard which, by means of two stout wires, was hung on the wall over the thin brick partition where the north window had been. In the Shrine was placed a portrait of the Master, Koot Hoomi. The doors of the Shrine were occasionally thrown open to Theosophists, that they might see the master's portrait. Hindus bowed reverently

[1] Let any one compare pp. 101–2 of the third edition with pp. 125–6 of the eighth edition. The plagiarized passage begins at "Ideas rule the world," and runs down to "speck of dirt." No acknowledgment of the omission is made. I owe this point to the Rev. John Hackett of Hampstead. Cf. also what occurs on p. 257, below.

before him and burned incense to him.[1] Both Indians and Europeans were accustomed to present their requests in the form of letters. The door would then be shut; and, when it was re-opened, a reply from the Master would be found within it. On one occasion a broken saucer was put in beside him. When the Shrine was re-opened, it was found intact. From this time onward many of the most striking phenomena were connected with the Shrine.

By the year 1884 the Theosophical Society had attained great proportions. There were over a hundred branches in India, and Hindus everywhere rejoiced in its work. Nor is their enthusiasm hard to understand. Theosophy provided a new defence of Hinduism for the thousands of educated men whose Western education had filled them with shivering doubts about their religion. It condemned Christian missionaries as impudent and ignorant intruders, who dared to criticize Hinduism and Buddhism, the two faiths which alone among all the religions of the world still taught clearly the truths of the Ancient Wisdom. All the great and good of every age had known and taught this wisdom; but, while it had been lost or beclouded elsewhere, Hinduism and Buddhism still retained its priceless principles; and in Tibet lived immortal teachers who were now, through Madame Blavatsky, revealing the Wisdom in all its glory to the whole human race. Yet even this most flattering proclamation would not have won its way as it did apart from the phenomena. There can be no question that it was these marvels that trumpeted the cause throughout India, and convinced the Hindu of the truth of the new propaganda.

11. In 1884 a great crisis in the history of Theosophy occurred. As Theosophists still assert that the whole was a missionary plot, and that Madame Blavatsky came out of it triumphant, we cannot dismiss it in a paragraph. In order

[1] Cf. the Rādhā Soāmis and the Deva Samāj, pp. 170 and 179, above.

A. JUDGE'S PLAN, ORIGINAL SIZE

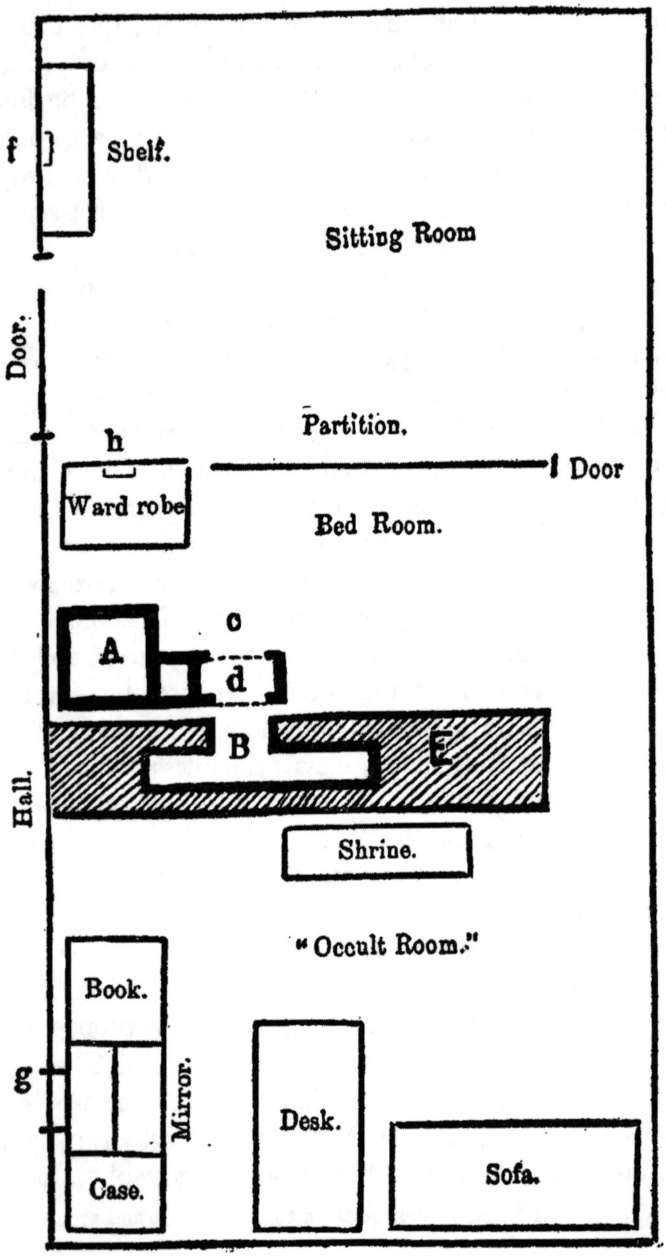

B. HODGSON'S PLAN, ⅗ OF ORIGINAL SIZE

PLAN OF OCCULT ROOM WITH SHRINE AND SURROUNDINGS

(From measurements taken by R. Hodgson, assisted by statements of Theosophic witnesses)

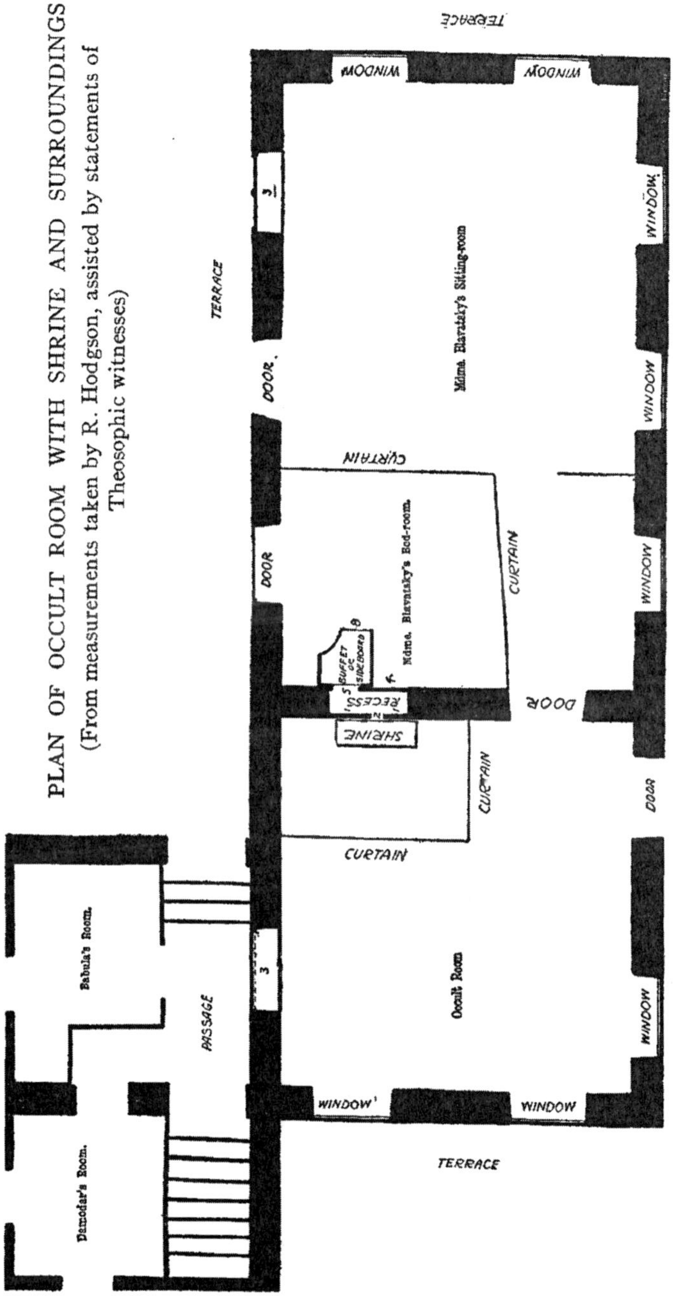

to place our readers in a position to judge for themselves, we shall give, in as brief a form as possible, an orderly outline of the significant events of the crisis and shall also indicate where the detailed evidence produced on both sides may be seen and examined.

a. On the 21st of February, 1884, Madame Blavatsky, Colonel Olcott and a young Calcutta Brāhman, Mohini Mohan Chatterji, sailed from Bombay for Europe. By Madame Blavatsky's explicit instructions, the Coulombs were left in charge of her rooms at the headquarters, Madras. They were to reside in them, and to look after her furniture and dogs. No one was to disturb them. There is the best evidence possible for these statements. The written instructions have been published;[1] and the following is a letter written by Madame Blavatsky, and printed in Dr. Hartmann's pamphlet published in September:[2]

> 46 Rue Notre Dame des Champs,
> Paris,
> April, 2–84.
>
> She swore to me that she would take care of my rooms, only asking me to let it be known that she alone had the right over all, and would have and keep the key. Having told Dr. Hartmann that he was welcome to my books and my desk in my absence, she made a vow when alone with me, and declared that if I allowed one single person to have access to my rooms, she would answer for nothing; — that the 'shrine' would be desecrated, etc.[3]

Damodar, a Hindu who had become a Theosophist and was one of Madame Blavatsky's secretaries, had the keys of the Occult Room and the Shrine.[4] Only these three had free access to the penetralia at headquarters. The affairs of the society were left by Colonel Olcott, the President, in the hands of a Committee of seven.

[1] *Collapse*, 19.
[2] Below, p. 240.
[3] *Report of Observations*, 32.
[4] *Proceedings*, IX, 225, 373–4.

b. On the 29th of February one member of this Committee, Dr. Hartmann by name, arrived at headquarters; and two or three days later a meeting of the Committee was held. In order that they might sit in quiet, Dr. Hartmann proposed that they should meet in Madame Blavatsky's room upstairs; but, to his amazement, the Coulombs refused to give them admittance. The consequence was a bitter quarrel between the Coulombs, on the one side, and the members of the Committee and the other residents at headquarters, on the other. Madame Coulomb said that she had many secrets which she would tell, if they continued to molest her.[1] She said there were sliding panels in the walls by which phenomena were created, and secret panels in the Shrine, by mean of which the letters from the Master and other things were introduced from Madame Blavatsky's room behind. She also talked of the money which she had lent Madame Blavatsky in Egypt and which had not been repaid.[2] Hence Dr. Hartmann and others wrote to Madame Blavatsky and Colonel Olcott, complaining of the Coulombs.

So serious did matters become in the meantime, that the Committee decided to impeach them in an informal manner, and expel them from headquarters. But on March 22nd, while they were drawing up the charges against them, Damodar laid before them a letter,[3] which he declared had been brought from Koot Hoomi by a chela in his astral body, advising them not to turn out the Coulombs. Naturally, the Committee were rather upset to find such an authority interfering to save the traitors. Yet, in the face of a message direct from the Master, they dared not turn

[1] *Collapse*, 24, 25, 34 ff. She had spoken earlier to many people in the same strain.

[2] Above, p. 213.

[3] Given in full in *Proceedings*, IX, 278.

them out of doors. Consequently, as Dr. Hartman says, an armistice was concluded with them.

After the peace was patched up, the Coulombs, Mr. Lane Fox and Damodar went to Ootacamund for a holiday. Meanwhile, the letters despatched early in March, reached the founders in Paris; and they replied, in letters written on the 1st and 2nd of April, to the Coulombs and to others. These letters reached Madras on the 25th of April. On the 26th, the very day when the mail from Europe reached Ootacamund, a letter [1] purporting to come from the Master, and directed to Dr. Hartmann, was forwarded to the latter by Damodar, from Ootacamund. This letter said that the Coulombs were plotting. Therefore, when they returned from Ootacamund, the Committee decided to expel them. On the 17th of May, M. Coulomb gave up the keys he held, and several of the sliding doors and panels which Madame Coulomb had talked about were discovered.[2] On the 23rd of May they were finally forced to leave headquarters.

c. We now turn to Europe for a moment. The Theosophical Society had by this time attained so much notoriety that the London Society for Psychical Research appointed, in May, 1884,[3] a Committee for the taking of such evidence as to the alleged phenomena as might be offered by members of that body at the time in England, or as could be collected elsewhere. The journey of the founders to Europe thus came at a very fortunate time, and the Research Society took full advantage of it.[4]

d. On the 9th of August Madame Coulomb called on the Editor of *The Madras Christian College Magazine*, and placed in his hands some forty letters, and asked him whether he cared to publish them, as they contained sufficient evidence

[1] Parts of it were published by Dr. Hartmann in his September pamphlet (p. 240, below) and these are reproduced in *Proceedings*, IX, 279.

[2] *Proceedings*, IX, 223. [3] *Ib.*, IX, 201. [4] *Ib.*, IX, 202.

to expose the fraudulent nature of the phenomena which had made so much stir in India. The Editor asked for a few days to look into the matter.[1]

A few days later the General Council of the Theosophical Society through their Chairman, Dr. Hartmann, sent out a circular letter of inquiry to a number of Theosophists who had visited headquarters, asking them what they knew about the Shrine.[2]

Meantime the Editor of the *Christian College Magazine* was examining the documents left in his hands. Most of them were letters from Madame Blavatsky to Madame Coulomb, but there were several other things, a letter from Mrs. Carmichael (the wife of an Indian Civilian) to Madame Blavatsky with a letter to Madame Coulomb written on the back, a receipt for a telegram, etc. The Editor submitted the documents to the most skilled opinion available in Madras, among others to certain bankers, and they pronounced them genuine.[3] But the letters authenticated themselves. No one could look through them and believe them to be forgeries. The question of the handwriting was quite a subordinate one. The letters contained scores of references to leading Hindus and Government Officials all over India with details of what happened when Madame Blavatsky was in their houses and when she met them casually. No forger would have dared to invent such details. If they had been forged, a few personal inquiries would have at once exposed them. The style was also Madame Blavatsky's, brilliant, vivacious, full of surprises and sudden changes. The documents were thus manifestly genuine. As they contained numerous instructions to Madame Coulomb for the production of phenomena, the Editor decided to publish a number of extracts from them, so as to expose Madame Blavatsky and her frauds.

[1] *Collapse*, 29. [2] *Proceedings*, IX, 223, 325. [3] *Ib.*, IX, 277.

Accordingly, an article appeared in the *Christian College Magazine*, on September 10th,[1] containing extracts from some dozen letters, with sufficient comment to make them comprehensible. The letters were almost all in French. The text and the English translation were given in parallel columns. The Editor quoted only such paragraphs as were necessary to prove the fraud, and omitted numerous passages dealing with the private affairs of individuals, both European and Indian; and most of the letters were not used at all.

The publication of this article caused immense excitement throughout India. Most of the newspapers recognized that it was a genuine exposure, but some doubted whether the Editor had not been hoaxed by forgeries. The leading Theosophists, on the other hand, put the whole matter down as a conspiracy on the part of the missionaries.

e. Mr. W. Q. Judge, who took part in the foundation of the society in 1875,[2] was in Europe in 1884, and was sent by Olcott from Paris to Madras.[3] He arrived there sometime in May or June.

f. Dr. Hartmann now drew up as vigorous a defence of Madame Blavatsky as he could and published it, sometime in September, with the title, *Report of Observations made during a nine-months' stay at the Head-quarters of the Theosophical Society at Adyar (Madras), India.*[4] A rough and inaccurate plan of the chief rooms at headquarters, probably the work of Judge,[5] appeared in it. It is reproduced above, plan *A*, page 234. Hartmann denied that the letters which had been published were genuine, and charged the missionaries with forming a conspiracy against the Theosophical Society. He confesses the existence at

[1] Reproduced in *Collapse*, 1–15. [2] See above, p. 218.

[3] *MPI.*, 125. The passage is quoted below, p. 248.

[4] *Proceedings*, IX, 230. [5] See pp. 452–3, below.

headquarters of such sliding panels, trapdoors, holes in the wall, etc., as could be used for the production of occult phenomena; but he asserts, that M. Coulomb made all these after Madame Blavatsky's departure, in order to ruin her reputation. The whole conspiracy, however, would be unmasked and the innocence of Madame Blavatsky established in a court of law.

We have noted Judge's arrival above because of the following grave incident in which he was concerned. The chief facts are given in a written statement by Dr. Hartmann from which we quote the following:

> Of the existence of a movable back to the Shrine and a filled-up aperture in the wall, none of us knew anything, and although superficial examinations were made, they divulged nothing; because to make a thorough examination, it would have been necessary to take the Shrine down, and we were prevented from doing this by the superstitious awe with which Mr. Damodar K. Mavalankar regarded the Shrine, and who looked upon every European who dared to touch or handle the "sacred" shrine as a desecration.
>
> At about the time when Major-General Morgan sent his invitation to Mr. Patterson to come to headquarters, that examination was made, and it was found that the back of the Shrine could be removed, and on moistening the wall behind the Shrine with a wet cloth, it was found that an aperture had existed, which had been plastered up. . . .
>
> I must confess that it seemed to me that if at that inopportune moment this *new discovery*, to which I then alluded in the papers (see *Madras Mail*), would have been made public, it would have had a bad effect on the public mind . . .
>
> A gentleman who was present, and who shared my opinions, was of the opinion that the *Shrine* had been too much desecrated to be of any more use, and he burned the Shrine in my presence.[1]

What they found was that the back of the Shrine consisted of three movable panels, and that there had been an aper-

[1] *Proceedings*, IX, 225.

ture in the thin brick partition behind;[1] so that there had actually been direct communication between Madame Blavatsky's room and the interior of the Shrine, precisely as Madame Coulomb had said.[2] The aperture had been plastered up when Madame Blavatsky sailed for Europe. Among those who examined the Shrine and made the discovery were Dr. Hartmann, Mr. Judge and Mr. T. Vijayaraghava Charloo (known as Ānanda);[3] and it was Judge who burned the Shrine.[4] The date of the discovery was September 20th.[5]

Dr. Hartmann and Theosophists generally have always maintained that the sliding panels in the back of the Shrine and the hole in the wall behind it, which made it possible to get access to the Shrine surreptitiously from Madame Blavatsky's room, were made by M. Coulomb *after* Madame Blavatsky sailed for Europe in February, 1884. It is passing strange that they destroyed the Shrine, if they were really convinced that M. Coulomb had made these arrangements in order to ruin Madame Blavatsky. Why did they not preserve this most notable piece of evidence of his villainy?

The truth is that it is totally impossible to believe that the sliding panels in the Shrine and the hole in the wall were made by M. Coulomb *after* Madame Blavatsky's departure; for while the Coulombs had charge of her rooms, Damodar had *the keys of the Occult Room and the Shrine*.[6] How then could M. Coulomb insert sliding panels in the back of the shrine, and dig a hole through the wall without the knowledge of Damodar? The burning of the Shrine shows that Judge and Hartmann had had some glimpse of this truth.

[1] See p. 232, above, and plan *B*, page 235. [2] See p. 237, above.

[3] *Proceedings*, IX, 224. On this page a full and clear account is given of the removal of the Shrine.

[4] *Ib.*, XXIV, 141. [5] *Ib.*, IX, 227. See p. 247, below.

[6] P. 236, above.

Clearly they were conscious that no defence of Madame Blavatsky was possible while the Shrine remained in existence.

g. It is important that Hartmann's bold promise of a lawsuit should be kept in mind. In making it Dr. Hartmann did not stand alone. Judge was especially bold in promising a full exposure in court;[1] and Theosophists in every part of India loudly proclaimed that the missionaries would be prosecuted, and their conspiracy laid bare. So strong was confidence at headquarters that again and again it was prophesied that they would rue the day when first they accepted the lying evidence of two dismissed servants.[2] The London Lodge published a pamphlet in which it was stated that the matter would go to Court; and Madame Blavatsky also stated in an interview with a representative of *The Pall Mall Gazette* that she was hurrying to India to commence proceedings against the missionaries.[2]

But, while this was what she said in public, she wrote in a very different strain to M. Solovyoff. We quote part of her letter. The date is early in October, 1884:

> "First of all, you can say to each and all in Paris that since, in spite of all my efforts, in spite of my having sacrificed to the society life and health and my whole future, I am suspected not only by my enemies but even by my own theosophists. I shall cut off the infected limb from the sound body; that is, I shall cut myself off from the society. They have all clutched at the idea with such delight, Olcott and Madame Gebhard and the rest, that I have not even met with any pity. I leave the moral to you. Of course, I shall not depart into the 'wilderness' till Olcott, who starts for India by the first steamer, has arranged matters at Adyar, and exposed and proved the conspiracy — they gave the Coulomb woman 10,000 rupees[3] as is now proved, in order to destroy the society; but when all this has settled down, then I shall go off, — where, I do not know yet;

[1] *Collapse*, 51–2. [2] *Ib.*, 49. [3] See below, p. 246.

it is all the same, besides, so long as it is somewhere that nobody knows.[1]

h. In October a second article appeared in *The Christian College Magazine*,[2] in which the missionaries, in reply to Dr. Hartmann's pamphlet and to other criticisms which Theosophists had raised against them, published a further instalment of letters, and indicated still more clearly the great strength of their position.

i. So keen was the interest in the Psychical Society on the question of the Theosophical phenomena and of the genuineness of the letters published in *The Christian College Magazine* that the Committee appointed by them to consider the phenomena determined to send one of their number to India to make careful scientific investigations on the spot. Mr. Richard Hodgson, B.A., of St. John's College, Cambridge, was sent out at the expense of Prof. Henry Sidgwick. He arrived in Madras on the 18th of December. On the 20th of December Madame Blavatsky and Colonel Olcott arrived at the headquarters in Madras.

The following is Mr. Hodgson's own statement of his attitude of mind:

Before proceeding it may be well for me to state that the general attitude which I have for years maintained with respect to various classes of alleged phenomena which form the subject of investigation by our Society enabled me, as I believe, to approach the task I had before me with complete impartiality; while the conclusions which I held and still hold concerning the important positive results achieved by our Society in connection with the phenomena of Telepathy, — of which, moreover, I have had instances in my own experience, both spontaneous and experimental, and both as agent and percipient, — formed a further safeguard of my readiness to deal with the evidence set before me without prejudice as to the principles involved. Indeed, whatever prepossessions I may have held were distinctly in

[1] *MPI.*, 94–95.

[2] Reproduced in *Collapse*, 15–42.

favour of Occultism and Madame Blavatsky — a fact which, I think I may venture to say, is well known to several leading Theosophists.[1]

Mr. Hodgson's actions fully bear out his statement. When he arrived in Madras, the Editor of *The Christian College Magazine* offered him hospitality, but he declined it; and a day or two later the Editor heard that he had gone to reside at the Theosophic headquarters; and there he resided all the time he was in India (nearly three months), except when he went on short visits to places at a distance from Madras. Madame Blavatsky acknowledges frankly that he was friendly to the Theosophist cause when he arrived in India. She writes to M. Solovyoff:

> It was he (*i.e.* Hartmann) who turned Hodgson, the representative sent by the London Psychical Society to inquire into the phenomena in India, from a friend, as he was at first, into an enemy.[2]

Mr. Hodgson acted wisely, I believe, in putting up at headquarters. He thus gave Madame Blavatsky, Colonel Olcott and all their followers the fullest possible opportunity of explaining every suspicious circumstance and giving all the evidence they possessed to prove that the letters which had been published were forgeries; while he himself was able to become acquainted with every corner of the rooms at headquarters, except in so far as the Theosophic leaders had destroyed the evidence.[3]

The Editor of *The Christian College Magazine* handed the incriminating letters to Mr. Hodgson for examination, on condition that they should be returned, as they were the property of Madame Coulomb, and were to be handed

[1] *Proceedings*, IX, 208.

[2] *MPI.*, 124. Quoted below, p. 248. Cf. also *Proceedings*, XXIV, 135.

[3] See above, pp. 241–2.

back to her as soon as all danger of a prosecution should have passed away.[1]

Mr. Hodgson interviewed the people who supplied the materials for building and repairs, traced the vases, saucers, flowers, etc., which appeared in the phenomena, to the shops or other places whence they came, and endeavoured to fit these facts into the accounts given by those who witnessed the phenomena. He tested all the details of the incriminating letters, cross-questioned witnesses, examined the places referred to, and compared the documents with

[1] As Theosophists have persistently declared that the Missionaries bought the letters for a very large price, the truth must be set down here. The Editor of *The Christian College Magazine* writes in April, 1885 (*Collapse*, 54–5):

"We did *not* buy the letters. They are still Madame Coulomb's property and will remain so. Two, at least, of the members of the Committee of Investigation — Dr. Hartmann and Mr. Subba Row — know this, and have known it since Sept. 27th of last year. On that date the Editor of *The Christian College Magazine*, accompanied by Mr. Gribble, the Rev. A. Alexander and the Rev. J. E. Padfield, visited the Headquarters of the Theosophical Society, where they met Messrs. Hartmann, Judge, Subba Row and Damodar. At the close of the interview Dr. Hartmann asked what we had paid Madame Coulomb, and remarked that it was rumoured we had purchased the letters for Rs. 10,000. He was informed that such a rumour was wholly false, that we had *not* purchased the letters, and that Madame Coulomb had only been paid at our ordinary rates for work done. On our return we asked the gentlemen who had accompanied us to write down separately their recollections of the interview. On reference to these documents we find the following remarks of Dr. Hartmann's recorded. We quote from Mr. Alexander's account: —

"'Dr. Hartmann replied . . . that this confirmed what he had always thought, that Madame Coulomb was acting not for money but for revenge.'

"We may add to this that the letters were put into our hands absolutely and unconditionally, with the single proviso that they should be returned when we were done with them. The first suggestion as to payment for work done came not from Madame Coulomb but from us; and from first to last we have paid her the comparatively paltry sum of Rs. 150."

One of the letters was lent to Mr. W. Emmette Coleman of San Francisco. He promised to return it, but did not do so. It was probably burned, along with his other papers, in the great fire in San Francisco. See p. 263.

acknowledged specimens of Madame Blavatsky's handwriting in matters of spelling, phraseology,[1] style, etc. No other person, whether Theosophist or not, had the opportunity of examining all the witnesses personally, of seeing all the rooms and other places involved in the matters at issue, and of handling all the documents. Any one who, from a sincere desire to get at what actually happened in these matters, will work patiently and carefully through the multitude of details supplied in all the sources, will realize with what extreme honesty and with what infinite pains Hodgson collected and sifted the evidence.

As he proceeded with this persistent scientific search for the facts, it became evident that the Theosophic leaders were not trustworthy witnesses, that they contradicted themselves and each other in multitudes of particulars. Each new piece of cross-questioning on Mr. Hodgson's part produced a new version of some occurrence. Madame Blavatsky,[2] Colonel Olcott,[3] Hartmann[4] and Damodar[5] all produced a very bad impression.

Here is what happened when Mr. Hodgson asked his first questions about the shrine in December, 1884:

> Madame Blavatsky professed ignorance on the subject, saying she had been unable to discover what had been done with the Shrine. Mr. Damodar and Mr. Hartmann both denied having any knowledge of it, and it was only after repeated and urgent requests to be told what had happened that I learnt from the halting account given by Mr. Damodar and Dr. Hartmann that the Shrine had been removed from the Occult Room (see Plan[6]) into Mr. Damodar's room at about mid-day of September 20th, that on the following morning, at 9 o'clock, they found the Shrine had been taken away, and they had not seen it since.

[1] See below, pp. 256–7.
[2] *Proceedings*, XXIV, 133.
[3] *Ib.*, IX, 210, 237–239, 309, 311, 335–6.
[4] *Ib.*, IX, 220–226. [5] *Ib.*, IX, 210, 226–237, 312. [6] Above, p. 235.

They threw out suggestions implying that the Coulombs or the missionaries might have stolen it.[1]

Mr. Hodgson questioned every Theosophist who had sent in written answers to Dr. Hartmann about the Shrine and any other one who could throw any light on its history, and in this way gradually pieced together a certain amount of information about it. All the evidence showed that no one had examined the Shrine carefully before the 20th of September. Every statement made about examinations before that date proved altogether untrustworthy. But he was kept in ignorance of the burning of the Shrine until the 13th of March.[2]

j. We may next see what Madame Blavatsky herself wrote about Dr. Hartmann. The letter was written from Naples in May, 1885, to M. Solovyoff, after her final return from India, but six months before Mr. Hodgson's report appeared:

If your heart is not attracted to Hartmann, you are quite right. This dreadful man has done me more harm by his defence, and often by his deceit, than the Coulombs by open lying. One moment he was defending me in the papers, the next he was writing such 'equivokes' that even the papers hostile to me could only open their mouths and say: 'There is a friend for you!' One day he defended me in letters to Hume and other theosophists, and then hinted at such infamies that all his correspondents went against me. It was he who turned Hodgson, the representative sent by the London Psychical Society to inquire into the phenomena in India, from a friend as he was at first, into an enemy. He is a cynic, a liar, cunning and vindictive, and his jealousy of the Master, and his envy for any one on whom the Master bestows the least attention, are simply repulsive. He has turned our devoted Judge, when despatched by Olcott from Paris to Adyar, into our enemy. He set against me at one time all the Europeans in Adyar, Lane Fox, Mr. and Mrs. Oakley,

[1] *Proceedings*, IX, 220. See the truth, above, pp. 241–2.

[2] Below, p. 250.

Brown; the Hindus alone, who hate him and have long since taken his measure, he was unable to stir. Now I have been able to save the society from him, by agreeing to take him with me under the plea that he is a doctor. The society, and Olcott at their head, were so afraid of him that they did not dare expel him.[1]

There thus need be no doubt as to Dr. Hartmann's character as a witness.

k. From the time that Madame Blavatsky and Colonel Olcott reached Madras, on the 20th December, 1884 (two days after Hodgson's arrival), the missionaries and the Coulombs watched and waited eagerly, looking for the promised suit-at-law which was to establish the innocence of Madame Blavatsky, prove the Coulombs forgers and expose the missionaries as conspirators. But week after week passed, and nothing happened. The blustering ceased. Hartmann, who had boasted by word of mouth and in print, did nothing. Colonel Olcott and Judge were mute. Madame Blavatsky initiated no proceedings in the Law Courts to clear her character. Finally, in February, there was issued from headquarters a pamphlet, the work of Dr. Hartmann in the main, and bearing the following title, *Report of the Result of an Investigation into the charges against Madame Blavatsky, brought by the Missionaries of the Scottish Free Church at Madras and examined by a Committee appointed for that purpose by the General Council of the Theosophical Society*. Madras, Scottish Press, 1885.[2] This pamphlet contains the written replies sent in by Theosophists in response to the letter circulated in August,[3] but no mention is made of the discoveries made by Dr. Hartmann and Mr. Judge in September,[4] nor of the effect of Hodgson's examina-

[1] *MPI.*, 124–5.

[2] *Collapse*, 48; *Proceedings*, XXIV, 134 n.

[3] See above, p. 239.

[4] See above, pp. 241–2.

tion on those who had sent in replies.[1] It is stated in the pamphlet that there is to be no prosecution of the missionaries. What a fiasco! A pamphlet instead of a prosecution!

What was it that choked the bluster of the Theosophists and stilled the last threat of a prosecution? In the inner circles of Theosophy it is acknowledged that Sinnett, Olcott and the others were afraid to have Madame Blavatsky with her unbridled tongue go into the witness-box: as a witness she was impossible. That doubtless weighed also, but the real cause of their terror, without any doubt, was the searching examination made by Hodgson. Until he came and subjected them to his trained scientific mode of inquiry, they doubtless believed they had an irrefragable case. But that ordeal made everybody at headquarters realize that no Theosophic leader could stand cross-examination for a quarter of an hour, and that many of the phenomena could be shewn to be fraudulent by a few carefully directed inquiries. To go to court would be black ruin. The following quotation will make this plain and will also explain the events that followed. Hodgson writes:

It was on the evening of March 13th, at a conference between Dr. Hartmann, Mr. and Mrs. Cooper-Oakley, Mr. Hume and myself, that Dr. Hartmann finally confessed that "nobody was allowed to touch that d—— Shrine," and he then related the incident described on p. 224 of my Report,[2] concerning the discovery of the sliding panel of the Shrine and the subsequent destruction of the Shrine itself. I had learned from Mr. A. D. Ezekiel, in Bombay, that he had discovered independently that there had once been a hole in the wall behind the Shrine, but that it had been carefully blocked up. Dr. Hartmann then admitted that traces of this hole had been discovered previously, but the discovery was kept a secret. On the following morning Mr. Hume drew up some statements to form proposed resolu-

[1] See above, p. 248. [2] See above, pp. 241–2.

tions for an informal meeting to be held in the evening by himself, the Oakleys, Hartmann, Ragoonath Row, Subba Row, and P. Sreenvas Row. These were to the effect that most of the phenomena in connection with the Theosophical Society were fraudulent, as appears from such of the Coulombs' statements as have been verified, and the independent investigations by myself, that the Society be reconstituted, that Madame Blavatsky, Olcott, Damodar, Babajee and Bhavani Shankar should resign their connection with it, that the disputed letters are genuine, and that Hartmann's pamphlet as well as the Defence pamphlet should be withdrawn, as being founded on an imperfect knowledge of the circumstances. These resolutions, as I was informed by Mr. Hume, were not carried, the Oakleys and Dr. Hartmann being unwilling to go so far as to condemn the phenomena as fraudulent. It was decided, however, that the pamphlets should be withdrawn.[1]

Hartmann confessed that the pamphlet published in February was thoroughly untrustworthy,[2] and gave Mr. Hodgson a written statement about the Shrine.[3] Finally, Madame Blavatsky herself confessed that the Shrine was made with three sliding panels in the back.[4]

The result of Mr. Hodgson's long patient inquiry was that he was driven to these conclusions: that every phenomenon, so far as he had been able to trace it, was fraudulent; that the letters handed over by Madame Coulomb were genuine; and that most of the Koot Hoomi letters were written by Madame Blavatsky herself, though a few were probably written by Damodar.[5]

[1] *Proceedings*, XXIV, 134. [2] *Ib.*, XXIV, 145.

[3] Reproduced in part, *Proceedings*, IX, 225, and quoted above, p. 241.

[4] *Proceedings*, IX, 221.

[5] For example, Damodar, who knew everything, wrote the letter, which pretends to come from Koot Hoomi, referred to above on p. 237, to prevent the Committee from expelling the Coulombs and discovering the shrine and the sliding panels, at least until orders should come from Europe. The letter from M., referred to above on p. 238, was clearly written by Madame Blavatsky in Europe and sent by the mail to Damodar to be delivered to

A few days after the conference just described Hodgson left for home. About the same time Judge slunk away to America without fulfilling his boasts;[1] and Damodar, knowing that his course was run, took a journey to the Himalayas, and was seen no more.[2]

l. When Madame Coulomb saw that Madame Blavatsky and her friends were afraid to prosecute and give her the opportunity of proving the truth of her statements, she determined to bring the matter before a court of law herself. But, since Madame Blavatsky had not publicly charged Madame Coulomb with forging the letters, it was impossible to prosecute her. Consequently, she instructed Messrs. Barclay and Morgan to proceed against General Morgan of Ootacamund, as he had been foremost in charging her with forgery. But at this juncture Madame Blavatsky's lady doctor went and begged Madame Coulomb's friends to postpone the case: Madame Blavatsky was so ill that it would inevitably kill her. They agreed. Several postponements were asked for and obtained; but finally the patient recovered. It was then decided to proceed with the case. As a preliminary measure, Madame Coulomb's solicitors wrote to General Morgan on March 25th, threatening him with criminal proceedings, should he fail to make an apology before April 2nd. General Morgan replied, in a letter dated March 31st, declining to apologize.

The very next day, the Theosophical Society gave Madame Blavatsky permission to leave India; and she embarked on a French steamer, the *Tibre*, at Madras on the 2nd of April, never to return. In order that no one

Dr. Hartmann. If it was sent by Morya himself, how did he require to use Damodar as his postman? Why did he not send it direct to Hartmann in Madras?

[1] *Proceedings*, XXIV, 141.

[2] The reason for his flight may be found in *Proceedings*, IX, 226–237.

might know beforehand that she was to sail, her passage and that of Miss Flynn, who went with her, were taken under the name of "Madame Helen and maid." She sailed on a medical certificate of dishealth; for her doctor thought that she ought not to stay through the hot weather. It was kidney-trouble she had suffered from. She had had a very similar attack in Elberfeld seven months earlier,[1] and she had another at Würzburg five months later.[2] But it is also perfectly clear that it was not this sickness that was the reason for her sudden and secret departure. Had she been ready to clear her character, she could have stayed a little longer without the slightest danger. As soon as it was rumoured that she had escaped, a representative of Messrs. Barclay and Morgan went down by rail to Pondicherry, where the French steamer had to call, went on board, and found the lady well and happy on deck, surrounded by a crowd of admirers. She unquestionably fled from India, in order to escape the ordeal of cross-examination as a witness in the Coulomb-Morgan trial. In a letter to M. Solovyoff, written at Naples on the 29th of the month, she says that she had been called a Russian spy, and adds:

> They certainly could not prove anything, but meanwhile, on mere suspicion, it might have been a matter of sending me to jail, arresting me, and doing who knows what to me. I have only now heard all this in detail; they did not tell me, and packed me off straight from my bed on to the French steamer.[3]

Dr. Hartmann also sailed in the same steamer. Thus, Judge, Damodar, Madame Blavatsky and Dr. Hartmann had all fled from Madras.

Two days after the steamer sailed the following note appeared in the *Madras Mail:*

[1] *MPI.*, 77, 87. [2] *Ib.*, 144. [3] *Ib.*, 119.

The Theosophists: — Colonel Olcott writes on behalf of the General Council of the Theosophist Society to say that "as a number of copies of a pamphlet entitled 'Report of the result of the investigations into the charges brought against Madame Blavatsky,'[1] have been circulated, it is my duty to state that the issue has not been ordered by the General Council, nor authorized by the Committee."[2]

Clearly, this action can have resulted only from a conviction on the part of the leaders that the pamphlet was untrustworthy; and that is precisely what Hodgson says they had come to.[3] The Theosophists of India thereby absolutely gave up the attempt to defend Madame Blavatsky.

On the 22nd of April a letter from Madame Coulomb appeared in the *Madras Mail* in which she explained that, since Madame Blavatsky had left the country, it was impossible to have the question of the authenticity of the letters satisfactorily settled, and she had in consequence decided to drop the case against General Morgan.

m. How sick the Theosophic leaders were of phenomena is patent from the fact that from this time these most useful miracles were banned. They were unnecessary; and they were dangerous. Every book labours to show that they are no essential element of the Theosophist programme. But has no one realized what the cessation of the phenomena means? Many of them were supposed to be the work of the Masters themselves. Hence, if we accept the Theosophic explanation of the Coulomb affair, we must conclude that those great Adepts, who, in the fulness of their omniscience, had planned them and carried them out, were compelled by a pair of forgers and a few conspiring missionaries to give up the policy they had adopted for the establishment of the truth in India!

[1] See above, p. 249. [2] *Proceedings*, XXIV, 135.
[3] See above, p. 251.

n. Meantime, the Committee appointed by the Society for Psychical Research to inquire into the phenomena of Theosophy had been dealing with certain parallel cases which had taken place in Europe, and had been led by all the evidence adduced to declare that they had been fraudulently arranged by Madame Blavatsky. This conclusion was based solely on the evidence available in Europe,[1] and is thus altogether independent of the Coulomb letters and the masses of evidence gathered by Hodgson.

o. When his report was laid before the Committee, they carefully weighed all the evidence and unanimously accepted his main conclusions. The report was published in December, 1885.[2]

No man is in a position to decide any one of the most important questions at issue until he has worked his way patiently through the mass of detailed evidence accumulated in this report. We cannot, in the space at our disposal, give any outline of the masses of evidence set forth in it. We simply note the most outstanding facts, and refer readers to all the relevant documents.

p. With regard to the phenomena, two points must be noticed here. First, the famous brooch case, detailed above,[3] was unmasked by journalists long before Hodgson had anything to do with the question. This affords us, then, undeniable evidence, quite apart from Hodgson, the missionaries and the Coulomb letters, that Madame Blavatsky, on one occasion at least, was guilty of a most impudent piece of fraud, and that she had made the most careful arrangements beforehand to deceive her hosts, an Indian Civilian and his wife. Secondly, the evidence which Hodgson offers to prove that other phenomena were fraudulent is of the same nature as that which exposed the brooch-trick, simple matters of fact, requiring no knowledge of telepathy

[1] *Proceedings*, IX, 397–400. [2] *Ib.*, IX, 201–396. [3] Pp. 228–31.

or any form of occultism for their appreciation, but understandable by all. Let readers turn to the *Report*.

q. As to the letters handed over by Madame Coulomb, the handwriting proved them to be Madame Blavatsky's; but it was not merely the handwriting that convinced every one who handled them of their genuineness and made it utterly impossible for the Theosophic leaders to prove them forgeries, but the masses of detailed allusions in them to Indian Civilians, prominent Hindus and other people,[1] details the truth of which no one could deny and no forger could have invented, details which proved absolutely true so far as Hodgson was able to probe them in each case. The instructions for the production of phenomena contained in the letters were proved genuine by the sliding panels and other arrangements found in the Shrine and in Madame Blavatsky's rooms and by many circumstances discovered by Hodgson.

r. In the case of the long philosophic letters purporting to come from the Masters, there is abundance of evidence to prove that most of them were written by Madame Blavatsky. The plagiarism from Mr. Kiddle and the stupid fictitious defence set up afterwards,[2] taken along with what we know of how *Isis Unveiled* was produced,[3] would suggest that the same mind produced both; but there is direct and convincing evidence as well. There are multitudes of errors in the English of these letters, errors in spelling, errors in dividing words at the end of a line, and errors in idiom; and almost every one of them can be paralleled in Madame Blavatsky's acknowledged correspondence. This was one of the forms of evidence which convinced Mr. Hodgson as to their authorship. Here are lists of some of the more noticeable of these errors:

[1] See, for example, the letter reproduced in *Collapse*, pp. 32–34, and the first letter on p. 211 of *Proceedings*, IX.

[2] Pp. 231–2, above.

[3] Pp. 223–5, above.

a. Misspells. your's, her's, fulfill, dispell, thiefs, leasure, quarreling, marshaling, alloted, in totto, circumstancial, defense.

b. Faulty division of words at the end of a line. incessan-tly, direc-tly, una-cquainted, fun-ctions, discer-ning, rea-ding, rea-dily, po-werless, atmos-phere, des-pite, corres-pondence, En-glishman, En-glish, misunders-tood.

c. Faulty idioms. I give you an advice; who, ever since he is here, has been influencing him; we mortals never have and will agree on any subject entirely; one who understands tolerably well English; you felt impatient and believed having reasons to complain; to take care of themselves and of their hereafter the best they know how; — the best she knew how; that the world will not believe in our philosophy unless it is convinced of it proceeding from reliable —; there are those, who, rather than to yield to the evidence of fact; in a direct course or along hundred of side-furrows; their active mentality preventing them to receive clear outside impressions; provided you consent to wait and did not abuse of the situation; Immutable laws cannot arise since they are eternal and uncreated, propelled in the Eternity and that God himself — if such a thing existed — could never have the power of stopping them; so more the pity for him.[1]

It must also be noticed here that Mr. Sinnett's books are no faithful representation of the Ms. letters. Most of the above errors, and many other awkward words and phrases, have been corrected;[2] and the passage plagiarized from Mr. Kiddle[3] is dropped altogether from the text in the later editions, and no note is appended to tell readers of the omission. This way of dealing with the Mss. is the more serious because Mr. Sinnett says on p. 100:[4]

The reader must be careful to remember, however, as I now most unequivocally affirm, that I shall in no case *alter* one syllable of the passages actually quoted.

[1] *Proceedings*, IX, 306–7.
[2] *Ib.*, IX, 305.
[3] See p. 231, above.
[4] *I.e.* of the 1st edition, p. 69 of the 3rd and p. 85 of the 8th edition.

Readers will form their own opinion of Theosophic editorial methods.[1] At a later date, Mr. W. Emmette Coleman, whom we have already mentioned,[2] brought forward a great mass of evidence of a different kind, which completely confirms Mr. Hodgson's conclusion. Here is his general statement:

> *Esoteric Buddhism*, by A. P. Sinnett, was based upon statements in letters received by Mr. Sinnett and Mr. A. O. Hume, through Madame Blavatsky, purporting to be written by the Mahatmas Koot Hoomi and Morya, — principally the former. Mr. Richard Hodgson has kindly lent me a considerable number of the original letters of the Mahatmas leading to the production of *Esoteric Buddhism*. I find in them overwhelming evidence that all of them were written by Madame Blavatsky, which evidence will be presented in full in my book. In these letters are a number of extracts from Buddhist books, alleged to be translations from the originals by the Mahatmic writers themselves. These letters claim for the adepts a knowledge of Sanskrit, Thibetan, Pali, and Chinese. I have traced to its source each quotation from the Buddhist scriptures in the letters, and they were all copied from current English translations, including even the notes and explanations of the English translators. They were principally copied from Beal's *Catena of Buddhist Scriptures from the Chinese*. In other places where the adept (?) is using his own language in explanation of Buddhistic terms and ideas, I find that his presumed original language was copied nearly word for word from Rhys Davids's *Buddhism*, and other books. I have traced every Buddhistic idea in these letters and in *Esoteric Buddhism*, and every Buddhistic term, such as Devachan, Avitchi, etc., to the books whence Helena Petrovna Blavatsky derived them. Although said to be proficient in the knowledge of Thibetan and Sanskrit, the words and terms in these languages in the letters of the adepts were nearly all used in a ludicrously erroneous and absurd manner. The writer of these letters was an ignoramus in Sanskrit and Thibetan; and the mistakes and blunders in them, in these languages, are in exact

[1] See also what M. Solovyoff reports, *MPI.*, 157.

[2] See above, pp. 223–4.

accordance with the known ignorance of Madame Blavatsky thereanent. *Esoteric Buddhism*, like all of Madame Blavatsky's works, was based upon wholesale plagiarism and ignorance.[1]

There is another fact. Most of these letters were written on a peculiar sort of hand-made rice-paper. After Madame Blavatsky's death, Judge fabricated a large number of Mahātma letters, as we shall see; and they too were written on this peculiar paper. Olcott then told his Theosophic friends that he himself had bought a quantity of this paper in Jummoo, Cashmere, in 1883; that Madame Blavatsky always carried a supply of it about with her; and that Judge must have abstracted some of it from her rooms in London.[2] M. Solovyoff tells us that, in a drawer of Madame Blavatsky's writing-table in Würzburg, he saw a packet of envelopes of this very paper.[3] Hence no serious student will doubt how these letters were composed.

s. Mr. Sinnett published a defence of the occult phenomena in 1886. Then Mrs. Besant attempted to answer Hodgson's *Report* in an article in *Time* in March, 1891. It is astounding to discover that for most of the evidence which Mr. Sinnett and Mrs. Besant bring, they rely on the pamphlet, *Report of the Result of an Investigation*, etc.,[4] which was chiefly compiled by Dr. Hartmann, Madame Blavatsky's "liar, cunning and vindictive,"[5] and which, within two months of its publication, was publicly repudiated by the leaders of Theosophy in India,[6] Dr. Hartmann himself having acknowledged it to be untrustworthy.[7]

Mr. Hodgson overwhelmed these articles with a reply in 1893.[8] Yet Mrs. Besant published *H. P. Blavatsky and the Masters of the Wisdom* in 1907, using the old repudiated

[1] *MPI.*, 363–4. [2] *Isis Very Much Unveiled*, 49; below, p. 268.
[3] *MPI.*, 152. [4] Above, p. 249. [5] Above, p. 248. [6] Above, p. 254.
[7] *Proceedings*, XXIV, 145; above, p. 251.
[8] *Ib.*, XXIV, 129–159.

source, and repeating certain shameful slanders, without even mentioning Hodgson's replies. Nothing has done so much to shake my confidence in Mrs. Besant's honesty as my study of this dreadful document. All later attempts at defence depend almost entirely on its statements. These books and pamphlets are by far the most unreliable literature that it has ever been my sad fate to have to study. A few samples of their quality are given in the Appendix, p. 447.

12. A new myth was created in 1885. According to the teaching of all the wise and good of the ancient world, the goddess Isis lifted her veil only to those who had lived lives of perfect chastity. Now Madame Blavatsky, according to Theosophic legend, was chosen by the Masters from amongst all modern men and women to receive the ancient wisdom in limitless measure from the highest sources. She unveiled Isis. Hence during the autumn of 1885, while she was at Würzburg, Germany, she began to tell her friends, that, despite her marriage to M. Blavatsky, despite many stories told of her after life, and despite her American marriage,[1] she had through all remained a spotless virgin.[2] Yet this is the woman whose confessions of gross and long-continued immorality live in her own letters to M. Aksakoff and to M. Solovyoff.[3] We are thus driven to acknowledge that she was capable of stupendous hypocrisy in addition to everything else. This myth has to be carefully borne in mind in the study of Theosophic literature written after 1885.

13. 1888 proved one of the most remarkable years in Madame Blavatsky's life. From that year dates the Esoteric School of Theosophy, which since then has been the kernel and the strength of the society. In the same year she published her greatest work, *The Secret Doctrine*. Then also

[1] See above, p. 221. [2] *MPI.*, 139–141. [3] See above, pp. 211–3.

Mr. G. R. S. Mead, now editor of *The Quest*, became her private secretary. He retained the position until her death in 1891.

The Esoteric School was created in order to initiate young Theosophists into the practice of occultism. The work was carried on in classes, each under the guidance of a secretary. A good deal of the instruction was taken from Ms. material prepared by Madame Blavatsky and afterwards published in the third volume of *The Secret Doctrine*. Each person initiated had to take two vows: to defend and advance the cause of Theosophy as far as lay in his power; and not to reveal anything taught in the Esoteric School. Each pupil received also a photograph[1] of a (pretended) portrait of one of the Masters and was bid gaze on it fixedly during meditation and try to visualize it in the corners of the room. The occultism of the school at this time seems to have been rather different to what it has become under Mrs. Besant and Mr. Leadbeater.

It was in October, 1888, that *The Secret Doctrine* was published. In the Introduction the authoress assures us that the teaching it contains comes from her Masters, who reside beyond the Himalayas. The truth it contains is now "permitted to see the light after long milleniums of the most profound silence and secrecy." The reason why "the outline of a few fundamental truths from the Secret Doctrine of the Archaic Ages" is now revealed is because European scholars during the nineteenth century have been studying the religions of Egypt, India and other lands and have been publishing to the world utterly false and misleading accounts of these great systems.[2]

The whole book is founded on what she calls "The Book of Dzyan," which consists of nineteen stanzas, and, according to Madame Blavatsky, is a very ancient work. It is

[1] See above, pp. 169, 170, 179. [2] Pp. xxi–xxii.

altogether unknown to European scholars; no copy of it lies in any European library; yet, she asserts, that it exists in one of the mysterious libraries of Tibet, in which are concealed all the sacred and philosophical works that have ever been written, in whatever language or characters, since the art of writing began.[1]

The Secret Doctrine is in two volumes, the first, on Cosmogenesis, being founded on the first seven stanzas of the Book of Dzyan, and the second, on Anthropogenesis, being founded on the remaining twelve. In this work readers will find Theosophy as it is actually taught to-day. The doctrine is much more developed and definite than it is in *Isis Unveiled.* Here the formation of the worlds and the evolution of man are treated in detail. As in the *Isis*, the treatment is unscientific in character throughout.

Analysis has shewn that large portions of the book were compiled in the same way as so much of the *Isis* was built up.[2] Hundreds of passages were borrowed without acknowledgment from modern books. Mr. Coleman writes as follows:

A specimen of the wholesale plagiarisms in this book appears in Vol. II, pp. 599–603. Nearly the whole of four pages was copied from *Oliver's Pythagorean Triangle*, while only a few lines were credited to that work. Considerable other matter in Secret Doctrine was copied, uncredited, from Oliver's work. Donnelly's Atlantis was largely plagiarised from. Madame Blavatsky not only borrowed from this writer the general idea of the derivation of Eastern civilization, mythology, etc., from Atlantis; but she coolly appropriated from him a number of the alleged detailed evidences of this derivation, without crediting him therewith. Vol. II, pp. 790–793, contains a number of facts, numbered seriatim, said to prove this Atlantean derivation.

These facts were almost wholly copied from Donnelly's book, ch. IV., where they are also numbered seriatim; but there is no

[1] Pp. xxiii–xxiv. [2] Above, pp. 223–5.

intimation in Secret Doctrine that its author was indebted to Donnelly's book for this mass of matter. In addition to those credited, there are 130 passages from Wilson's Vishnu Purana copied uncredited; and there are some 70 passages from Winchell's World Life not credited. From Dowson's Hindu Classical Dictionary, 123 passages were plagiarised. From Decharme's Mythologie de la Grèce Antique, about 60 passages were plagiarised; from *Myer's Qabbala*, 34. These are some of the other books plagiarised from: Kenealy's Book of God, Faber's Cabiri, Wake's Great Pyramid, Gould's Mythical Monsters, Joly's Man before Metals, Stallo's Modern Physics, Massey's Natural Genesis, Mackey's Mythological Astronomy, Schmidt's Descent and Darwinism, Quatrefage's Human Species, Laing's Modern Science and Modern Thought, Mather's Cabbala Unveiled, Maspéro's Musée de Boulaq, Ragon's Maçonnerie Occulte, Lefevre's Philosophy, and Buchner's Force and Matter.

The Book of Dzyan was the work of Madame Blavatsky — a compilation, in her own language, from a variety of scources, embracing the general principles of the doctrines and dogmas taught in the Secret Doctrine. I find in this "oldest book in the world" statements copied from nineteenth century books, and in the usual blundering manner of Madame Blavatsky. Letters and other writings of the adepts are found in the Secret Doctrine. In these Mahatmic productions I have traced various plagiarised passages from Wilson's Vishnu Purana and Winchell's World Life, — of like character to those in Madame Blavatsky's acknowledged writings. Detailed proofs of this will be given in my book. I have also traced the source whence she derived the word Dzyan.[1]

It is greatly to be regretted that Coleman's promised book never appeared. The evidence he had accumulated would have been interesting in the extreme. His library was destroyed in the fire which followed the great earthquake in San Francisco in 1906; and he died in 1909. The third edition of *The Secret Doctrine*, edited and published in London in 1897, gives references to a considerable proportion of the

[1] *MPI.*, pp. 358–9.

borrowed passages which Coleman speaks of; so that there is no question about them. But Theosophists who have studied the work carefully, while willing to acknowledge the presence of these recognized quotations, believe that the book of Dzyan and certain other passages cannot be traced to modern works. Since Mr. Coleman did not publish his studies, the question is still undecided.

14. Madame Blavatsky[1] died at the age of sixty on the 8th of May, 1891.

It may be well to introduce here a pen-and-ink portrait of her which appeared recently:

She was playing her usual game of "Patience" when I came upon her first of all one evening. She looked up and arrested your attention by the steady gaze of her large, pale blue eyes. Most people regarded them as the redeeming feature of an otherwise excessively plain face. They were set to advantage in a somewhat wide angle on either side of what did duty for a nose but which she playfully described as "no nose at all, but a button." Her mouth was wide with lips that were close-set, thin, and mobile, and when she laughed she opened her mouth and eyes wide with the abandon of a child. I have never seen a woman of mature years laugh with such child-like naturalness as she. Her complexion may be described as coffee-coloured, a yellowish brown, and the face had no square inch that was not scored by a thousand wrinkles. This and the whites of her eyes, which were not white at all but yellow, gave one the impression of "liver" or the tropics, and either would have been a safe guess. The size and shape of her head was very remarkable. No student of phrenology would convict her of material tendencies or attribute to her anything but a highly spiritual and intellectual nature, for the vault of the head from the bore of the ear upwards was exceptionally high, as was also the forward development, and these were sustained by an adequately broad base, while the lateral development was comparatively insignificant. Her iron-grey crinkly hair ran in fascinating little ripples to where it was gathered in the most

[1] See her portrait, Plate IX, facing p. 195.

unconventional of knots on the nape of the neck, as if it were something to be got out of the way merely, and stuck through with a broad comb. The inevitable cigarette called immediate attention to her hands. They were really beautiful hands, but uncanny; so like a child's with their dimples and soft cushions; and every phalange of her lithe, tapering fingers was double-jointed. They seemed to be endowed with a life of their own. They were seldom still for more than a few seconds together. Later on she gave some sort of reason for this. Holding her hands perfectly still over a table, the palms curved so as to form a sort of inverted cup, she remained so for perhaps two minutes or more, when suddenly there was a loud explosion like the crack of a rifle and one expected to see that the table itself had split from end to end.[1]

She was a woman of very unusual powers. Her personality was potent and attractive in a very high degree. She had great gifts as a story-teller and conversationalist. She was greatly loved by her friends, and was most affectionate to them in turn. She drew people towards her, and won their confidence, influencing every one who came within her radius so deeply that people found it hard to escape from her control. She had the genius to will and to rule. She was what Theosophists call "a psychic" of a very high order. This word denotes those little-understood sympathies and faculties which make the spiritualistic medium, the telepathist, the thought-reader, the clairvoyant, the hypnotist. Probably some of the lesser phenomena which she exhibited were quite real. She was also a woman of great energy and industry; for, in spite of frequent illness and racking pain, she worked almost incessantly for many years. She had the shaping gift of imagination, which, combined with a natural power of direct and telling expression, enabled her to produce books which have captivated thousands.

In character she was an extraordinary mixture. She was

[1] W. R. Gorn Old in the *Occult Review* of March, 1914.

bountifully generous to her friends and to every one in need. She was devoted to her family and her country. She must have had sterling qualities to inspire friends as she did. Yet Colonel Olcott tells us that she was not loyal to her friends, that she used them all as pawns;[1] and another unimpeachable witness says, "You never knew when you had her." We have already seen how far she was from being truthful; and all who knew her say she was extremely unguarded with her tongue, and also with her pen.[2] She was liable to outbursts of furious rage, when her great face became livid with passion and almost demonic in expression.[3] She would then execrate every one in appalling language, and make the most outrageous statements which were not meant to be taken seriously.[4] She expected those who loved her to do for her whatever she asked: conscience had no rights as compared with friendship.[5] Seen against this background of elemental character, the colossal frauds and pretences of her Theosophic career seem a little more credible than they do at first sight.

The truth is, she is best described as a Bohemian. She was always smoking,[6] was loose in speech and in manner, took her freedom in everything.[7] She was as far as possible from being a saint.[8] She hated all conventions, and enjoyed nothing so much as tilting at them and breaking through them. Indeed, from her own point of view, the whole propaganda was but a half-serious, half-comic attack on the solemn sobrieties and stupidities of modern science and

[1] *ODL.*, I, 463.

[2] *MPI.*, 71. This accounts in some degree for the recklessness with which she wrote masses of compromising material to Madame Coulomb. Most of her letters show this characteristic.

[3] Sinnett, *Incidents*, 18, 19; *ODL.*, I, 463; *MPI.*, 152. [4] *ODL.*, I, 463.

[5] *MPI.*, 59. [6] *ODL.*, I, 449–453. [7] *Ib.*, 440–462.

[8] Cf. her own words to M. Solovyoff, "I am by no means a saint; I am far from being one, little father." *MPI.*, 19.

the strait-laced ideas of Christianity. Her volcanic temperament and surging senses rebelled against all such things. Yet she was serious also. She saw that there was much more in ancient occultism and magic than the middle nineteenth century could believe, and she was convinced that Hinduism and Buddhism deserved better treatment than they had received. Despite all that she wrote about Christianity, the Orthodox Greek Church still touched her heart.

LITERATURE. — N.B. Books marked with an asterisk to be used with extreme caution. — HISTORY: * *Old Diary Leaves*, by H. S. Olcott, New York, Putnam's Sons, four vols., 1895, 1900, 1904, 1906, 6*s*. net each. * *Incidents in the Life of Madame Blavatsky*, by A. P. Sinnett, London, Redway, 1886, new edition, T. P. S. 1913. *A Modern Priestess of Isis*, by V. S. Solovyoff, translated by Walter Leaf, London, Longmans, 1895, out of print. TEACHING AND PHENOMENA: * *The Occult World*, by A. P. Sinnett, London, Trübner, 1881. * *Esoteric Buddhism*, by A. P. Sinnett, London, Trübner, 1883. THE MADRAS EXPOSURE: *The Collapse of Koot Hoomi*, Madras, C. L. S. I., 1904, as. 4. *Proceedings of the Society for Psychical Research*, IX, pp. 201–400, London, Trübner, 1885, 4*s*. 6*d*.; XXIV, 129–159, London, Trübner, 1893, 3*s*. 6*d*. Also Solovyoff's *Modern Priestess of Isis*. For THEOSOPHIC DEFENCES, see Appendix. MADAME BLAVATSKY'S WORKS: *Isis Unveiled*, New York, Bouton, London, Quaritch, 1877, 2 vols. (Point Loma Edition, 18 Bartlett's Buildings, London, E. C., 17*s*.) *The Secret Doctrine*, London, T. P. S., 1888, 2 vols. (A reprint of this edition, Point Loma, 1909, 42*s*.) Third volume, London, T. P. S., 1897. Third edition revised and annotated, London, T. P. S., 3 vols. 50*s*.

Mrs. Besant

In 1888 Mr. W. T. Stead, editor of *The Review of Reviews*, handed Mrs. Besant a copy of *The Secret Doctrine* to review; and that book made her a follower of Madame Blavatsky. She passed at one leap from Atheism to Theosophy; and, since the death of the foundress, she has been by far the most potent personality within the society.

From the beginning Olcott had been President and Judge Vice-President, while Madame Blavatsky herself had only held the position of Corresponding Secretary. When she died, Judge cabled from America to the London office, "Do nothing till I come." Within a few days after his arrival in London, he produced two messages which he declared had been sent by the Master Morya, Madame Blavatsky's own special monitor. Mrs. Besant accepted the missives as genuine, and publicly proclaimed in a great meeting in London that there could be no doubt about the existence of the Mahātmas, as communications had been received from them since the death of Madame Blavatsky. These messages continued to arrive. Mr. Judge's wisdom and the high place which he ought to have in the Society was their constant burden. Mrs. Besant was convinced of their genuineness; Olcott was in India; and in consequence Judge rose to great prominence in the movement. As a result of some of these wonderful epistles Olcott was so cowed that he actually resigned his position as President of the Society early in 1892. Shortly afterwards he withdrew his resignation, but at first without effect; for at the Annual Convention of 1892 Judge was elected President for life. This election, however, does not appear to have been ratified. A little later Mrs. Besant went to India. When all the documents were laid before Olcott, it became clear to him that Judge had forged them, and that he had abstracted from Madame Blavatsky's rooms in London the hand-made rice-paper [1] on which they were written and the seal with which most of them were sealed. Mrs. Besant examined all the evidence and recognized Judge's guilt. Olcott then wrote to Judge on the 12th of February, 1894, giving him the option of (*a*) retiring from all the offices he held in the Theo-

[1] It was the same paper as the Koot Hoomi letters were written on. See above, p. 259.

sophical Society, and leaving Olcott to make a general public explanation or (*b*) having a Judicial Committee convened and the whole of the proceedings made public. Judge refused to resign. It was therefore decided that all the documents should be placed in Mrs. Besant's hands, that she should preside over a judicial inquiry to be held at the Annual Convention in London in July, 1894, and that all the evidence should be published. This latter pledge was given in order to satisfy Indian Theosophists, who were insistent that the fraud should be exposed.

But, when the Judicial Committee met, Olcott and Judge being present as well as Mrs. Besant, a most extraordinary thing happened. After most serious deliberation, the Committee came to the conclusion that it was contrary to Theosophic principles to decide whether Judge was guilty or not. The trial was impossible! It was also agreed that the evidence which had been gathered should not be published. Clearly, the inner history of this most shameful transaction is that Judge, who knew all that had happened in Madras in 1884 and much else, threatened that, if he were exposed, he would expose everybody, but agreed to continue to work with the Colonel and Mrs. Besant on condition that the affair should be hushed up in such a way that his character should not suffer. All this the leaders endeavoured to carry out.

But many Theosophists felt that such immorality must not be condoned and concealed. One of the officials, Mr. W. R. Gorn Old, therefore urged the leaders at the London headquarters to have the evidence published. He was told that that was impossible: *Mrs. Besant had burned all the documents!* Like Judge in Madras,[1] she had found fire a most convenient means for getting rid of inconvenient evidence. But she did not know that, before the incrimi-

[1] See above, pp. 241–2.

nating documents were handed over to her in India, facsimile copies of all had been taken by Mr. Old. Even when he made this fact known at headquarters, and offered to hand the copies over for publication, the leaders refused to act. Then, Mr. Old, disgusted beyond measure because the officials would not carry out the promise made in India, that all the evidence should be published, and were determined as far as possible to hide the fraud, resigned his position and left the society. He then handed over the facsimiles of the documents to his friend, Mr. Edmund Garrett; and the whole story was published in *The Westminster Gazette*, October 29–November 8, 1894. It was thereafter republished in book form under the title *Isis Very Much Unveiled*. For his action Mr. Old was vehemently attacked by Theosophists as a traitor and a pledge-breaker; but, if Mrs. Besant and Colonel Olcott were justified in promising to publish all the evidence, how did Mr. Old do wrong in doing what they had promised to do? It was they who broke their pledges. He was also charged with having done it from sordid motives. As a matter of fact, through resignation of his offices in the Society, he lost a comfortable income, and he refused the honorarium of £80 offered him by the editor of *The Westminster Gazette* for his services.

It was probably this most unexpected publication of the evidence, blazoning his forgery to all the world, that drove Judge to the next step. He had agreed to work along with Olcott and Mrs. Besant; but, now that the evidence, which they had gathered against him, and which they could not repudiate, had been published, the only course open to him was to deny the facts and pose as a martyr. This he did. He broke away from the main Theosophical Society, carrying with him a majority of American Theosophists. These he formed into the Universal Brotherhood and Theosophical Society, and was elected their President for life. He lived, however, only eleven months longer. His place was taken by Mrs. Katherine Tingley. The headquarters of this rival organization are at Point Loma, California.

Neither Mrs. Besant nor Colonel Olcott ever attempted to deny any of the statements made in *The Westminster Gazette*. The whole fabric of gross and shameful fraud and concealment stands undeniable.

Since 1893 Mrs. Besant has spent most of her time in India, and has been very successful in building up Theosophy there. Her activity has run in the main along four lines. She has lectured a great deal in every part of India, making the defence and exposition of Hinduism her chief theme. Secondly, she has done a great deal for the education of Hindus. Hindus had established many colleges between 1879 and 1898; but, like Government colleges, they gave no religious instruction. The Central Hindu College, which she founded in Benares in 1898, is modelled on a missionary college, Hinduism taking the place of Christianity. From that centre she strove to spread this type of education throughout the Hindu community, founding schools in many places for both boys and girls. Thirdly, she has proved a most prolific and most effective writer. Tens of thousands of her books have been sold in many other lands as well as India. Lastly, she has given a good deal of time to occultism; but that we shall deal with later.

Mr. C. W. Leadbeater, who had been a curate of the Church of England, became a Theosophist in 1884, and since that time, with the exception of a break of some four years, he has been one of the officials of the society. He has worked in India, Ceylon, America and England. He is a very able writer.

He has also become notorious because of his occult investigations. We have seen that a secret society for the practice of occultism was formed within the Theosophic Society by Madame Blavatsky in 1888. Since her death Mrs. Besant and Mr. Leadbeater have been the leaders of the Esoteric School. They have re-organized the School, introduced a hierarchy of gurus and systematized the instruction, keeping certain very definite ends in view. They have also conducted a long series of occult investigations themselves, the results of which have been published from time to time. One of their chief methods is to read what they call the Etheric Record of past events,[1] and thereby reconstruct portions of ancient history.

Mr. Leadbeater on one occasion, on consulting the record, came to the startling conclusions, that Jesus and Christ were two distinct persons; that both were men, neither being the Logos, or the Son of God; that Jesus was born in 105 B.C.; that Christ was the great Master; that Jesus, wise and devoted though he was, merely yielded up his body for Christ to use; that the twelve Apostles never lived; and that there is scarcely a scrap of historical matter in the Gospels. The teaching now is that one ego was incarnated at a very early date as Hermes, again as Zoroaster, then as Orpheus, finally as Gautama the Buddha. Another ego was Christ. He used the body of Jesus as his vehicle. Jesus was born in 105 B.C., and was again incarnated as Apollonius of Tyana.

Much of this Mrs. Besant published in her book, *Esoteric Christianity*. It is also embodied in Mr. Leadbeater's own work, *The Christian Creed*, published in 1904. In 1903 Mr. G. R. S. Mead published *Did Jesus Live 100 B.C.?*, an attempt to collect and estimate all the evidence contained in Talmudic and Christian sources, bearing on the time when Jesus lived. He does not come to any decision on the main question.

[1] See below, p. 278.

5. In 1905 certain very serious charges were brought against Mr. Leadbeater. He was then in England, and held the office of Presidential Delegate in the British section of the society. It was said that he had given immoral teaching to boys in America, and had even gone the length of immoral acts. The leaders of the American Section of the society were greatly disturbed over the matter, and wished to have him expelled from the society. Since they did not possess this power themselves, it was decided that they should send a Commissioner to London to lay the matter before Colonel Olcott, the President-founder. Colonel Olcott called a special meeting, consisting of the Executive Committee of the British Section, the Commissioner from America, and a representative from France. The whole matter was carefully discussed and Mr. Leadbeater was examined. He confessed frankly enough to the charge of having given a number of boys the teaching complained of; and, under great pressure, he acknowledged that he might have been guilty also of some of the acts complained of. The printed minutes, legally authenticated, lie before me, as I write; so that there can be no question as to the absolute accuracy of these statements. Finally, Mr. Leadbeater's resignation was accepted, and he dropped out of the society. Mrs. Besant declared that he would not be restored until he repudiated his opinions on these matters.

6. Colonel Olcott died early in 1907, and Mrs. Besant became President of the Theosophic Society.

7. In January, 1909, Mrs. Besant announced in the *Theosophist* that the General Council had decided to allow Mr. Leadbeater to return to the society. Since then he has resided at the headquarters in Madras. He had not repudiated his teaching, nor has he yet done so. About the same time a defence of his teaching, written by an American Theosophist named Van Hoek, was circulated

in the Society. Two of the English leaders, backed by many members, appealed to the General Council to withdraw this document, but they refused. The result was that, under the leadership of Mr. G. R. S. Mead, a body of some 700 British Theosophists, including nearly all the cultured and influential members in the country, and a number in other lands, left the society.

8. Since the moment when Mr. Leadbeater settled at headquarters, occultism has come to the front, and is now the main activity of the society. Nor is that all. Mr. Leadbeater had already published most amazing accounts of what, as he asserted, he had seen in clairvoyance. But these were readings of the records of the past; while prophecy is now held to be one of the chief functions of occultism. We are told that the world is just about to enter on a new era of history. A great World-teacher will very soon enter upon his work. The human being whose body is to be the physical vehicle for the ego of this World-teacher is already in the Theosophical Society, and is to be trained for his task by Mrs. Besant and Mr. Leadbeater. Mrs. Besant will soon be seen to be one of the greatest rulers of the world of gods and men. Even those who stand nearest to her scarcely realize how great she is, and will be. Mrs. Besant, in turn, affirms that Mr. Leadbeater is a most exalted being, on the very threshold of divinity. In consequence, both these leaders and the Maḍrasi boy who is to be the vehicle of the coming Teacher are adored and praised by lowly bending groups of Theosophic initiates.

It was only gradually that all this was made public. Clearly, however, most careful preparation had been made for the supreme announcement. The new policy is meant to be a master-stroke to capture at once Christianity, Buddhism and Hinduism for the Theosophical Society. In England the coming one was called Christ, while in India and Ceylon he was called the Bodhisattva or Maitreya. He is said to be the ego which used the body of Jesus and was then called Christ. A new world-wide organization was created to prepare people for the Epiphany. At first it was called the Order of the Rising Sun, but three months later[1] was changed to the Order of the Star in the East. A most urgent propaganda was launched among the students of the Hindu College, Benares, in all the Theosophic lodges of the world, and among Christian people in England and elsewhere.

One of the most extraordinary accompaniments of this startling movement has been the publication of a book, written by Mrs. Besant and Mr. Leadbeater in collaboration, and called *Man: Whence, How and Whither*. This work is essentially a vast mythology, stretching away back some thirty thousand years. It is the pretended record of the repeated incarnations of the small group of people at present resident at the Theosophic headquarters at Adyar, Madras; and what we are asked to believe is that we have in the history represented in this record the preparation for the great events that will take place, when the great World-teacher makes his appearance. For example, we are told that in 13,500 B.C. "Jesus" was the wife of an emperor of southern India, while in 12,800 B.C. he was the brother of Madame Marie-Louise Kirby, and the father of Mrs. S. Maude Sharpe (General Secretary of the English Section), of Julius Cæsar, and of T. Subba Rao, the Teshu Lama being at that time his daughter.[2]

9. The new propaganda with its outrageous statements and limitless claims has led to considerable upheavals within Theosophy. The persistent preaching of the new doctrine

[1] April, 1911.

[2] For some account of the book see *Mrs. Besant and the Present Crisis in the Theosophical Society*, by Eugène Lévy.

to the students of the Hindu College, Benares, and the formation of numerous societies and classes for the study of its literature and other such purposes, enraged the mass of solid Hindus connected with the College. They protested seriously for some time, but got no redress. Finally, they were able to make things so hot for Mrs. Besant's personal followers on the teaching staff, that they resigned in a body and left. Mrs. Besant has thus lost nearly all her influence in the citadel of Hinduism.

There were also many members of the Society in India who resigned, probably as many as 500; but she still retains her hold over the great bulk of the Indian membership. A few seceded in England and in America. On account of a sharp disagreement between Mrs. Besant and Herr Steiner, the German leader, all the lodges in Germany, consisting of 2400 members, and several in Switzerland, were driven out of the movement. Germany has thus been forced to form a fresh organization. The new name is the Anthroposophical Society.

The third result has been a crop of lawsuits in Madras. The chief case arose from the fact that a Madrasi Brāhman, named G. Nārāyaṇa Aiyer, handed over his two sons to Mrs. Besant to be educated. The elder of these boys, J. Kṛishṇamurti, is called *Alcyone* in Mr. Leadbeater's occult investigations; and he is said to have been chosen as the vehicle of the coming Christ. Mrs. Besant placed the boys under Mr. Leadbeater's care in the matter of their studies. The father objected on the ground that Mr. Leadbeater is an immoral man.[1] Mrs. Besant consented to keep the boys apart from Mr. Leadbeater, but put them again under his care, and finally refused to separate them from him. The father then raised an action against her in the Madras courts, and won his case.[2] Mrs. Besant ap-

[1] See p. 273, above.

[2] See *The Alcyone Case*.

pealed, but lost again. She then appealed to the Privy Council in England; and the original case has been upset on a technical point.[1] Mrs. Besant brought lawsuits for defamation of character against two citizens of Madras, but both were dismissed. In the course of the four trials in Madras a great deal of very unfavourable evidence was produced against Leadbeater and Mrs. Besant. The following is an extract from the Judgment in the first case:

> Mr. Leadbeater admitted in his evidence that he has held, and even now holds, opinions which I need only describe as certainly immoral and such as to unfit him to be the tutor of the boys, and, taken in conjunction with his professed power to detect the approach of impure thoughts, render him a highly dangerous associate for children.[2]

In one case the judge declared that Mrs. Besant had defended Leadbeater's immoral teaching. In another the judge said Mrs. Besant had not shewn common honesty in her dealings with the father of the boys.

10. The Theosophic cause has suffered so seriously in India through the new propaganda and these lawsuits that Mrs. Besant has been making frantic efforts during the last nine months to achieve a new position by means of new activities. The first of these is a Theosophic movement in favour of social reform. This is a very noticeable change; for, until now, the Society has been reactionary on all social questions with the exception of early marriage, and Mrs. Besant has published long, elaborate defences of many superstitious observances in Hinduism connected with caste and the family. Hindus are being enrolled for the purpose of advancing social reform; and each stalwart appends his name to seven pledges.[3]

[1] *The Times, Weekly Edition*, May 8, 1914.
[2] *The Alcyone Case*, p. 260.
[3] *ISR.*, XXIV, 43.

Another proposal has been to form a *Young Men's Indian Association*, confessedly in imitation of the Young Men's Christian Association, and for the purpose of saving young men from Christian influence. The original idea was to make it a Hindu organization of a Theosophic type, but several of the Madras leaders refused to have anything to do with an organization that touched religion; and, in consequence, the proposal is now a purely secular one. There have been great difficulties in getting the project launched. When I was last in Madras,[1] all that had been done was to arrange for the opening of a small hostel, containing a reading room, but without a Superintendent.

11. We give next a very brief outline of the teaching given by Theosophists. Our sketch is drawn from Mr. C. W. Leadbeater's *Textbook of Theosophy*, and consists largely of quotations from it. We begin with a couple of sentences, descriptive of 'the Etheric Record,' which, we fancy, are necessary as a sort of preface to the whole:

> Theosophy has much to tell us of the past history of man — of how in the course of evolution he has come to be what he now is. This also is a matter of observation, because of the fact that there exists an indelible record of all that has taken place — a sort of memory of Nature — by examining which the scenes of earlier evolution may be made to pass before the eyes of the investigator as though they were happening at this moment.

We can now plunge into the major principles of the system:

> Of the Absolute, the Infinite, the All-embracing, we can at our present stage know nothing, except that It is; we can say nothing that is not a limitation, and therefore inaccurate.
>
> In It are innumerable universes; in each universe countless solar systems. Each solar system is the expression of a mighty Being, whom we call the LOGOS, the Word of God, the Solar Deity. He is to it all that men mean by God.

[1] In March, 1914.

Out of Himself He has called this mighty system into being. We who are in it are evolving fragments of His life, Sparks of His divine Fire; from Him we all have come; into Him we shall all return.

Next below this Solar Deity, yet also in some mysterious manner part of Him, come His seven Ministers, sometimes called the Planetary Spirits.

Under Them in turn come vast hosts or orders of spiritual Beings, whom we call Angels or Devas.

Here in our world there is a great Official who represents the Solar Deity, and is in absolute control of all the evolution that takes place upon this planet. We may imagine Him as the true KING of this world, and under Him are ministers in charge of different departments. One of these departments is concerned with the evolution of the different races of humanity, so that for each great race there is a Head who founds it, differentiates it from all others, and watches over its development. Another department is that of religion and education, and it is from this that all the greatest teachers of history have come — that all religions have been sent forth. The great Official at the head of this department either comes Himself or sends one of His pupils to found a new religion when He decides that one is needed.

Therefore all religions, at the time of their first presentation to the world, have contained a definite statement of the Truth, and in its fundamentals this Truth has been always the same.

It is foolish for men to wrangle over the question of the superiority of one teacher or one form of teaching to another, for the teacher is always one sent by the Great Brotherhood of Adepts, and in all its important points, in its ethical and moral principles, the teaching has always been the same.

In the earlier stages of the development of humanity, the great Officials of the Hierarchy are provided from outside, from other and more highly evolved parts of the system, but as soon as men can be trained to the necessary level of power and wisdom, these offices are held by them. In order to be fit to hold such an office a man must raise himself to a very high level, and must become what is called an Adept.

A large number of men have attained the Adept level . . . but always some of them remain within touch of our earth as members of this Hierarchy which has in charge the administration of the affairs of our world and of the spiritual evolution of our humanity.

This august body is often called the Great White Brotherhood.

A few of these great Adepts, who are thus working for the good of the world, are willing to take as apprentices those who have resolved to devote themselves utterly to the service of mankind; such Adepts are called Masters.

One of these apprentices was Helena Petrovna Blavatsky.

To attain the honour of being accepted as an apprentice of one of the Masters of the Wisdom is the object set before himself by every earnest Theosophical student. But it means a determined effort. There have always been men who were willing to make the necessary effort, and therefore there have always been men who knew. The knowledge is so transcendent that when a man grasps it fully he becomes more than man, and he passes beyond our ken.

Mr. Leadbeater next gives a chapter describing certain intricate chemical processes whereby a solar system is said to be formed from "the æther of space." Our own globe is a fair sample of all the planets; and it is said to be really seven interpenetrating worlds; the physical earth and six others which are beyond the ken of our ordinary senses but are visible to the eye of the clairvoyant or occultist, when far enough advanced. These six suprasensual worlds do not stand apart from the physical earth, but interpenetrate it at every point, occupying the same space which it occupies but also stretching far beyond it. The seven worlds are named in descending order, Divine, Monadic, Spiritual, Intuitional, Mental, Emotional (or Astral), Physical.

Each of these worlds has its inhabitants. The evolution of life is described in another chapter.

Man, according to Theosophy, is in essence a Spark of the divine Fire, belonging to the Monadic world mentioned above, and is called a Monad. For the purposes of human evolution the Monad manifests itself in lower worlds. It manifests itself in three aspects in the Spiritual, Intuitional and higher Mental worlds. This is the Theosophic soul, a Monad, a trinity, a self. This Monad is immortal, is born and dies many times, but is in no way affected by birth or death. Before birth he draws round him veils from the lower mental and astral worlds, and only then obtains his physical body. During life man in his bodies makes progress, slow or rapid: and according to his behaviour is his experience. As to death and the hereafter we read:

> Death is the laying aside of the physical body: but it makes no more difference to the ego than does the laying aside of an overcoat to the physical man. Having put off his physical body, the ego continues to live in his astral body until the force has become exhausted which has been generated by such emotions and passions as he has allowed himself to feel during earth-life. When that has happened, the second death takes place; the astral body also falls away from him, and he finds himself living in the mental body and in the lower mental world. In that condition he remains until the thought-forces generated during his physical and astral lives have worn themselves out; then he drops the third vehicle in its turn and remains once more an ego in his own world, inhabiting his causal body.

Man makes for himself his own purgatory and heaven, and these are not places, but states of consciousness. Hell does not exist; it is only a figment of the theological imagination; but a man who lives foolishly may make for himself a very unpleasant and long-enduring purgatory. Neither purgatory nor heaven can ever be eternal, for a finite cause cannot produce an infinite result.

After life for a shorter or longer time in the higher worlds the man is reborn, in order to make more progress. According to Theosophy, a man can never be born an animal. Nor is any final failure possible:

> This is a school in which no pupil ever fails; every one must go on to the end.

There is one further point which it is necessary to express here. As all religions are held to be in reality the same, Theosophy is said to place us at the standpoint where this unity becomes visible; and its function, we are told, is to strengthen every religion and to antagonize none.

12. But hitherto we have said nothing about that which is the core of the whole, namely occultism. We have seen that Madame Blavatsky started a secret society within the Society for the practical study of occultism in 1888.[1] Since then this Esoteric School has contained all the most convinced Theosophists. It seems clear, that under Mrs. Besant and Mr. Leadbeater, the organization has been greatly developed and the work of the school transformed. At present there is within the school an inner group called the Esoteric Section, and within that again a smaller group who have given special pledges to Mrs. Besant.[2] The chief investigations are carried on at headquarters in Madras by Mr. Leadbeater and Mrs. Besant: but the members of the school are found all over the world; and in most of the lodges classes are held in which young members receive their earliest lessons.

As members are bound by a pledge not to divulge what goes on in the school, it is extremely difficult for an outsider to realize what the aims, the methods and the results of Theosophic Occultism are. Even those who have broken

[1] P. 261, above. [2] See her portrait, Plate IX, facing p. 195.

absolutely with Theosophy feel they are still bound by the old pledges and will not speak out. Several things, however, may be said:

A. There is a regular hierarchy of gurus (*i.e.* teachers). They teach forms of meditation which are meant to still the mind and to make it receptive, receptive not only to teaching but to impressions on the sub-conscious plane. There are secret manuals which are put into the hands of junior members, and they are taught to practise this meditative discipline privately. The gurus use telepathic impressions and hypnotic suggestions to bring the minds of their disciples under their control. Everything that is taught must be accepted on the authority of the teacher: nothing can be tested. When these processes have been continued for some time, the mind becomes almost paralyzed, and is ready to receive and believe anything that comes through the teacher, and to disbelieve everything adverse.

The pupil as he advances meets the leaders in the esoteric section of his lodge.

B. The word which Leadbeater uses to describe his methods of research is Clairvoyance; but from many hints in the literature, and from words which have dropped from Theosophists in conversation I am convinced that hypnotic methods are much used.

C. We are frankly told that clairvoyant powers have no connection with intelligence, spirituality or purity of character:

> A constantly growing minority, however, of fairly intelligent people believe clairvoyance to be a fact, and regard it as a perfectly natural power, which will become universal in the course of evolution. They do not regard it as a miraculous gift, nor as an outgrowth from high spirituality, lofty intelligence, or purity of character. . . . They know that it is a power latent in all men, and that it can be developed by anyone who is able and

willing to pay the price demanded for its forcing, ahead of the general evolution.[1]

D. Results. In the process of working through masses of Theosophic literature and interviewing scores of individuals who have been connected with Theosophy I have become convinced that the following results arise from occultism:

i. On pupils the result is their complete subjugation to their gurus [2] and through their gurus to the leaders of the Theosophical Society. Scarcely anything is read except Theosophic literature; and the mind becomes incapable of believing that the guru or the leader can be wrong. We may realize how eager the leaders are to obtain this result from the fact that the members of the innermost group of all have each taken a personal pledge to Mrs. Besant, a pledge of "absolute obedience without cavil or delay." Apart from this result on the mind, it would be hard to understand how, in spite of the frequent exposures of the leaders, the mass of Theosophists continue their adhesion without a break.

ii. It is well known that the continued practice of spiritualism drives all mediums to fraud. However honest they may be, however real the bulk of the phenomena appearing through them may be, a moment comes when reality fails them, and the temptation to pretend and to deceive is overwhelming. The same danger haunts the Theosophic leaders. The pursuit of occultism necessarily involves them in a constant straining after results and the consequent acceptance of illusions. They live in a world half-true, half-false.

[1] *Man: Whence, How, and Whither*, quoted in Lévy, 110.

[2] Madame Blavatsky used the word "psychologize" for this process. In a letter written from America to a Hindu in Bombay, she called Olcott "a psychologized baby" (*Proceedings*, IX, 311); and writing of Bavaji to M. Solovyoff in 1886, she says, "He is an obedient and clever boy! He is an obedient weapon in my hands! 'Je l'ai psychologisé.'" (*MPI.*, 184.)

Necessarily, the mind ceases to distinguish sharply between truth and falsehood. A clear case from Mrs. Besant's own life may be cited here. One evening in a lecture in London she declared, to the amazement of the whole audience, that Madame Blavatsky had been again incarnated. After the lecture her own friends asked her how she had come to say such a thing. She replied, "O, I just felt like it." She had not a particle of evidence. Probably she did not realize that she was romancing and misleading her audience. Another instance is her pamphlet in defence of Madame Blavatsky.[1] Similarly, the Theosophists felt sure they had an irrefragable case until Hodgson cross-examined them: they had not realized in the slightest their own extreme inaccuracy. Necessarily, the blurring of the distinction between truth and falsehood weakens the conscience in other directions also. This sheds a little more light on the Theosophic mind. Madame Blavatsky's frauds, Olcott's inaccuracy and lies,[2] Judge's shrine-burning[3] and forgeries,[4] Sinnett's editorial achievements,[5] Leadbeater's immoralities,[6] and Mrs. Besant's behaviour in the Judge case,[7] all are made a little more intelligible. There was loose morality in some of these cases to begin with; but occultism and its attendant phenomena did the rest.

13. The enslaving of the minds of the members, however, will not stand as a full explanation of the survival of the system. If in spite of exposures which would destroy almost any society, members still remain true to Theosophy, it is clear that it must meet certain needs of our day which otherwise do not find satisfaction. It will therefore be worth while to attempt to discover what its chief attractions are.

[1] Appendix, p. 447. [2] *Proceedings*, IX, 237–239. [3] Pp. 241–2, above.
[4] See above, pp. 268–9. [5] Pp. 232, 257, above, and *MPI.*, 157.
[6] P. 273, above. [7] Pp. 268–70, above.

A. One of the most outstanding features of the nineteenth century was the rise of accurate knowledge of the religions of the world. The religions of antiquity, especially of Egypt, Babylonia, Assyria, Persia, India and China, have been explored by a great company of scholarly Orientalists. The faiths of the ruder peoples have been described by an army of missionaries, travellers, traders and anthropologists. The whole has been built up into a new and most imposing science, the science of religions. Further, during the last half-century our knowledge of the human mind, and especially of its more abnormal activities, has grown very rapidly. In consequence, psychological interests and methods of study hold a great place in modern thought.

The thinking men of our time are vividly conscious of these masses of fresh knowledge. Even if they do not care to study psychology and the religions in detail, they want to know what practical attitude a reasonable man ought to take towards the religions, and also towards telepathy, hypnotism, clairvoyance and such like. The Church of Christ thus far has failed to give clear expression to her mind on these matters. Yet, it is high time she should do so, for guidance is wanted; and if the Church is not able to suggest a reasonable attitude, thinking men will follow the guidance of other schools of thought.

Now the Theosophical Society is first of all sympathetic to all religions. It has assumed a generous attitude, the attitude of appreciation and friendliness. Nor is that all. The society has its text-books and classes, its teachers and lecturers, and invites men and women to come and study, to come and enjoy the rich feast which Oriental religions offer to the student. The Christian doctrine of the brotherhood of men is also taught: Theosophists are bid receive men of all religions as brothers. The bulk of the work they have done in the exposition of religions is unscientific and seriously misleading. They have usually filled men's heads with froth instead of knowledge. Yet the fact remains that they have attempted to do in a wrong way the work the Church of Christ ought to have done in the right way. This is unquestionably the first attraction which Theosophy presents to the outsider; and it is the attraction which has drawn to it the great majority of the more intellectual men who at one time or another have belonged to it.

B. The second attraction is the promise of occult knowledge and secret power. A very small number of really notable men, *e.g.* Sir William Crookes and M. V. S. Solovyoff, the Russian man of letters, were attracted to Madame Blavatsky by this side of her work, although they soon discovered the hollowness of her pretences.[1] But it is this aspect of the system also which draws the mass of the devoted Theosophists of the West. The sheer fascination of secrecy lays hold of them, the hope of exclusive knowledge, the promise of a path to occult development. Then, once these people enter the Esoteric School, the system holds them like a vice. One friend who has escaped from the toils describes most vividly the fierce mental and spiritual struggle which it cost to regain freedom.

C. In India and Ceylon it is perfectly clear that the great mass of members have been drawn by neither of these two attractions but simply and solely by the Theosophic defence of Hinduism and Buddhism. Thousands of Orientals, whose minds had been filled with shivering doubts about their religion by the Western education they had received, have fled to Theosophy for refuge with great joy and relief. The defence goes a very long way. The depths to which Mrs. Besant habitually descends in defending Hinduism will hardly be believed. There is scarcely an ex-

[1] *MPI.*, 7.

ploded doctrine, scarcely a superstitious observance, which she has not defended with the silliest and most shameful arguments. No one who has not scanned the files of *The Central Hindu College Magazine* or the reports of Mrs. Besant's lectures in India has any idea of the indescribable rubbish which Theosophy has presented to its Hindu members. But there is another side to all this. It is a simple matter of fact that for several decades Hindu and Buddhist thought and civilization were most unjustly depreciated and unmercifully condemned by missionaries, by Europeans in general and even by some Hindus. Only a few Orientalists escape this censure. There was thus really good reason for a crusade in defence of these systems.

14. To estimate the value of the work done by Theosophy is rather a difficult task. It has certainly popularized, in Europe and America, a number of the best Oriental books, such as the Upanishads and the *Gītā*, and has taught Theosophists to sympathize with Orientals and to think of them as brothers; while in India it has helped to restore to the Hindu and the Buddhist that self-respect which tended to evaporate amid the almost universal depreciation of Oriental thought, life and art.

But there is a vast amount to be placed on the other side of the account. Theosophy under Madame Blavatsky condemned and ridiculed Orientalists, and yet took from them, almost without acknowledgment, practically all the trustworthy knowledge of the East it possessed. Further in spite of all its pretences and all its noise, Theosophy has made no contribution whatever to our knowledge of Oriental religions. It has not discovered a single fresh historical fact, nor brought a fresh text to the notice of scholars, nor produced a notable translation or commentary. Thousands of copies of Mrs. Besant's translation of the *Gītā* have been sold; but no scholar would dream of referring to it for the translation of a difficult line. Apart from the writings of Mr. G. R. S. Mead and one or two others, we must pronounce the whole vast literature of the Theosophical Societies worthless from the point of view of scientific knowledge. Where is there a single scholar, historian or philosopher to be found amongst its members? One and all are repelled by the charlatanism of the literature. There is, last of all, the gross disservice it renders by filling the heads of its ordinary members with the cosmological and historical rubbish which is dumped in such heaps by the high-priests of occultism at headquarters, and with the impudently worthless trash published in defence of superstitions which thoughtful Hindus would do anything to get rid of.

15. Mrs. Besant constantly proclaims both in India and in England that a man can become a Theosophist and yet remain a true Christian; nay, she goes further and says that Theosophy will make a man a better Christian. Is this contention justifiable? The facts contained in the following paragraphs will enable readers to judge:

(1) Instead of the Heavenly Father of Jesus Christ, with whom every man may come into closest personal relationships in worship, prayer and communion, Theosophy offers us, as the Supreme, *an unknowable IT*.[1]

(2) Theosophy detaches religion from God. The ancient wisdom which it teaches is not a revelation from the Unknowable, but proceeds from the human Masters who are in charge of the department of religion in our world.[2]

(3) Necessarily there is no prayer in Theosophy, since the Supreme is unknowable.

(4) There is no worship of God in Theosophy. It is the Masters, and such people as Alcyone, Mrs. Besant and Mr. Leadbeater who receive adoration.

[1] Above, p. 278. [2] Above, p. 279.

(5) The Gospels are condemned as utterly unhistorical.[1]

(6) Jesus and Christ are declared to be distinct persons.[2]

(7) Neither Jesus nor Christ is the Son of God: they are said to be mere men.[3]

(8) The whole story of Jesus as given in the Gospels, and also by Tacitus, is made unhistorical; for He was not born under Augustus, in the days of Herod the King, but a century earlier, in B.C. 105.[4] He is said to be one of the Masters on earth now and to spend most of his time in the Lebanon.

(9) It was another quite obscure fanatical preacher who was condemned to death and executed in Jerusalem about 30 A.D.[5]

(10) According to Theosophic teaching, Jesus was not crucified for the sins of men. No such death could be an atonement for the sins of others. It could only be punishment for His own sins in a former life; for the sway of the doctrine of Karma knows no exception.

(11) The Second Coming of Christ which Mrs. Besant refers to is not the Second Coming of the crucified Jesus, the Son of God, but the return of a man named Christ, who, according to Mrs. Besant's story, for a time used as His vehicle the body of a man named Jesus, who was born 105 B.C.

(12) Christianity teaches that, "It is appointed unto men once to die; and after death cometh judgment"; while Theosophy teaches that every human being is born and dies many times.

This catalogue might be made much longer; but we believe it is quite long enough. We ask our readers to consider seriously whether Mrs. Besant acts rightly, when she stands up before a great audience of Christian people in England, who know nothing of these Theosophic doctrines which she has in her mind, and tells them that to become Theosophists will not make them disloyal Christians.

[1] Leadbeater, *The Christian Creed*, 15. [2] *Ib.*, 13, 29. [3] *Ib.*, 15, 27, 29.
[4] Above, p. 272. [5] Leadbeater, *The Inner Life*, I, 183.

Every Christian teacher and minister ought to inform himself of the true nature of this poisonous anti-Christian system; for attempts are being made in many places to introduce it into the Church.

For the relation between Theosophy and the Rādhā Soāmi system, see above, p. 172, and for its influence on the Parsees, p. 344, below.

LITERATURE. — JUDGE: *Isis Very Much Unveiled*, by Edmund Garrett, London, Westminster Gazette Office, 1894, 1*s*. THE LEADBEATER CASE: See *The Alcyone Case* (below). TEACHING: *Esoteric Christianity*, by Annie Besant, London, T. P. S., 1901, 5*s*. net. *Did Jesus Live 100 B.C.?* by G. R. S. Mead, London, T. P. S., 1903, 9*s*. net. *The Christian Creed*, by C. W. Leadbeater, London, T. P. S., 1904, 3*s*. 6*d*. net. *A Textbook of Theosophy*, by C. W. Leadbeater, Madras, Theosophist Office, 1912, 1*s*. 6*d*. net. *Man; Whence, How, and Whither*, by Annie Besant and C. W. Leadbeater, Madras, T. P. H., 1913. ALCYONE: *Mrs. Besant and the Alcyone Case*, by Veritas, Madras, Goodwin and Co., 1913, 3*s*. (A detailed account of the first trial in Madras.) *Mrs. Besant and the Present Crisis in the Theosophical Society*, by Eugène Lévy, London, Heywood Smith, 1913, 1*s*. net.

4. SECTARIAN MOVEMENTS IN HINDUISM

The rise of the modern spirit and the example set by the great movements we have already discussed had the effect of stirring each of the chief Hindu sects to self-defence and to various efforts for the strengthening of the community.

A. The Mādhvas

It was the Mādhvas of South India who first bestirred themselves to mutual help and organization. They are a Vishṇuite sect, and are followers of Madhva, a philosophic thinker, who formed his system and created his sect, in the Canarese country in Western India, in the thirteenth century. The sect is strongest in the part of the country where it arose, but it is found scattered throughout the South; and the Chaitanya sect of Bengal and Brindaban sprang from its influence. Like all the other theistic sects, they are Vedāntists, their form of the Vedānta being dualistic. Kṛishṇa is their favourite incarnation. A considerable number of cultured and well-to-do men are Mādhvas.

Thirty-seven years ago, a member of the sect, Mr. Kanchi Sabba Raoji, who had had a good English education, and was a Deputy-Collector of the First Grade under the Madras Government, conceived the idea of forming a society to unite the Mādhvas, to stimulate the systematic study of Mādhva literature, and to look after the Mādhva temples. In 1877 he succeeded in forming the *Mādhva Siddhāntonnahinī Sabhā*, or Association for the Strengthening of the Mādhva System. An annual Conference is held, at which speeches are delivered, examinations in the sacred books conducted, and prizes and honours conferred. A well-managed Bank, with a capital of three lacs of rupees, is connected with the society, and is able to give an annual grant in aid of its work. The Mahārājas of Travancore and Mysore, and a large number of wealthy titled gentlemen, are patrons and life-members of the society; and all the leading educated Mādhvas of the South are members. The Conference meets at Chirtanur, near Tirupati, in the Madras Presidency.

From the *Thirty-Fourth Annual Report*[1] it appears that the founder of the society did all he could to stimulate the paṇḍits of the sect to study the literature. His hope was that, if the paṇḍits could be made educated men, it would be possible to bring the mass of the people to an intelligent knowledge of their religion, and to raise the whole standard of thought and life throughout the sect. The *Report* says that most of the men whom the founder dealt with have

[1] Published by Thompson & Co., Madras, 1912.

passed away, and that worthy successors are hard to find. All capable young Mādhvas seek an English education, and are altogether unwilling to become paṇḍits.

In recent years, the sect has produced a number of books to help its people in the circumstances of to-day. Most of these are in the vernaculars, but a few are in English. S. Subba Rao has translated Madhva's *Commentary on the Vedānta-sūtras*,[1] and has done the work well; but the most noteworthy book is the *Life and Teachings of Sri Madhvacharyar*, by C. M. Padmanabha Char, of Coimbatore.[2]

B. The Chaitanyas

1. Early in the sixteenth century, a young Bengali sannyāsī, named Kṛishṇa Chaitanya, belonging to Nuddea (then, as now, celebrated as a seat of Sanskrit learning), founded a new sect which worships Kṛishṇa and Rādhā. The theology he taught was the system of Madhva, but in other matters he was a follower of the earlier Vishṇuites of Bengal. He was a man of extremely emotional temperament, and won his success by a tempest of devotion. He would repeat the sweet name of his Lord till he lost all self-consciousness, and imagined himself Kṛishṇa or his beloved Rādhā. He and his followers would sit together for hours, singing hymns in praise of Kṛishṇa with instrumental accompaniment, until they lost themselves in ecstasy and love. This was called *saṅkīrtana*, united praise. Then they would sally out, drums beating and flags flying, and would march through the streets, dancing and singing to Kṛishṇa with such contagious joy and holy rapture, that the whole town would be swept along on the tide of devotion. This was called *nagarkīrtana*, town-praise. The composition of popular hymns was thus as character-

[1] Madras, Natesan, Rs. 3, as. 8. [2] To be had of the author. Rs. 3.

istic of Chaitanya's followers as it is of the Salvation Army. In consequence there arose from his movement a new rich literature of religious song in the vernacular.[1] These poems and hymns did much to mould the mind of Rabindra Nath Tagore.[2] During Chaitanya's lifetime, the movement was wholesome and uplifting, but it soon degenerated to carelessness and uncleanness. The pure flame was kept burning in a few families; but the fall had been so serious that during the first half of the nineteenth century, the sect was very little thought of in Bengal.

2. We have already seen that Keshab Chandra Sen belonged to one of the good old Vaishṇava families, that one of his earliest associates in his religious work was Bijay Kṛishṇa Gosvāmī, a lineal descendant of one of the personal companions of Chaitanya, and that they successfully introduced into the Brāhma Samāj the enthusiastic devotional methods which we have just described.[3]

Both these forms of praise have also been adopted by the Christian Church in Bengal. *Saṅkīrtana* may be witnessed in any gathering; and, when the annual united Conference is held in Calcutta in October, a *nagarkīrtana* procession passes through the northern parts of the city.

3. But the Neo-Kṛishṇa movement of Bengal is above all things a literary movement. When Bijay Kṛishṇa Gosvāmī finally left the Brāhma Samāj in 1886, he and some friends sought to create a modernized Vaishṇavism, a mystic Hinduism meant to be a revival of the Chaitanya spirit; and their preaching was not without result; but no organization resulted from their labours. The literary revival, on the other hand, has been very successful. It was Christianity and Christian criticism that led to the movement. The steady toil of the Mission Colleges of Calcutta had

[1] Sen's *History of Bengali Language and Literature*, chap. V.

[2] See p. 385, below.

[3] See pp. 41 and 47, above.

produced among educated Bengalis a distinct liking for the Gospels and a craving for a perfect character such as Christ's for daily contemplation and imitation. The official Librarian of the Bengal Government wrote in 1899:

> There is no denying the fact that all this revolution in the religious belief of the educated Hindu has been brought about as much by the dissemination of Christian thought by Missionaries as by the study of Hindu scriptures; for Christian influence is plainly detectable in many of the Hindu publications of the year.

On the other hand, Orientalists and missionaries had openly declared that the incarnation-stories of Rāma and Kṛishṇa were myths, and that the *Gītā* did not come from Kṛishṇa. The aim of the whole movement is to destroy this criticism, and to persuade the Bengali to put Kṛishṇa in the place of Christ and the *Gītā* in the place of the Gospels.

The new literature falls into three groups, dealing respectively with (*a*) the historicity of the traditional life of Kṛishṇa, (*b*) his life and character, regarded as an example for imitation, (*c*) the *Gītā*. Of all the books of the Neo-Kṛishṇa literature *Kṛishṇacharitra*, a Bengali prose work by the great novelist Baṅkim Chandra Chatterji, has been by far the most influential. The main purpose of the work is to prove the historicity of the man-God Kṛishṇa; and, though its reasoning is but a house of cards, it has been used as the critical arsenal of the whole movement. Many books have also been written in English on the life and character of Kṛishṇa, notably *Lord Gaurāṅga* by Sishir Kumar Ghose. A daily text-book, called *The Imitation of Śree Kṛishṇa*, acknowledges by its title and its form the Christian influence which inspired it. Of texts and translations of the *Gītā* there is an endless catalogue; and there have been several books written to prove that the *Gītā* lays the foundations of a universal religion.

But there is a wider interest connected with this literature. The *Gītā* has won its way to recognition throughout the world, and is widely read in Europe and America. It was one of the first Sanskrit books introduced to Europe; for it was translated into English in 1785 by Charles Wilkins. Since then it has received a great deal of attention from Western Scholars. Edwin Arnold's translation, *The Song Celestial,* did much to make it known; and the Theosophical Society has introduced it to thousands.

A Bengali, named Surendranath Mukerji, a nephew of Mr. Justice Anukul Chandra Mukerji of Calcutta, had rather a romantic history in America. He was a follower of Chaitanya, and became a sannyāsī, taking the name Premānanda Bhāratī. He was usually called Bābā Bhāratī. He went to New York in 1902, and lectured on Kṛishṇa with great success not only in New York, but in Boston, Los Angeles (where he built a Hindu temple), and elsewhere. In 1907 he returned to India with a few American disciples, and opened a Mission in Calcutta. But funds failed, and he returned to America. He published two books, one on *Kṛishṇa* and one on *Light on Life.* He died in Calcutta in January, 1914.

The Vaishṇavas of Orissa and the Northern Telugu country held a Convention at least once. It took place at Berhampore, Ganjam, in December, 1910. The Chairman was Bābā Bhāratī. Religious education in schools and the translation of Vaishṇava literature into the vernacular seem to have been the chief matters under discussion.

LITERATURE. — *Chaitanya's Pilgrimages and Teachings,* translated into English by Jadunath Sarkar, London, Luzac, 1913, 3*s.* net. (A translation of the central portion of the best of the early Bengali biographies of Chaitanya.) *Gītā and Gospel,* by J. N. Farquhar, Madras, C. L. S., 6 as. (The Appendix gives an account of the Neo-Kṛishṇa Movement in Bengal and a list of the chief books down to 1903.) *Kṛishṇacharitra* by Baṅkim Chandra Chatterji, Calcutta, 1886 and 1892. (Bengali prose. Meant to prove Kṛishṇa historical.) *The Bhagavadgītā*, translated by M. M. Chatterji, New York, 1887. (A Theosophic attempt to put the *Gītā* on a level with the New Testament.) *Lord Gauraṅga*, by Shishir Kumar Ghose, Calcutta, 1897. Two vols. (A life of Chaitanya in English prose. A very inflated work.)

C. The Śrī-Vaishṇavas

The sect of Rāmānuja, called the Śrī-Vaishṇavas, holds a very striking position among the Hindus of the South. They own many of the greatest and wealthiest temples; a large proportion of the members of the sect are Brāhmans; and English education has made great headway amongst them. One would not have been surprised if they had become organized for self-defence and advance much earlier than most sects. But they are divided into a pair of very hostile sub-sects, called Vaḍa-galais, and Teṅ-galais; and many of the members of both subdivisions are strictly orthodox. They were thus rather late in developing modern movements.

They have had one scholar, however, who has done his very utmost to uphold the dignity of the sect by his writings both in English and the vernacular, Mr. A. Govindāchārya Svāmī of Mysore City. Since 1898 he has published a long list of books, the most noteworthy of which are: *Rāmānuja's Commentary on the Gītā*, the *Holy Lives of the Āzhvārs*, and the *Life of Rāmānuja*. A little monthly in English, named the *Viśish.ādvaitin*, was also published for some time, but it has been discontinued.

Then in 1902 a group of Śrī-Vaishṇavas resident in the Mysore State formed a society named the Ubhayavedānta Pravartana Sabhā, or Association for the Promotion of both forms of the Vedānta, which has continued to do good work ever since. It is clearly modelled on the Mādhva Sabhā, as will be seen from the following statement of aims:

(1) To encourage the study of Viśishṭādvaita works in Sanskrit and Tamil;

(2) To hold an annual examination at Melkote (Tirunārāyanapuram), the most sacred Vaishṇava Shrine in the Mysore State, and to award prizes to successful candidates; and

(3) To facilitate the propagation of Viśishṭādvaita philosophy by providing, as funds permit, for the holding of religious classes, delivery of lectures, employment of itinerant teachers and preachers, etc.

Another society with similar aims was recently formed in Madras, the Śrī Viśishṭādvaita Siddhānta Saṅgam. From a report of a general meeting published in the *Hindu* on March 3rd, 1914, it seems clear that the society wishes to encourage religious education in the vernacular among the young people of the community, so that they may not lose their religion.

LITERATURE.—*Śrī Bhagavadgītā with Śrī Rāmānuja's Commentary*, translated by A. Govindāchārya, Madras, Vaijayanti Press, 1898, Rs. 5. *The Holy Lives of the Āzhvārs* (*i.e.* the Ālvārs), by A. Govindāchārya, Mysore, G. T. A. Press, 1902, Rs. 1 as. 8. *The Divine Wisdom of the Drāvida Saints* (*i.e.* the Āḷvārs), by A. Govindāchārya, Madras, C. N. Press, 1902, Rs. 2. *The Life of Rāmānuja*, by A. Govindāchārya, Madras, Murthy & Co., 1906, Rs. 2 as. 12. (A translation of a thirteenth-century Tamil life.)

D. *Four Vaishṇava Sects*

In the month of May, 1911, the four chief Vaishṇava sects, the Śrī-Vaishṇavas, the Mādhvas, the Vallabhas and the Nimbārkas, took part in a united Vaishṇava Conference held at Allahabad. Several papers of considerable interest were read, and were afterwards published in the

Brahmavādin for October and November, 1912. The Conference met also in 1913, at Jaora in Malwa, but no Report has yet been published.

E. The Śaiva Siddhānta

Among the many sects which honour Śiva the Śaiva Siddhānta is decidedly the most interesting; for it has a great history, and possesses a very rich literature, both in Sanskrit and Tamil. It is also one of the largest and most influential bodies in South India. A considerable proportion of its people are now cultured men of position and influence. English education is spreading steadily amongst them; and the pressure of European thought is keenly felt.

Śaiva Sabhās, *i.e.* Śivaite Associations, have sprung up in several places, notably at Palamcottah and Tuticorin. The Śaiva Sabhā of Palamcottah dates from 1886, and has had an honourable history. Its objects are the propagation of the principles of the Śaiva Siddhānta among Śaivas and others, the supervision of religious institutions, when funds are mismanaged, the cultivation of the Dravidian languages and the betterment of social conditions in South India. The means employed are classes, lectures, the publication of literature, a library, and in recent years, an annual Conference (see below). The Sabhā owns a printing press.

The sect has been fortunate in drawing the attention of a number of scholarly missionaries; and in recent years they have had several scholars of their own, who have worked faithfully for the elucidation of the literature. Of these the chief have been Mr. V. V. Ramanan and Mr. J. M. Nallasvāmī Piḷḷai.

Until 1895 very little was known about the sect. A few essays had appeared by Hoisington, Pope and Cobban, but that was all. In that year, however, Mr. Nallasvāmī Piḷḷai published an English translation [1] of what is regarded as the fundamental scripture of the Siddhānta, the *Śiva-jnāna-bodha*, "Instruction in Śiva-Knowledge." It is a short manual of dogma in Sanskrit, accompanied by an elaborate Tamil commentary by Mey-kaṇḍa-devar, a famous theologian of the thirteenth century. In 1900 Mr. Nallasvāmī Piḷḷai and his friends succeeded in starting a monthly English magazine, *The Siddhānta Dīpikā*, or Lamp of the Siddhānta, for the purpose of giving expression to the best thought of the sect. It has done good work. Many translations are published in it. An English translation of the Śivaite commentary on the *Vedānta-sūtras*, which is by Nīlakaṇṭhāchārya and is called the *Śaiva Bhāshya*, appeared in its pages, and is now being issued in book form. In 1900 Dr. G. U. Pope's edition and translation of Māṇikka Vāchakar's *Tiruvāchakam* [2] drew wide attention to the sect. Three years ago Mr. Nallāsvāmī Piḷḷai published a very useful volume, called *Studies in Śaiva Siddhānta*.[3] We ought also to mention a booklet by the Hon. Mr. P. Arunachulam, of the Ceylon Civil Service, *Studies and Translations from the Tamil*.[4]

Since 1906 the sect has held an annual Conference, the Śaiva Siddhānta Mahāsamājam, at various towns in the north of the Tamil country. The last for which a Report has reached me was held at Conjeeveram in December, 1912. Papers are read and resolutions passed, and the whole Conference helps to encourage and uplift the sect. The last Conference was held at Vellore on the 26th, 27th, and 28th December, 1913. An interesting appreciation of the gathering appeared in *The Harvest Field* for January,

[1] Madras, Somasundara Nayagar. [2] Oxford, the University Press.

[3] Madras, Meykandan Press, 1911, Rs. 3.

[4] Madras, Siddhānta Dipika Office, 1898, as. 4.

1914. Since 1909 the Śaiva Sabhā of Palamcottah has held an Annual Conference in Palamcottah, which is very similar in character to the Mahāsamājam. The latter draws its supporters mainly from the north, while the former influences the south of the Tamil country.

In March last I had the privilege and pleasure of interviewing the head of the Tirujnāna Sambandha Svāmī Maṭha in Madura. His name is Svāminātha Deśika. He received me most courteously, explained the course of instruction followed in the monastery, and also told me about his own tours among his disciples. He said that he sympathized with the Śaiva Siddhānta Mahāsamājam, but could not agree with it in all things, and that he did not attend the annual gathering, because, among other reasons, he does not feel that, as a sannyāsī, he can travel by railway.

F. The Liṅgāyats

In the twelfth century, at Kalyān in the south of the Bombay Presidency, Basava, the prime minister of the state, founded a new Śaiva sect called the Vīra Śaivas, *i.e.* the heroic, or excellent Śaivas. No Brāhman was allowed to act as priest in the sect,[1] and the members renounced caste altogether; but the old poison has crept in amongst them again, and they demand recognition for their caste distinctions in the census papers. There seems to be no theological doctrine marking them off from other Śivaites; but each person wears a miniature *liṅga* (Śiva's phallic symbol) in a reliquary hung around his neck, and holds it in the palm of his left hand during his private worship. Hence they are usually called Liṅgāyats. The men who act as their priests and gurus are called Jaṅgamas and may belong to any caste. Jaṅgama-worship is one of the

[1] Cf. the Tiyas, below, p. 312.

most essential parts of the cult of the sect. The Jaṅgama sits down in yoga-posture, and his disciple sits down before him and performs the sixteen operations of worship, precisely as is done in the case of an idol. The chief books of the sect are *Siddhānta Śikhāmaṇi*, *Kriyasāra*, *Liṅgadhārana Chandrikā*, *Vīra Śaiva Dharma Śiromaṇi*, and the bhāshya mentioned below. The Basava Purāṇas are popular books of far less consequence.

Thirty years ago the Liṅgāyat Education Association was formed for the promotion of modern education within the community. Large gifts from the wealthiest members of the sect, supplemented by smaller sums from others, sufficed to create an endowment (now amounting to Rs. 225,000), the proceeds of which are used to help poor Liṅgāyat boys to get an education. This central fund has its office in Dharwar. In recent years other organizations have arisen elsewhere, notably the Mysore Liṅgāyat Education Fund, which was organized in Bangalore in 1905, and a hostel for Liṅgāyat students, the Virashaiva Ashram, Kalbadevi, Bombay. In consequence, the community is making progress in education, and many of the younger Liṅgāyats are getting into Government service.

Some ten years ago the All-India Liṅgāyat Conference met for the first time to discuss problems, both religious and secular, which affect the life and standing of the sect. In 1905 the Conference met at Bangalore, and the organization of the Mysore Education Fund was one of the results of the gathering. The Conference of 1913 met at Belgaum. There have been divisions of opinion on various questions, especially religious questions; and, in consequence the Conference has resolved to restrict itself to educational, economic and other secular problems; and all religious subjects are to be dealt with by the *Śivayogmandir*, which is clearly under the control of the Jaṅgamas.

Literature is not being neglected. The Liṅgāyat commentary on the *Vedānta-sūtras* is by Śrīpati Paṇḍitārādhya and is called *Śrīkara Bhāshya*. One-half of this commentary was printed many years ago in Canarese character, but, until recently, no copy, either manuscript or printed, of the second half was known to exist. A good Ms. of the latter has now been found, and Dewan Bahadur Putana Chetty, until recently one of the Councillors of the Mysore State, has arranged to have the whole text edited by competent paṇḍits and printed in *devanāgarī*. The philosophic standpoint of this commentary is said to be *śakti-viśishṭādvaita*. Liṅgāyats state that there were two earlier Liṅgāyat commentaries, by Renukāchārya and Nīlakaṇṭhāchārya respectively, but no Mss. of these works now exist.

G. *The Left-hand Śāktas*

Śakti is a Sanskrit word meaning strength, energy. It is used in every Hindu sect to designate the wife of a god as his energy in action. Lakshmī is the *śakti* of Vishṇu; while Umā is the *śakti* of Śiva. But a number of sects give nearly all their attention to the *śakti* of Śiva, to the neglect of Śiva himself. These sects are known as *Śāktas*. They usually call the *śakti Devī*, *i.e.* the Goddess; but Kālī, or Durgā, is also frequently used. Their sectarian books are called Tantras.

These Devī-worshipping sects fall into two groups, distinguished the one from the other as the Right-hand Śāktas and the Left-hand Śāktas. The Right-hand Śāktas are scarcely distinguishable from ordinary Hindus, except in this that they worship Kālī; but the Left-hand Śāktas have several very distinct characteristics. We need not discuss their theology here in detail: for us the significant point is their worship. According to them Moksha, *i.e.*

release from transmigration, can be achieved in this evil age only by their peculiar ritual. They meet in private houses, and worship in secret. A group of worshippers is known as a *chakra* or circle. In the room there is either an image of the goddess or a *yantra*, that is, a diagram which mystically represents the goddess. The actual cult consists in partaking of the *Pañchatattva*, *i.e.* the five elements. They are also called the *Pañchamakāra*, *i.e.* the five m's, because the Sanskrit names of the elements all begin with the letter m: they are wine, meat, fish, parched grain and sexual intercourse. A worship-circle always consists of both men and women; and people of any caste or of no caste are admitted. The actual observances are foul beyond description, always involving promiscuity, and often incest.

No modern organization, so far as the writer is aware, has undertaken to modernize or defend this system; yet there have been tentative defences by two individuals. By far the greatest and best book belonging to the sect is the *Mahānirvāṅa Tantra*. A translation of this work was published in 1900 by Manmatha Nath Dutt Śāstrī, M.A.[1] In his Introduction[2] the following paragraph occurs:

> However abhorrent these rites may appear on the face of them, there is no doubt that there is a great esoteric meaning behind them. All these, meat, wine, fish and women are objects of temptation. If a worshipper can overcome this temptation, the road to eternal bliss is clear for him. It is not an easy affair for a man to have a youthful and beautiful damsel before him and worship her as a goddess without feeling the least lustful impulse within him. He is to take wine, after dedicating it to the goddess, not for the purpose of intoxicating but for that of concentrating his mind on the object of his devotions. He is to take meat and fish, not because they are palatable dishes but because he must be in good health for performing religious rites.

[1] Calcutta, the Elysium Press. Rs. 10. [2] P. xxi.

Thus we see that in Tantrik religion, a worshipper is to approach God through diverse objects of pleasure. He is to relinquish his desire and self and convert the various pursuits of enjoyment into instruments of spiritual discipline.

Last year, a European published, under a *nom de plume*, a new translation [1] of the same work, with an Introduction, in which, while he does not openly state that he regards the system as good or right, he yet suggests some sort of defence at every point.

H. The Smārtas

The word *smārta* is an adjective formed from *smṛiti*. The Smārtas are those Hindus found in many parts of India who follow Śaṅkara, the great mediæval exponent of the Vedānta, in his monistic exposition of the Vedānta, his unsectarian recognition of all the gods of Hinduism, and his insistence on strict adherence to the rules of ritual and of conduct laid down in the ancient *sūtras*, which come under that section of Hindu sacred literature which is called *smṛiti*.

Many Hindu scholars seek to commend Śaṅkara's philosophy to the world. Here we mention briefly an organization of a more practical character, which seeks to strengthen and defend the whole Smārta position, namely, the Advaita Sabhā of Kumbakonam. The best thing I can do to bring this movement vividly before readers is to transcribe the following passage from a most courteous letter which reached me last January from Mr. K. Sundararaman, who was a Professor of History in a college, but has now retired and lives in Kumbakonam.

The Society was started in 1895 — chiefly at the instigation of some of the learned Pandits of the Tanjore District — among

[1] *Tantra of the Great Liberation*, by Arthur Avalon, London, Luzac, 10*s*. net.

whom must be mentioned first and foremost, the greatest modern Vedantist of South India, Raju Sastri of Mannargudi town.

An annual assembly of Brahman Pandits of the school of Sankaracharya is convened usually in the month of July. It has always met in the town of Kumbakonam, where there is a Mutt (or monastery) presided over by one who claims to be a lineal successor of the famous founder of the Advaita School of Vedanta. The Pandits who attend are chiefly drawn from the Southern or Tamil Districts of the Madras Presidency. Others are welcome, and there have been years during which Pandits have come in from Godavery and Krishna Districts which form part of the Telugu country. In the year 1911, the Annual Session met at Palghat, as an exceptional case.

There are four permanent Examiners for the Sabha, who are all of them men of great merit and fame. They prefer to conduct their examinations orally, on the ground that such examinations are more efficacious as a test of worth. They also set papers to such as are unwilling or unable to stand the searching oral test. Some time is also given to the older and abler Pandits to carry on *Vakyartha* or scholastic disputations on selected topics under the superintendence of the four Examiners.

In the evenings, popular lectures are given by Pandits to spread a knowledge of the Vedanta religion among the lay members and the women of the Brahman Community, and also to interest them in the work of the society.

The annual session lasts usually for a week, but sometimes it has lasted 2 or 3 days more. During its course, the assembled Pandits are fed at the Society's expense. At its close, presents are made to them according to merit, and their travelling expenses are also paid. The Examiners are at present paid Rs. 50 each, besides their travelling expenses.

The Pandits are attracted, *not* by the money gifts, but by their devotion to the branch of learning for the cultivation of which they spend their time and energy, and by their earnest desire to help forward its more systematic and thorough study. The spectacle is one rare in an age when men's interests are predominantly materialistic.

The sabha has engaged a learned Pandit — who is one of the four Examiners of the Sabha and who resides at Kumbakonam

— to teach the Vedanta philosophy as contained in the writings of Sankaracharya and of some of the later writers of his school. He has also the obligation to deliver every year a course of lectures on a selected topic or work in two leading centres of one of the Tamil Districts. There is a small endowment of Rs. 5,000 out of which this Pandit is paid one half of his salary. The other half of his salary is met from the subscriptions sporadically collected each year. The entire annual income from all sources does not exceed Rs. 2,000.

The work of the society is very humble in its character, and it also works too much on antique lines. Its work may, in course of time, get modernized; and then it will live. As at present carried on, it gives not much of a promise for the future.

Professor Sundararaman's own position will also be of interest. He believes that the whole of the ritualistic system of Hinduism comes from God, that every detail of it is right, that the punctilious observance of all its rules would bring health, strength and prosperity to the Indian people, and that the decline of India during the last two thousand years is the direct outcome of the neglect of these rules by large masses of the population. The following is a paragraph from one of his letters to the press: [1]

The consequences of rebellion against ritualistic Hinduism are writ plainly on the face of the history of India for two thousand years and more. Buddha began the first revolt, and since then he has had many successors and imitators. The unity and might of the once glorious fabric of Hindu society and civilization have been shattered, but not beyond hope of recovery. That recovery must be effected not by further doses of "Protestant" revolt,[2] but by the persistent and patient endeavour to observe the injunctions and precepts of the ancient Dharma [3] in its entirety.

[1] *ISR.*, XXII, 23.

[2] This is a reference to the samājes, especially the Brāhma and Prārthanā Samājes.

[3] *I.e.* the religious law.

I have been informed that, in Kathiawar, there is another Smārta organization, the leader of which is Mr. Nathu Sarma of Porebandar and Bilkha.

5. Caste Organizations

A. Caste Conferences

The modern spirit and the difficulties of the times have stirred the leading castes, as well as the leading sects, of Hinduism to united action. The earliest of all the Caste organizations was the Kāyastha Conference, which was first held in 1887. These gatherings were already very common by 1897; for Ranade refers to them in an address delivered that year.[1] Caste Conferences may be local, or provincial, or may represent all India. Like other conferences, they are held during the cold season, very often during the Christmas week. Printed reports of these gatherings are very seldom issued; so that I have had to rely on notices in the newspapers for my information.

I have noted Conferences of Brāhmans and of Brāhman sub-castes, Kshatriyas, Rājputs, Vaiśyas, Kāyasthas and Kāyastha sub-castes, Vellālas, Reddys, Nairs, Jats, Patidars, Daivadnyas, Namaśūdras, etc.

There are two main motives in these conferences. On the one hand, they share the widespread impulse to defend the whole of Hinduism, and, very naturally, within that wider object, their own caste privileges. But on the other, there is a strong desire to promote the prosperity of the caste; and that of necessity demands the introduction of such reforms as may help the caste in the difficult circumstances of the present. Frequently the caste appeals to the Government for special privileges which they once enjoyed or which they would like to obtain. Resolutions

[1] *Essays*, 165.

are passed on the subject of the age of marriage, of funeral expenses, and of marriage expenses. Education usually bulks rather large, and female education is frequently advocated. There is a great desire to attain greater unity in the caste. Frequent proposals are made for making marriages possible between sub-castes which at present do not intermarry.

For some time social reformers were inclined to disapprove of these Caste Conferences. The following is from a leader in the *Indian Social Reformer:*

> The idea of caste conferences has always been repugnant to us, even when they have for their object the prosecution of social reforms. The caste sentiment is so ingrained in the Hindu mind, it so deeply permeates every fibre of our being, and it so thoroughly colours our outlook, that it seems to us that the only effective course for those who wish to see this state of mind altered, is resolutely to cut themselves off from anything savouring of the idea. . . .
>
> An occasional European like Mrs. Annie Besant may allow her intellect to play with the idea of caste without much practical effect. Her nervous system is strung to different social ideals, and mere intellection does not produce conduct. But with one who is born a Hindu and who believes caste to be the great monster we have to kill, only one attitude is safe and possible. He must not associate himself with any movement which, under whatever name or pretext, aims at setting up caste as its goal and standard. To the subtle poison of caste, its self-complacency, and its pharisaism, the Hindu nervous system has for centuries been accustomed to respond. Unconsciously, the best and most resolute of reformers are apt to have the old monster taking liberties with them if they slide into the attitude of acquiescence in such movements. These observations apply to caste conferences which meet with the object of effecting reforms in the habits and customs of their respective castes. They apply more forcibly to such movements as the Saraswat Conference recently held at Belgaum, whose sole object is to amalgamate and perpetuate this particular caste. The charac-

ter of the movement is sufficiently clear from the fact that the one resolution about social reform, regarding the marriageable age, which was sought to be introduced, had to be dropped for fear of breaking up the Conference.[1]

But experience seems to show that the progressive tendency is in most Conferences stronger than the conservative. The following is from the same journal as the above:

> Judging however by the broad lines on which the resolutions passed at the annual gatherings of most of these bodies are based, there is good reason to think that they all tend to the propagation of liberal ideas on religious and social questions throughout the land.[2]

Most magazines are inclined to take quite a hopeful view of these gatherings. How the leaven works even among rather backward communities, may be seen from the following brief report of a meeting of one group of Sikhs in the Paṇjab:

> The Sikh Jats assembled the other day in a meeting held at Budhi, District Jullundar, with the object of giving up the evil customs prevalent among them and effecting useful and necessary reforms. Resolutions were passed enjoining the curtailment of expense on occasions of marriages and other festivities and forbidding drink and nautches on such occasions. It was further resolved that the *siapa* should also be abolished, and that on no occasion should indecent songs be allowed.[3]

Two groups of people which, strictly speaking, belong to the great Outcaste population of India must find mention here; and that for two reasons. First, both of these communities are amongst the very best of the Outcastes. Secondly, there have arisen among them organizations of sufficient energy and value to raise them to a place in modern India alongside caste people. See the other Outcaste stirrings below.[4]

[1] *ISR.*, XX, 423. [2] *Ib.*, XXI, 241. [3] *Ib.*, XX, 557. [4] Pp. 368–70.

B. The Tiyas

Scattered up and down the west coast of Southern India there live three Outcaste communities which are of the same stock, and which, taken together, number 1,800,000. In South Kanara they are called Villavas, in Malabar Tiyas and in Travancore Elavas. They now differ from each other in a variety of ways, and neither intermarry nor dine together, but originally they were one. The new movement aims at emancipating them from the disabilities of their position as Outcastes, advancing them economically and educationally, and fusing the three groups into one body. The spirit of the race and the position in which the awakening found them are both clearly reflected in the following extracts from an address presented by them to Mrs. Besant, the Theosophic leader, in 1904:

> We are very pleased to hear that although born a Christian you are prepared to die a Hindu. . . . When you visited Calicut you were admitted as a guest in one of the palaces belonging to a member of the Zamorin's family. This was rendered possible by the fact of your having become a convert to Hinduism. But as we are Hindus by very birth we are prevented from approaching the place. . . . Even the sight of us within close proximity is a source of pollution. . . . If under such circumstances we are to gain admission to places accessible to you, we find a way to it through you. And it is this:—It is impossible for us to be born Christians. We shall therefore become Christian converts first and then turn Hindus as you have done. This will relieve us of our disability as you have cured yourself of your disability.

Although they are Outcastes, they have long been recognized as possessing the right of studying and practising the old Hindu medicine, and also Astrology. Consequently, in many families a knowledge of Sanskrit is handed down from father to son. For this and other reasons they have not been nearly so crushed and depressed as most Outcaste tribes are.

In one of the old medical families, settled three miles north of Trivandrum in Travancore, a boy was born who was called Nanu Ashan. He knew a little Sanskrit, having been taught the medical lore traditional in his family. But, besides that, he managed one way or another to persuade some Hindu scholar or scholars to give him something of a Hindu theological training. I have failed to learn who his teachers were, or what sect or school they belonged to. He became an ascetic, taking the name of Nārāyaṇa. He is now known as Śrī Nārāyaṇa Gurusvāmī.

About 1890 he began to urge his community to make a new beginning religiously. Hitherto they had been devil-worshippers like the mass of the Outcastes. He urged them to build temples for themselves, and to worship the Hindu gods in orthodox fashion, but to appoint members of their own community as priests. Gradually the movement caught on. It has spread to the North and the South; and there are now thirty temples in all. A small Sanskrit school is usually attached to each temple. The movement is thoroughly orthodox in everything except in its non-Brahman priests. So much for the religious leader.

The other leader is a layman. Within Travancore State the Eḷavas were under serious disabilities. Government service was closed to them, and their children were not allowed to study in the schools. A young man (now Dr. Palpu of the Mysore Medical Service) succeeded, in extremely difficult circumstances, in getting an education for himself; and then set to work to get the disabilities removed. Government service under the Travancore Government is now open to the community, and most of the schools are open also.

An organization was started in 1903 to draw the people together and to work for their betterment. It is called the S. N. D. P. Yogam, or in full, the Śrī Nārāyaṇa Dharma Paripālana Yogam, *i.e.* Union for the Protection of the Śrī Nārāyaṇa Religion. This union, which represents the three sections of the community, has its headquarters in Trivandrum. Local Yogams have been started in some thirty-three places, notably in Parur, Calicut and Tellicherry. An Annual Conference is held, now at one place, now at another. Sometimes an Industrial Exhibition accompanies the Conference. The Yogam supports a number of preachers, some of whom are sannyāsīs. They move about the country, giving lectures in the temples and elsewhere, and teaching the people. Most of the temples are related one way or another to the Yogam, and some are directly managed by it. They have an educational fund, from which money is advanced as loans to poor students. At Alwaye, where Śaṅkara, the great Vedāntist, was born, they have a monastery which they wish to transform into a Sanskrit-English College. A good deal of money and effort is being used to spread industrial and agricultural education and to advance the community economically. Social reform is also sought. A magazine, the *Vivekodaya*, is published from the office in Trivandrum.

The religious side of the movement has very little reality in it. Most of the leaders have adopted it, as some of them said to me, merely to catch the interest of the masses,[1] and to keep them from becoming Christians. On the other hand, the new system is perhaps a little better than the old devil-worship. It is also of considerable interest to the student as a modern parallel to the rise of the Liṅgāyats.[2]

[1] Cf. the Ārya Samāj, above, pp. 118–20. [2] P. 301, above.

C. *The Vokkaligas*

The Vokkaligas also are technically Outcastes, but really are as fine a people as great masses of Śudras are. They are the peasant class of the Mysore State, and number about a million and a quarter, one fourth of the whole population of the State. They are a simple, hardy, kindly people, but, otherwise, they were very backward until the new movement waked them.

In 1906 seven individuals came together, and said, "It is time that we bestir ourselves to see that the poor have the benefit of education." They found a rich man, and promised to work, if he would provide money. He promised to give Rs. 10,000.

It was resolved to hold a Conference in Bangalore. The peasants came in thousands; enthusiasm grew; and Rs. 50,000 were subscribed on the spot. Thus the Vokkaligara Sangha, or union, was formed, and the work began. The aims of the movement are as follows:

(1) To adopt means for the awakening of the people by sending lecturers into the villages to preach to them the value of education, the advantage of improving their methods of cultivation, the benefit accruing from paying attention to sanitation, hygiene, domestic science, etc.

(2) To hold periodical Conferences in different parts of the State, at which all questions relating to the amelioration of the community are dealt with. A spirit of unity, concord, and brotherly feeling is sure to result from such meetings.

(3) To establish the headquarters of the Association in Bangalore, where arrangements will be made for the boarding and lodging of the students coming from the country for study. It is intended to make it the centre of activity. Courses of illustrated lectures on all useful subjects, a reading room, a library, a museum, on a small scale, of the arts and crafts of the community, a gymnasium, athletic grounds, evening classes in technical subjects, are all proposed to be instituted. Similar

institutions on a smaller scale may be erected in the principal towns of the State as funds permit.

(4) To establish and maintain Demonstration Farms, showing modern methods of cultivation and machinery employed for the purpose. The organisation of exhibitions to show to the people how to secure better housing conditions, and better sanitary and healthy surroundings are also intended.

(5) The publication of a newspaper and other periodicals to educate the people and to spread among them wholesome and progressive ideas. It is intended to make illustrated journalism a feature of this branch of work.

(6) To work in co-operation with the Government in their efforts to bring about the progress of the State.

The Sangha now owns a press which does printing in both English and Canarese, a building worth Rs. 30,000, with a hostel for one hundred boys on a site given by Government, and a newspaper, the *Vokkaligara Patrika*, one of the best in the State. The aim of the movement is to get the peasant boys to come for education. They live at the hostel; those who can afford it pay; those who cannot are paid for by the Society. The boys attend the Government schools; there is the closest cooperation and good will between the Government and the Peasants' Movement. The best methods of Western organization have been adapted to the needs of the organization and the spirit of service dominates all the work. After seven years, with its position now well established, the Peasants' Movement realizes how much work is yet to be done. The special development now to be undertaken is the improvement of agricultural education and methods, and the simple, sober, religious, intelligent character of the peasants makes them good material on which to work. Four Conferences have been held. Lecturers go into the interior on the occasions of fairs and festivals where large numbers of people collect to make known to them the aims and objects of the Association, to enrol new subscribers for the Association's newspaper, and also new members of the Association.[1]

6. The Bhārata Dharma Mahāmaṇḍala

A bold attempt has been made during recent years to gather together the whole of the Hindu people in a single organization, partly in self-defence, partly for further instruction in religion.

1. By the year 1890, as a result of the work of the Ārya Samāj, of Rāmakṛishṇa and the Theosophists, there was a general uprising of the educated Hindu spirit in defence of Hinduism. Out of this widespread desire to strengthen the old faith there sprang a number of organizations. In the Panjab the movement was started by a Brāhman, who had been a cook, but is now known as Paṇḍit Dīn Dayāl Śarma. Infuriated by the attacks of the Ārya Samāj on orthodox Hinduism, he attacked the Samāj in turn, and taught the people to retain their idols and live in orthodox fashion. He had had no Sanskrit training nor English education, but he was a brilliant speaker and he was so successful that a number of paṇḍits and titled men gathered round him. Then in 1895 they founded the Sanātan Dharma Sabhā in Hardwar and Delhi. In 1896 Svāmī Gyānānandaji started in Muttra a movement called the Nigamāgama Maṇḍalī. In Bengal the Dharma Mahāmaṇḍalī[2] arose. In Southern India Paṇḍit Śāstrīji Pade founded the Bhārata Dharma Mahāparishad. All these organizations aimed at defending orthodox Hinduism, but they were not connected with one another.[3]

[1] See *ISR.*, May 17th, 1914, pp. 435 and 438.

[2] A Sanātana Dharma Rakshinī Sabhā had been formed in Calcutta as early as 1873. See *Dayanand Sarasvati* (Natesan) 28.

[3] *Mahamaṇḍal Magazine*, vol. I, no. 4, pp. 1–2.

By 1900 these movements had made so much progress that a national Conference was held at Delhi under the presidency of the Mahārāja of Darbhaṅga. One noteworthy episode in the Conference was a great procession in which the President walked barefooted, carrying a copy of the Vedas, and attended by nearly a hundred thousand people.[1]

2. In 1902 it became possible to unite the various bodies in one large organization, and the Bhārata Dharma Mahāmaṇḍala was formed at Muttra. Svāmī Gyānānandaji became Organizing Secretary, and Gopīnāth, a graduate, worked along with him. Paṇḍit Dīn Dayāl continued to do very valuable work for the movement. The Mahāmaṇḍala was registered, and a constitution was drawn up. In 1905 the headquarters of the Association were moved to Benares, where they are to-day.

The following are said to be the objects of the Association:

(*a*) To promote Hindu religious education in accordance with the Sanatan Dharma, to diffuse the knowledge of the Vedas, Smritis, Purans and other Hindu Shastras and to introduce, in the light of such knowledge, useful reforms into Hindu Life and Society.

(*b*) To promote and enrich the Sanskrit and Hindi literatures in all the branches.

(*c*) To introduce such useful reforms as may be warranted by the Shastras in the management of the Hindu Charitable and religious institutions and Tirthas, *i.e.* sacred places.

(*d*) To establish, affiliate and control Branch Sabhas in different parts of India.

(*e*) To found and maintain new and to support the existing Hindu Colleges, Schools, Libraries and publishing establishments in consonance with the object of the Association.

[1] *Madras Decennial Missionary Conference Report*, 306–7.

(*f*) To adopt all proper and lawful means and measures to carry out the above objects.

The work of the Association is distributed among five departments, The Preaching Department, The Religious Endowments Department, The Department of Sacred Learning, The Library and Research Department, and The Publishing Department.

The Mahāmaṇḍala publishes an Anglo-Hindī monthly, the *Mahāmaṇḍal Magazine*, and several provincial magazines, in the vernacular; and the Research Department has its own organ, called *Vidyā Ratnakar*. One of the chief difficulties of the Association is to find preachers "worthy of the name": an attempt is being made to meet this need by means of a training-school at headquarters.

The Mahāmaṇḍala advertises a long list of books for sale; and the following note comes at the end of the advertisement:

For

UPANISHADS
VEDAS
SMRITIS
PURANAS
TANTRAS
HINDI PHILOSOPHICAL WORKS

and all kinds of Sanskrit and Hindu religious books,
Apply to the Manager, Gurudham, Benares City.

Numerous booklets for free distribution are also appearing.

Under the general supervision of this great national body come a number of Provincial Associations, and under these in turn are some 600 local societies, called Sabhās in the towns and villages. There are provincial offices and organizations in Calcutta, Bombay, Lahore, Ajmere, Muttra and Darbhanga. There is no provincial organization in Madras.

For eight years the newly formed organization enjoyed abounding prosperity under the guidance of Svāmī Gyānānandaji. In 1910, however, he decided to retire from the position of organizing secretary. He was able to give a very satisfactory account of his stewardship during the eight years. The Association had been recognized as a body representing the whole Hindu community by the heads of the chief Hindu sects and religious orders. Some 600 branches had been opened, and about 400 institutions had become affiliated. Nearly 200 preachers were employed; a considerable literature had been put into circulation; and large sums of money had been subscribed.

The Mahāmaṇḍala has never recovered from the loss of this organizer's work. For two years after his retirement there was constant weakness, and bickering. In 1912 the chief secretary was forced to resign through vigorous action taken by the Bengal Provincial Organization, and Mr. Sarada Charan Mitra, who was until recently a Justice of the High Court of Calcutta, became Chief Secretary in his place; and it is hoped that work will now go on satisfactorily. The Mahārāja of Darbhaṅga is the General President of the Mahāmaṇḍala, and by his wealth and prestige adds greatly to its strength; but the leading personality in the movement at present is Paṇḍit Madan Mohan Malavīya, who is one of the most prominent men in the United Provinces as an educationalist and politician, and who has been the leading spirit in all that has been done to found a Hindu University.

3. Through its extreme orthodoxy the Mahāmaṇḍala has won the adherence of numerous ruling princes and sectarian pontiffs; and tens of thousands of young Hindus are ready to applaud both its theological position and its propaganda; but of the many thousands who shout approval there are very few indeed who are willing to lay a

hand to the work. The contrast between orthodoxy and such bodies as the Brāhma Samāj or the Ārya Samāj in this regard is very striking, and very significant: there is no spontaneous living energy in the orthodox community. Then, thinking Hindus all over the country disapprove very seriously of the reactionary character of its teaching. The editor of the *Indian Social Reformer*, referring to the fact that the Mahāmaṇḍala wishes to uphold the old rule, that no Hindu may cross the sea, comments severely on the unhealthy character of the whole propaganda;[1] while the *Leader* of Allahabad says:

> We receive from time to time papers relating to the internal strife in the Bharat Dharma Mahamandal with the request that we should express our opinion on the merits of the personal controversies that have been going on. We are sorry we must decline the courteous invitation. To our mind the best that could happen to the country, the Hindu community and the Mahamandal itself is that that organization should decree its own abolition. It is so very reactionary in its religious and social tendencies and activities that far from promoting the well-being and advancement of the community, it does a lot of harm — whenever it does anything at all, that is to say. Its members are so wealthy and influential that if they are so minded they can make themselves a powerful help to progress. But the misfortune and mischief is that they do not.[2]

The Mahāmaṇḍala stands above all things for the defence of the whole of Hinduism, the Sanātana Dharma, the Eternal Religion, as they call it. The foundation of such an organization is in itself almost a portent. Hinduism has never in the course of its whole history been a single organization. It has been a natural growth, springing up and spreading like the grass, the flowers and the forests of India. No one has ever been able to count its sects, or to

[1] *ISR.*, XXII, 121. [2] *Ib.*, XXII, 518.

classify its multitudes of wandering ascetics. Nor until now has the Hindu ever felt the need of union for defence. Apologetic against Jains and Buddhists one does find in the ancient literature; and there are frequent references to persecution also; but these things were left to philosophers and kings: the ordinary Hindu went his way unheeding. How great then is the pressure of the modern spirit and of Christian criticism to-day!

It is also worthy of notice that, although the purpose of the organization is to defend and maintain the ancient religion unchanged, the modern spirit shows itself in much of the work of the Association. First of all, like every other modern religious movement in India, the Mahāmaṇḍala finds itself driven to set forth the Hindu system as the religion for all mankind. To defend a religion which is but the religion of the Hindus is felt to be impossible for the modern mind. Hence we have the extraordinary spectacle of this organization, created for the express purpose of defending the religion which in all its own sacred books is expressly restricted to the four highest castes — Brāhmans, Kshatriyas, Vaiśyas and Śūdras, — making the following declaration:

> But the Sanatan Dharma is not marked by any such spirit of narrowness or exclusiveness. It is not a particular *creed* promising salvation to its followers alone; it is the universal Dharma for all mankind.[1]

Again, in all the sacred literature of Hinduism the rule is laid down that the Vedas must not be made known to any one except initiated members of the three twice-born castes, Brāhmans, Kshatriyas and Vaiśyas. No woman, and no Śūdra may hear the sacred words, not to speak of Outcastes and foreigners. This rule may be found thou-

[1] *Mahāmaṇḍal Magazine*, vol. I, no. 1, p. 8.

sands of times in all the great books, legal and philosophical. In the earliest of Hindu law-books we read:

> If a Śūdra listens intentionally to a recitation of the Veda, his ears shall be filled with some molten tin or lac. If he recites Veda texts, his tongue shall be cut out. If he remembers them, his body shall be split in twain.[1]

Yet this most orthodox movement, backed by the heads of all the greatest Hindu sects, sells copies of any part of the Vedas to any one who cares to buy them, and encourages their study, no matter what a man's caste may be.[2] Clearly, the freedom as well as the universality of Christianity is working with irresistible force within the very citadel of Hinduism.

Perhaps the most striking evidence of the working of the leaven that has yet appeared is a paper which occurs in the first number of the official organ of the movement, *The Mahāmaṇḍal Magazine.* It is a clear, well-written, forcible paper by Professor Phani Bhusan Adhikari, M.A., on *The Need of a Critical History of Hinduism.* The following quotations from this article will show where this thoughtful defender of orthodox Hinduism stands; but the paper as a whole is most significant and well worth study:

> But Hinduism has erred too much on the side of its catholicity. Its philosophy has made it unpractical, as every philosophy does its adherents. What would have otherwise been an excellent virtue has proved to be a pernicious vice. Hinduism is *unpractical,* and who knows to what extent the unpractical nature of the Hindu character may have been due to the catholicity of its religious spirit? In adopting everything within itself, it does not appear to have made a selection between the useful and the useless; and in cases where this selection has been of the useful, it is reluctant to give up what, once so useful, has now become not only useless but positively injurious. . . .

[1] *Gautama Dharmasūtra,* XII, 4–6. [2] See above, p. 318.

Now, if we take a somewhat wide survey of what popularly goes by the name of *Hinduism* (and Hinduism is now too much popular), we find that it consists mostly in the observance of certain practices, the meaning of the use of which is hardly known to or can be explained even by those who pose as authorities on the religion. . . .

Those who have eyes to see will observe that the present-day Hinduism of the popular type consists in the scrupulous performance of certain rites and the unquestioning maintenance of certain forms the meaning of which is almost unknown. It is these which under the name of *Sanatana Dharma* is the *all* of popular Hinduism. . . .

For permanent results of a beneficial nature, some other method of action has become desirable to adopt. The method that suggests itself for the purpose is *historical* and *critical* (although both go hand-in-hand in a subject like religion). This is the method which has been found highly useful in preserving the essentials of Christianity.

The Hindu nation is passing now through what may be called a transition-period. The situation is very critical. There are signs all around of a break with the old which has been found to be effete and in some cases positively unhealthy for the life of the nation in the present altered conditions. . . .

What is wanted is a band of scholars forming an association with a common object. . . .

7. The All-India Śuddhi Sabhā

In the nineties a movement arose in the Panjab for readmitting to the Hindu community people who had passed over to other faiths.[1] Since a Hindu becomes impure through embracing another religion, the method adopted is to subject those who return to a purifying ceremony. Hence the name Śuddhi Sabhā, purification society. At a later date other provinces formed similar organizations; and now there is an All-India Śuddhi Sabhā, which holds

[1] Ranade, *Essays*, 164. *Census of India*, 1911, vol. I, 128.

an annual Conference. In 1913 the Conference was held at Karachi in the Christmas holidays. The Ārya Samāj still take a large share in the work; but other bodies, and notably the Prārthanā Samāj, are interested.

8. The Jains

The Jain system arose within Hinduism in the sixth century B.C., a little before Buddhism; and, like Buddhism, broke away from the parent faith at an early date and became a distinct religion. It is, like Buddhism, an atheistic system. The supreme religious aim of the system is to free the soul from matter. Its chief doctrine is that there are souls in every particle of earth, air, water and fire, as well as in men, animals and plants; and its first ethical precept is, Do not destroy life. In consequence, the Jain has to obey many rules in order to avoid taking life in any of its forms. Another of the original beliefs is that the endurance of austerities is a great help towards salvation. From the very beginning, the community was divided into monks and laymen, the former alone subjecting themselves to the severest discipline. In Jainism the Tīrthakaras hold the place which the Buddhas hold in Buddhism. By the Christian era the Jains, like the Buddhists, had begun to use idols. Images of the Tīrthakaras are worshipped in their temples.

The above brief account of the rise of Jainism is drawn from the writings of Western scholars who have studied the original authorities. But there is a group of scholarly Jains who do not accept these statements. Their account of the history runs as follows:

> The Jain system was founded in Ayodhyā untold ages ago by Ṛishabha. It was reformed by Pārśvanāth in the eighth century. The last reformer, Mahāvīra, rose in the sixth century. Jainism has been a rival of Hinduism from the beginning.

All my information about modern movements among the Jains I owe to two friends, Mrs. Sinclair Stevenson of Rajkot, Kathiawar, and Mr. J. L. Jaini, Barrister-at-Law. Mr. Jaini has revised and accepted as correct the whole of my essay from this point onwards.

At an early date the Jain community broke into two sects. What divided them was the question whether Jain monks should wear clothes or not; and the names of the sects still indicate this difference. One sect is called Śvetāmbara, that is, clothed-in-white; the other Digambara, that is, clothed-in-atmosphere, because their monks wear no clothes.

After the Christian era the Jain community seems to have grown rapidly in numbers and influence. They were prosperous and wealthy business people. In various parts of India they obtained royal patronage, and abundance of resources. In both the North and the South there are remains of architecture from the early centuries which show that the sect was very prominent. They had numerous scholars who created a great literature on the original sacred books of the sect, and also cultivated with success all the sciences which were current in India in mediæval times.

But their power was broken in the South by the rise of the Śivaite and Vishṇuite sects; and at a later date the same cause steadily weakened and depressed them in the North. It seems clear that for many centuries there has been a continuous drift of the Jain population into Hinduism; while Hindu thought and practice have as continuously found their way into Jain temples and homes. In Śvetāmbara temples to-day the ministrants are usually Hindus; and nearly all Jain families call in Brāhmans to assist them in their domestic ceremonies.

The steady drift towards Hinduism is still in progress, as

the following table will show. The three last Reports of the Census of India give the following as the figures for the Jain population:

1891	1,500,000
1901	1,334,000
1911	1,248,000

In 1473 A.D. a movement arose amongst Śvetāmbara Jains in Ahmabadad against idolatry, with the result that a group broke away and formed a non-idolatrous sect. They are called Sthānakavāsīs. The three sects, Digambaras, Śvetāmbaras and Sthānakavāsīs, divide the Jain community fairly evenly between them, each numbering about 400,000 souls.

Colebrooke published a certain amount of information about the Jain sect early in the nineteenth century, but their early history was not understood until the Pali literature of Ceylonese Buddhism became available towards the end of the century. A number of the Jain texts have been translated into English in recent years, and many Jain inscriptions have been deciphered; but much still remains to be done to make the history and the teaching of the sect fully intelligible.

2. Jains began to take advantage of Western education both in Bengal and in Bombay almost as early as any other community; and they have prospered exceedingly in business under British rule. They are a very wealthy community. The pearl trade of the East is almost altogether in their own hands. Hence Jains are scattered in many parts of the world, notably in Britain, France and South Africa. One Jain has received the honour of knighthood, Sir Vasonji Tricumji of Bombay.

Yet the better men of the community are deeply conscious that the Jains are in a very perilous position. The following quotations will show what some of the leaders think:

> Are we on our way to attain that level of life? I think we are not. Firstly, because we are dwindling down year after year. Secondly, our little community is a house divided against itself. Thirdly, we have reduced our power to the lowest limit by cutting the community into numberless castes.[1]
>
> Alas! the body of Jainism is in a very bad way. It is not only ill, but perhaps it is already lifeless. . . . Knowledge of Jainism is almost extinct. Very few original texts are extant; they are unknown to the Jaina masses, even to their learned leaders, and are very rarely read even in private, not to speak of public meetings. The spiritual or rather anti-spiritual food of the masses is derived partly from crude half Jaina, half non-Jaina truths or half truths and partly superstitions upon which their lives are based in our towns and villages. . . . The Jaina community is dying; perhaps it is already dead; at any rate its condition is very serious.[2]

In consequence, a keen desire for organization and reform began to manifest itself about 1890; and rather valuable results have followed. There has been no movement created comparable with the Brāhma Samāj or the Ārya Samāj; nor have the Jains had noteworthy leaders like Ram Mohan Ray or Dayānanda Sarasvatī. Yet for the last twenty years there have been groups of young men who have earnestly worked for the uplifting of the community, and there has been one Jain leader who is well worthy of mention here.

This notable man, Rajchandra Ravjibhai,[3] was a Sthānakavāsī, and was born in Morvi State, Kathiawar, in 1868. He received no English education. He was a jeweller in Bombay for some eight or nine years and died in 1900.

[1] *Digambar Jain*, Kartik, 1969, p. 33.

[2] *Jain Gazette*, May, 1911, pp. 74–75.

[3] See his portrait, Plate XI, facing page 376.

He was a gifted man and a poet, and so is usually called Rajchandra Kavi: "Kavi" means poet. A good deal of his influence was due to his extraordinary memory which enabled him to attend to one hundred things at once. He was a reformer, and yet more of an idealist than a reformer. Although a Sthānakavāsī, he was so eager to see the three sects united that he used to say there was no harm in worshipping in a Śvetāmbara temple. He declared that neither *mūrti* (idol) nor *mumati* (mouth-cloth [1]) led to *moksa* (release) but a good life. He held that the moral ideal underlying the legends was the great thing, not the legends themselves. He thus sought to weaken the religious sanction of old customs rather than to produce any immediate and radical change in conduct. The following quotation gives his attitude towards reform:

> His views on the social and political questions of the day were liberal. He said that there ought not to be anything like caste distinctions amongst the Jains, as those who were Jains were all ordered to lead a similar life. Among all the agencies for reform, he assigned the highest place to the religious reformer, working with the purest of motives and without ostentation. He found fault with the religious teachers of the present day, because they preached sectarianism, did not realise the change of the times, and often forgot their real sphere in the desire to proclaim themselves as *avatars* (incarnations) of God, and arrogated to themselves powers which they did not possess. In his later years, it was clear that he was preparing to fulfil his life's mission in that capacity. But unfortunately death intervened and the mission remained unfulfilled.[2]

As a result of English education and the influence of such advanced men as Kavi, there is a common leaven working throughout the Jain community, and especially among the

[1] The mouth-cloth is worn by Jain ascetics, lest they should inadvertently swallow an insect.

[2] *Pioneer*, 22nd May, 1901.

educated men. This new spirit manifests itself in various ways, first of all, in sectarian conferences.

3. The Digambara sect were first in the field. They held their first annual Conference about 1893. A year or eighteen months later, as a result of the work of the Conference, a group of the younger men belonging to all the three sects organized themselves as the Jain Young Men's Association. Then in 1903 the Śvetāmbara sect began to hold a Conference; and the Sthānakavāsīs followed in 1906. These three sectarian conferences have proved on the whole the most successful of all the efforts made during this period; but a good deal has also been done by local groups unconnected with any conference; and it is probable that in the future still greater things will be accomplished by those who are seeking to unite the three sects in one.

The aims which these organizations have in view are, in the main, to unite, strengthen and build up the community, so that individuals may not drift away from it, and to introduce such education and fresh life as will adapt the Jains to modern conditions. All parties seem to recognize that these great ends cannot be achieved unless their religious teachers, whether *sādhus* (celibate ascetics) or priests, receive a good modern education, so as to enable them to lead the community in the difficult circumstances of to-day, and to meet, on the one hand, the assaults of materialism, and, on the other, the criticism of the Ārya Samāj and of Christianity. Jains want their sādhus to become educated, capable, modern men like missionaries. All realize also that it is of the utmost importance that the boys and girls of the community should receive not only a modern education, but such religious and moral training as shall make them good Jains. There is also a clear realization that the old religion must be uplifted; but as to how this is to be done there is no unanimity. The policy advocated by the educated young men is a good deal different from that favoured by conservatives, whether sādhus, priests or laymen.

The chief methods employed by the various organizations are (*a*) institutions for giving a religious education to the sādhus and priests, (*b*) hostels for students, in which each student is required to study Jain books and live a Jain life, (*c*) newspapers in the vernaculars and in English, (*d*) the publication of literature, both the ancient sacred texts and modern books, and (*e*) the introduction of religious and social reform. We had better now look at the leading organizations in turn.

4. The All-India Digambara Jain Conference, Bhāratvarshīya Digambara Jain Mahāsabhā, the office of which is at Khurai, C.P., was founded about 1893. It has proved a very useful organization; yet it has had its difficulties. At the annual gathering at Muzaffarnagar in 1911 there was a tremendous dispute, which ended in a suspension of the Conference. Later on peace was made. It has succeeded in creating several valuable institutions, notably the Syādvāda Mahāvidyālaya at Benares, in which the priests of the sect receive something of a modern training, an orphanage in Delhi, a number of Hostels in various parts of the country, and a Widows' Home in Bombay. The Digambaras support a number of newspapers, the *Digambara Jain*, a monthly magazine, published in Surat, and containing articles in several languages, the *Hindi Jain Gazette*, the *Jain Mitra*, and a woman's paper called the *Jain Nārī Hitkārī*.

5. The Śvetāmbaras met for the first time in Conference at Marwar in 1903, and they have met seven times since then. The Conference has an office in Bombay, and issues a paper, the *Conference Herald*. Books for the moral and

religious training of Jains in school and college are being produced in five grades. Hostels for students have been organized in several places, and a training college for sādhus at Benares, the Yasovijaya Jain Pāṭhśāla, in which they receive an English education and a training in the sacred books. The Conference has also undertaken to index the books in the Treasure-houses, *i.e.* libraries, at Cambay, Jessalmir, Patan, and elsewhere. This work is attended with considerable difficulty, owing to the Jain habit of concealing their sacred books.

One of the chief points of Jain devotion is the building of temples. These are not erected to meet the needs of the population, but as works of piety. Consequently, there are vast numbers of Jain temples, quite out of proportion to the number of Jains. The Conference sees to the restoration and repair of the most important of these.

Like Hindus, the Śvetāmbara Jains have discovered that a large amount of the income of their temples is misused, and various plans are being tried by the Conference to rectify the matter. At Palitana and Junagadh Committees have been formed to supervise the disbursement of these monies.

There is a desire among certain laymen to lessen the prominence given to idol-worship. Two well-known men ventured to publish something on this subject about five years ago, but the result was a storm of opposition, which has not yet died down.

Laymen are also rather eager to lessen the power of the sādhus in the Conference, because they are uneducated and reactionary. This too has led to quarrelling.

Śvetāmbara laymen are doing a good deal of useful work apart from the Conference. They issue four or five monthly papers, and one vernacular fortnightly, the *Jain Śāsana*, published at Benares. They also are doing what they can in the way of bringing out versions of their Scriptures, and revising and correcting them. Rich merchants provide the necessary funds. They depend a good deal on English and German scholars for the work of editing and translating these texts.

6. The Sthānakavāsīs met first in Conference in 1906. The office of Conference is at Ajmere, and their paper is called *Conference Prakāsh.* The subjects discussed at the Conferences fall under the following heads, education (boarding schools, religious education for boys and girls, orphanages, a training college for teachers), libraries, publication of sacred texts and a proposed union of all Jains. Though idolatry is the subject on which this sect feels most keenly, it is never mentioned in Conference, because there are always members of the other sects present whom they do not wish to offend. Many feel also the need of dealing with caste, but they do not venture to raise the question. Certain other aspects of social reform are, however, eagerly pressed. A Jain history from the Sthānakavāsī point of view is being prepared. The Conference sends out itinerant preachers to acquaint the people with the decisions of Conference and to collect fourpence from every house towards the expenses of the annual gathering and the preaching scheme.

Outside the Conference, small groups of Sthānakavāsīs are doing useful work. In many towns and large villages libraries are being founded. They are meant specially for Jain books, but secular works are also admitted. Local Jain societies establish hostels for Jain boys, and arrange for religious teaching to be given an hour before the ordinary schools meet. A monthly paper, the *Jain Hitecchi,* is supported; and another is being started. The objects sought by these papers are, to remove the superstitions and increase the knowledge of the people, and to insist on a higher standard of training for sādhus.

7. But the more advanced men are by no means satisfied with what is being done in the Conferences belonging to the three sects. They feel that the three groups must become united, if the community is to survive, and that there is far greater need for reform and modernization than the average Jain realizes. The following quotations will show what these leaders think:

> Obviously our orthodox people are very anxious about our religion; and could they grasp the situation, we should not be far from a satisfactory solution of the crucial problem of Jain progress. The failure of the orthodox is due to one cause. They are attempting the hopeless task of transforming the twentieth century into the days of Shri Mahaveer. They would forget the history of twenty-six centuries. By founding Pathashalas of the primeval type, they would think of producing our Akalanks and Nikalanks. What is the result? They hardly attract any intelligent boys to these antiquated seminaries and after years of arduous toiling, they find themselves as far from their ideal as ever before. The experience is discouraging not only to the orthodox but to every one who cherishes the sublime hope of vivifying Jain ideals.
>
> What is the remedy? To my mind it consists in modernising the institutions where we have to train up typical Jain spirituality through the ages to come. That is not done by the absurd insertion of a few readers or book-keeping in the curriculum of our Pathashalas. The aim of these nurseries of Jain lives ought to be to associate the best in the discoveries of the West with the highest in the lore of the past. They should be Colleges in which the Jain boys would imbibe Jain principles in their best form and yet would become able to hold their own against the literary and scientific savants of the west. Such should be the place from which Jain types would be evolved—types that shall not be at a disadvantage in any walk of life and shall yet live up to Jain ideals. That would be the Aligarh of the Jains.[1]

Like certain Muḥammadan leaders whom we have mentioned above,[2] these men think it necessary to lay stress on

[1] *Digambar Jain*, Kartik, 1969, pp. 33-34. [2] P. 98.

the spirit of Jainism, rather than on the literal observance of all the old rules. Here is an attempt to state what the spirit of Jainism is:

> Well, then, what is the Light left in our custody by Lord Mahavira? . . . Briefly characterised the Light teaches us (1) Spiritual independence which connotes individual freedom and unlimited responsibility. The soul depends upon none else for its progress, and none else is responsible for the degradation and distress which the soul may be affected with. . . . (2) It teaches us the essential universality of the Brotherhood of not only all men but of all that lives. The current of life in the lowest living organism is as sacred, subtle, sensitive, mighty and eternal as in Juliet, Cleopatra, Cæsar, Alexander, Christ, Mahomet, and Lord Mahavira himself. This is the undying basis of our fraternity for all.[1]

This advanced group became organized in 1894 or 1895 as the Jain Young Men's Association. It is now called the Bhārata Jaina Mahāmaṇḍala, or All-India Jain Association. Its office is in Lucknow, and it is governed by its Officers and a Managing Committee. The chief officer is the General Secretary, but he is assisted by three Joint Secretaries, one from each of the three sects. The objects of the Association are:

(*a*) The union and progress of the Jaina community.
(*b*) The propagation of Jainism.

The Association holds an anniversary, usually about Christmas. There are also provincial and local organizations affiliated to the main body. Special men are told off to do departmental work of several types, one of the most prominent being female education. The Association issues a monthly magazine in English, the *Jain Gazette*.

[1] *Digambar Jain*, Kartik, 1969, pp. 26–27.

The Association has been peculiarly active during the last three years. The energy of Mr. J. L. Jaini, Barrister-at-Law, has proved of very great value to it in various directions. In 1910 the International Jain Literature Society was founded in London. All the leading Jains in Europe and all the chief European Jain scholars have become members. They propose to edit and publish Jain literature. In 1911 the Ṛishabha Brahmacharya Āśrama was founded at Meerut for the training of sādhus. The same year a branch of the Jain Literature Society was formed in India; and the Central Jain Library was founded at Arrah in Behar, for the purpose of collecting books and manuscripts, and cataloguing Jain literature. The Library issues a monthly magazine in Hindi, which is named the *Jaina Siddhānta Bhāskara*, and is published in Calcutta. Finally, as these words are being written, August 24, 1913, the Mahāvīra Brotherhood is being founded in London, for the purpose of uniting Jains resident in Europe and helping them to live the Jain life.

It may be well to notice that books in English are being published by Jains to introduce Jainism to Europeans. Of these we may mention an *Introduction to Jainism*, by A. B. Latthe,[1] M.A., *Jainism in Western Garb, as a Solution to Life's Great Problems*,[2] by Herbert Warren, an Englishman who has become a Jain, and a third volume by Mr. J. L. Jaini, which is about to be issued by the Jain Literary Society.

Modern Indian religious movements find very close parallels among the Buddhists of Burma and Ceylon; but my knowledge of the religion and of the local conditions is too scanty to enable me to sketch the religious situation in those lands with accuracy.

[1] Bombay, Natha Rangaji, 1905. [2] Madras, Thompson & Co., 1912, 1s.

9. The Sikhs

1. Nānak (1469–1538), the founder of the Sikh sect, was a disciple of the famous teacher Kabīr. Except in two matters, his system is practically identical with that of many other Vaishṇava sects. It is a theism, and the main teaching of the founder is highly spiritual in character. Yet the whole Hindu pantheon is retained. The doctrine of transmigration and karma and the Indian social system remain unaltered. The guru holds the great place which he has in all the later Vaishṇava and Śaiva systems. He is not only a teacher but a saviour, and receives worship. The two points on which Kabīr and Nānak were unlike earlier teachers were these: they condemned the whole doctrine of divine incarnations; and they never ceased to protest against idolatry, thus preventing their followers from using Hindu temples. On one other point the two men seem to have been agreed: they did not wish their followers to become ascetics, but advised them to go on with their ordinary avocations.

Since the guru held such a great place in Nānak's teaching, it was necessary to appoint another man to succeed him at his death. Nine gurus were thus appointed, one after the other; and the series would have gone on indefinitely, had it not been for a momentous change introduced by the tenth guru. Nānak had left behind him a liturgy for the sect called the *Japjī*, and also a considerable body of religious poetry. In this matter he was like many of the teachers of North India who lived before him. These poems were carefully treasured by the Sikhs; the second guru invented the Panjābī alphabet, called Gurumukhī, as the script for them; and the fifth guru gathered them together and made a book of them, including also a large number of pieces from Kabīr and fifteen other saints. This volume is called the *Ādi Granth,* or "Original Book." The tenth guru added a great deal of fresh material; and the result is the *Granth Sahib,* or Noble Book of the Sikhs. Before he died, this guru told the Sikhs that they must not appoint another guru, but must take the *Granth* for their guru. Since that time this sacred book has been the centre and the inspiration of the sect.

But Govind Singh, the tenth guru, introduced another change of still greater importance. At the time when he was Sikh leader, at the end of the seventeenth and the beginning of the eighteenth century, Aurangzeb, the last great Mughal Emperor, was pressing the sect very hard. He did all in his power, by means of persecution and administrative pressure, to turn them into Muslims. Govind Singh had the genius to perceive how the Sikhs could be organized so as to be able to resist the Mughals. He formed all those who were willing to enter into a covenant with him into what he called the *Khālsā.* The ceremony of initiation, *Khanda-di-Pāhul,* Baptism of the Sword, gave it a religious character. Within this league Caste disappeared, and each man became a warrior, vowed to fight for his faith to the death, and to regard every other member of the league as a brother. They called themselves "Lions," each adding the word Singh to his name. The result was an army of heroes as unconquerable as Cromwell's Ironsides. Certain definite customs were laid upon them, which marked them off from other men, and increased the feeling of brotherhood among them. Infanticide, widow-burning and pilgrimage were prohibited. Wine and tobacco were proscribed. The consequences were two. The Khālsā became strong to resist the Mughals, but their organization cut them off from their fellow-countrymen, and made them practically a new caste.

The transformation of the Church into an army produced

another evil result; living preaching ceased among the Sikhs, and their religious life began to go down. Hinduism began to reappear among them. Though their founder had condemned the doctrine of incarnations, they soon came to regard each of their ten gurus as an incarnation of the Supreme; and, in spite of his advice, orders of ascetics began to appear among them.

The recognition of the *Granth Sahib* as the guru of the community has also proved unhealthy. The book is worshipped like an idol in the Golden Temple at Amṛitsār: a priest fans it, while the people throw offerings of flowers to it, and bow down before it. At night it is put to bed, to be waked in the morning for another day of worship. In a Sikh monastery in Conjeeveram, I was shown the altar where fire-sacrifice is regularly performed to the *Granth*. Nor is the rule against pilgrimage kept. Here and there one meets groups of Sikh ascetics on pilgrimage, visiting all the chief Hindu temples. When asked how they, as Sikhs, opposed to all idolatry, go to idolatrous temples, they answer that they go to look at the idols, not to worship them. This is surely as clear a case of the fascination of idols as one could wish to have.

After the fall of the Mughal Empire, the Sikhs became organized in two small democratic republics, called Taran Dal and Budha Dal. Then these subdivided into twelve missils, or petty states. Finally, Ranjit Singh united them all, and became the king of the Panjab. He ruled from 1800 to 1839. To their religious memories and warlike pride there was thus added the consciousness of nationality.

2. Ranjit Singh had been statesman enough to keep the peace with the British, who already held all the territory to the east of the Panjab; but he was not long dead before the Sikh leaders, in the pride of their old military

prowess, began to make raids on British territory. This the British would not endure. War followed in 1845, and the Sikhs were defeated; but even that was not sufficient. They would not keep the peace. Hence a second war, in 1848–1849, resulted in the annexation of the Panjab to British India.

The province was singularly fortunate in the British officers sent to administer it. John Lawrence, Eadwardes, Nicholson, Montgomery, Reynell Taylor were men of striking character, of great capacity and of Christian life. Hence the Panjab remained quite loyal throughout the Mutiny in 1857–1858; and the Sikhs have been one of the stoutest and most valuable elements in the Indian army ever since the annexation of the province.

3. Fresh religious influences came in with the empire. Christian missionaries entered the province in 1849, and since then have spread all over it; the Brāhma Samāj appeared in Lahore in 1863; the Ārya Samāj began its aggressive and stormy career in 1877; and since 1898 the atheistic Deva Samāj has made its influence felt not only in Lahore city but in some of the country districts.

4. The Sikh community, for various reasons, has tended to become weak and impoverished. The following paragraphs are from their own paper:

They are poorer than their Hindu or Moslem brothers. They borrow money from the village *Sahukars* or money-lenders, to carry on their agricultural occupation, under very hard and exacting terms. All grain in excess of their bare necessities is snatched from them by some device or another. 'A person who has to be anxious for his livelihood cannot aspire to be wealthy' goes the Punjabi saying. Sikh peasantry could, therefore, hardly support their children for higher education. There are very few Sikh merchants and traders, and Sikh banking and trading companies hardly exist. This general state of poverty prevailing among them is the greatest hindrance in their way to progress and prosperity. Calamities, such as famine, locusts, plague, war, etc., have added to their burdens and anxieties and rendered the condition of the Sikhs indescribably wretched.

We have often been drawing the attention of our leaders to the comparatively backward state of education, and daily decreasing number of the Sikh young men who receive instruction in the public and private schools of the Punjab.

With the decline of spiritual religion among them, there has come to them what has come to every other reformed Hindu sect, an overpowering tendency to drift back into ordinary Hinduism. Hatred of Muḥammadans is traditional amongst them, and quite strong enough to influence conduct. The Hindu community is big and influential; and Hindu worship is showy and attractive, and appeals to the feelings, while Sikh worship is exceedingly simple. There are only four places of worship of any size belonging to the sect in the whole of the Panjab. For a long time very little was done to strengthen the Sikhs in their religion. The chiefs tended to become cold. The *Gyānīs*, or learned men, who knew the *Granth* and interpreted it, had lost a great deal of their fervour and learning. The drift towards Hinduism thus became almost irresistible. Idols found their way not only into the homes of the people but into the Sikh temples. Caste crept back, and all the evils of Hindu social life. Education was not increasing among them.

5. But the new forces set in motion by the British Government, Christian Missions and the Samājes at last began to tell upon the Sikhs. Above all, the provocative attacks of Dayānanda and the Ārya Samāj stirred them to fury. About 1890 a body of reformers arose amongst them, and summoned their leaders to action for the revival of Sikhism and the uplifting of the community. A college for Sikhs

called the Khālsā College was founded at Amṛitsār. A central association called the Chief Khālsā Dīwan, with its office at Amṛitsār, was created; and local associations, called Singh Sabhās, were formed all over the country for the strengthening and purification of Sikh life. An agitation was started in favour of the extension of education and of social reform.

Considerable results have already arisen from this reforming policy. A weekly paper in English, the *Khālsā Advocate* was started in 1903, and still continues to express the views of the progressives. In 1869 the Government of India commissioned a German missionary, Dr. Ernest Trumpp, to translate the *Ādi Granth* into English, in order that they might understand their Sikh subjects better; and the volume was published in 1877. Trumpp found the work exceedingly difficult for various reasons, and acknowledged that his translation must be imperfect in many particulars. When Western education spread among the Sikhs, they became very dissatisfied with his work; and in 1893 they asked Mr. A. M. Macauliffe, a member of of the Indian Civil Service, to make a new translation for them. Mr. Macauliffe, who was deeply impressed with the value of the Sikh religion, agreed to do so. He worked in the closest possible collaboration with the Sikh Gyānīs, and published his work in six volumes in 1910.

By 1905 the reforming spirit had gone so far that the Sikh leaders found it possible to cast out the Hindu idols which had found their way into the central place of Sikh worship, the Golden Temple at Amṛitsār. By word and action they have shewn that they wish to revive the spirit of their military organizer, the tenth guru. They want to reincarnate the courage, the freedom and the independence of these days. They wish to be truly Sikhs. They realize that they must resist Hinduism as well as the Ārya Samāj, if they are to escape from caste and the other social evils of the Hindu system.

The chief lines of reform which are being pressed by the leaders are the same as those advocated by Hindu social reformers. They protest against caste and child-marriage; they plead that widows ought to be allowed to remarry, if they choose to do so: they agitate against expensive weddings; they plead for temperance; and a good deal of progress has been made. They have a Widows' Home with thirty inmates at Amṛitsār; also Orphanages; and attempts are made to help the Depressed Classes.

It is in education that the Sikhs have made most progress. The Khālsā College in Amṛitsār is under a European Principal and is carefully governed by a representative Committee. It has done good service to the community. The latest available report, that for 1911–1912, gives the number of students as 159. Everything seems satisfactory except the religious instruction. There is a large hostel in connection with the college, and another in Lahore. In addition to the college, the community supports 46 boys' schools, High, Middle and Primary.

There is a large and very successful Boarding School for Girls at Ferozepore. It has 305 pupils, 273 of them boarders. There are 32 other girls' schools.

Two Theological Seminaries, one at Tarn Tarn and another at Gujranwala, receive grants from the Chief Khālsā Dīwan.

For many years Sikh educational institutions languished for lack of financial support. In 1908 the leaders started a Sikh Educational Conference, which meets annually, now in one town, now in another. It reviews the educational situation, suggests improvements, and keeps Government informed of its wishes; but the chief service it renders to the community is the raising of funds. About Rs. 15,000 are now handed to the Chief Khālsā Dīwan every year to be divided amongst their educational institutions.

The Chief Khālsā Dīwan also publishes a fair amount of literature, mainly in Panjābī, but partly in English, setting forth the lives of the gurus and the Sikh faith in its early purity. It has a Tract Society with a dépôt for the sale of this literature in Amṛitsār, and another in Lahore. There is a Sikh Bank. There is a Young Men's Sikh Association in Lahore and a Khālsā Young Men's Association in Amṛitsār, imitations of the Y. M. C. A.; and a young men's paper, *The Khalsa Young Men's Magazine*, is published. Finally the Chief Khālsā Dīwan has some twelve or fifteen missionaries in the Punjab, and about as many more in other parts of India, who preach to Sikhs and others.

Fresh life is stirring in the Sikh community, and the activities we have detailed all tend towards progress. Yet a very great deal remains to be done. The chief question of all is, Can the Sikh faith be made a living and inspiring force in the circumstances of modern India or not?

LITERATURE. — *The Ādi Granth*, by Dr. Ernest Trumpp, London, Trübner, 1877, 63*s*. *The Sikh Religion*, a translation of the *Granth*, with lives of the Gurus, by M. A. Macauliffe, Oxford University Press, 1912, 63*s*. net. *Sri Guru Nanak Dev*, by Sewaram Singh Thapar, Rawalpindi, Commercial Union Press, 1904, Re. 1 as. 4. *Sikhism, A Universal Religion*, by Rup Singh, Amritsar, Coronation Printing Works. *Bhai Mahnga or the Search after Truth*, Amritsar, The Chief Khalsa Diwan, 1911.

10. THE PARSEES

1. There were certain parts of the programme of the Rahnumai Mazdayasnan Sabhā[1] and of the teaching of Mr. K. R. Cama[2] which many Parsees thought rather

[1] See above, p. 84. [2] See above, p. 85.

dangerous. They were afraid that the removal of certain parts of the traditional system as superstitions, the laying of extreme emphasis on the *Gathas* and on the moral elements of Zoroastrianism, and the proposal to pray in Gujarātī instead of in the ancient sacred language of the *Avesta*, would weaken the religion itself and shatter the faith of the masses.

One of the leaders of this party in early days was Mr. Hormusji Cama (a member of the same family to which Mr. K. R. Cama belonged), who in Europe in the sixties came into contact with the best Zoroastrian scholars and published, at his own expense for gratuitous distribution, Professor Bleeck's English rendering of Professor Spiegel's German translation of the *Avesta*. A society, the Rahe Rust, or True Way, was organized to oppose the reformers; and a journal, the *Suryodaya*, or Sunrise, carried on vigorous controversy with the *Rast Goftar* [1] on all the chief points of dispute. Mr. Hormusji Cama was the conservative protagonist in this long-continued fight.

2. When the Theosophical Society transferred its headquarters to India in 1879,[2] a number of this type of Parsees joined it, and in the course of years the new system got a firm hold. The Theosophic policy in Zoroastrianism was the same as in Hinduism, — full defence of the whole religion. The crudest and most superstitious observances were allegorically explained as expressions of the highest spiritual wisdom:

> They preach to the less educated classes of people that there is high efficacy in offering flowers and milk and cocoanuts to the waters; they preach to the people as an act of special religious merit to fall prostrate before and kiss imaginary pictures of their prophet; they exhort people to make a show of penitence by a vigorous slapping of cheeks. They represent to the people

[1] See above, p. 84. [2] See above, p. 226.

that the sole efficacy of their prayers consist in the material form resultant upon the physical vibrations created by their utterances.[1]

As in Hinduism, so here, the mounting spirit of nationalism and community-feeling coalesced with the impulse to defend the whole of the traditional faith; and there arose the cry: "Everything Zoroastrian is good; everything Western is bad; we must defend ourselves against the pestilential materialism of Europe." Behind this bulwark of patriotic communal feeling all the conservative elements of the Parsee race ranged themselves; and the tide of nationalism swept for a time the mass of the young educated men into the party, and carried away even a few of the older members of the reforming group.

Gradually this party began to pose as the expounders of orthodox Zoroastrianism. The original message of the prophet, they asserted, was identical with the Ancient Wisdom, and included pantheism, the practice of yoga, and the doctrine of reincarnation and karma. They flouted the scientific methods of exegesis pursued by scholarly Parsees, and endeavoured to defend superstitious and even idolatrous practices in the light of Theosophy. They stood by Mrs. Besant when she brought Mr. Leadbeater back into the Theosophical Society in January 1909.[2] A clear expression of the position of this group of Parsees will be found in *The Message of Zoroaster*, by A. S. N. Wadia, published by Dent.

It was this group that caused the violent scenes that marred the first and second Zoroastrian Conferences.[3] After that Conference, they separated themselves from the reformers; and, in consequence, the Parsee community has been rent into two parties.

[1] *Journal of the Iranian Association*, March, 1913, p. 247.
[2] See above, p. 273. [3] See above, p. 89.

This conservative group works mostly through the Zoroastrian Association, an old organization which has fallen into their hands. They are toiling eagerly for the amelioration of the community. They are doing good work by erecting houses for the poorer classes; and they have started a Census to discover how much poverty there is in the community. The paper which represents their position is *The Jami Jamshed.*

3. A Zoroastrian propaganda has arisen in America. The name used for the system is Mazdaznan. The founder, who calls himself His Humbleness Zar-Adusht Hannish, is said to be a man of German and Russian parentage, whose real name is Otto Hannisch. He called himself a Persian, and said he had come from Tibet (like Madame Blavatsky and M. Nicolai Notovitch), where he had penetrated the deepest secrets of the Dalai Lama.[1] His teaching is a mixture of Zoroastrian, Hindu, Buddhist, Christian and Muslim elements. The side most emphasized in America seems to be the effect of breathing and other exercises on health. They celebrate the birth of Jesus on the 23rd of May. Mazdaznan Temples have been erected in a few places. In the Boston temple there is a brilliant representation of the sun. Perhaps the following may serve as a sample of Mazdaznan teaching:

> As an introductory step Mazdaznan offers the formula of "Assurance, or Ahura's Prayer," which when uttered on the breath, assures oxygenation and purification of the blood, increased circulation and rhythmic heart action.

Assurance, or Ahura's Prayer

Our Father who art in Peace,
Intoned be Thy name;
Thy realm arise;

[1] P. 27, above.

Thy will incarnate upon the earth as in heaven.
This day impart Thy Word
And remember not our offenses
That we may forgive those who offend us.
Thru temptation guide us
And from error deliver us. Be it so.

The movement seems to have a few adherents in India.

11. The Muḥammadans

The rise of the spirit which finds expression in the Hindu movements we have dealt with above led to similar activity among Muḥammadans. Many observers agree in saying that most educated Muslims are turning away from the rationalism of Sir Syed Ahmad Khan[1] to orthodoxy.

1. In 1885 there was founded in the city of Lahore the *Anjuman-i-Himayet-i-Islam*, i.e. the Society for the Defence of Islam; and since that date branch associations have been formed in many towns throughout India. The objects of the Association are set forth as follows in a prospectus of the society:

I. (*a*) Rationally and intelligently to answer, through verbal discussion or in writing, any accusations advanced against Islam, and to further its propagation.

(*b*) To impart suitable and necessary education to Muslim boys and girls, and save them from abjuring their own true faith.

(*c*) To take upon itself the maintenance and education, to the best of its ability, of Muhammadan orphans, and to render all possible educational aid to poor Muslim boys and girls, so as to save them from falling into the hands of the followers of other religions.

[1] P. 99, above.

(*d*) To improve the social, moral and intellectual condition of the Muslim community and initiate measures conducive to the creation and preservation of friendly feelings and concord between the different sects of Islam.

(*e*) To bring home to the Muhammadans the advantages of loyalty to the British Government.

II. For the realisation of its objects, the Anjuman shall appoint preachers, issue a monthly magazine, establish educational institutions and orphanages, and make use of other necessary means.

Several accounts of the working of the parent Association in Lahore have been placed in my hands, which give information about its educational activities. The purpose, clearly, is to give Muslims a good modern education, and, along with it, religious instruction of a more orthodox type than is given in Aligarh institutions. They are eager to increase female education, and have nine girls' schools in Lahore. They have two very large boys' schools in the same city, and also an Arts College, called the Islamia College, with 200 pupils on the rolls and a European Principal. Islamic Theology is taught daily in each of the classes. Attached to the College is the Rivaz Hostel with 131 boarders. There is then the Hamidia School with 27 pupils, an academy for advanced Arabic scholarship. They have also an Orphanage in the city in which some simple industrial training is given. Of the educational efforts of the associations in other towns I have failed to get reports.

Nor have my Muslim correspondents told me anything about the other activities of the *Anjuman*. I am therefore driven to give here the experience of missionaries:

The methods of defence adopted by this great organisation have been, in brief, *the establishment of Muhammadan vernacular and Anglo-vernacular schools for the education of Muslim*

> *youth*, the publication of a literature, books, tracts and newspapers, for the refutation of anti-Muslim publications as well as for the commendation and propagation of the religion of Islam. In addition to this a Muslim propaganda has been organized, especially to withstand and hinder the work of missions. Even Zenana teachers are supported, whose first duty is to break up, if possible, the missionary Zenana and Girls' Schools. Pressure is brought to bear upon Muslim parents and families to exclude the Christian ladies and workers. Moreover, preachers are supported and sent here and there to preach against the Christian religion and to use every effort to bring back to the Muslim fold any who have been converted to Christianity. Christian perverts are sent out as the chosen agents of this propaganda.
>
> The results of the labours of the Anjuman-i-Himayat-ul-Islam are apparent in a revival of interest among Muslims in their own religion. The Mosques have been repaired and efforts have not been fruitless in securing a better attendance. The boycott inaugurated against missionary work has reduced the attendance of Muslims at the chapels and schools, and has no doubt closed many doors once open to Christian teaching.[1]

Clearly this organization is a Muslim parallel to the Bhārata Dharma Mahamaṇḍala, though it has not gained so much publicity.

2. In recent years the chief efforts made by Muslims in defence of their religion have had as their object the production of preachers, teachers and missionaries of a more modern type. They wish them to be cultured men, fit to lead and teach those who have had an English education; and they wish them to be well-trained theologians, able to defend Islam against Christian, Ārya and Hindu criticism, and to carry the war into the enemy's territory.

In 1894 a Defence Association was formed, the *Nadwat-ul-Ulama*, or Society of Muslim Theologians, which has its central office in Lucknow. The principal objects of the Association are stated as follows:

[1] *Madras Decennial Miss. Conf. Rep.*, 334.

(1) The advancement and reform of education in Arabic Schools.

(2) The suppression of religious quarrels.

(3) Social reform.

(4) The pursuit of the general welfare of Mussulmans and the spread of Islam.

The methods which this society employ for the defence and strengthening of Islam are five:

(1) Most of their money and activity has been spent in founding and maintaining in Lucknow a divinity school of a new type meant to provide a more enlightened education for the Muḥammadan clergy. It is called the *Dar-ul-ulum* (*i.e.* School of Theology) of the Nadwat-ul-Ulama and dates from 1898. They wish to establish such institutions elsewhere. A branch has already been opened at Shahjahanpur, and another in Madras. The young men undergo a very serious training, lasting at least eight years, in all branches of Muḥammadan theology; and in addition they are taught English, Geography and Mathematics. They receive no training in Christianity or Hinduism. The curriculum as a whole is a great advance on the old education. There are about 100 students at present; but much larger numbers are expected in future. A great building is being erected for the Seminary on the north bank of the Goomti River.

(2) Missionaries are sent out to preach.

(3) An Urdu monthly magazine, *En Nadwa*, is published, in which attempts are made to reconcile Muslim thought with modern science and thought.

(4) There is an orphanage in Cawnpore.

(5) An Annual Conference is held.

Under another society a theological seminary, the *Madrasa-i-Ilāhiyāt*, has been organized in Cawnpore. I understand it owes its existence mainly to a desire to repel the attacks of the Ārya Samāj, several Muslims, including one Moulvie at least, having gone over to Hinduism under Ārya influence. The aims of the institution are two:

a. To protect Islam from external attacks.

b. To send missionaries to preach Islam among Non-Muslims, and ignorant Muslims.

Six subjects are taught, the *Koran*, Islamic theology and philosophy, the defence of Islam, Christianity, Western science, and Sanskrit. There are seven students at present. None of them know English; but I was told that some of the missionaries already sent out do know English. A printing press is attached to the school; and a series of tracts has already been published against the Ārya Samāj.

A third seminary recently founded is the *Anjuman-i-Naumania*, which is carried on in the Shahi Mosque, Lahore. The Secretary writes, "Ours is a purely religious school teaching Arabic literature and sciences through the medium of our vernacular." From another source I learn that the institution receives considerable financial help from Muslims who have had a university education.

Fourthly, a learned Muḥammadan, named Hakīm Ajmal Haziq-ul-Mulk, who is a doctor and resides in Delhi, has the idea of combining Orthodox Muḥammadanism with Western culture. He has already trained four graduates of Aligarh as Moulvies.

The most important and most orthodox of all Muslim seminaries in India is the *Dar-ul-ulum*, or School of Theology, at Deoband, near Saharanpur. It has about 500 students. All Muslims acknowledge that it is very old-fashioned. Yet even here the pressure of modern times is being felt: an English class has recently been opened, and attempts are being made to reform the divinity course in several directions.

In Jubbulpore there is a little group of Muslims who have had an English education and are very eager to defend their religion. They told me that they had already started a High School in the town, the purpose of which is to preserve and to spread Muḥammadanism. They have also opened a little school on the same lines as the seminary in Lucknow. It is as yet but a little venture; but they hope to raise the standard and train young men to know the *Koran* thoroughly, and also to deal with men of other religions.

An All-India Muslim Students' Brotherhood with its headquarters at Aligarh has just been formed.

Finally, there is a Muḥammadan Book and Tract Depot in Lahore, where a large variety of volumes, both in Urdu and English, are offered for sale. Any English work which can be used apologetically, *e.g.* Carlyle's *Hero as Prophet*, is published and sold cheap.

3. The movements already dealt with are all among Sunnis; but the Shiahs are also active. They hold an annual Conference [1] which is meant mainly to rouse their community on the subject of education and to find money for its extension. I am told also that there is at present a great upward movement of the Feringhi Mahal School. Their work is mostly literary. They translate English works into Urdu. They are approaching far more than formerly the philosophy of the West.

12. Sectarian Universities

The most successful of the educational efforts yet made for the defence and strengthening of Hinduism has been the Central Hindu College, Benares, founded by Hindus under the leadership of Mrs. Besant and the Theosophical Society.

[1] *ISR.*, XX, 234.

It is strong, efficient, successful, and it actually teaches Hinduism. Hence a desire has arisen to take the further forward step of creating a Hindu University which should arrange curricula, hold examinations and confer degrees. In this way, not the actual work of teaching only, but the aims of education, the subjects taught and the standards demanded would be under Hindu control. Naturally the Muḥammadan community at once followed suit and proposed a Muslim University. Both parties began the collection of funds.

These proposals are so contrary to the spirit of University culture and so likely to stand in the way of every movement for the increasing of friendliness and harmony amongst the various religious communities of India that it seems certain that the Government of India would have vetoed them absolutely, had there not been something (all unknown to the public) to hinder their action. They have, however, definitely decided that, if such Universities are set up, they shall be local teaching Universities, and not territorial organizations like the existing Universities. This obviates the most serious dangers. Meantime Mrs. Besant has fallen from her high place in Benares;[1] and the proposals for the present seem to hang fire.

[1] P. 276, above.

CHAPTER V

RELIGIOUS NATIONALISM

1895–1913

In this last section of our period a frightful portent flamed up in India, anarchism and murder inspired by religion. But, fortunately, there seems to be good reason for believing that the outbreak of violence will prove a lurid episode in a time of great and better things. Facts seem to justify our marking off these years sharply from the preceding; for new ideals and passions which are visible in their best literature and noblest activity as well as in anarchism distinguish it clearly from earlier times. Yet there is a certain continuity: the new spirit is a further stage of the movement which began a century ago, a further unfolding of what has been latent in the Awakening from the beginning. The notes of what we tentatively call Religious Nationalism seem to be as follows:

A. Independence. A distinct advance in thought and action made itself manifest about 1870. Young India began to think of political influence and to defend the ancient religious heritage. Yet there was a sort of half-dependence on the ideals and the thought of others, which gives the time an appearance of unripeness. In this new era we have the assertion of the full independence of the Indian mind. The educated Indian now regards himself as a full-grown man, the equal in every respect of the cultured European, not to be set aside as an Asiatic, or as a member of a dark race. He claims the right of thinking his own thoughts; and he is quite prepared to burn what he has hitherto adored and to create a new heaven and a new earth. This adult self-confidence was immeasurably strengthened by the victory of Japan over Russia. Every Asiatic felt himself recreated by that great event. To all Asiatic lands it was a crisis in race-history, the moment when the age-old flood of European aggression was turned back. The exultation which every Indian felt over the victory lifted the national spirit to its height and gave a new note of strength to the period.

B. A new nationalism. The patriotism of to-day makes the feeling which inspired the Congress seem a very bloodless thing indeed. Men now live at fever-heat, carried beyond themselves by a new overmastering devotion to the good of India. But there is clear sight as well as passion. The new nationalism is much more serious and open-eyed than the thin old politicalism. It is burdened, tortured, driven forward by the conviction that the whole national life needs to be reinspired and reborn. Full proof of the depths to which the Indian mind has been stirred may be seen in this, that in all the best minds the new feeling and the fresh thought are fired by religion, either a furious devotion to some divinity of hate and blood, or a self-consecration to God and India which promises to bear good fruit. Finally, whether in anarchists or in men of peace, the new nationalism is willing to serve and suffer. The deluded boys who believed they could bring in India's millennium by murdering a few white men were quite prepared to give their lives for their country; and the healthy movements which incarnate the new spirit at its best spend themselves in unselfish service.

1. Anarchism

Before we attempt to describe the murderous propaganda we had better endeavour to realize what curdled to such bitterness the spirit of many of the most generous young Indians of our days. What were the causes of the sudden storm of furious hate?

1. *The fact that India is under a foreign government.* The first thought of the man filled with the new spirit is that this is utterly wrong, something which simply ought not to be. India ought to be guided by her own ideals and ruled by her own men. Her present rulers loom up as tyrannical aggressors, thieves of the nation's rights, ruthless destroyers of her priceless ancient heritage.

2. *The race-hatred and race-contempt of Europeans.* I am not one of those who believe that the Englishman behaves worse in his imperial position than other nationalities would do, if they were in his place. Indeed, I am inclined to think that, in comparison with others, he stands fairly high. Yet the fact remains that there is a percentage of Europeans in India — soldiers, mechanics, shop assistants, business men, with a sprinkling even of professional men, army officers, and civilians — who continually shew contempt and hatred for Indians and speak of them as an inferior race, and who from time to time assault Indian servants and subordinates, and treat educated Indians with the grossest rudeness. This behaviour of a small minority of our fellow-countrymen, which at all times has produced very serious results, necessarily stirred the fiercest passions, when national feeling and Indian self-respect rose to flood-tide.

We must also frankly acknowledge that every piece of self-complacent, ill-informed, unsympathetic criticism of Indian religion, society and life, whether written by tourist, missionary or official, helped to inflame the sense of wrong and to embitter the resentment which the imperial position of Britain necessarily creates.

3. *Lord Curzon.* Perhaps no man was ever so well prepared for the viceroyalty as Lord Curzon was. Certainly

no man ever toiled harder in the position, or worked more disinterestedly for the good of India. His insight and his unsparing labour are already producing their fruits in higher efficiency in education and many other departments of Indian life. Yet it was his tragic destiny to be more furiously detested by the educated Indian than any other Englishman. The cause lay in his self-confident and arrogant spirit and manner. Twenty years earlier they would have scarcely provoked comment; but, contemporaneous with the rise of the Indian mind to independence and national dignity and with the emergence of Asia from her secular slavery to Europe, they stung India to fury and worked wild ruin.

4. *The inner antagonism between Hindu and Western culture.* When the modern Indian reached self-consciousness and self-confidence, there could not fail to come a violent reaction from the attitude of reverence for the West which had guided his scholar-footsteps. Trained to think by his modern education, he could not fail to turn back to the ancient culture which lived in him and make the most of it. The period of training had been too repressive, too fully dominated by the West. The reaction was bound to come. Thus the old passionate devotion to Hinduism flared up and increased the passion of the anarchist; and his perception of the inner antagonism between Hindu and Western culture-ideals at once justified and embittered his hatred.

5. *Exaggerated praise of India and condemnation of the West.* This more than anything else was the cause of the ruinous folly which marked so much of the teaching and the action of the anarchists. Dayānanda, the Theosophists, Vivekānanda, Sister Niveditā and all that followed them talked in the wildest and most extravagant way in praise of Hinduism and Indian civilization and in condemnation of

Christianity and the West; so that they actually led the average educated Hindu to believe the doctrine, that everything Indian is pure, spiritual and lofty, and that everything Western is materialistic, sensual, devilish. I do not believe that these leaders had any sinister political motive for this policy. Sir Valentine Chirol is inclined to go too far in this matter. What they did they did in the hope of making their followers devoted and enthusiastic Hindus, and of rousing them to toil for the benefit of India. But you cannot sow the wind without reaping the whirlwind. If it be true that Hinduism and Indian civilization are purely spiritual and good, and that Christianity and Western civilization are grossly materialistic and corrupt, then the average Hindu was quite right in drawing the conclusion that the sooner India is rid of Europeans and Western influence the better: we are already on the very verge of the doctrine of the anarchists. These leaders are directly responsible for a great deal of the wildest teaching of the assassin press. It is not merely the general attitude that is common to the revivalists and the anarchists. It is as clear as noonday that the religious aspect of anarchism was merely an extension of that revival of Hinduism which is the work of Dayānanda, Rāmakṛishṇa, Vivekānanda and the Theosophists. Further, the historical is almost as close as the logical connection. Dayānanda started the Anti-cow-killing agitation in 1882.[1] The movement grew until, in 1888, it had reached colossal proportions; and in 1893 Tilak made it one of his most potent tools. Kṛishṇavarma was a pupil of Dayānanda; Lājpat Rai was for many years one of the chief leaders of the Ārya Samāj; and Vivekānanda's brother Bhūpendra was one of the most influential of the anarchist journalists of Calcutta.

The history of Indian anarchism cannot be written yet.

[1] P. 111, above.

The most salient facts may be found in Sir Valentine Chirol's *Indian Unrest*;[1] but every careful reader of that useful volume must feel very distinctly that there are many facts as yet unknown which are needed to make the growth of the movement intelligible. We mention here only the names of the leaders.

So far as can be seen at present, Bal Gangadhar Tilak, a member of the sept of Brāhmans that led and governed the Marāṭhas, formed the earliest centre of the propaganda known as anarchism. The Anti-cow-killing agitation already referred to was one of several experiments which he tried in seeking to rouse his people to energetic political action; but in 1895 he organized a great celebration of the birthday of Śivaji, the chieftain who, in the latter half of the seventeenth century, made the Marāṭha tribes an iron army and a united nation to resist the Muḥammadans. This widespread commemoration of the Marāṭha leader in 1895 is significant, because in it for the first time all the features of the Extremist propaganda stand out clear; and there is unquestionable proof that it contained the poison of anarchy; for within two years it worked itself out in murder in the streets of Poona. For this reason we take 1895 as the date of the arrival of the new spirit in Indian history.

Two other men can be discerned as generators of the anarchical spirit, alongside of Tilak, between 1900 and 1905. These are Śyāmaji Kṛishṇavarma in London and Bipin Chandra Pāl in Calcutta. The former, who had been a personal friend and pupil of Dayānanda, lived in India House, London, edited the *Indian Sociologist*, and filled many a young Hindu student with the poison of hate and murder. Here perhaps was the chief centre of the cult of the bomb. Bipin Chandra Pāl edited a journal, called

[1] London, Macmillan, 1910, 5*s*. net.

New India, the settled policy of which was to publish every tale that could be found and exaggerated to fill the Indian mind with the bitterest hatred and profoundest contempt for Europeans, and to urge Indians to train themselves physically to be able to fight those blackguards.

The following paragraphs by the Rev. C. F. Andrews of Delhi describe very faithfully the effect of the Russo-Japanese war upon India:

> At the close of the year 1904 it was clear to those who were watching the political horizon that great changes were impending in the East. Storm-clouds had been gathering thick and fast. The air was full of electricity. The war between Russia and Japan had kept the surrounding peoples on the tip-toe of expectation. A stir of excitement passed over the North of India. Even the remote villagers talked over the victories of Japan as they sat in their circles and passed round the *huqqa* at night. One of the older men said to me, "There has been nothing like it since the Mutiny." A Turkish cousul of long experience in Western Asia told me that in the interior you could see everywhere the most ignorant peasants "tingling" with the news. Asia was moved from one end to the other, and the sleep of the centuries was finally broken. It was a time when it was "good to be alive," for a new chapter was being written in the book of the world's history.
>
> My own work at Delhi was at a singular point of vantage. It was a meeting-point of Hindus and Musalmans, where their opinions could be noted and recorded. The Aligarh movement among Muhammadans was close at hand, and I was in touch with it. I was also in sympathy with Hindu leaders of the modern school of Indian thought and shared many of their views. Each party spoke freely to me of their hopes and aims. The Musalmans, as one expected, regarded the reverses of Russia chiefly from the territorial standpoint. These reverses seemed to mark the limit of the expansion of the Christian nations over the world's surface. The Hindus regarded more the inner significance of the event. The old-time glory and greatness of Asia seemed destined to return. The material aggrandisement

of the European races at the expense of the East seemed at last to be checked. The whole of Buddhaland from Ceylon to Japan might again become one in thought and life. Hinduism might once more bring forth its old treasures of spiritual culture for the benefit of mankind. Behind these dreams and visions was the one exulting hope — that the days of servitude to the West were over and the day of independence had dawned. Much had gone before to prepare the way for such a dawn of hope: the Japanese victories made it, for the first time, shining and radiant.[1]

Now, in contrast with these glowing lights, let us place some of Lord Curzon's acts as they seemed at the time to educated Indians. He gave an address at Calcutta University Convocation in which he suggested to a listening nation that they were a nation of liars. He created and passed a Universities' Act which was meant to introduce a number of much-needed reforms into the higher education; yet, honestly or dishonestly, almost the whole native press interpreted it as meant to curtail Western education among Indians, and thereby to weaken their influence in the country. Then there came, in 1905, the Partition of Bengal. It is now perfectly clear that some serious change in the administration of the province was urgently required; and there seems to be no reason to doubt that Lord Curzon believed he was carrying out the best policy; but he paid but little attention to Bengali feeling and opinion, and some of the speeches which he delivered in a tour through the province were provocative in the last degree. In any case, his action infuriated the educated classes of Bengal; the whole country was soon rocking in sympathy with them; and an unscrupulous propaganda roused the wildest passion, excited the students beyond measure and led to many riots.

It was these events that gave the Anarchist party their

[1] *The Renaissance in India*, 4–5.

opportunity. Immediately a new type of journalism appeared in Calcutta. The chief writers were Aravinda Ghose, who had been educated in England, and had then spent some years in the service of the Gaekwar of Baroda, his brother Barendra, Bipin Chandra Pal and Bhūpendra Nath Dutt, a brother of Svāmī Vivekānanda; while Tilak and his followers continued the campaign in the West, and Lāla Lājpat Rai and some other Āryas did all they could to rouse the Panjab. A long series of murders and attempted murders of Europeans and Indians was the direct result of this writing and of the secret plotting of men who are not yet fully known.

Perhaps the most amazing fact in the whole sad history is this, that the Moderate party, which until now had controlled the National Congress and had led the educated community, were swept off their feet and dragged behind the Anarchists, almost without a word of protest, until the Congress met at Surat in 1907; when the two parties actually came to blows, and the gathering had to be broken up. This fact, and the terrible catalogue of murders which was steadily lengthening out, at last convinced the Moderates that they must dissociate themselves from the teaching of the Anarchist party. Then the tide began to turn. Fewer of the high-strung, unselfish students fell into the toils of the men who planned the murders. In June, 1908, Tilak was arrested and sent to prison for six years for seditious writing. Lord Morley, who was Secretary of State for India, and the Viceroy, Lord Minto, had the new Councils Act passed in 1909, which proved that Britain is really anxious to go forward and give educated India a gradually increasing share in the government of the Empire. The King's visit touched the hearts of the people of India as nothing has done for many years; and the rearrangement of the two Bengals helped to heal old wounds.

The results have been priceless. There is now a clear perception of the fact that Indians must coöperate with the British Government in order to bring in the better day for India. Things look distinctly promising.[1]

The following are the chief notes of Anarchist teaching:

1. Indian civilization in all its branches, — religion, education, art, industry, home life and government, — is healthy, spiritual, beautiful and good. It has become corrupted in the course of the centuries, but that is largely the result of the cruelty and aggression of the Muḥammadans in former times and now of the British. The Indian patriot must toil to restore Indian life and civilization.

2. Western civilization in all its parts, — religion, education, art, business and government, — is gross, materialistic and therefore degrading to India. The patriotic Indian must recognize the grave danger lurking in every element of Western influence, must hate it, and must be on his guard against it.

The inevitable result of this has been race-hatred such as has never been seen in India before. The Anarchist press was filled with the uttermost hate and bitterness.

3. India ought to be made truly Indian. There is no place for Europeans in the country. Indians can manage everything far better than Europeans can. The British Government, Missions, European trade and Western influence of every kind, are altogether unhealthy in India. Everything should belong to the Indians themselves.

4. Hence it is a religious duty to get rid of the European and all the evils that attend him. The better a man understands his religion, the more clear will be his perception that Europeans and European influence must be rooted out. All means for the attainment of this end are justifiable. As

[1] Since these words were put in type, the war has come, and Tilak and Lājpat Rai are loyally helping the Government.

Kṛishṇa killed Kaṁsa, so the modern Indian must kill the European demons that are tyrannically holding India down. The blood-thirsty goddess Kālī ought to be much honoured by the Indian patriot. Even the *Gītā* was used to teach murder. Lies, deceit, murder, everything, it was argued, may be rightly used. How far the leaders really believed this teaching no man can say; but the younger men got filled with it, and many were only too sincere.

5. The whole propaganda was marked by a complete disregard of historical truth. The most frightful distortions of past events, and the foulest slanders both of the Government and of individual Europeans went the round of the press, and did their poisonous work.

LITERATURE. — *The New Spirit*, by Bepin Chandra Pal, Calcutta, Sinha, Sarvadhicari & Co., 1907, Rs. 1 as. 4. *Life of Aravinda Ghosha*, by Rama Chandra Palita, Calcutta, the author, 1911, Rs. 1 as. 8. *Indian Unrest*, by Sir Valentine Chirol, London, Macmillan, 1910, 5*s*. net.

Anarchism flung itself against the British Government and fell back broken. The whole movement was a pitiful piece of waste, — waste of energy, patriotic feeling, literary skill and human life. One cannot look back upon it without a very heavy heart, as one thinks of all the dignity and worth of the character and feeling which were perverted and flung away. But the same high love for India and will to be spent for her sake have found healthy channels for themselves along various lines. In all these movements the main notes of the period ring out very distinctly: the end in view in each case is the national advancement; the religious sanction is always in the background, even if it is not distinctly expressed; the work is of the nature of unselfish service; and high passion inspires the whole. We subdivide the movements into four groups, industrial, social, artistic and poetic.

2. Industry, Science, Economics

The Swadeshi Movement (*svadeśī* = belonging to one's own country), an agitation for the strengthening of Indian industries, arose in Bengal in Lord Curzon's viceroyalty under the stimulus of national excitement. Indians were urged to buy goods of Indian design and manufacture; articles and books were published, exhibiting the vast natural resources of India, the abundance of cheap labour available, and shewing how much India loses through importing what might quite well be made in the country. The movement was later contaminated by an organized Boycott of British goods, which was accompanied by much violence and social tyranny, disturbed business for a while, and embittered relations between the races, but entirely failed to divert the natural course of trade. The legitimate movement, however, has been distinctly useful. The educated classes began to think of economic questions, and every Indian industry was encouraged and quickened. Under the same impulse a society was formed in Calcutta for the purpose of sending young men to Europe, America or Japan to receive industrial or scientific education. When these students began to return from study, a supply of trained workers became available for the furthering of native industries. Between 1905 and 1907 a considerable number of new manufacturing and trading companies were formed in various parts of India, but above all in Bengal. Cotton, jute, leather, soap, glass and other manufactures were attempted. There was at least one steam navigation company. Several Banks and Insurance Companies arose. All have not proved successful by any means from the business point of view; indeed, in the end of 1913, a number of Indian banks collapsed; but experience has been gained; and in a number of cases considerable progress has been achieved.

There has also been an increase in the number of students reading science, agriculture and economics at the Universities; and several Indians have written wisely and well on economic questions.

3. Social and Political Service

a. Help for the Depressed Classes

One sixth of the whole population of India, a vast mass of humanity outnumbering all the people of England, Scotland, Ireland and Wales, have for some two thousand years been held down by Hindus at the bottom of society, in indescribable ignorance, dirt and degradation, on the ground that they are so foul as to be unfit for ordinary human intercourse. According to the orthodox theory, every man born among these people is a soul which in former lives lived so viciously that his present degradation is the just punishment for his former sin. They are called Outcastes, Untouchables, Pañchamas, or the Depressed Classes. What sort of a national danger this mass of crushed humanity is to India, every student of sociology and politics will readily realize. These people belong to many different races, and are found in every part of India, sometimes in small, sometimes in large groups. Their poverty is in most cases pitiable. Their religion consists in pacifying diabolic powers by means of animal sacrifice and various forms of barbaric ritual.

More than a century ago Christian missionaries attempted to win some of these groups for Christ; and at quite an early date they met with some success; but it was not until the year 1880 that anything startling occurred. The years from 1876 to 1879 were marked by a frightful famine, which brought indescribable suffering and lamentable loss of life in many parts of the South of India. Christians could not stand idly by in these circumstances:

Hundreds of thousands of people were dying in the Tamil and Telugu countries. Government was doing what it could in face of the hopeless mass of misery. There were few railroads, and grain brought from other countries by sea rotted on the beach at Madras while people two hundred miles away starved for lack of it. At this crisis missionaries everywhere co-operated with Government in the work of relief, raising funds among their own supporters at home, carrying out earthworks, and so finding employment for many poor people, and doing all that pity and their close contact with the people enabled them to do to help the sufferers.[1]

The result was that to these poor down-trodden people the contrast between Hinduism which held them down, and Christianity which did all that it possibly could to save them, began to be dimly visible; and, after the famine was over, they came to the missionaries in thousands for baptism. Such movements have occurred in several distinct parts of India. When such a movement begins, it usually lasts for a number of years, and then dies down. Or, it may slacken and then increase again.

Wherever it has been possible to give sufficient attention to this work, very remarkable results have been secured. When missionaries began to appeal to these people, Hindus jeered at them, saying they might as well attempt to uplift the monkeys of the forest. Certainly, at first sight, they are most unpromising material, physically, socially, mentally, morally. Yet the truth of Christ and loving Christian service have worked miracles. They have responded nobly, and great advances in physical well-being, in education, in society and the family, and also in religion, have been won.

One of the most remarkable features of the work is this, that Hindus and Muḥammadans all over India at once give the baptized Outcaste a new standing. He is no longer

[1] *The Outcastes' Hope*, 32–3.

untouchable and beyond the pale, but is received as other Christians are.

For many years the work went on without causing much comment from the Hindu side; though, now and then, some educated man would refer to Christian success among these people either in scorn or in bitter anger. But, just about the time when the new nationalist spirit was spreading far and wide, fresh currents of thought began to shew themselves both among the Outcastes themselves and among educated men.

Groups of these Outcastes who had not become Christians had begun to realize that the doctrine which for so long had justified their miserable condition was false, and that it was not held by missionaries or the British Government. The hope that they might be able to throw off their chains began to rise in their hearts. These new stirrings appeared in different parts of India. First of all, came the Tiyas of Malabar, and, later, the Vokkaligas of Mysore. In the case of both these peoples the rising is so remarkable that we have dealt with them alongside of Caste movements.[1] Another noticeable case is the rising of the Mahars of the Marāṭha country. They met in Conference at Poona in November, 1910, and drew up a Memorial to the Earl of Crewe, Secretary of State for India, begging that certain privileges which their fathers enjoyed in the Indian army should be restored to them. In this connection they speak of the many Mahars who fell wounded or died fighting bravely side by side with Europeans, and with Indians who were not Outcastes. But much more important than this claim of theirs is the spirit shown in the Memorial, and the statements they make to the Secretary for India. The following are a few sentences taken from it:

[1] Above, pp. 311 and 314.

As British subjects we cannot, we should not submit to ordinances which are entirely foreign to British ideas of public justice and public honour. We are sick of the bondage which the barbarism of Hindu customs imposes upon us; we long to enjoy the perfect freedom which the British nation and the British Government desire to offer impartially to all those who are connected with them as British subjects.

We would, therefore, earnestly appeal to the Imperial Government to move on our behalf. We have long submitted to the Jagannath of caste; we have for ages been crushed under its ponderous wheels. But we can now no longer submit to the tyranny.

Our Hindu rulers did not recognize our manhood, and treated us worse than their cattle; and shall not that nation which emancipated the Negro at infinite self-sacrifice, and enlightened and elevated the poorer people of its own commonwealth, condescend to give us a helping hand?

The kindly touch of the Christian religion elevates the Mahar at once and for ever, socially as well as politically, and shall not the magic power of British Law and British Justice produce the same effect upon us even as followers of our own ancestral faith?

A similar story may be told of the Namaśūdras of Bengal. They are amongst the very lowest classes of the country; yet we find them in Conference in April, 1910, seeking to plan for their own advancement, and stirring each other up to various items of social reform.[1] A few months later a still more interesting event took place in the Panjab:

An incident which would appear to be queer, under existing conditions, is reported to the *Hindustan* from Jullundur. To the reflecting mind it appears to be but the beginning, feeble though it be, of a spirit of retaliation against the most inhuman and degrading treatment meted out by Hindus and Mussalmans alike to the depressed classes for centuries past. The sweepers of Jullundur have started a society called the *Valmika Samāj* to defend their interests. They do not think themselves to be in any way inferior to their Hindu or Mussalman compatriots.

[1] *ISR.*, XX, 397.

At the last Dussehra fair they opened a shop vending sweetmeats for the benefit of members of their own community. The following is the translation on the board: — "Let it be known to the *High-born* that Hindus and Mussalmans are prohibited to buy sweets here. Chuhras and all others are welcome."[1]

Somewhere about 1903 the whole problem began to be discussed in the Indian press. Orthodox Hindus still condemned the missionary propaganda in violent terms, but far-sighted men gave utterance to other ideas. Here is what the Hon. Mr. G. K. Gokhale said at a public meeting in Dharwar in 1903:

I think all fair-minded persons will have to admit that it is absolutely monstrous that a class of human beings with bodies similar to our own, with brains that can think and with hearts that can feel, should be perpetually condemned to a low life of utter wretchedness, servitude and mental and moral degradation, and that permanent barriers should be placed in their way so that it should be impossible for them ever to overcome them and improve their lot. This is deeply revolting to our sense of justice. I believe one has only to put oneself mentally into their places to realize how grievous this injustice is. We may touch a cat, we may touch a dog, we may touch any other animal, but the touch of these human beings is pollution. And so complete is now the mental degradation of these people that they themselves see nothing in such treatment to resent, that they acquiesce in it as though nothing better than that was their due. Moreover, is it, I may ask, consistent with our own self-respect that these men should be kept out of our houses and shut out from all social intercourse as long as they remain within the pale of Hinduism, whereas the moment they put on a coat, and a hat and a pair of trousers and call themselves Christians we are prepared to shake hands with them and look upon them as quite respectable? No sensible man will say that this is a satisfactory state of things.[2]

[1] From the *Punjabee*. Reproduced in *ISR.*, XXI, 98.

[2] Quoted in the Memorial of the Mahars.

At a later date Mr. Gokhale's political instincts led him to give utterance to another wise word:

> The problem of the depressed classes really went to the root of their claim to be treated on terms of equality with other civilized communities of the world. They were all of them asking — he might even use the word clamouring — for equal treatment by other communities. He thought they were entitled to do that, and they would be unworthy of their manhood if they did not agitate for it. But they would deserve to have it only when they were prepared to extend the same treatment to those who expected it at their hands.[1]

The Ārya Samāj was probably the first body that proposed to outflank the missionary movement:

> While the people of India increased in 1891–1901 at the rate of $1\frac{1}{2}$ per cent, native Christians increased at the rate of over 30 per cent. Just consider for a moment what Christian missionaries are accomplishing in India, though they come here from the remotest part of Europe. They beat even the Arya Samajists, in spite of their preaching the indigenous faith of the country. The reason is that the Arya Samajists have not yet learnt to work among the masses who form the backbone of India. It is high time for us to realize that the future of India lies not in the hands of the higher classes but of the low caste people, and if we devote the best part of our enegry in raising the status of the masses, we can make every Indian household resound with the chanting of Vedas at no distant date. But where are the men, where is the sacrifice? [2]

Later, certain Hindus took up the same position; but others pointed out that the policy of raising the Outcaste is contrary to Hinduism and must certainly tend to break up the religion. The following is a sentence from the *Mahratta:* [3]

> Now we know that the result of educating the depressed classes must be in the long run to weaken, if not utterly destroy caste.

[1] *ISR.*, XX, 88. [2] From the *Arya Messenger.* [3] November 7, 1909.

Yet, in spite of many cries of danger, the conscience of India has been waked. Men realize that it is *wrong* to hold down the Outcaste. Then the new Nationalist consciousness feels so distinctly the need of unifying the nation and of strengthening every element in the population that the problem of transforming these fifty millions of crushed Indians into vigorous citizens is felt to be one of the most pressing national problems. Hence the best men have turned to action.

The Brāhma Samāj and the Prārthanā Samāj were the first bodies outside the Christian Church that gave any attention to the depressed classes; but their work has never risen to such dimensions as to make it of great importance. The Prārthanā Samāj in Mangalore has been working among these poor people since 1898, and the Brāhmas have a little work going on in East Bengal. In 1906, however, things began to take a more practical turn. The Depressed Classes Mission Society of India was founded in Bombay that year. It shows clearly the influence of the most recent developments of the national spirit; for the philanthropic aim of the work is largely sustained by national feeling; and people of any religion may take part in the work. As a matter of fact, however, the leaders throughout have belonged to the Prārthanā Samāj, though they have received a great deal of support from Hindus. The following gives a sketch of the aims of the Society, its work and its finances:

The object of the Society shall be to maintain a Mission which shall seek to elevate the social as well as the spiritual condition of the Depressed Classes viz. the Mahars, Chambhars, Pariahs, Namsudras, Dheds, and all other classes treated as untouchable in India, by

(1) Promoting education,
(2) Providing work,
(3) Remedying their social disabilities,

(4) Preaching to them principles of Liberal Religion, personal character and good citizenship.

Work of the Society

The present organization and work of the Society, which is described at length in the last annual report, a copy of which accompanies this representation among other enclosures, may be summarized as follows: —

The Society has under it fifteen centres of work in and outside of the Bombay Presidency, viz. Bombay, Poona, Hubli, Nagpur, Yeotmal, Thana, Satara, Mahableshwar, Malvan, Dapoli, Akola, Amraoti, Bhavanagar, Mangalore, Madras. Of these the first five, being incorporated branches, are under the direct control of the Executive Committee of the Society and the rest, being only affiliated, are independent in the management of their own local affairs. The Headquarters are in Parel, Bombay, and the Society is registered as a charitable Body under Act XXI of 1860. It has at present in all thirty educational institutions of which five are Boarding Houses, four are technical institutions, one is a middle school and the remaining are primary schools. The number of pupils on the roll on the 31st December last was 1,231 and the total expenditure of the Society on its educational work last year was Rs. 20,304.11.5 for which the total Grant-in-Aid received from the Government and the local municipalities for the year was Rs. 1,956. Of the thirty institutions sixteen are incorporated and fourteen are affiliated to the Society.[1]

It will be seen that this Society, which was started in Bombay some seven years ago, has roused people in many parts of Western and Southern India to the duty of doing something for the Outcaste. The Society is therefore an organization of real value, and may do still larger work in the future. It will be noticed that the work of the Mission is practically confined to education, except in so far as it seeks

[1] From an address presented to H. E. the Governor of Bombay, on the 30th of July, 1913. *ISR.*, XXIII, 580.

to rouse public opinion. A similar society exists in Calcutta, but it has not grown to any strength.

Several of the sectarian groups are attempting to gather in Outcastes to their fold, and all of them follow the educational method which the Depressed Classes Mission uses. I have not been able to get detailed reports of these activities, perhaps because in most cases the work done is small. The Ārya Samāj probably does more than the others. The Deva Samāj has three schools in distinct centres in the Panjab. The local Sikh Associations called Singh Sabhās do what they can to induce Outcastes to become Sikhs. Some Hindus in the Mysore State have organized what they call *The Hindu Education Mission* to help the children of the Outcastes of Mysore. Three day schools and two night schools have been already started. The Theosophists of Madras have also a few schools for the same class. Muḥammadans in the Panjab, and also in Malabar have succeeded in persuading groups of Outcastes to become Muslims.

But by far the most significant and important fact to be observed with regard to this whole question is the fact that the conscience of India has been roused by what missions have done; and it is now perfectly clear that, whether sooner or later, whether through the Christian Church or through other agencies, the Outcastes of India will inevitably escape from the inhuman condition in which Hinduism has imprisoned them for two thousand years. Thus in far-distant India, and in the twentieth century, Christ fulfils once more His promise to bring release to the captive. Perhaps the clearest proof of the change in the attitude of the Indian public generally to this question will be found in a small volume, called *The Depressed Classes*, containing twenty-three addresses and papers by Hindus, Christians, Theosophists, Āryas, Brāhmas, and Prārthanā Samājists.

Many signs of the working of this new spirit may be observed. The Director of Public Instruction in the Bombay Presidency observes that during the last few years a great change has come over local boards and other bodies; there is now far less objection to Outcaste children taking places in the ordinary schools.[1] Mr. T. B. Pandian has succeeded in raising money to dig a number of wells for Outcastes in the Tamil country.[2] Quite recently the Hindu community in a centre in the Panjab held a ceremony to begin the practice of allowing these untouchable Outcastes to use the ordinary wells.[3] So the leaven works.

Yet it is very important to observe that, though the activities of the Depressed Classes Mission are of considerable value, the fact that it can do no vigorous religious work seriously weakens its results. "The kindly touch of the Christian religion elevates the Mahar at once and for ever," as the Mahars said in their address to the Earl of Crewe; while the Depressed Classes Mission can merely give a little education and moral advice.

LITERATURE.—*The Outcastes' Hope*, by G. E. Phillips, London, Y. P. M. M., 1912, 1s. net. *The Depressed Classes*, by many writers, Madras, Natesan, 1912, Re. 1.

b. Universal Education

One of the most striking manifestations of the new national spirit is the Bill which Mr. Gokhale laid before the Viceroy's Council in the winter of 1911–1912, for the purpose of extending primary education all over the country. The method proposed was to give local authorities the power, under certain conditions, to make primary education compulsory amongst the people under their jurisdiction. For various reasons the Bill was rejected, but it served a very

[1] *ISR.*, XXI, 184. [2] *Ib.*, XX, 621. [3] *Ib.*, XXIII, 25.

useful purpose in familiarizing the educated classes with the reasons why universal education is desirable, and in evoking the opinions of the native press on the subject. Thus, though it failed to pass, the Bill undoubtedly forwarded the cause. Some step for the furtherance of universal education will have to be taken ere long.

c. The Servants of India Society

In Poona there is a Hindu College called the Fergusson College, the professors of which receive very small salaries and do their work for the love of India. The quality of the education is high; and a number of most devoted public servants have been trained in its work. Amongst these the most brilliant is the Hon. Mr. Gopāl Kṛishṇa Gokhale, C. I. E. He served as one of the professors of the College for twenty years, from 1885 till the end of 1904. He then set himself to the formation of a society, the aim of which should be devoted and life-long service to the people of India.

The following paragraphs give the substance of an interview which the writer had with Mr. Gokhale in the National Liberal Club, London, in June, 1913.

The Society, which was established in 1905, is called the Servants of India Society. Its headquarters are in Poona, where there is a Home specially built for the training of the workers; and there are Branches in four of the provinces of India, Bombay, the Central Provinces, Madras and the United Provinces.

Only University graduates or men who have done successful public service are admitted as members. When a young man wishes to become a member, he lives in Mr. Gokhale's house for a short time, or in the Home, so that he may learn by experience what the society is, and so that the other members

PLATE XI

RAJCHANDRA RAVJIBHAI

THE HON'BLE G. K. GOKHALE, C. I. E.

RABINDRA NATH TAGORE

may have an opportunity of gauging his temperament and character. If he is thought suitable and if he wishes to go into the work, he becomes a student. For five years he receives a salary of only thirty rupees a month, and spends every year four months in study in the Home in Poona, six months in practical work in that Branch of the society to which he belongs and two months at home. The purpose of the whole movement is to create by means of practical work a higher type of worker. The progress of India is the great aim in view. There is a clear perception that, if India is to be a nation, the communities must become united. Hence in all the work of the society the aim of bringing Hindus and Muḥammadans together in real brotherhood is kept in view. Young Hindus are sent to live among Muḥammadans, to help them by loving service to the utmost of their power, just as missionaries do.

The society is open to young men of any race or religion; and there is a keen desire on the part of the leaders to get members other than Hindus. One Muḥammadan is already a member. There is no attempt made to bind the men together religiously. There are no common prayers in the Home. Each man is left to order his own devotions as he thinks best. Yet Mr. Gokhale holds that the aims in view, and the serious renunciation which membership imposes, are in themselves deeply religious. No demand is made that a student should give up caste; yet brotherly feeling in the Home is so rich and deep that no caste distinctions are kept. Members are not asked to become celibates; but life in the Home during the four months of training is monastic. The students are completely under the guidance of the First Member, Mr. Gokhale. During the five years of their training they are not allowed to deliver public addresses or to write to the magazines, without first submitting the matter to the First Member.

The work of the society is carried on under the direction of the Branches. Those who are members give their whole time and work to public service, while the students give their annual term of six months. A few of them are told off annually to make arrangements for the meetings of the National Congress. They do all they possibly can to help such movements as primary education, female education, and the uplifting of the Depressed Classes. In Berar a great deal has been done to help the Co-operative Credit Societies of the Province. During the serious fodder-famine from which Gujarāt suffered in 1912, ten members and six volunteers were fully engaged for ten months, and did priceless service.

After the five years of studentship are over, a member receives only fifty rupees a month of salary, even if he be a married man with a family. There are at present twenty-six members in all. The expenses of the society already run from twenty to forty thousand rupees per annum. Mr. Gokhale raises the bulk of this large sum himself from private friends.

The following paragraphs copied from a brief prospectus of the society [1] will give a clear idea of the spirit of the undertaking:

For some time past, the conviction has been forcing itself on many earnest and thoughtful minds that a stage has been reached in the work of nation-building in India, when, for further progress, the devoted labours of a specially trained agency, applying itself to the task in a true missionary spirit, are required. The work that has been accomplished so far has indeed been of the highest value. The growth during the last fifty years of a feeling of common nationality, based upon common traditions and ties, common hopes and aspirations, and even common disabilities, has been most striking. The fact that we are Indians first, and Hindus, Mahomedans and Parsees or

[1] *The Servants of India Society*, to be had from the Society.

Christians afterwards, is being realized in a steadily increasing measure, and the idea of a united and renovated India, marching onwards to a place among the nations of the world worthy of her great past, is no longer a mere idle dream of a few imaginative minds, but is the definitely accepted creed of those who form the brain of the community — the educated classes of the country. A creditable beginning has already been made in matters of education and of local self-government; and all classes of the people are slowly but steadily coming under the influence of liberal ideas. The claims of public life are every day receiving wider recognition, and attachment to the land of our birth is growing into a strong and deeply cherished passion of the heart. The annual meetings of Congresses and Conferences, the work of public bodies and associations, the writings in the columns of the Indian Press — all bear witness to the new life that is coursing in the veins of the people. The results achieved so far are undoubtedly most gratifying, but they only mean that the jungle has been cleared and the foundations laid. The great work of rearing the superstructure has yet to be taken in hand and the situation demands on the part of workers devotion and sacrifices proportionate to the magnitude of the task.

The Servants of India Society has been established to meet in some measure these requirements of the situation. Its members frankly accept the British connection as ordained, in the inscrutable dispensation of Providence, for India's good. Self-Government within the Empire for their country and a higher life generally for their countrymen is their goal. This goal, they recognize, cannot be attained without years of earnest and patient effort and sacrifices worthy of the cause. Much of the work must be directed toward building up in the country a higher type of character and capacity than is generally available at present; and the advance can only be slow. Moreover the path is beset with great difficulties; there will be constant temptations to turn back; bitter disappointments will repeatedly try the faith of those who have put their hand to the work. But the weary toil can have but one end, if only the workers grow not faint-hearted on the way. One essential condition of success in this work is that a sufficient number of our countrymen must now come forward to devote themselves to the cause in the spirit in which religious work is undertaken. Public life must be spiritualized. Love of country must so fill the heart that all else shall appear as of little moment by its side. A fervent patriotism which rejoices at every opportunity of sacrifice for the motherland, a dauntless heart which refuses to be turned back from its object by difficulty or danger, a deep faith in the purpose of Providence which nothing can shake — equipped with these, the worker must start on his mission and reverently seek the joy which comes of spending oneself in the service of one's country.

Mr. M. K. Gandhi,[1] who did such excellent service in the struggle with the South African Government for justice for the Indian, has signified his intention of becoming a worker under the Society.

d. The Seva Sadan

The progress of thought and the march of events, working together in India, have forced many women's problems to the front during the last few years.

The *Seva Sadan*, or Home[2] of Service, was founded in Bombay in July, 1908, by Mr. B. M. Malabari, the Parsee Reformer whose pamphlet on Child-marriage and Widow-celibacy published in 1887 is mentioned above,[3] and Dayaram Gidumal, a Hindu from Sindh, a retired judge. These two vigorous men collected large sums of money and guaranteed a steady income for the institution. During the last three years they paid in Rs. 45,000 between them, and raised an Endowment and Building Fund of Rs. 82,000. But Malabari is dead, while Gidumal has fallen away from

[1] See *M. K. Gandhi*, a sketch of his life and work. Madras, Natesan, as. 4.

[2] I owe practically all my information on the Seva Sadan to a letter from Miss B. A. Engineer, the General Secretary, and a few pamphlets which she kindly sent me.

[3] See p. 87.

social reform; so that the Seva Sadan must now rely on other friends.

Perhaps the following lines cut from one of their publications will most readily give a clear idea of the work:

OBJECT:—Social Educational and Medical Service (Seva) through Indian Sisters, regular and lay.

The Society maintains the following institutions:—

1. A Home for the Homeless.
2. An Industrial Home with various departments.
3. A Shelter for the distressed.
4. A Dispensary for Women and Children.
5. Ashrams (or Sisterhoods)—Hindu, Parsi and Mahommedan.
6. A Work-Class, also Home Classes in Chawls (*i.e.* large tenement houses).

All these are for the benefit of women.

A resident lady doctor gives her whole time to the work; and two others give a certain amount of help. A social service nurse is also available for outdoor work; and there are lay sisters, Hindu, Parsee and Muslim, who move about among the poor. Young probationers are sent for training to various medical schools.

The society also publishes tracts for free distribution on medical, sanitary and moral subjects.

The Home has now its own building in Gamdevi Road, Bombay. The annual expenditure is about Rs. 20,000.

There are branches in Poona and Ahmedabad which are also doing excellent work.

One might reasonably mention here certain other forms of social work, such as Widows' Homes, the Social Service being done by students, and especially the Nishkāma Karma Maṭha,[1] which is very similar in purpose and in work to the

[1] See below, p. 403.

Seva Sadan; but our aim in this chapter has been to group together the new movements which shew a decidedly nationalist purpose, while in other chapters we have dealt with those which are more sectarian in character,[1] or are clearly inspired by social considerations.[2]

4. Fine Art and Music

The Government School of Art, Calcutta, has been for several years the centre of a very promising revival of Indian painting, sculpture, wood-carving and other fine arts. Mr. E. B. Havell, who was for several years Principal of the School, has been the leader of the movement; but he has been ably seconded by a group of very promising Indian painters, the most prominent of whom is Mr. Abanindra Nath Tagore. The purpose in view is to produce a genuinely Indian school of art. A number of beautiful reproductions of both ancient and modern pictures have been published at moderate prices by the Indian Society of Oriental Art, which is closely connected with the Calcutta School; and in London the India Society is doing similar work.

Mr. Havell and Dr. A. K. Coomaraswamy, who is connected with Ceylon, have for several years led a crusade to convince the world that Indian art has high spiritual qualities which set it at least in the front rank of the world's art, if not in advance of all other art. This high argument, which is parallel to the claims made on behalf of Hinduism, Buddhism and other Oriental faiths by the revivalists, has proved of large value; for it has led to a far more intelligent appreciation of Indian sculpture and painting than was possible in former years, and to the recognition of fine qualities in them hitherto unnoticed, and has also given great

[1] Chap. IV. [2] Chap. VI.

encouragement to Indian artists; but it seems clear that it has failed to bring sober critics to the acceptance of all that Messrs. Havell and Coomaraswamy teach. No one who wishes to understand India ought to fail to look through Mr. Havell's exquisite book, *Indian Sculpture and Painting*, and the volumes of reproductions published by Dr. Coomaraswamy.

Until quite recently the cultivation of music in India was left largely to nautch-girls. Here also the new national spirit has proved creative. Keen interest in the best Indian music, both vocal and instrumental, is being shewn in several quarters. *The Gandharva Mahāvidyālaya*, or Academy of Indian Music, was established in Lahore in 1901, but has now its headquarters in Girgaum, Bombay. Local musical societies have appeared in a number of places, one of which, the *Poona Gayan Samāj*, or Song Society, may be mentioned. Sir George Clarke, when Governor of Bombay, and also Lady Clarke, did all they could to encourage these efforts. Within the Christian Church, the Rev. H. A. Popley of Erode, in South India, has done excellent service in adapting the best Indian music to Christian uses. Several Europeans have recently written books on Indian music.

LITERATURE.—*Indian Sculpture and Painting*, E. B. Havell, London, Murray, 63*s*. *Essays on Indian Art, Industry and Education*, E. B. Havell, Madras, Natesan, Rs. 1 as. 4. *Essays on National Idealism*, A. K. Coomaraswamy, Madras, Natesan, Rs. 1. *The Music of Hindustan*, by A. H. Fox Strangways, Oxford, Clarendon Press, 1914, 21*s*. net.

5. POETRY

The fourth son of Debendranath Tagore[1] is Rabindranath Tagore,[2] who is by far the most prominent literary

[1] See p. 39, above. [2] See his portrait, Plate XI, facing page 376.

man in India to-day. For many years he has been the acknowledged king of Bengali literature. His songs and hymns are on every lip, and everything he writes is treasured. When he delivers an oration in Bengali, or when he sings some of his own songs, his power and charm are inexpressible. Quite recently he translated a number of his short devotional poems into rhythmical English prose; and, by the advice of his friends, they were published in England, under the title *Gitanjali*. He is now recognized as one of the greatest literary men of the Empire; and European opinion as such is expressed in the award of the Nobel prize for literature to him.

But the chief fact to be realized about him is that he is the very flower of the new nationalist movement, representing at their very highest the noblest motives that have stirred the people of India since the new century began. His position is central. Though he is the son of Debendranath Tagore,[1] he no longer holds his father's religious position. He expects, as he said to me a few months ago, that the regeneration of India will come through gradual change within the body of Hinduism itself rather than from the action of any detached society like the Brāhma Samāj. Even when he tells his readers in *Sādhanā* that his religious faith is a purely Indian growth, owing nothing to the West, he is still the child of his day; for the modern Nationalist has no difficulty in finding every Christian principle and practice in ancient Hinduism.

Mr. Tagore sums up in himself all the best characteristics of modern nationalist thought and feeling. He is an eager educationalist, maintaining at Bolpur, Bengal, a Boarding School in which two hundred boys receive an education combining the best traditions of the old Hindu teaching with the healthiest modern methods. A good modern

[1] P. 39, above.

education is given; the health of the body is secured by athletics; and music and daily worship, in the simple and severe manner of the Brāhma Samāj, are used to purify and strengthen the religious nature.[1]

Mr. Tagore feels as keenly on social questions. Never shall I forget the magnificent oration which I heard him deliver in Bengali, on *Indian Society*, in the Minerva Theatre, Calcutta.[2] The loftiness of the speaker's character, his brilliant diction, and the superb strength and music of his utterance moved me very deeply, and produced an extraordinary effect on the great audience. His proposals were scarcely practical, and no one has attempted to carry them out in action; but one could not fail to realize his insight into the urgency of the whole social problem or to feel the heart-throb of nationalism in every sentence.

The universal appeal of *Gitanjali*[3] is due largely to the lofty religious feeling which inspires the work, and to the sincerity and simplicity of the style, touched with the colour and fragrance of the East, but largely also to the character of the religious ideas of the poems. There is sufficient Hindu phraseology and form, drawn from the exquisite Bengali lyrics of the Chaitanya movement,[4] to distinguish these poems from European work and to give them a most engaging freshness; yet the dominant beliefs are Christian and in full harmony with modern thought. There is no karma, no transmigration, no inaction, no pessimism, no world-weariness and hatred of sense in this lofty verse; but there is the perception that nature is the revelation of God; there is everywhere the joy of meeting Him in sun and shower; there is the dignity and

[1] The school is described in the *Modern Review*, May, 1913.

[2] July 22, 1904. The address was reported in the *Bengalee* next day.

[3] *Gitanjali*, by R. N. Tagore. London, Macmillan, 1913, 4*s*. 6*d*.

[4] P. 294, above.

worth of toil, deliverance won only by going down where God is, among "the poorest and lowliest and lost," the duty of service, the core of religion found in righteousness, life won by dying to self, sin recognized as shame and thraldom, and death as God's messenger and man's friend.[1]

[1] This essay was written before the striking appreciation appeared in the *Times Literary Supplement* of May 16, 1914, and before the author had seen the review in the *Spectator* of Feb. 14, 1914.

CHAPTER VI

SOCIAL REFORM AND SERVICE

1828–1913

SOCIAL service and reform are so closely intertwined with religious thought and effort in every land, and especially in India, that it may prove useful to students to have a connected account, however brief, of the various movements and organizations which have influenced the people of India socially during the past century.

1. HISTORICAL OUTLINE

The Indian social movement is a direct outcome of Christian missions and Western influence; and all communities have felt the impact in a greater or less degree. The primal impulse was communicated by the Serampore Missionaries to Ram Mohan Ray, and by him to the Hindu community; and, throughout the whole history, Christian teaching, effort and example have done more than anything else to quicken the movement.

Ram Mohan Ray scarcely touched the question of caste, but he condemned polygamy, and he spoke and wrote against widow-burning with so much force and convincing power as materially to prepare the way for Lord Bentinck's act.[1]

Under Lord Bentinck the British Government entered on a new policy of very great significance, the putting down of certain social and religious customs which had for many

[1] Above, p. 33.

centuries been usual in India but which were outrageously inhuman. Widow-burning was prohibited in 1829; *thagī*, or the strangling of travellers, was then put down, and the crusade against female infanticide was begun. Under later rulers human sacrifice and religious suicide were prohibited.

In 1849 a secret society for social reform was founded by Hindus in Bombay, and in 1851 the Parsees of the city formed a Religious Reform Association.

Besides their daily teaching in College, Duff and the other educational missionaries of Calcutta used to deliver public lectures in the city in which social as well as religious questions were discussed. As a result of this Christian teaching a secret society was formed in Calcutta, in which Hindus pledged themselves to educate their wives and daughters. In 1849 Īśvara Chandra Vidyāsāgara, along with a European official, Mr. Drinkwater Bethune, founded the first Hindu school for girls in Calcutta. About the same time Vidyāsāgara also began the agitation which led to the Government Act of 1856 legalizing the marriage of Hindu widows.

A little earlier Lord Dalhousie passed an Act prohibiting the gross obscenities which until then had been common in the streets of Indian cities. It was found necessary to insert a clause into the Bill providing that its restrictions should not apply to the images, temples and cars of the gods.

The next prominent name in social reform is Keshab Chandra Sen. He was the first non-Christian who adopted the whole social programme of Christian Missions, namely, the thorough reform of the Hindu family, the repudiation of caste and the practice of philanthropy. Through his influence new non-idolatrous rites for domestic ceremonies were introduced among Brāhmas; and they gave up child-marriage, polygamy and enforced widowhood, and began to press forward the education of girls. Brāhma marriages were legalized by Lord Lawrence's Government in 1872. Sasipada Banerjea did a good deal of excellent social work at Barahanagar near Calcutta. The New Dispensation and the Sādhāran Brāhma Samāj are still true to Keshab's teaching and practice in social matters.

The interest of the story passes next to the Bombay Presidency, where from 1870 onwards Maṅkar, Ranade and Vishṇu Śāstrī Paṇḍit carried on a vigorous and fruitful agitation in favour of the remarriage of Hindu widows.

About 1870 the movement appeared also in the North. In that year Syed Aḥmad Khan began his long-continued agitation in favour of modern education and social reform among Muḥammadans; and from 1875, when the Ārya Samāj was founded, we must also reckon Dayānanda as helping the cause of reform along certain lines. He not only condemned idolatry but opposed child-marriage and favoured female education. His crusade against caste was more nominal than real.

From 1880 onwards the great mass movements of the Depressed Classes towards Christianity began.[1] These have not only added hundreds of thousands to the Christian Church, but have powerfully affected thinking men of all religions throughout India, and have started movements of untold significance among Brāhmas, Āryas, Hindus and Muḥammadans.

In 1887 the first Widows' Home organized by a Hindu was opened by Sasipada Banerjea at Barahanagar near Calcutta. In the same year B. M. Malabari, a Parsee, published a large pamphlet entitled *Infant Marriage and Enforced Widowhood in India.* This pamphlet, with its unsparing criticism and its great array of weighty names, roused widespread discussion, and did much to move public opinion. It was largely as a result of this agitation that the Govern-

[1] See above, p. 366.

ment of India felt free to pass, in 1891, their Age of Consent Act, whereby cohabitation with a wife under the age of twelve is prohibited. It has been found impossible to enforce the Act with anything like strictness; but it has proved distinctly helpful in more ways than one.

Meanwhile social reformers had organized themselves and had met in 1888, for the first time, in the National Social Conference, which since that date has formed the centre of much social effort and has proved a powerful agent for the formation of public opinion. A few facts about its history are given below.

From about 1890 onwards one can trace the influence of a large number of organizations in social matters. Most of these new bodies are exceedingly conservative, the Rāmakṛishṇa Mission, the Sectarian movements, whether Hindu, Jain or Muḥammadan, and the Caste Conferences; yet every one of them does something to promote female education and to raise the age of the marriage of girls. Even the ultra conservative Nambutīri Brāhmans of Travancore are beginning to move.

Since the opening of the new century there has been a notable increase in earnest attempts to render social service to the most needy. The Rāmakṛishṇa Mission has not only given itself to education but to medical work and to flood and famine relief. The Ārya Samāj has also done great work in famine relief. But the most important organizations are the various societies, Brāhma, Ārya, Hindu, Muslim, which are seeking to help the Depressed Classes, the many new Widows' Homes, the Seva Sadan and Mr. Gokhale's Servants of India Society.

LITERATURE. — *The Administration of the East India Company*, by J. W. Kaye, London, Bentley, 1853 (describes the great reforms). *The Suppression of Human Sacrifice, Suttee and Female Infanticide*,

Madras, C. L. S. I., 1898, 2½ as. (abridged from Kaye). *Confessions of a Thug*, by Meadows Taylor, London, Trübner, 1*s*. *Rambles and Recollections*, by W. H. Sleeman, Oxford University Press, 7*s*. 6*d*. net. *Social Reform in Bengal*, by S. N. Tattvabhushana, Calcutta. *Infant Marriage and Enforced Widowhood in India*, by B. M. Malabari, Bombay, 1887. *Religious and Social Reform*, by M. G. Ranade, Bombay, Claridge, 1902. *The Speeches and Writings of Sir N. G. Chandavarkar*, Bombay, 1911, Rs. 2 as. 8.

2. The National Social Conference

It was the Bombay Presidency, and, in the main, the Prārthanā Samāj, that created the new movement. The earliest Social Reform Association was formed in Sind in 1882. The National Social Conference was organized and met for the first time at Madras in 1888.[1] The real leader was Mr. M. G. Ranade, but, with his usual modesty, he remained as much in the background as possible. Sir T. Mādhava Rao presided at the first Conference, and afterwards the most prominent place was usually taken by Rai Bahadur Raghunath Rao,[2] a Hindu belonging to the Madras Presidency, who had been Prime Minister of the State of Indore, and was older than Ranade. The methods of the Conference are practically the same as those in use in the Congress. Representatives meet from every part of India. The subjects on the agenda are discussed, and resolutions are passed. The Conference usually meets in the same city as the Congress, and just after it. At the close of the Conference the members usually dine together, irrespective of caste, race and religious distinctions. While a few Muḥammadans and others attend, the great majority of those who take part in the Conference are Hindus; and the whole policy of the movement tends to be Hindu in its affinities and interests.[3] The following set of resolutions passed in

[1] Ranade, *Essays*, 179. [2] This leader died in 1912. *ISR.*, XXII, 422.
[3] See Resolution XI, below.

the Conference held at Allahabad in December, 1910, will give some idea of its interests and work:[1]

I. (*a*) That in the opinion of this Conference greater and more persistent efforts should be made by the educated community themselves to promote the Education of Women. That with a view to give effect to this recommendation this Conference is of opinion that a larger number of schools should be opened in towns and that a graduated series of text books be prepared for use in such schools and that local Committees be appointed to collect funds and to establish and conduct such schools.

(*b*) That this Conference while appreciating the help which Government has extended to the cause of the Education of Women in this country is of opinion that the proportion of expenditure on the Education of Women is much less than it should be and it earnestly prays that Government may be pleased to spend a larger proportion of revenues under this head.

II. That this Conference strongly recommends that every effort should be made to persuade parents not to marry their boys before the age of 25 and their girls before 16.

III. This Conference is of opinion that the time has come when steps should be taken to abolish the parda system.

IV. That this Conference welcomes the efforts that are being made in several parts of the country to raise the moral, material and social condition of the depressed classes, and urges that further efforts be made to obtain for these classes full recognition as an integral part of the general body of the community.

V. That this Conference records its opinion that no attempt should be made in the census to introduce artificial distinctions among classes recognized as belonging to our community and in this connection views with great

[1] *ISR.*, XXI, 221.

concern the recent circular issued by Mr. Gait regarding the depressed classes.

VI. That the miserable condition of young widows should be improved by starting or further strengthening Widows' Homes in each province, by giving young widows technical education and permitting such of them as wish to marry to do so without let or hindrance.

VII. That this Conference is of opinion that the requirements of Act III of 1872 of repudiation of religious belief on the part of parties to marriage is unnecessary and inexpedient, and urges that the law be so amended as to omit this undue interference with religious beliefs.

VIII. That every effort should be made to induce sub-castes of the same caste to interdine and intermarry.

IX. That a working fund be established for the organization of the annual Social Conference for collecting and publishing its proceedings and for carrying on the necessary office work during the year.

X. That this Conference reiterates the resolution passed at previous Conferences urging on all social reform bodies the necessity of strenuous efforts in favour of temperance and social purity, and regrets the action of the exhibition authorities to allow a dancing girl to perform within the precincts.

XI. That in the opinion of this Conference it is a pressing duty of the Hindu community to provide facilities for the re-admission of repentant converts.

XII. That all obstructions to the re-admission of foreign returned Indians be removed.

XIII. That in the opinion of this Conference it is urgently necessary that there should be some legislation controlling the administration and management of charitable and religious trusts which as experience has proved have been utterly mismanaged by their trustees.

The year 1897 marks a further advance in the movement. Two permanent provincial organizations for furthering social reform arose that year, *The Bombay Presidency Social Reform Association*, and *The Madras Hindu Social Reform Association*. These bodies at once began to hold annual Provincial Conferences.[1] In 1900 Bengal followed suit.[2] These provincial assemblies, which are usually held at the same time and place as the provincial gatherings for political purposes, have proved extremely useful. Distances are so great in India that it is very hard to gather men from every quarter for a Conference, but the problem is much easier in a province. Local conferences are also held representing single districts or other sections of the country. The first of these were also held in 1897, in the Godavery and Mangalore districts.[3] Wherever a group of the friends of freedom and progress happen to be, there it is comparatively easy to hold a social conference.

Since 1904 an Indian Ladies' Conference (*Bhārat Mahilā Parishad*) has been held at the same time and place as the National Social Conference, to discuss subjects affecting women's life. The following Resolutions were passed in Hindī at the seventh Conference held at Allahabad at Christmas, 1910:

1. That in the opinion of this Conference the best way of the advancement of the country is female education and the Conference requests all Indians to make arrangements for spreading female education.

2. That in the opinion of this Conference it is not enough to teach girls reading and writing. They ought to be taught how to manage the household, how to attend a sick person, sewing, etc.

3. That in the opinion of this Conference child-marriage is

[1] Ranade, *Essays*, 165–6, 279. Cf. for Bombay, *ISR.*, XX, 136, 148, 292, 304; XXII, 375; and Madras, *ISR.*, XIX, 580; XX, 375, 462.

[2] See *ISR.*, XXII, 44.

[3] Ranade, *Essays*, 165.

the root of all evils. It is the duty of the well-wishers of the country to remove this evil.

4. That this Conference is of opinion that it is absolutely necessary to lessen the rigour of the *parda*.

5. That this Conference thinks that the children should not be made to wear ornaments.

6. That the condition of Hindu widows is pitiable, and in order to save them from many troubles it is necessary to open Widows' Homes where they can be educated.

Ladies have also met in conference in a few provincial centres in recent years, notably Benares,[1] Guntur,[2] Vizianagram[3] and Travancore.[4]

In 1890 *The Indian Social Reformer*, a twelve-page weekly in English, began to appear. Its office is in Bombay. Its editor, Mr. K. Natarajan, belongs to the Madras Presidency. The paper has had a very honourable record. It stands for religion, for morality, for social and political progress, and has consistently maintained a courageous and manly policy. Its influence as an encouragement to social reformers in small places, where orthodox opposition is fierce and powerful, must be very great.

3. Female Infanticide

As British rule was extended in India, administrators discovered, to their horror, that female infanticide prevailed to a most alarming extent in the Centre and the West. In some villages there was scarcely a girl to be seen; in others there were four or five times as many boys as girls, all the rest having been destroyed. Under Lord Bentinck administrative action was taken to put down the inhuman practice. The crusade took many years; and even now there may be some places where it is still secretly practised; but on the

[1] *ISR.*, XX, 439.
[2] *Ib.*, XX, 498.
[3] *Ib.*, XXI, 222.
[4] *Ib.*, XXIII, 161.

whole it has been stamped out, and no Indian would wish to see it revived.

4. Child-Marriage

The Hindu law since about 500 B.C. has been that the father who does not marry his daughter before the menses appear commits sin; and since the Christian era, if not earlier, the law has been held to be a serious religious obligation and has been almost universally obeyed.[1]

Christian influence began to make itself felt early in the nineteenth century, and bore fruit among the Parsees in Bombay, in the Brāhma Samāj under Keshab Chandra Sen and in the Ārya Samāj under Dayānanda. B. M. Malabari, a Parsee journalist, started in 1884 an agitation on child-marriage and widow-celibacy which convulsed Hindu society, and deeply influenced public opinion. He wished Government to take action, especially in the matter of child-marriage.[2] His pamphlet, containing the opinions of many prominent Hindus and Government officials, was published in 1887.[3] Much useful discussion was provoked. Missionaries supported him warmly throughout the country. Soon, a case occurred, which proved conclusively how serious the matter was becoming:

> Public attention was called to the matter by the case of Rukhmabai in Bombay, a case which showed that relief was demanded not for Christian girls alone, but for Hindu girls as well. Rukhmabai was a Hindu girl, educated in the Free Church Mission School and afterwards as a Zenana pupil. She was clever and accomplished, and the man, Dadaji by name, to whom she had been married in infancy, being repulsive and illiterate, she refused to live with him. He appealed to the law to compel her to do so. The case was carried from court to court, till the High Court ordered Rukhmabai either to live with

[1] *Crown of Hinduism*, 94–96. [2] Ranade, *Essays*, xxiv ff.
[3] See p. 389, above.

Dadaji as his wife or go to prison for six months. A compromise, however, was then effected. A sum of money, sufficient to buy another wife, was paid to Dadaji. But it was decreed that, according to Hindu law, Rukhmabai must never marry. She went to London to study medicine, took the degree of M.D., and returned to India to take charge of a hospital for women.[1]

In 1890 a tragic occurrence brought another aspect of the subject forcibly before the minds of all men. A Bengali girl, named Phulmanī Dāsī, eleven years of age, died in Calcutta in consequence of what in all other civilized countries would be described as an outrage on the part of her husband, who was a man of thirty. He was arrested and tried for culpable homicide. The only defence he made was to quote the clause in the Penal Code which fixed the age of ten years as the lowest limit for married life. Yet he was convicted, and sentenced to twelve months' rigorous imprisonment. The consequence was a loud outcry from the orthodox community. They complained that it was utterly unjust to punish a man for doing what was prescribed by his religion and distinctly permitted by law.

The case caused great indignation in Christian circles. Europeans demanded, in the words of Max Müller, "that the strong arm of the English law be not rendered infamous by aiding and abetting unnatural atrocities." There was a loud cry that the age should be raised, and that the penalty should be increased. The Government of India therefore introduced a bill into the Legislative Council, raising the age from ten to twelve.

The Bill roused the most violent opposition amongst Hindus. The following sentences give some idea of the excitement and fury raised by the proposal:

> Never before, within living memory, had Bengal been so agitated. Crowds of excited Hindus paraded the streets all

[1] *Kenneth S. Macdonald*, 183–4.

day and far into the night, yelling at the pitch of their voices, "Our religion is in danger." Those who were still sane enough to argue protested that the Bill was an infringement of the Queen's Proclamation of 1858, by which she pledged her Government to a policy of non-interference with the religions of her Indian subjects. . . . A monster meeting of protest was held on the *maidan*, for no public building in Calcutta would accommodate all those who wished to be present. The attendance was estimated at one hundred thousand, and speeches were delivered from twelve platforms. . . . No such public demonstration had ever been seen in Calcutta. When it became apparent that the appeals to the Government of India and to the Secretary of State were in vain, it was resolved as a last resort to make a supreme effort to move Kali, the patron goddess of Calcutta, to intervene. A *mahapuja*, or whole day of fasting, prayer and sacrifice was proclaimed at Kalighat, the great shrine of this popular deity, in one of the suburbs of Calcutta. . . . It was estimated at the time that two hundred thousand rupees (over £13,000) were spent on the ceremony. Three hundred pundits, many of whom had been brought from Benares, led the devotions. One devotee wished to sacrifice himself upon the altar, and was with difficulty restrained from his purpose. Others, like the priests of Baal, cut themselves with knives.[1]

But Government passed the Bill in spite of all protests. The date was 1891. Those who are best able to judge believe that it has had a good effect; but it is quite well known that the law is still broken in multitudes of cases.

About twenty years ago Colonel Walter, then Agent to the Governor-General in Rajputana, suggested to the leaders of Rajput society an arrangement which has produced excellent results. By the unanimous decision of these men it was decided that no girl should be married before she was fourteen, and that the marriage expenses should in no case exceed a certain proportion of the father's yearly income. A society, called the Walterkṛit Rājputra Hita-

[1] *Kenneth S. Macdonald*, 188–9.

kārinī Sabhā (the Rajput Benevolent Society created by Colonel Walter) sees to the enforcement of these rules. It would be well if similar institutions could be introduced elsewhere.[1]

In 1901 the Gaekwar of Baroda passed the Infant Marriage Prevention Act, which fixed the minimum age for marriage in the State at twelve for girls and sixteen for boys. Early in 1912 the Census Commissioner of Baroda published his impressions of the results of the act. *The Times of India* thus summarizes his views:

> In the ten years under review no less than 22,218 applications were made for exemption from the provisions of the Act and 95 per cent of them were allowed. Over 23,000 marriages were performed even without this formality of an application for exemption, in violation of the Act. The parties responsible were fined from a few to a hundred rupees, and the Superintendent thinks that there must have been an equally large number of marriages which were connived at by the village patels who are also the marriage registrars. The age returns are notoriously unreliable, but even thus there were 158 per thousand males and 277 per thousand females married and widowed, under 10 years of age.

Clearly the act is much too far in advance of the public conscience.

A certain amount of progress has been achieved in this matter as a result of these acts and of the persistent agitation of the reformers; but it is universally recognized that the mass of Hindu society has been scarcely touched as yet.

5. Boy-Marriage

In ancient India boys of the Brāhman, Kshatriya and Vaiśya castes were expected to go to school for a religious education for an extended period, and were married only on

[1] Risley, *The People of India*, 188.

their final return from school. But for many centuries the vast mass of boys have not taken the old religious training. Hence nothing has stood in the way of marriage; and in many parts of the country it has long been customary to marry boys at the age of eight, ten or twelve.[1]

Social Reformers have appealed powerfully against this most unwise custom, and modern education has tended to restrict the practice; but the plan referred to in the following paragraph is probably the best that has yet been thought of for dealing with the difficulty:

> At the last meeting of the Travancore Popular Assembly Mr. K. G. Sesha Iyer advocated the exclusion of married boys from Government Schools. The Central Hindu College at Benares has been enforcing this exclusion for several years past. The rule ought to be adopted everywhere. Seeing that the ancient ideal of students in India was celibacy until education was finished, there ought to be no opposition from orthodox Hindus. To prevent any possible hardship to married boys, who are not responsible for their marriage, it may be laid down that the rule will be enforced five years hence.[2]

6. Polygamy

Every Hindu marriage is *in posse* polygamous. Though the great majority of Hindus are monogamous in practice, yet there is a law which allows a man to take a second wife if the first proves childless or quarrelsome; and from the earliest times until to-day kings and wealthy men have been accustomed to marry many wives.[3]

Ram Mohan Ray himself had two wives, when he was a young man; but, later, under Christian influence, he condemned polygamy. Social reformers have continued to agitate against the practice, and public opinion has been

[1] *Crown of Hinduism*, 86. [2] *Modern Review*, May, 1913.
[3] *Crown of Hinduism*, 91–93.

partially modified, but the old conditions still prevail. There has been very little betterment, except in the Samājes.

7. Widows

About 500 B.C. it became the rule that only childless Hindu widows should marry, and from about the time of the Christian era, it has been the law that no Hindu widow, not even a virgin child-widow, shall marry.[1] Some three or four centuries later the practice of *satī* became recognized as legitimate, *i.e.* when a man died, his widow was allowed to mount the pyre and be burned along with his body if she wished to do so. Widows who did not mount the pyre had thenceforward to live a life of serious asceticism. In many parts of India to-day, as soon as a woman is widowed, her hair is shaven away and she must live tonsured all the rest of her life.[2]

By the beginning of the nineteenth century widow-burning had reached huge proportions in India, especially in Bengal. The vast majority of widows certainly were not burned; but several hundreds actually mounted the pyre every year in Bengal alone. In certain kingdoms, especially in the South, a vast holocaust of women took place when the king died. Individual Englishmen protested vehemently against the practice; and here and there an English administrator took the law into his own hands, and prevented the burning of a widow; but for many years the British Government hesitated to interfere. The Serampore missionaries protested very loudly on the subject both in England and in India; and Ram Mohan Ray added his powerful voice to theirs. Finally, in 1829, in spite of the opposition of many leading Hindus and of some Englishmen, Lord Bentinck prohibited the practice within the British prov-

[1] *Crown of Hinduism*, 96–98. [2] *Ib.*, 98–101.

inces. It was many years later before it was put down in native states.

Perhaps no educated Indian to-day would wish to revive the practice; for all now recognize that it came into use at a comparatively modern date; but, even in these days, a Hindu widow occasionally carries out the old custom by burning herself. When such a thing happens, the Hindu community still thrills with reverence and sympathy. It may be also mentioned that Dr. A. K. Coomaraswamy published in *The Sociological Review* for April, 1913, a paper, in which he attempts to set forth the essential nature of the Hindu ideal of woman, and he gives his paper the title, *Satī; A Defence of the Indian Woman.*

It was Paṇḍit Īśvara Chandra Vidyāsāgara who began the agitation in favour of allowing Hindu widows to remarry, if they wished to do so. The Government of India passed an Act legalizing such marriages in 1856. About 1870 an agitation was started in the Bombay Presidency for the purpose of rousing Hindus to such sympathy with widows as would make widow-marriage really possible in Hindu society.[1] The Social Reform Movement has made this one of its main aims, and has done a great deal to commend the remarriage of widows in all parts of the country. In consequence, a certain number of such marriages do take place in all grades of Hindu society, and in most parts of the country; but they are exceedingly few, and it is questionable whether they are increasing.

Social reformers have not done very much to lighten the burden of suffering which the widow has to endure throughout her life. Only one point has been vehemently attacked by them, namely, the tonsure. Appeals on this subject now and then appear in the columns of the *Indian Social Reformer;* and in 1909 a small volume called *The Ton-*

[1] Ranade, *Essays*, xvii, xviii.

sure of Hindu Widows, by M. A. Subramaniam, B.A., B.L., was published in Madras.[1]

During the last twenty years groups of Hindus in various parts of the country have begun to maintain Widows' homes in imitation of Christian missions. The earliest Home outside the Christian Church was established at Barahanagar near Calcutta in 1887 by Sasipada Banerjea,[2] and did good work for some time; but it is no longer in existence. In 1889, a Christian lady, Paṇḍitā Rāmabai, opened the *Sāradā Sadan*, or Home of Learning, for Hindu widows in Bombay.[3] Soon after it was moved to Poona. But within a few years so many of the widows had been baptized that Hindus became very hostile. Most of the widows were withdrawn, and Hindu subscriptions ceased. But the work accomplished was manifestly good and necessary; and Hindus began to clamour for a similar institution under Hindu management. Hence the *Hindu Widows' Home Association* was organized in Poona in 1896, and a Home was opened, which has steadily grown in strength and usefulness. During the year 1912 there were 105 inmates in the Home, of whom 95 were widows. The annual expenditure is now about 17,000 Rupees.[4] The whole institution seems to be thoroughly well managed by the founder, Mr. D. K. Karve. In 1906 a Boarding School for high-caste Hindu girls and widows was opened close beside the Home. Then in 1912 the *Nishkāma Karma Maṭha* (Monastery for Unselfish Work) was started for the purpose of creating a band of competent women workers to staff the Boarding School. I was able to visit these institutions in February last, and was much struck with the character of the buildings

[1] Cf. *ISR.*, XX, 185, 296; and *Indian Review*, March, 1910.

[2] *Social Reform in Bengal*, 12.

[3] See *The High-caste Hindu Woman*, by Paṇḍitā Rāmabai, New York, Revell.

[4] *Report* for 1912; *ISR.*, XIX, 596, 605; XX, 151, 261.

and the excellence of the arrangements. So far as I know, no widows' home was founded by Hindus between 1896 and 1906; but it was probably during that interval that the Deva Samāj,[1] the Ārya Samāj[2] and the Digambara Jains[3] founded their homes. I have seen no reports of these institutions, and do not know the dates when they were founded. In 1907 a Hindu Widows' Home was founded in Mysore City; and in 1910 there were thirty-two pupils, of whom seventeen were resident. The total cost was met by Rai Bahadur Narasimha Iyengar.[4] The same year the Mahilā Śilpāśrama, or Women's Industrial Refuge, was founded in Calcutta by Mrs. P. Mukerjee, a niece of Mr. Rabindra Nath Tagore. Over a dozen widows reside in it, and a number of others come from the outside to receive instruction. It is supported by public subscription, supplemented by Government and Municipal grants.[5] In 1908 the Sikhs opened their Widows' Home in Amṛitsār. In 1910 Mrs. Pitt, the widow of an Indian civilian, opened a Widows' Home in Bangalore, which is to be conducted on purely Hindu lines. It is intended to teach women the privilege of social service.[6] In 1911 a Home was opened in Dacca of which Mrs. Dutta is the Founder-Secretary.[7] In July, 1912, a group of Hindus organized a Brāhman Widows' Hostel in Madras, and in September of that year the Government of Madras undertook the bulk of the financial responsibilities. It is too early to say anything about the success of this new venture.[8]

[1] At Ferozpore and Bhatinda.
[2] One is at Jullundur. Chirol, *Indian Unrest*, 111.
[3] In Bombay.
[4] *ISR.*, XX, 522.
[5] My informant is Mr. Hem Ch. Sarkar of the Sādhāran Brāhma Samāj.
[6] *ISR.*, XXI, 26, 500.
[7] *Ib.*, XXIV, 390.
[8] *Ib.*, XXIII, 532.

8. The Zenāna

From very early times the ladies of royal harems in India lived in something like seclusion, and wealthy families naturally copied kings in some degree. There was also a great deal of distrust of women expressed in Hindu law, and men were therefore bid guard their women with great care. Yet there was no general custom of shutting women up in the house. When, however, at the end of the twelfth century, the Muḥammadan invasion came, two motives arose which combined to make the Hindus seclude their women. Their conquerors, who now held the highest social position in India, kept their women shut up in the women's apartments; and it was natural for Hindus to imitate them. Then, in the wild violence and lawlessness which characterized Muslim rule for centuries, Hindu women were unsafe, unless they were shut up and guarded. Hence all high-caste Hindus, living in provinces where Muḥammadans were numerous and powerful, adopted the Zenāna system. A high-caste woman to-day very seldom leaves the zenāna. If she goes out, it is in the dusk of the morning or the evening, and only for a hurried visit to the temple or the river. On occasion she may go to the house of a relative for a wedding or some other important ceremony, but, if she do, she goes in a closed carriage or palanquin. Parsees and Jains adopted the custom as well as Hindus. In those parts of the South where Muḥammadan rule did not arise or did not last long, some of the old freedom still remains; and the women of the lower orders live a very free life.

Christian teaching and Western example have made a very serious impact on educated opinion in this matter; and the women of the Brāhma Samāj are now as free as Christian women; but the only other community which has stepped out into full freedom is the Parsees. But there has been a distinct and very welcome change amongst educated Hindus during the last twenty years. A small but increasing number in Calcutta and in Bombay take their wives and children out driving with them in the evening; and in every educated centre the women themselves are increasingly eager to meet European ladies socially, to gather together in little clubs and societies, and occasionally to hold women's meetings and conferences. One sympathizes with the fear lest a sudden change should do more harm than good; but, without any doubt, progress in this matter might with safety be a good deal accelerated.

9. Marriage Expenses

Loud and bitter complaints are raised in many parts of India by Hindus about the extortionate payments demanded by the bridegroom's family from the father of the bride. The evil seems to be largely a result of the progress of Western education; for a young man who has done well at College is a most desirable bridegroom, and naturally the price has tended to rise as steadily as the demand. The tyrannical custom, which compels a father to spend huge sums upon feasting, processions and presents to Brāhmans on the occasion of a daughter's wedding, presses very heavily on the poor. Most fathers are driven to borrow huge sums, and, in consequence, pass the remainder of their lives in bondage and fear.

Reformers have tried to mitigate these evils, but nothing very substantial, except the action of the Walterkṛit Sabhā,[1] has to be chronicled. Quite recently in Calcutta, a father could see no way to raise money for his daughter's marriage except by mortgaging his home. The daughter,

[1] Above, p. 398.

whose name was Snehalatā, burned herself to death in her own room to release her father from the impasse.[1] Her suicide roused intense feeling, and meetings were held to move public opinion, but with what result has still to be seen.

10. Domestic Ceremonies

In ancient Hindu Law-books twelve domestic *saṁskāras* or sacraments, are enumerated as binding on every Hindu of the Brāhman, Kshatriya and Vaiśya castes, and the details of the ceremonies are laid down in priestly manuals. Each is filled with polytheistic ideas and idolatrous practices; so that modern men are inclined to object to them. Debendranath Tagore prepared a new set of ceremonies for Brāhmas from which everything idolatrous was excluded, and Keshab carried the process still farther.[2] The other Samājes have followed suit, but orthodoxy remains orthodox.

11. Devadāsīs (Hierodouloi)

In Hindu literature of all ages, even in the *Ṛigveda* itself, wherever references to heaven occur, we find very frequent mention of the Gandharvas and the Apsarases, the former being male musicians, the latter female dancers and singers. The Apsarases are equally famed for their dazzling beauty and their easy morals. When some human ascetic carried his austerities to such a pitch that the merit due to him threatened to endanger the gods, the regular expedient was to send down one of these irresistible nymphs to draw him away from his self-torture.

This is probably a reflection of the customs of Hindu Kings. Each had a troop of male musicians in his resi-

[1] *ISR.*, Feb. 15th, 1914, 210. Two other cases followed. *ISR.*, May 17th.

[2] Above, pp. 41, 43, 48.

dence and companies of dancing and singing women of rather loose character. This custom is still kept up by Hindu princes.[1]

Every well-appointed Hindu temple aims at being an earthly reproduction of the paradise of the god in whose honour it was built. He and his spouse or spouses are there in stone, also his mount, his car, and all else that he needs. The Gandharvas are represented by the Temple-band, the Apsarases by the courtesans who sing and dance in the service. These are dedicated to the service of the god; but they give their favours to his worshippers. They are usually called *Devadāsīs*, handmaidens of the god, Hierodouloi; but in the Bombay Presidency each shrine has its own name for its women, *Muralis*, *Jogavins*, *Bhavinis*, *Naikinis*, *Kalawantis*, *Basavis*,[2] *Devadāsīs*, *Devalis*, *Jogtis*, *Matangis*, *Sharnis*, Muralis being used in a general way for all.[3] They dance and sing in the temple-services and also when the images are carried out through the town in procession. Hence the common name for them everywhere is Nautch-girls, Dancing-girls. The songs they sing are usually obscene. They receive certain allowances from the temple. Until recently they lived within the temple precincts, but now they usually occupy some street or lane close by. In North India they are not permanently attached to the temple. They live in the bazaar, practise music and dancing, and ply their trade. The temple-authorities hire as many as they require for each occasion. In some temples in the Bombay Presidency there are male prostitutes also.

How foul the atmosphere is in which this custom thrives may be realized from the hideous sculpture visible on the

[1] V. Smith's *Asoka*, 89.
[2] Cf. Dubois, 133.
[3] Shinde's *Muralis*, 2; *ISR.*, XXIII, 606.

gates and walls of many Hindu temples in Central and Southern India and from the following quotation:

> And then again, it is not that only females are dedicated to the temples but also males who are called Waghyas of Khandoba, Aradhyes of Ambabai, Potrajas of Dyamawwa, Jogyas of Yallamma, and who are forbidden to marry or to live the ordinary civil life and therefore lead a more or less dissolute life. Their number however is not so considerable as that of the female victims nor is their looseness so noticeable. There is a third class of devotees, who are neither male nor female but are mostly eunuchs. These hideous beings are more indecent than immoral and they naturally follow the trade of procurers, pimps, and such other disgusting and un-natural practices. Whether they are for some wicked purpose castrated or born defective and how they come to be connected with the temples cannot be said; but they are generally connected with the temples of the female deities Ambabai and Yallamma. Quite a number of them might be seen at any time loitering and dancing about the little temple of Bolai near the Sassoon Hospital in Poona.[1]

Courtesan ministrants, in precisely similar fashion, lived in the temples of Babylonia, Syria and Egypt, and took part in the ritual; and thence the custom spread to Cyprus, the Greek islands and elsewhere. The Greek name for them was Hierodouloi, Sacred Slaves.[2]

To these facts is due the low estimate in which music and dancing, especially the latter, have been held in most countries of the East. Salome degraded herself to the level of a courtesan in dancing before Herod. The cultivation of music and dancing has never been a respectable art in India, but has always been left to Nautch-girls.[3]

A century ago these women were much more in the public eye in India than they are to-day. L'Abbé Dubois writes:[4]

[1] Shinde's *Muralis*, 4.
[2] Art. *Hierodouloi, ERE.*
[3] Dubois, 337.
[4] 585.

Their duties, however, are not confined to religious ceremonies. Ordinary politeness requires that when persons of any distinction make formal visits to each other they must be accompanied by a certain number of these courtezans. To dispense with them would show a want of respect towards the person visited, whether the visit was one of duty or politeness.

Hindus have also been accustomed to hire them to dance and sing in their houses at weddings, on other festive occasions, and even when entertaining European officials: their dancing and singing have been part of the programme, like the performances of jugglers.

Missionaries have long protested in the name of morality and decency against the whole system, and have especially begged that European officials should give no countenance to such a thing. Brāhmas and social reformers have joined in these protests. The presence of these women at the temple-services and in the great processions leads to a great deal of vice among young Hindus; and their introduction into the homes of the people on festive occasions has done endless harm. Their gestures in dancing are lewd and suggestive; and their songs are immoral and obscene. Many a man has spoken of the dire results such exhibitions have upon the young.

Western example and education have had their influence upon the coarsest parts of Hinduism. The frightful obscenities which we hear about from eighteenth-century writers have almost altogether disappeared. What remains is bad enough, it is true; but the grossest things have been removed. Dancing girls are much less prominent in the temples of the West and the North than they used to be.

Lord Wenlock, who was Governor of Madras from 1891 to 1896, was the first prominent official who distinctly refused to countenance the nautch.[1] His example has

[1] *Kenneth S. Macdonald*, 71.

proved very powerful: so that nowadays one seldom hears of an English official consenting to be present on any occasion when dancing-girls are present. The majority of educated Hindus have also given up the custom of having them in their homes at weddings and such like. This is a reform of very great value indeed; and we may trust that in future things will go still further.

In many parts of the country it is customary to marry a girl to an idol, a flower, a sword or some other material object, in order that she may be free from the entanglements of a genuine marriage.

In the year 1906 a large body of gentlemen, including many Hindus, approached the Governor of Bombay, calling his attention to the whole practice of divine marriage, and praying that measures might be taken by the Government to put down the dedication of girls to prostitution. The following is a brief statement:

> The Memorialists ask that the attention of the Police shall be called to the infrequency of prosecution, and that they shall be directed to show greater vigilance in bringing offenders to account. They request that public notices shall be posted in many places, and especially at Jejuri, where the temple of Khandoba enjoys an infamous pre-eminence in this destruction of innocent children; and that temple-authorities shall be warned of their liability to prosecution as accessories to crime, if they permit such ceremonies to take place within the precincts of the temple.[1]

In the following year the Bombay Government issued a resolution on the subject. They feel the need of action but recognize that it is impossible to do much until public opinion is riper. They promise, however, to prosecute temple-authorities who take part in the dedication of girls; and they suggest that the Hindu community should

[1] *Harvest Field*, June, 1906.

provide orphanages or homes in which girls rescued by Government may be placed.[1]

Two years later Sir George Clarke, Governor of Bombay, issued a proclamation, calling the attention of District Magistrates to the powers of the law and to the necessity of enforcing them seriously.[2]

The Mysore Government next took action. In 1909 they issued an order, in which they prohibit the performance of any religious ceremony which has an intimate connection with dedication to the profession of a prostitute or dancing-girl. This prohibition applies to every temple under the control of the Mysore Government.[3] About the same time, the head of the Śaṅkeśvara monastery, a modern representative of Śaṅkarāchārya, issued an order in which he declares that the custom of dedicating girls has not the sanction of any sacred book of the Hindus, and therefore must be put a stop to.[4] Later still the Travancore Government took the matter up.[5]

But though the movement has thus made considerable progress, there are those who oppose it for various reasons.[6] The first of these is the fear that the musical art may suffer if they are discouraged. How absurd this argument is, we need not say. Yet it had weight enough with certain Government officials to lead them to introduce dancing-girls into the Arts and Industries Exhibition at Allahabad in the winter of 1910–1911, and to give prizes to the most skilful of these artistes.[7] As one might expect in such a country as India, Government example at once led to serious results. Here is what the Rev. C. F. Andrews of Delhi wrote to the press on the subject:

[1] *Indian Witness*, August 15, 1907.
[2] *ISR.*, XIX, 568.
[3] *Harvest Field*, 1909, p. 190.
[4] *ISR.*, XIX, 565.
[5] *ISR.*, XX, 461.
[6] *ISR.*, XX, 127 and 123.
[7] The Social Conference objected. See p. 393, above.

An intimate friend of mine, who was known by all the city to refuse under any circumstances to be present at a wedding where a nautch was a part of the ceremonies, was asked a few days ago to a wedding, and was on the point of accepting it, when he discovered that a nautch was to be held. When he remonstrated with some indignation, saying that his own abstention from nautches was well known in the city, the reply was immediately made that now things were different. The Government itself was encouraging nautches, and one was being held every night at the Government Exhibition.[1]

Fortunately, the press of India, whether European or Indian, almost unanimously condemned the action of those who had charge of the Exhibition;[2] and public opinion was so clearly expressed that we may hope that little final evil will come of it.

Fortunately, Lord Morley's attention had been drawn to the whole problem; and, on the 3rd of March, 1911, he addressed a despatch to the Government of India on the question:

My attention in Council has lately been called to the various methods by which female children in India are condemned to a life of prostitution, whether by enrolment in a body of dancing girls attached to a Hindu Temple; by symbolical marriage to an idol, a flower, a sword, or some other material object; or by adoption by a prostitute whose profession the child is brought up to follow. I observe with satisfaction that an increasing section of Hindu Society regards the association of religious ceremonies with the practice of prostitution with strong disapproval. In Madras, where the Institution of Temple Dancing Girls still survives, an Indian District Magistrate, Mr. R. Ramachandra Row, has expressed the opinion that Temple servants have been degraded from their original status to perform functions 'abhorrent to strict Hindu religion'; and in Bombay a society for the protection of children has been formed with the co-operation of leading Hindu citizens.

[1] From the *Leader*. See *ISR.*, XXI, 292. [2] *ISR.*, XXI, 306.

I desire to be informed of the probable extent of the evil; how far the provisions of the Penal Code, sections 372 and 373, are in themselves sufficient to deal with it effectually, and whether in your opinion, or that of the Local Governments, adequate steps are being taken to enforce the law as it at present stands, or whether any, and if so, what amendments of the law are required to give reasonable encouragement and suppress the grave abuse. The matter is one in which the weight of public authority may well be lent to the furtherance of reforms advocated by the enlightened leaders of the communities to which the children belong whom the law was intended to protect.

The Society for the Protection of Children in Western India, which consists of men belonging to all faiths, keeps watch over the progress of events, and seeks to rouse public opinion, and to help Government in every way possible. The pamphlet on *Muralis* quoted above was published by them.

As this book goes to press, the Government of India is passing a law for the better protection of girls.

LITERATURE.—*Hindu Customs, Manners and Ceremonies*, by J. A. Dubois, Oxford University Press. *The Crown of Hinduism*, by J. N. Farquhar, Oxford University Press. *The Muralis*, by V. R. Shinde, Bombay, Sharada Kridan Press, half an anna. *Lotus Buds*, by Amy W. Carmichael, London, Morgan & Scott. *India and its Problems*, W. S. Lilly, 231–237.

12. EDUCATION OF BOYS

In Ancient India, when the Hindu system took shape, it was the rule that every boy of the three highest castes should go to some teacher and spend several years in acquiring a religious education. All girls, and all boys of every other caste or class, were by law excluded from this education. As the centuries passed, the percentage of those taking the religious education became less and less.

Doubtless various systems of secular education were used from time to time, but none of them took deep root in the country. When the Muḥammadans conquered India, Muslim education became the passport to government service and high social position. Here again it was only the few who were educated.

At the beginning of the nineteenth century the illiteracy of India was almost complete. The number of those who received any education was exceedingly small; and in the universal confusion of the times things were steadily getting worse. It was the missionaries who began to give the people education. But what they gave them was not any Indian discipline, but a Western training, mediated in the schools by the vernaculars. A few European laymen soon began to help. Then Ram Mohan Ray perceived the facts of the situation, and became the champion of Western education. Government came round to the same point of view in 1835.

The one large fact which we must keep firm hold of in thinking of education in modern India is, that Western education (which the country clearly must have) comes from an alien civilization and environment, and that in inoculating the community with this most necessary remedy considerable disturbance will inevitably be produced. This far-reaching fact is usually neglected altogether by those who condemn modern education in India as a failure.[1] The comparison of the results of Roman education in the provinces of the Empire would lead men to a saner estimate of the factors at work. It is quite as necessary to keep this same truth in mind, if we are to understand why the education of boys grows so slowly in India. The conservatism of the people and their pitiful

[1] Parts of Chirol's writing on education are weakened by a failure to take this most important fact into full consideration.

poverty are certainly powerful retarding agents. Yet both taken together do not hamper progress nearly so much as the inherent antagonism of the religious systems to Western thought and life.

Two very healthy symptoms may here be mentioned to cheer the reformer and the student. The first of these is Mr. Gokhale's bold attempt to secure universal education in India through Government action. The Bill which he laid before the Viceroy's Council was rejected; and, personally, I am inclined to believe it was well for India that it should be rejected; yet the way in which the Indian press received the proposal showed that the educated class have travelled far in opinion these last twenty years, and that there is in them the possibility of still greater advance. The second healthy symptom is this, that competent Indian observers assure us that the last few years of extreme national interest and excitement have so stirred the common people in certain parts of India that there is now a keen desire for widespread education, and such a willingness to allow children to attend school as has not been known before.

In 1902, 22.2 per cent of the boys of school-going age in India were at school; in 1912 the percentage had risen to 29.

13. Education of Girls

The ancient ideal for high-caste Hindus was that, when children reached the age of eight to twelve, the boys should go to school, and the girls should be married.[1] The deep distinction here implied has not only been taught the Hindu people for two thousand five hundred years, but has been worked into their very nature and character by a series of institutions such as no other country has ever possessed. Girls have been married before reaching

[1] *Crown of Hinduism*, 93–94.

puberty. Their husbands have been free to marry as many wives as they chose to have. No husband has eaten with his wife. The widow has been prevented from remarrying, while the widower has had severe pressure brought to bear upon him to induce him to remarry, if he was disinclined. For some fifteen hundred years, the Hindu widow was taught that the noblest thing she could do was to burn herself upon the pyre with her husband. For six hundred years, high-caste women have been closely shut up in the zenāna. Finally there was another fact which told for a long time:

> Courtesans, whose business in life is to dance in the temples and at public ceremonies, and prostitutes are the only women who are allowed to learn to read, sing, or dance. It would be thought a disgrace to a respectable woman to learn to read; and even if she had learnt she would be ashamed to own it.[1]

This feeling does not tell so powerfully now as it did a century ago.

When we take all these factors into consideration, we are not astonished to find that the proposal to give Hindu girls an education has made very little progress in the community. The whole Hindu scheme of things has operated to keep the people from giving their girls an education.

It was missionaries who began the education of girls. They were followed, at a considerable interval, by a few European laymen, the Government, and the Brāhma Samāj. Later still, the other Samājes, the Rāmakṛishṇa Mission and Theosophy began to help; and now most Hindu organizations do something to further the cause. Progress is slow, yet while only 2.5 per cent of girls of school-going age were in school in 1902, there were 5 per cent in 1912.

[1] Dubois, 337.

14. Caste

The main rules of caste which a Hindu has to observe relate to marriage, food, occupation and foreign travel. No man may marry outside his caste, and usually he is restricted to certain sub-sections of his caste, while, in many parts of India, sectarian distinctions narrow the range of choice still farther. Certain kinds of food are absolutely proscribed in each caste; there are rules as to the caste of the person who may cook for the members of the caste; no man may eat with a person of lower caste than himself; and there are strict rules as to those from whose hands one may receive water. The occupation rule is in most cases very strict for low-caste people but very lax for the high castes. No Hindu may cross the ocean.[1]

The marriage rule is very strictly kept by all classes. There are very few, even among those who have had an English education, who dare to break the matrimonial rules; for they are the very foundation of caste observance. Not only the social reform organization but most of the sectarian unions [2] and the caste conferences [3] suggest that restrictions on marriage between members of sub-castes should be given up, but very little progress has yet been made. It is only the most advanced reformers who propose that distinctions of caste should be altogether neglected in marriage.

The law as to what is legitimate or illegitimate in the matter of diet must always have been subject to minor changes. Educated men living in the large towns take large liberties nowadays outside their own homes in this matter, but they are usually strict at home. Mr. Shridhar Ketkar, in the second volume of his *History of Caste in*

[1] *Crown of Hinduism*, 163–166.

[2] See above, pp. 291 ff.

[3] See above, pp. 308 ff.

India, gives a very illuminating account of the state of affairs in the matter of diet in the Bombay Presidency.[1]

Until recent times the rule that a man must not eat with a person of lower caste than himself was upheld with the extremest stringency. In past days, people have been outcasted because they had *smelt* beef! Even now in certain localities orthodoxy is very strict. Yet Western thought and common sense are gradually telling on educated men. The Brāhmas are quite free in interdining, and most members of the Prārthanā Samāj are ready to dine not only with Hindus of any grade but with Christians, Muḥammadans and foreigners. Indeed social reformers all tend to seek liberty in this matter. The ordinary educated Hindu desires freedom, so that he may dine with old classmates and with Europeans who have been happily associated with him in public life, education or business. Yet many shrink back, and the mass of educated men still hold the orthodox position. There is much ground yet to be possessed.

What may perhaps be described as the boldest action taken by social reformers in recent years was carried out in Bombay in November, 1912. Under the auspices of a new organization, called the Aryan Brotherhood, a Conference of people opposed to caste was held from the 9th to the 12th of November, and closed with a dinner at which one hundred and fifty men and women dined together, openly setting at defiance the laws of caste. Those who were present at the dinner had come from many parts of Western India; and a considerable number of them found themselves outcasted, as soon as they returned to their homes. In several places, the orthodox party showed that they were determined to push things to the uttermost. It is well known that Brāhmans of the highest rank who are counted orthodox take tea in

[1] Chap. VI.

Irani shops in Bombay, and even occasionally dine quietly with Muḥammadans or Europeans. So long as this is done secretly, nothing is said; but a public defiance of all the rules of caste is another matter. Some of those outcasted yielded at once, and were reinstated after performing *prāyaśchitta* (an atonement ceremony), but others are holding out. It seems clear that this piece of bold action will produce good results.[1]

The rule that no Hindu may cross the ocean was imposed because it is clear that no Hindu can go to another country by sea and keep caste rules about food. When Ram Mohan Ray went to England, he sought to preserve his caste by taking a Brāhman cook with him. The desire to get an education in Europe or America has proved the most powerful motive leading to the breach of the rule; but the exigencies of business have also proved effective; and a few orthodox Hindu princes have yielded under the overwhelming desire to be present at some great state ceremonial in England. For a long time orthodoxy remained utterly implacable. The man who had crossed the ocean could not be received back into caste unless he underwent the prescribed atonement, *prāyaśchitta*, a most disgusting and barbarous ceremony. Those who would not pay the penalty were outcasted. Hence there grew up in Calcutta a small but interesting and influential community who, for the sake of education, had suffered excommunication. Most of them found refuge in the Brāhma Samāj. For long the battle was most serious,[2] and in many parts of India it is so to the present day; but nationalism has triumphed in Calcutta. One of the most noticeable results of the unbounded excitement of 1905–1907 was the creation of a society in Calcutta for the sending of Bengali students to Europe, America or

[1] *ISR.*, XXIII, 49, 133, 139, 176, 233.

[2] Ranade, *Essays*, 161.

Japan to receive a modern education. So popular has the movement been and so powerful its leaders, that, when students return to Calcutta, they are received back into caste without any fuss. Quite recently the Bhatias of Bombay have split into two sections over the problem.

The movement for the uplifting of the Outcaste is probably the most significant of all the facts that fall to be chronicled under the head of caste. But it has been already dealt with,[1] so that we need not touch it here.

15. Temperance

Many a Hindu has been reckless enough to declare that Europeans brought drink to India, and debauched a teetotal nation. The facts are, however, that there has been a good deal of drinking in India since the very dawn of history. Priests and people in the time of the *Ṛigveda* were so fond of the drink called *soma* that they not only offered it to the gods as one of the best gifts they could give, but actually deified it. Soma is one of the leading gods of the *Ṛigveda*. From the Epics it is also evident that there was a good deal of drinking among the warlike tribes in the pre-Christian centuries. The laws of Manu show us that in settled Hindu life throughout North India various kinds of intoxicating liquor, drink shops, drinking parties and drunkards, were not uncommon; and the dramas corroborate this evidence.

It is perfectly true that Hindu law for many centuries has been seriously opposed to the use of alcoholic drink; and high-caste Hindus, as a class, have been practically total abstainers. Yet even this general statement requires to be qualified; for in Bengal, at the great festivals, every family gives *siddhi* to visitors; and in the Left-

[1] Above, pp. 366 ff.

hand Śākta Sect intoxicating liquor is one of the five *tattvas* used as means of salvation. Many of the lower castes have been accustomed to drink from time immemorial.

Modern life, unfortunately, has done a good deal to introduce drink among the educated classes and to spread the drinking habit among the coolies on tea-gardens. It is probably true also that the planting of licensed liquor shops in the lower parts of the great cities of India has led to an extension of the drinking customs of the common people.

There was thus ample room for a temperance propaganda. A vigorous crusade was carried on for several years by Mr. W. S. Caine and a number of helpers, with the result that many Hindu castes were induced to give up drink altogether. The movement still continues to do good work, through the Churches, the Samājes, and Temperance Societies consisting of men of every faith. Besides using moral suasion with communities and individuals, these bodies do useful service by watching lest the action of the Excise Department lead to an increase in drink-shops and drinking, and by making suggestions to Government for the better control of the traffic. An Annual Temperance Conference is held in one of the great cities.

16. Social Service

It was Keshab Chandra Sen who first suggested that the Brāhma Samāj should copy Christians in the matter of philanthropy. All the Samājes have taken this up seriously. The Ārya Samāj especially has done work of very great value in relieving the famine-stricken and those who suffered in the great Kangra earthquake. The Rāmakṛishṇa Mission has several times done fine service in relieving sufferers from flood, famine and pestilence. The Ārya Samāj, the Deva Samāj and the Rāmakṛishṇa Mission all follow the lead of the Christian Church in doing medical work. The Brāhma Mission on the Kasi Hills also gives medical help.

But the new currents started by the great national excitement of recent years have helped to bring into existence a new type of effort which may yet prove of considerable value. For many years certain Christian Colleges and schools have led out their students into simple social service. Usually this has taken the form of schools for neglected tribes and castes, or simple medical relief; but, in recent years, the value of social work as training for the young Christian has been so clearly perceived that the whole subject has been carefully discussed, and many new lines of activity have been started. This Christian movement found articulate expression in an excellent book, *Suggestions for Social Helpfulness*, by the Rev. D. J. Fleming, of Lahore. This volume is now out of print, but its place has been taken by a still better book, *Social Study, Service and Exhibits*, by the same author.

During the last three or four years the movement has appeared in Government and Hindu Colleges; and it is steadily spreading. In most cases the work attempted is a school for Outcaste children. This service is being done by students of the Presidency College, Calcutta, by students of the Central Hindu College, Benares, and by others. In some cases, careful social study has been started. For example, the students of Patna College, organized in the Chanakya Society, have surveyed the chief industries of Patna City, of Dinapore, of Mozufferpore and of some other places in Behar. In many centres the Young Men's Christian Association has organized groups of Hindus for social service along various lines.

In close connection with the Servants of India Society's work there was started recently, under the Presidency of Sir N. G. Chandavarkar, the Social Service League, Bombay. The objects of the League are:

> The collection and study of social facts; the discussion of social theories and social problems with a view to forming public opinion and securing improvements in the conditions of life, and the pursuit of social service.

Only those who are prepared to work are received as members. A similar League, under the Presidency of Mrs. Whitehead, is working in Madras.

LITERATURE. — *Social Study, Service and Exhibits*, by D. J. Fleming, Calcutta, The Association Press, 1913, 10 as. *The Theory and Practice of Social Service in India*, by K. M. Munshi, Bombay, the Social Service League (a prize essay).

17. THE CRIMINAL TRIBES[1]

The movement for the reformation of the Criminal Tribes is scarcely parallel with the other efforts at social reform which we have just reviewed; for, thus far, it has been almost exclusively the work of the Salvation Army and the Government; but it is a matter of so much importance and interest, and fits so well into the chronicle of this chapter, that the story had better be told.

The phrase Criminal Tribes is used strictly of *tribes whose regular caste-occupation is some form of crime.* The form of crime which a tribe practises is part of the caste-organization, and is carried on under very strict rules.

[1] I am indebted for much of my information on this subject to Mr. O. H. B. Starte, I. C. S., who travelled home on the same steamer with me in April, 1914. He has been engaged during the last four years in establishing and controlling experimental settlements amongst the Criminal Tribes in the southern part of the Bombay Presidency.

Thus, among the Ghantichors of the Bombay Presidency it used to be the rule that a young man could not marry until he had stolen a nose-ring off a woman's face. The same tribe is bound by another rule, that they must steal only by day: until quite recently, if a man stole by night, he was outcasted. The reason why these regulations are so well understood and so carefully observed is that they are to the tribesmen religious laws. In most cases the tribe holds that the gods have imposed their particular crime-occupation on them; that, so long as they follow it in accordance with caste rules, they are true men and faithful to their religion; and that, if they were to give it up, the gods would wreak their displeasure on them. Hence, before starting out on a criminal expedition, they offer prayers to their divinity, and when they return, they dedicate to him a percentage of their spoils. The Chhapparbands of the Bombay Presidency, for example, whose caste profession is the making of counterfeit coins, give 12½ per cent. Most of these tribes are Hindus, but some are Muḥammadans; and amongst the Muḥammadans it is usually to the shrines of the Pirs (saints) that they dedicate the stated portion of their gains.[1]

No trustworthy estimate of the numbers of these religious criminals can be given; for no careful survey has yet been made. Some tribes are completely and dangerously

[1] The secret society of robber-stranglers known as *Thags*, which was put down by the British Government in the second quarter of the nineteenth century (p. 17, above), was an organization conducted on the same principles as a criminal tribe, but it had a much wider basis. It was composed of both Hindus and Muḥammadans, and the Hindus belonged to many different castes; yet all took the same oaths, practised the same ritual and worshipped the same divinity, the goddess Kālī. The date of its origin and the name of its founder are alike unknown. Doubtless it sprang into existence at some time when the Delhi Government was so disorganized as to give predatory gangs unusual opportunities for plundering. See Meadows Taylor, *Confessions of a Thug*, London, Trübner, 1s.

criminal; others are less aggressive, part being actively criminal, the rest only passively so; others are mixed, some sections being perfectly honest, others hardened criminals. But, though a definite census has not been taken, they are known to be very numerous; for they are found in every part of India; and we may be certain that the total population of those tribes which are completely and dangerously criminal is not less than 300,000. If they could be changed into good citizens, a large part of the Indian police force could be disbanded.

The growing efficiency of the British Government, and two modern police-methods — the taking of finger-prints and gang-prosecutions — have broken the self-confidence of many of these tribes. They begin to find the resources of civilization too strong for them. They are in a chastened mood, and are thus in some degree prepared to respond to the suggestion that they should become honest men. The majority are willing to enter Settlements.

Government is also, in a manner, pledged to go forward with their reclamation: such is the implication of the Criminal Tribes' Act of 1911.

Government Settlements for the purposes of reclamation were tried at various times in the past, but with limited success. It is only during the last six years that results have been won which justify the hope that the further improvement of methods may lead to a complete transformation of these tribes.

A. In 1908 work was begun in a small Settlement at Gorakhpur by the Salvation Army with Government help, and others have been opened since. The long experience the Army has had in dealing with the criminal class all over the world has prepared them for the task. Government provides suitable buildings when such are available, or gives grants-in-aid for the erection of new buildings. It also gives a monthly grant for expenses, and in many cases provides land for cultivation. Trades, such as silk-reeling, carpentry, weaving, etc., are taught to many of the younger members of the tribes. The Salvation Army provides experienced officers of the right type of character. Their work has not been all success by any means; and they themselves confess that they are only learning how to deal with these difficult people; yet such results have been won as to justify a wide extension of the effort. The Army have now 25 Settlements in India and one in Ceylon. A pamphlet by Commissioner Booth Tucker, called *Crimino-curology*,[1] gives a vivid account of their work.

B. At the end of 1909 the Government of Bombay opened an experimental Settlement at Bijapur in the South of the Presidency, under direct Government supervision. In the beginning their efforts were confined to Chhapparbands, Harranshikaris and Ghantichors. At a later date work was opened at other centres. The method has two sides. The people live in a Settlement, and work is provided for them, either in the Settlement or outside, so that they may become accustomed to earning an honest livelihood. A considerable number of them have been placed in spinning and weaving mills, others have been taught masonry or carpentry. Experience has shewn that the members of the Settlement attain to a virility and knowledge of the economic value of their own labour much more speedily if work is found for them under independent employers than if work is provided directly under the Settlement authorities. Hence the present policy is to establish the Settlements in places where there is a keen demand for labour. They are kindly treated and helped in every possible way. But, in order that they may not slip away from discipline and return to

[1] Simla, The Royal Army Temperance Association Press.

crime, they are registered and watched; and absconders are punished.

Very encouraging results have been already won. An extension of the work is now contemplated; but the question is being considered whether, in order to obtain the necessary moral influence, some of the Settlements should not be controlled by voluntary agencies.

The independent experience so gained fully corroborates the conclusions which Salvation Army Officers have reached as to the possibility of reclaiming these people and the methods to be employed. The provision of regular work for a considerable period of time under strict discipline, and the placing of them under the guidance of people of high character, who will treat them at once with the utmost kindness and the utmost firmness, and will use all possible moral suasion to change them, seem to be the principles which will lead to success. Government alone can bring to bear the pressure necessary to secure discipline, and private philanthropic effort alone can supply in a satisfactory way the men and women needed for the moral side of the work of reclamation.

The work is still mostly of an experimental nature, but the experiments now being carried on in different parts of India are leading to such definite conclusions that it is highly probable that the near future will see a very wide extension of the work.

There are thirteen Salvation Army Settlements in the United Provinces, five in the Panjab, five in the Madras Presidency and two in Bihar and Orissa. The American Baptists in the Telugu country have one Settlement, and one is under the control of the Manager of a Mica mine. The Wesleyans in Benares are working among the Doms, a semi-criminal tribe.

Arrangements are being made for the opening of more

Settlements under private management. Hitherto only Christian bodies have been willing and able to undertake the task, and until quite recently the Salvation Army alone has had Settlements; but long-established Missions, with their communities, Churches, Industrial Schools and Industries, and their knowledge of the local conditions, are in many respects in a position of great advantage for dealing with the problem, though at present they have not the experience of the Salvation Army. It may also be noted that the Panjab Government recently invited several of the leading Hindu and Muḥammadan societies to take a share in the work. The problem is so large that there would appear to be ample scope for all suitable voluntary agencies to aid in its solution.

CHAPTER VII

SIGNIFICANCE OF THE MOVEMENTS

I. The most prominent characteristic of the long series of religious movements we have dealt with is *the steady advance of the ancient faiths.* The earlier organizations were very radical indeed in the treatment they proposed for the troubles of the time, and adopted great masses of Christian thought and practice. But as the years passed, men found courage to defend an ever larger amount of the old theology, until a number undertook to prove every scrap of the ancient structure good. Hinduism, Islam, Buddhism, Jainism and Zoroastrianism each leaped up into new vigorous activity, every prominent sect experiencing a mysterious awakening. Finally, under the impulse of national feeling, the tables were completely turned: not only the religions but everything Oriental was glorified as spiritual and ennobling, while everything Western received condemnation as hideously materialistic and degrading. An immense quantity of literature pours from the press, and considerable sums of money are subscribed for defence purposes, above all for sectarian education.

Hence the Hindu, the Jain, the Buddhist, the Parsee and the Muslim are to-day filled with overflowing confidence each in his own religion; a confidence which tends to be hostile to spiritual life as well as to a reasonable estimate of the old faiths. Many a man has a pride in his tone, and shews an arrogance towards outsiders, which are scarcely characteristic of health, whether religious or intellectual. *The Modern Review*, perhaps the best and most representative of the monthlies at present, frequently contains a good deal of bombast; and the youthful graduates who speak and write on Hinduism have usually far too much of Vivekānanda's swagger about them. Hundreds of men of the student class, under Dayānanda's influence, believe that the ancient Hindus were as far advanced in the natural sciences[1] as modern Europeans are, and that they had invented not only firearms and locomotives but telegraphs and aeroplanes as well.

Yet the arrival of the new spirit was necessary for the health of the country. The long decades during which not only the European but the cultured Hindu looked down upon the religion, philosophy and art of India effectually opened the door to the influence of the West, without which the Awakening would have been impossible; but they as effectually depressed the Indian spirit to a point at which the doing of the best work was impossible. Hence the return of self-respect was sorely needed; and that has come since the twentieth century opened.

II. But there is another aspect of the situation which requires to be clearly realized. The triumphant revival of the old religions, with their growing body-guard of defence organizations, has been accompanied by *continuous and steadily increasing inner decay*. This most significant of all facts in the history of these movements seems to be scarcely perceived by the leaders. They believe that the danger is past. This blindness arises largely from the fact that they draw their apologetic and their inspiration almost entirely from Rāmakṛishṇa, Vivekānanda, Sister Niveditā, Dayānanda and Mrs. Besant; and it is clear that neither capable thinking nor clear-eyed perception can be bred on such teaching as theirs.

[1] P. 116, above.

We shall here attempt only a very brief statement of the evidence for this inner decay in the case of Hinduism. While the apologists have been busy building their defences these last forty years, Western influence has been steadily moulding the educated Hindu mind and rendering it altogether incapable of holding the ideas which form the foundation of the religion. Hence we have many defences of idolatry but no faith in it. In spite of all that has been said in favour of the Hindu family, no educated Hindu has found any religious basis for pre-puberty marriage, for widow-celibacy, for polygamy, for the zenāna. The modern man simply cannot believe that his dead father's spirit comes and eats the rice-cake offered at the *śrāddha*, far less that his place in heaven is dependent on it. Much has been said to make caste seem a most reasonable form of social organization; yet thinking Hindus no longer hold that which is the foundation of the system, the doctrine that each man's caste is an infallible index of the stage of spiritual progress his soul has reached in its transmigrational journey. The Depressed Classes Mission is clear proof that Hindus no longer believe that the Outcaste is a soul whose past record is so foul that physical contact with him is spiritually dangerous to the caste Hindu. What student believes that that is true of the European Principal and Professors of his college? Yet, if these things are incredible, caste has no religious basis left. Then the Vedic Schools are dying. Asceticism is clearly dying. The great Śaṅkarāchārya founded four monasteries, at Śriṅgeri in Mysore, at Dvārikā in Kathiawar, at Badrināṛāyaṇa in the Himalayas, and at Puri. In February last, at Rajkot, Kathiawar, I had a personal interview with the Śaṅkara who is the head of the Dvārikā monastery. Instead of a fine company of intelligent men studying the Vedānta, he has only some half a dozen boys of six or seven years of age as his disciples. They came marching into the verandah where we were seated, each little fellow dressed in a rough brown blanket and carrying the wand of a *brahmachārī*, and saluted the *āchārya*. He also informed me that the Badrinārāyaṇa monastery is now extinct.[1]

III. *The causes which have combined to create the movements are many.* The stimulating forces are almost exclusively Western, viz. the British Government, English education and literature, Christianity, Oriental research, European science and philosophy, and the material elements of Western civilization; but the beliefs and the organization of the ancient faiths have been moulding forces of great potency. The Ārya Samāj is an interesting example of the interaction of rationalism and modern inventions with belief in transmigration and the inerrancy of the Vedic hymns. The Deva Samāj shews us Western evolutionary science in unstable combination with Hindu guru-worship. Theosophy is a new Gnosticism which owes its knowledge to Western Orientalists but takes its principles from Buddhism and its fireworks from occultism.

IV. While the shaping forces at work in the movements have been many, it is quite clear that *Christianity has ruled the development throughout.* Christianity has been, as it were, a great searchlight flung across the expanse of the religions; and in its blaze all the coarse, unclean and superstitious elements of the old faiths stood out, quite early, in painful vividness. India shuddered; and the earlier movements were the response to the revelation. But the same light which exposed all the grossness gradually enabled men to distinguish the nobler and more spiritual elements of the religions. Consequently the Hindu, the

[1] A great deal of evidence on the subject of the decay of Hinduism is gathered in the author's *Crown of Hinduism*, pp. 34, 42, 113–15, 148–51, 177–87, 191, 273–6, 334–9, 342, 421–4, 446–7.

Jain, the Parsee and the Muḥammadan set these in the foreground, crushed out the worst as far as possible, and sought to build up fresh organizations which should be able to bear the searching glare continually flung on them by the great Intruder from the West. Hence, while most of the material used in the reconstruction is old, Christian principles have guided the builders. In every case the attempt is made to come up to Christian requirements. Frequently the outcome is extremely slender; yet the purpose can be seen. Christianity has been the norm; and no part of the most orthodox movement is fully comprehensible except when seen from the Christian point of view.

1. Christianity has made men feel that the only possible religion is *monotheism*. The Brāhma, Prārthanā and Ārya Samājes declare themselves as truly monotheistic as Christianity. Parsees and Muḥammadans make the same claim. All the Śaiva and Vaishṇava sects, and also the Sikhs, urge that they are true monotheists; yet their teaching recognizes the existence of all the gods of the Hindu pantheon. Various forms of pantheism (for example, Theosophy, and the systems taught by Rāmakṛishṇa, the Rādhā Soāmis and the Smārtas of the South) demand recognition as monotheistic, on the ground that monotheism and pantheism should be reckoned as synonyms.[1] Why should theological terms be used with pedantic strictness? Finally, even in the case of atheistic forms of thought (for example, Jainism, the Buddhism of Ceylon and the teaching of the Deva Samāj) the vogue of monotheism is clear. People shrink from the word atheist. Individual Jains and Deva Samājists will affirm that all they mean is that they cannot see the necessity for a Creator; while in Ceylon theistic phraseology is very common in all revival literature.

[1] Mr. Shridhar Ketkar says this frankly. See his *Hinduism, its Formation and Future*, 47.

2. When this idea of the one spiritual God is held intelligently, it necessarily *excludes polytheism, mythology, idolatry and man-worship.* Face to face with this powerful conception, the modern religious movements of India fall into three groups. The first of these contains the Brāhma, Prārthanā and Ārya Samājes. All these have been so deeply influenced by the idea that they hold it in comparative purity, and, along with the Parsees and the Muḥammadans, summon all men to give up these degrading superstitions. Next come the Rādhā Soāmis, the Chet Rāmīs, and the members of the Deva Samāj, who, though they have given up polytheism and mythology, have succumbed to man-worship, and will doubtless be led on by it to idolatry. In the case of nearly all the other movements, there is a desire to remain orthodox: so that polytheism, mythology, idols and guru-worship are all retained. Yet the effect of Christian criticism is very noticeable. In most of the groups guru-worship, at least in its most degrading aspects, is carefully concealed. The modern thinking man is ashamed of it. Vivekānanda and his fellow-disciples worshipped Rāmakṛishṇa, but Christian influence led them to minimize it: "We offer him worship bordering on divine worship." In the case of idols, the need of an apologetic is seriously felt, and numerous attempts have been made to reach a reasonable defence, attempts about as successful as Aaron's explanation of how the golden calf came into existence. No thinking man to-day can accept a phallic symbol as a worthy representation of the God of the whole earth; so Vivekānanda asserted, without a vestige of evidence, that the *liṅga* is no phallus but a model of a sacred hill. The most pitiful allegorizations are put forward as defences of the mythology. In every case the apologetic confesses, in form, if not in words, that it is the Christian spirit which has to be faced.

3. The Christian doctrine that *God is the Father of men* and that every man is a child of God, with its corollary, that all men are brothers, is accepted with practical unanimity in all the movements. In the Brāhma and Prārthanā Samājes, and by Śivanārāyaṇa, these doctrines are seriously accepted and made the basis of a new life. But the force and pervasiveness of the teaching are seen still more clearly in the fact that in the case of all the other movements (with the exception of those which deny the existence of God) the doctrine is accepted and taught, even though other parts of the theology are radically inconsistent with it. The Śaiva and Vaishṇava sects claim the Fatherhood of God and the Brotherhood of Man as Hindu doctrines, and yet hold hard by the Hindu doctrine of the essential inferiority of woman and the Caste system with its inhuman laws for Outcastes and Mlecchas. Theosophists, Rādhā Soāmis and Smārtas, though they make the Supreme impersonal and unknowable, yet find themselves driven to call Him the Heavenly Father. The Christian doctrine of the love of God, which is a necessary element in the Fatherhood, passed into the teaching of the Brāhma and Prārthanā Samājes, and has deeply influenced most of the other movements. It has led to increased emphasis being laid on the doctrine of *bhakti*. The belief, that all men, as children of God, are brothers, and that morality may be summed up in the word brotherliness, has also worked wonders. Here is the secret of the strange fact that men who still hold by the doctrine of transmigration and karma feel increasingly that caste is wrong, and are being gradually driven, by their consciences, first to acknowledge that the untouchable Outcastes are their brothers, and then, more slowly and reluctantly, to receive them as such. The same belief has given Indians a truer idea of the value of the human personality and shews itself in the convic-

tion that an Indian of any class is as great and valuable as a European, and in the new attitude to women and children. This fresh way of looking at every human being is implied in all the activities of the new Nationalism. Another implicate of the Fatherhood has made a tremendous impression. Every modern religious movement in India calls itself the religion for all men. What a striking result this is in India becomes clear only when one recollects what an extremely exclusive religion orthodox Hinduism is. Yet even the superlatively orthodox Bhārata Dharma Mahāmaṇḍala makes the claim of universalism, and offers to sell to any one the books which, according to Hindu law, must be seen by no woman and by no man outside the three twice-born castes. How is it that no such claim was ever made until Christianity appeared on the scene? On the basis of human brotherhood Christ insists vehemently on the duty of kindly philanthropic service, and no part of His teaching has produced larger results in India. Feeble attempts are made here and there to trace the teaching to Hinduism; but all well-informed men recognize that it was introduced into India by Christian missions. This mighty force shews itself in every element of the social reform movement, but above all things in what Christians have done for the Outcastes, and in the rise of the movement among Hindus.

4. *The righteousness of God*, as taught by Jesus, has also exercised a profound influence. The conception necessarily involves the Christian ideas of repentance, forgiveness, the transformation of character, the holy life and the passion for saving men. All these in their fulness were adopted by Keshab Chandra Sen; those who follow him, both in Bengal and Bombay, still preach them; and most of them may be traced in the exquisite cadences of *Gitanjali*. In all the other movements there has been a serious clinging to the conceptions of the old religion. Yet, modern men could

not but seek to get rid of the filth, superstition and corruption revealed by the searchlight of Christ. Many of these things are exposed in the writings of Ram Mohan Ray, of Śivanārāyaṇa and of Dayānanda. There has been a serious attempt, on the part of the orthodox, to destroy, to drive underground or to deny the worst features of Left-hand Śāktism, temple-prostitution, temple-miracles, priestly fraud and corruption, and unclean superstition. Even Vivekānanda acknowledges the presence of masses of superstition in Hinduism:

> The old ideas may be all superstition, but within these masses of superstition are nuggets of gold and truth.

Mrs. Besant alone has had the courage to defend many of the gross superstitions which the honest Hindu is heartily ashamed of. On the other hand, it is now universally recognized that no religion is worth the name that does not work for spiritual ends and produce men of high and noble character. Hindus lay all the stress nowadays on the best parts of Hinduism, and make as little as possible of law, custom and ritual. There is no movement that does not set the Upanishads and the *Gītā* in the foreground. So keenly is this felt in Jainism and Islam that, where the laws of the religion are external and old-world, modern apologists tell us that we must follow not the literal commands but the spirit of Jainism, the spirit of Islam; and there is many an orthodox Moulvie in India to-day who denies that the Koran allows slavery, polygamy or the killing of men who refuse to accept Islam. It is very significant that the Deva Samāj and Madame Blavatsky unite in proclaiming to the world how many hardened criminals their particular doctrine has saved.[1]

5. Christianity insists that *the worship of God must be*

[1] Above, p. 181, and *MPI.*, 265–6.

spiritual, and therefore that animal and vegetarian sacrifices, ceremonial bathing, pilgrimage and self-torture ought to be given up. For the same reason worship ought to be conducted in the vernacular, so that it may be understood by the people; otherwise it has little or no value for them. The Brāhma, Prārthanā and Ārya Samājes have responded very fully to these ideals; and the Rādhā Soāmi Satsaṅg, the Deva Samāj and Śivanārāyaṇa have not fallen far short of them. A sort of simple non-conformist service in the vernacular has been the norm for all these bodies. Sacrifice, pilgrimage and ceremonial bathing have been completely given up. The spirituality of true worship also finds powerful expression in *Gitanjali*. The conviction that prayer ought to be in the vernacular has led to fresh proposals among both Parsees and Muslims, although little result has followed. There have been a few attempts made to transform sacrifice to spiritual uses. Thus Keshab allegorized the *homa* sacrifice and the ceremonial waving of lights, called *Āratī*. In the Ārya Samāj and in the teaching of Śivanārāyaṇa we find fire-sacrifice retained, not as part of the worship of God but as a means of purifying the air! The other movements cling to old Hindu worship practically without change; but cultured men are more than half ashamed of it; the defences offered are very half-hearted; and the details are frequently condemned by individuals.

The Christian contention that sacred books can be of no value, unless they are understood by the people, has led all the movements, Jain, Sikh, Parsee and Muslim, as well as Hindu, to produce translations of the sacred books they use and to write all fresh books in the vernaculars.

6. The Christian doctrine of *the Person of Christ* has been adopted in a modified form in a number of the movements. Keshab Chandra Sen is the most noteworthy instance; but, besides him, we note, in the Hindu sphere, the Chet

Rāmīs and the Īsāmoshipanthīs, and among Muḥammadans, the Aḥmadīyas and the Nazarenes.

But much more important than these cases of direct acceptance of certain aspects of the Person of Christ is the indirect influence the doctrine has exerted. The most striking case of all is the prophecy of the Coming Christ which has caused such an upheaval in Theosophy. Next in importance is the increased emphasis laid during recent years on the Vishṇuite doctrine of divine incarnations, and the altered form it has taken. The old animal incarnations are dropped out of sight, and all the stress is laid on Rāma and Kṛishṇa, above all on Kṛishṇa. The reason for his prominence is to be found in his place in the *Gītā*. Kṛishṇa and the *Gītā* can thus be put forward as a satisfactory Hindu substitute for Christ and the Gospels. Hence, in order to make it possible to place Kṛishṇa on an equality with Christ, numerous attempts have been made to whitewash his character as it is represented in the Epic and the Purāṇas, and many books have been written to prove the historicity of his life as it appears in the *Mahābhārata*. A similar motive led a Calcutta Hindu to publish a little devotional volume called *The Imitation of Shri Krishna.* It is worth noting also that the Rādhā Soāmis call their Sant Satguru the Son of God.

7. The most characteristic and vital of all Hindu doctrines is transmigration and karma. It is also more anti-Christian than any other aspect of the religion; for it involves not only the theory that each individual passes through many lives and deaths, but also the doctrines that a man's place in society is an infallible index of the stage of soul-progress he has reached; that the suffering he undergoes is strictly equivalent to his past sins; that women are born women because of former sin, and widows are widowed for the same reason; that to seek to ameliorate

the social condition of an individual or a tribe is futile, since the exact amount of the misery or happiness each man will suffer or enjoy is inevitably fixed by his karma; that Caste is the only right form of society, because social grades are divinely proportioned to human desert; that divine forgiveness is impossible; and that, since God stands apart from karma, He is necessarily actionless. So powerful and pervasive is the doctrine that there is scarcely a part of the religion that has not been modified by it. How potent then has Christianity been in controlling the religious thought of the past century! The doctrine has been expelled completely from the teaching of the Brāhma and Prārthanā Samājes; and everywhere else it has been deeply wounded. Every aspect of the social reform movement is a direct attack upon it; and indeed each of the social implications of the doctrine is rapidly losing its hold. Men revere the doctrine to-day but do not understand it. To them it is merely an explanation of the inequalities of life; but no educated Hindu is ready to follow even that line to the end.

8. In all the movements we trace a strong desire *that their leaders should be like missionaries*, that their priests and teachers should be men of training, of high moral character and spiritual power. Each body desires to give its teachers a modern training in theology, so that they may be able to teach the people and to defend the system from outside attack. The great majority of sādhus, priests and gurus are recognized as being worse than useless. Apart from the Brāhma and Prārthanā Samājes, very few of the movements have been able to secure trained leaders. One hears everywhere that there is great difficulty in getting good preachers. All the clever young men want to enter secular employment. The sectarian movements have organized examinations and offered prizes to stimulate study; while the Parsees, the Jains and the Muḥammadans

are making serious attempts to organize modern systems of theological training.

9. A peculiarly arresting proof that Christianity has ruled the whole religious development of the last century is to be found in the *Social Reform Movement*. From beginning to end the ideas that have led to reform have been purely Christian, and have had to win their way in face of the deepest conceptions of Hindu theology and social organization. Buddhist and Jain teaching are quite as hostile, and Islam also, in most cases. All this shines out so conspicuously in our sixth chapter that we need say no more here.

10. The dominance of Christianity in the religious development of the last hundred years may be clearly seen in this that, *almost without exception, the methods of work in use in the movements have been borrowed from missions*. This is the more noticeable since India, in the past, had the genius to produce a series of methods of religious propaganda unmatched in the history of the world.

The schools of the priests, which at quite an early date were thrown open to the three twice-born castes, is the first method of Hinduism. In them arose most of the greatest literature of the religion; and, for well-nigh three thousand years they dominated the mind of India. When the passion for release from transmigration awakened the early Hindus to philosophic inquiry, there appeared the second method, groups of wandering monks (and nuns also), who practised and taught their respective ascetic theories of release. All the forms of Hindu philosophy were propagated in this way. The same is true of Buddhism and Jainism, except that in these movements monasteries appeared at an early date, and greatly eased the rigours of asceticism. In mediæval days there appeared the third method, the wandering monk with his commentary on the *Vedānta-sūtras*, challenging to debate any one who had a rival theory of the Vedānta, or a rival philosophy and retiring from time to time to a monastery to study and write. Śaṅkara, Rāmānuja and Madhva are the best examples. The fourth method appeared very early in the Tamil South, an emotional devotee, poet, musician and singer, wandering from shrine to shrine, using only the vernacular, singing and dancing in ecstasy, or swooning away in rapture before the idol which he adored. Rāmānanda was the creator of the fifth method, which proved very successful in North India, the wandering preacher and theologian, fit to meet scholars, but ready to preach to the people in their own tongue, and always ready to put his prayers and meditations into pithy vernacular verse. This type, known as the *Bhagat* (*i.e.* the *Bhāgavata*, the devotee of the Lord, Bhagavān), might be a monk, like Rāmānanda, or a married man, like Nānak or Tulsī Das. Chaitanya was a Brāhman, who had been a brilliant figure in the schools ; but he introduced into the North the ecstatic singing and dancing of the South.

It is very remarkable that no single movement in our days uses these remarkable methods. We have seen no new Sanskrit commentary on the *Vedānta-sūtras*. No vernacular poet moves from shrine to shrine dancing and singing, followed by crowds of enraptured devotees. Dayānanda and Rāmakrishṇa were monks; but in neither case did any organized movement appear until monastic modes of effort had given place to missionary methods. Keshab introduced Chaitanya's dancing and singing into the Brāhma samāj, but they are of no service to-day as modes of propaganda. Only modern forms of effort are efficient. The occultism of the new Theosophy is the one outstanding method at present in use which is not missionary in origin, and, as far as one can see, it is not Indian either.

On the other hand, every sort of missionary method and organization has been copied. A modern movement belonging to whatever religion is in almost every detail a replica of a mission. Many of the methods are old, having been long in use in Europe and America, but many are quite fresh, developed to meet the peculiar circumstances of modern India. We shall merely give a list of the more notable of the methods copied, and leave readers to carry the inquiry farther themselves. The modes of congregational worship, the educated ministry, preaching, lecturing, pastoral work, prayer meetings, itinerancy, conferences, make the first group. Sunday schools, Bible classes, Young People's Societies, Bands of Hope, social gatherings and other forms of work for young people make another. The principles and methods of the mission school and college, girls' schools, boarding schools, hostels, industrial and technical schools, schools for the blind, the deaf and dumb, orphanages, widows' homes and zenāna visitation, form the educational group. All forms of medical work, and also the Christian leper asylum, have beeen copied. Work among the Outcastes and the wild tribes is one of the most noticeable of all cases. Literature of every type, in English and the vernaculars, for men, young men, women and children, forms another group. Philanthropy and social service can escape no one's notice. Every movement has copied the Y. M. C. A., and a few have tried to reproduce the Salvation Army. The very names used by Christians are adopted and used by non-Christians. The whole movement is a *Revival;* the work is conducted by Hindu, Ārya or Muslim *Missionaries;* and on many of them the title *Reverend* is conferred; Vivekānanda organized a *mission*, and many others have followed him; Gītā *Classes* are conducted; *Prayer Meetings* are held; and *Young Men's* Hindu (or Ārya, Jain, Muslim, Buddhist) *Associations* are organized; and the language of the Bible and of Christian prayer is on every lip.

V. After the evidence we have already adduced none need be gathered to show that Christ's parable of the leaven is proving itself true in India. Sir Narayana Chandavarka of Bombay, in the following words, speaks out what many recognize to-day:

> The ideas that lie at the heart of the Gospel of Christ are slowly but surely permeating every part of Hindu society and modifying every phase of Hindu thought.

VI. Every student will notice how remarkably close the parallel is between the revival of the ancient religions of the Roman Empire in the early Christian centuries and these movements in India in our own days. The similarity is far greater than we have been able to bring out in our pages, since our studies run on other lines. A number of the salient points have been already touched on in fugitive papers by different writers; but the subject is well worth working up into a monograph.

APPENDIX

1. *H. P. Blavatsky and the Masters of the Wisdom*, by Annie Besant. Theosophical Publishing Society, London. 1907.

2. *Episodes from an Unwritten History*, by Claude Bragdon. Rochester, the Manas Press. 1910.

3. *Incidents in the History of the Theosophical Society*, by Joseph H. Fussell. Point Loma, California, the Aryan Theosophical Press.

4. *A Historical Retrospect of the Theosophical Society*, by H. S. Olcott. Madras, published by the Society. 1896.

The first purpose of this Appendix is to give readers some idea of the extreme unreliability of the historical literature of Theosophy, and the second is to show the publishers of these books that they are thoroughly inaccurate and misleading, and on that ground to appeal to them, to withdraw them from circulation.

1. *H. P. Blavatsky and the Masters of the Wisdom.*

a. "In August, 1851, we find her in London, and there, on a moonlight night, as her diary tells us, beside the Serpentine, 'I met the Master of my dreams.' He then told her that he had chosen her to work in a society, and some time afterwards, with her father's permission, she went into training for her future mission, passing through seven and ten years of probation, trial and hard work." P. 7.

"On November 17th, 1875, she founded, in pursuance of the order she had received, the Theosophical Society." P. 10.

Here we have the Theosophic myth at work. For the whole of the stupendous story of her intercourse with these "Masters" Madame Blavatsky never produced any trustworthy evidence. There is only her own bare assertion. She has never given any definite geographical information to enable scholars to find the Lodge of the Brotherhood in Tibet or the vast libraries which she asserts exist there. Since those days Sarat Chandra Das, a Calcutta Hindu, has travelled in Tibet, visited libraries and talked with many monks. The British expedition sent by Lord Curzon actually went to Lhassa; so that Tibet is now well known. Two of the most honoured Hindu scholars in Calcutta, Paṇḍit Hara Prasād Śāstrī and Paṇḍit Satischandra Vidyābhūshaṇa have wandered all over the hills within British territory, visiting monasteries and libraries. They have brought many Mss., both Sanskrit and Tibetan, to Calcutta. How is it that there is not a scrap of corroboration of Madame Blavatsky's wonderful story? No one knows anything about the existence of the Masters, their Lodge or the Libraries.

On the other hand, as we have shewn above, in Madame Blavatsky's own letters there is overwhelming evidence to prove the whole false.

In the passages before us we are asked, on the evidence of an entry in Madame Blavatsky's "diary," to believe that she was guided by the Masters from 1851 to 1875. Now, what are the facts? *The "diary" is no diary at all, but a book of drawings.* If it were a real diary; if it provided us with information which enabled us to understand Madame Blavatsky's early life; and if the passage referred to were an integral part of the narrative, and demonstrably written in 1851; then it would be solid evidence. *But the passage quoted is the only entry in the whole book.* No one can tell when it was written. What then is its value as evidence?—Simply nil. It may have been written by Madame Blavatsky at any time during the last twelve years of her life. But how are we to characterize Mrs. Besant's audacity in calling the book in question a diary?

b. "Before dealing with the communications received during a short time in the famous 'Shrine' at Adyar, it is necessary to describe the rooms which afterwards became famous. Madame Blavatsky occupied two out of three rooms of the upper story, opening on to a large hall. There was a sitting-room, which opened into a bedroom, and this again into a third room; the wall between the bedroom and this third room was made of two partitions with twelve inches between them, lightly built, there being no support below, and with a door in the middle, the door being thus sunk in a recess. This third room was set apart for occult purposes, and was called the Occult Room. On the partition wall, loosely hanging, was a cupboard, originally over the door, in which were placed two pictures of the Masters, a silver bowl, and other articles; the cupboard had a solid back and shelves, and was merely hung on the wall, so that it could be removed easily. This cupboard was called 'The Shrine.' The wall was smoothly plastered over, and various people — after it had been tampered with by the Coulombs — bore witness to the fact that at least up to February 17th, 1884, — H. P. B. left Adyar on February 7th — it was intact. General Morgan states that he first saw the Occult Room in August, 1883, when he visited Adyar in Madame Blavatsky's absence, and, probably in consequence of a remarkable phenomenon that happened on his visit, he examined the Shrine and its surroundings with great care; he affirms that, up to January, 1884, when he left the headquarters, 'any trickery was impossible.'" Pp. 20–21.

The authoress goes on to quote a number of similar statements made by Mrs. Morgan, Col. Olcott and several other Theosophists with regard to the Shrine; and she repeats her main affirmation about it again:

"Mr. Hodgson did not see the cupboard, and Dr. Hartmann, who did see it, and examine it, says it had 'a solid unmovable back,' and this is confirmed by others." P. 44.

Now what are the facts with regard to these large masses of evidence? They have been already given, but may be summarized as follows:

(1) Every scrap of this evidence is quoted from the pamphlet, *Report of the Result of an Investigation into the Charges against Madame Blavatsky*, which contains the statements of Theosophists written (in response to the circular of August, 1884) before Mr. Hodgson arrived in India, but not published until February, 1885. P. 249, above.

(2) It was compiled in the main by Dr. Hartmann, Madame Blavatsky's "liar, cunning and vindictive." P. 248, above.

(3) In September, 1884, five months before the pamphlet was published, the Shrine was examined by Judge, Dr. Hartmann and other Theosophists, and the sliding panels were found. Pp. 241–2, above.

(4) Three of these Theosophists removed the Shrine, and Judge burned it. Pp. 241–2, above. This is the amazing fact which is necessary to explain Mrs. Besant's statement that "Mr. Hodgson did not see the cupboard," and which she most carefully suppresses. Neither the discovery of the panels nor the burning of the Shrine is mentioned in the pamphlet, *Report of the Result*, etc., though it was published five months later.

(5) When Hodgson asked Dr. Hartmann and Damodar about the Shrine, they said they did not know what had happened to it, and suggested that it had been stolen by the missionaries or the Coulombs. Pp. 247–8, above.

(6) Most of the people whose testimony Mrs. Besant quotes were questioned by Mr. Hodgson personally, and acknowledged that *they had never examined the back of the Shrine*, thus repudiating all the evidence which Mrs. Besant quotes. Each of the following singly confessed this to Mr. Hodgson, thus proving that their statements printed in the pamphlet were at the least very careless declarations: Mrs. Morgan, Mr. Subba Row, Mr. Damodar, Mr. P. Sreenevasa Rao, Mr. T. Vijiaraghava Charloo (Ananda), Babajee, Mr. P. Rathnavelu, Mr. T. C. Rajamiengar. The details of their confessions are given by Mr. Hodgson (*Proceedings*, IX, 220–226; 325–341). He adds with reference to Mr. St. George Lane-Fox, "Mr. Lane-Fox desired my special attention to the fact that an excessive superstition was attached to the Shrine by the natives. The feeling with which they regarded it would absolutely interfere with any careful investigation of either the shrine or its surroundings" (*Ib.*, 327). Dr. Hartmann himself agreed with this statement (*Ib.*, 226). Thus Mr. Hodgson could find no evidence that any one examined the Shrine before September, 1884.

(7) On March 13, 1885, about a month after the publica-

tion of the pamphlet, Dr. Hartmann confessed, in the presence of Mr. and Mrs. Cooper-Oakley, Mr. A. O. Hume, and Mr. Hodgson, that "nobody was allowed to touch that d— shrine"; and he then told the story of the discovery of the panels and the burning of the Shrine. These facts were effectually concealed from Hodgson until that date. Pp. 250–1, above.

(8) Mme. Blavatsky confessed to Mr. Hodgson that the Shrine was made with three sliding panels in the back. P. 251, above.

(9) Dr. Hartmann confessed that his pamphlet was untrustworthy, and gave Mr. Hodgson a written statement about the Shrine, which is quoted above. Pp. 251 and 241, above.

(10) In April, 1885, the pamphlet was publicly repudiated in *The Madras Mail* by the Theosophic leaders. Pp. 253–4, above.

How then shall we characterize Mrs. Besant's statement of the evidence as to the Shrine?

c. Mrs. Besant quotes *in extenso* a letter written by Mr. A. O. Hume to the Calcutta *Statesman*, in September, 1884, with reference to the letters handed over by Madame Coulomb. We need quote only the last sentence, which is as follows:

"Parts of the letters may be genuine enough; one passage cited has a meaning quite different from that in which I see that the *Times of India* accepts it, but believe me, Madame Blavatsky is far too shrewd a woman to have ever *written* to any one, anything that could *convict* her of *fraud*." P. 37.

Now it is quite true that Mr. Hume sent this letter to the *Statesman;* but Mrs. Besant omits altogether to tell her readers that, within a few months, his mind changed completely. This fact was published by Mr. Hodgson twenty-two years before Mrs. Besant wrote her booklet:

"When the Blavatsky-Coulomb letters were first published, Mr. Hume expressed his opinion publicly that Madame Blavatsky was too clever to have thus committed herself; latterly, however, and partly in consequence of the evidence I was able to lay before him, he came to the conviction that the letters in question were actually written by Madame Blavatsky." *Proceedings*, IX, 274.

Mrs. Besant declares she studied Mr. Hodgson's Report carefully: does not her action in this case, then, come as near wilful misrepresentation as possible?

d. "Mr. Hodgson, the gentleman sent by the S. P. R., was present at this memorable Convention Meeting of December, 1884, the Colonel, in the innocence of his heart, extending to him a warm welcome. Mr. Hodgson's appearance of friendship was, however, a mere pretence to cover his real aim; he simulated honest inquiry only the more surely to destroy." P. 40.

Dr. Hartmann and Mr. Judge charged the Coulombs with forgery and the missionaries with hatching a conspiracy. Mrs. Besant now charges Mr. Hodgson with shameful treachery; and if we accept this charge, we must believe that the Society for Psychical Research were from beginning to end duped by this dishonest scheme. But, apart from these considerations and from Mr. Hodgson's own statement and behaviour, how are we to characterize Mrs. Besant's conduct in publishing this foul slander twelve years after the publication of *A Modern Priestess of Isis*, in which Madame Blavatsky herself says that Hodgson was at first a friend? (P. 248, above.)

e. "Mr. Hodgson, in his Report, publishes a 'plan of the Occult Room with shrine and surroundings (from measurements taken by R. Hodgson, assisted by the statements of Theosophic witnesses).' On page 220 Mr. Hodgson says that 'the accompanying rough sketch, made from measurements of my own, shows the positions.' The reader will now see why I laid stress on the fact that Mr. Judge had, in the summer of 1884, bricked up the hole, plastered the wall, and then re-papered it; this having been done in the summer of 1884, how could Mr. Hodgson have made a rough sketch of the positions from his own measurements in the spring of 1885? It may be asked: 'How then did Mr. Hodgson obtain his plan?' The answer is simple; Mr. Judge gives it. He said: 'I made a plan of how it had been left by Coulomb, and that plan it is that Hodgson pirated in his report, and desires people to think his, and to be that which he made on the spot, while looking at that which he thus pretends to have drawn.' All that Mr. Hodgson could have seen was a blank wall. I reprint here the comment I made in *Time* on this remarkable proceeding: 'I venture to suggest that the pirating of another person's plan, with "measurements" of things that no longer existed when Mr. Hodgson visited Adyar, is not consistent with good faith. Yet the whole terrible charge against Madame Blavatsky rests on this man's testimony. The Society of Psychical Research, which has taken the responsibility of the report, has no knowledge of the facts, other than that afforded by Mr. Hodgson. Everything turns on his veracity. And he issues another man's plan as his own, and makes imaginary measurements of vanished objects.' " P. 43.

This attack is practically the same as that published by Mrs. Besant in *Time* in 1892. Mr. Hodgson replied in detail to the attack in *Proceedings*, XXIV, 136–141, issued in June, 1893. He not only shewed that all the minor charges were unjustifiable, but published a copy of the only plan of the Shrine made by a Theosophist which he ever saw. It had appeared in the *Report of Observations*, etc., a pamphlet published by Dr. Hartmann in September, 1884. (See above, p. 240.) This must be the plan Mrs. Besant refers to, as the pamphlet was prepared and issued during the time when Mr. Judge was in Madras. This plan is reproduced above (plan A, page 234), with Mr. Hodgson's plan (plan B) beside it, that readers may see with their own eyes how utterly absurd it is to say that the latter was copied from the former.

Yet here we have Mrs. Besant repeating the old attack in 1907, without the slightest reference to Mr. Hodgson's complete disproof of the slander, and without a single scrap of evidence, except the statement of Judge, to substantiate the charge.

Further, Judge, on whose testimony Mrs. Besant relies, is the man who had to do with the removal and burning of the Shrine, and he is the man whose frauds and forgeries Mrs. Besant and Colonel Olcott discovered in 1894. (See above, pp. 241–2, 268–71.) What sort of a witness is he?

Now, if the plan republished by Mr. Hodgson is *not* Mr.

Judge's plan, Mrs. Besant is in honour bound to publish Mr. Judge's one, that the world may see that Mr. Hodgson plagiarized it. But if the reproduced plan *is* Mr. Judge's plan, then will not Mrs. Besant withdraw from publication this cruel and baseless slander on the dead?

f. "Mr. Hodgson's third charge is that certain letters alleged to be from the Mahātmā Koot Hoomi were written by Madame Blavatsky, or in some cases by Damodar." P. 48.

"The before-mentioned experts varied together as to the authorship of the letters submitted to them; first they said they were not done by Madame Blavatsky; then, this not satisfying Mr. Hodgson, they said they were. As against this valuable opinion of theirs may be put that of Herr Ernst Schutze, the Court expert in caligraphy at Berlin, who gave evidence on oath that the letter of Master K. H. 'has not the remotest resemblance with the letter of Madame Blavatsky,' and who wrote: 'I must assure you most positively that if you have believed that both letters came from one and the same hand, you have laboured under a most complete mistake.'" P. 48.

This statement looks very convincing at first sight; but let us set the facts around it and see what becomes of it.

When Mr. Hodgson got a number of these letters submitted to him, he found that the penmanship varied in them a good deal. He then placed them as far as possible in chronological order, when it became plain that the early letters retained many of the characteristics of Madame Blavatsky's handwriting, while in the later examples a number of these characteristics were eliminated. Studied as a series, they at once suggest that all are by the same hand and that there had been a progressive differentiation of the handwriting.

It was merely several small slips of writing belonging to this lengthy correspondence, conducted in a disguised hand, which were submitted to the English experts, and which they declared had not been written by Madame Blavatsky. When the long chronological series was submitted to them, they recognized the progressive differentiation and came to the conclusion that all were written by Madame Blavatsky.

Now to come to the German expert. Mr. Sinnett tells us (*Incidents in the Life of Madame Blavatsky*, 323–4) that the documents submitted to him were a Koot Hoomi letter of September, 1884, and a letter written by Madame Blavatsky in *October, 1885*. Now it had been suggested many months before this latter date that Madame Blavatsky had written the letters in question. Clearly, if the expert was to make his examination under scientific conditions, a letter written by Madame Blavatsky *before* the question arose should have been given him for comparison. How could he judge a question of handwriting, if the accused was given an opportunity of resorting to disguise? Further, Mr. Hodgson gives a number of facts which clearly suggest that Madame Blavatsky attempted the same trick with him. *Proceedings*, IX, 281, 290–1; XXIV, 148–9. Thus the German expert's verdict is worthless, simply because the evidence was not submitted to him.

The English experts, on the other hand, had before them specimens of Madame Blavatsky's writing dating from *before* the Coulomb exposure, and also a considerable number of K. H. letters of various dates. They thus worked under scientific conditions, while the German expert did not.

Again we remark that all these facts are detailed by Mr. Hodgson (*Proceedings*, IX, 282 ff.; XXIV, 147–149); yet Mrs. Besant ignores them entirely, and indeed suggests by her language that there are no such material facts.

No one would say that the mere opinion of experts on the handwriting would be sufficient to settle the question of the authorship of these letters. As we have shown above (pp. 256–9), several other lines of proof combine to indicate that they were written by Madame Blavatsky and her immediate disciples.

We have submitted only a few fragments of Mrs. Besant's booklet to examination. Limits of space alone prevent us from carrying the process farther. The bulk of the rest of the material is quite as rotten as the portions we have reviewed.

2. *Episodes from an Unwritten History.*

This work is in the main dependent on No. 1, and we need not deal with the corresponding passages here. But to give some idea of the utter unreality of the story we shall quote two passages:

a. "The work designated to Judge by the Founders was magnificently performed, and notwithstanding his secession from the parent society in 1895, taking with him most, though not all, of his colleagues, his name rightly ranks first, after those of the two Founders, among the great workers and leaders in the Theosophical cause." P. 25.

What must be the condition of the Theosophic conscience which writes such a panegyric of Judge? See above, pp. 241–2, 268–71.

b. Writing of Madame Coulomb, this author says:

"Prince Harisinghji of Kathiawar, to whom she had applied on more than one occasion for two thousand rupees, tired of her importunities, complained at last to Madame Blavatsky, who promptly put an end to an intolerable situation by dismissing from her service Madame Coulomb." P. 42.

This last statement is absolutely false. See the evidence produced above (p. 236), shewing that the Coulombs were left in full charge of Madame Blavatsky's rooms.

3. *Incidents in the History of the Theosophical Movement.*

In the discussion of the Madras exposure this pamphlet is dependent on Mrs. Besant, and repeats the gross and baseless slander about the plan of the shrine-room (pp. 452–4, above). We need not deal with it again. But there are other slanders:

a. "It was afterwards learned and published in the Madras *Daily Mail* that the missionaries of the Madras Christian College had offered to pay Mme. Coulomb a thousand rupees to procure certain letters of Madame Blavatsky." P. 7.

This is utterly false. See the facts on p. 246 n., above.

b. "Both M. and Mme. Coulomb later, when their actions were exposed, confessed to this plot." P. 7.

Could a grosser slander be conceived? Madame Coulomb, so far from confessing to a plot, instituted a lawsuit in defence of her character (p. 252, above), and when it became impossible to proceed with it, published a long letter in *The Madras Mail*, stating her position once more with the utmost emphasis (p. 254, above).

4. *A Historical Retrospect of the Theosophical Society.*

a. Writing about Judge, Olcott says:

"In the autumn of 1893, charges had been made against this officer's character, a widespread and intense excitement had resulted, and a majority of the Sections were urging me to remove him from office. A Judicial Committee was convened at London in 1894 to try the charges, but adjourned without doing so because of certain technical points which were put forward and held to be good. The discontent was not allayed by this action but greatly increased, feeling ran high, an overwhelming majority of the American Branches stood by him, and an angry discussion was carried on within and outside our own press. This was the state of affairs when the Ninth Annual Convention of the American Section met at Boston, Mass., on the day specified. The Delegates almost in a mass made Mr. Judge's cause their own, and voted to secede from the parent Society and organize as an independent society." P. 17.

What sort of a historical account is this of the amazing events we have outlined above (pp. 268–71)? Olcott here simply keeps up the policy of concealment agreed upon in the Judicial Committee.

We appeal to all who read these pages, Theosophists, reviewers and the general public: Is it not high time that the Theosophical Publishing Society, London, the Manas Press, Rochester, U. S. A., the Aryan Theosophical Press, Point Loma, California, and the Theosophical Society, Madras, should withdraw these most unhistorical publications from circulation?

GLOSSARY OF INDIAN TERMS

āchārya:	scholar, theologian, minister.
astral:	belonging to the astral world, see p. 195.
bhakti:	devotion, love for God.
bhāshya:	commentary, especially on the *Vedānta-sūtras*.
brahmachārī:	celibate student.
chela:	disciple.
Daṇḍīs:	ten orders of sannyāsīs, organized by Śankārācharya and named from the *daṇḍa* or beggar's stick which each sannyāsī carries.
guru:	a Hindu teacher, worshipped as God.
mantra:	a short expression, prose or verse, used as a sacred utterance, and believed to possess mystic power.
mleccha:	a name used by Hindus for foreigners, like the Greek 'barbaros' and the Jewish 'Gentile.'
Moulvie:	a Muslim theologian.
Om:	the most sacred of all mystic syllables in use among Hindus.
paṇḍit:	a learned man, especially learned in language.
paramahaṁsa:	a title conferred on a sannyāsī of high philosophic and religious attainments.
purda:	a word meaning 'curtain,' used instead of zenāna.
sādhu:	a word used for any modern Hindu ascetic.
Śaiva:	Śivaite.
saṁskāras:	domestic ceremonies.
sannyāsī:	a celibate monk, see p. 73.
sat:	real, true.
satguru:	true guru.
śrāddha:	Hindu ancestor-worship.
svāmī:	lit. 'lord,' a title conferred on sannyāsīs.
Vaishṇava:	Vishṇuite.
zenāna:	the women's apartments in an Indian house.

INDEX

Published by

Facsimile Publisher
Ashok Vihar, Delhi-110052 (India)
Website: www.facsimilepublisher.com

Distributed by

Gyan Books Pvt. Ltd.
5, Ansari Road, Daryaganj, New Delhi-110002 (India)
E-mail: books@gyanbooks.com, Website: www.gyanbooks.com